Dignity and Defiance

Founded in San Francisco in 1992, the Democracy Center works globally to advance social justice through a combination of investigation and reporting, training citizens in the art of public advocacy, and organizing international citizen campaigns. Through all of these efforts the center works to help build a global citizenry that understands the public issues before it and is able to take effective public action. A special emphasis of our work is economic globalization and the movement for global democracy and justice.

Also by the Democracy Center:

The Initiative Cookbook: Recipes and Stories from California's Ballot Wars

The Democracy Owners' Manual: A Practical Guide to Changing the World

Dignity and Defiance

Stories from Bolivia's Challenge to Globalization

Edited by Jim Shultz
and Melissa Crane Draper

UNIVERSITY OF CALIFORNIA PRESS
Berkeley · Los Angeles · London

University of California Press, one of the most
distinguished university presses in the United States,
enriches lives around the world by advancing
scholarship in the humanities, social sciences, and
natural sciences. Its activities are supported by the UC
Press Foundation and by philanthropic contributions
from individuals and institutions. For more
information, visit www.ucpress.edu.

University of California Press
Berkeley and Los Angeles, California

University of California Press, Ltd.
London, England

Library of Congress Cataloging-in-Publication Data

Dignity and defiance : stories from Bolivia's challenge to
globalization / edited by Jim Shultz and Melissa Crane
Draper.
    p.   cm.
  Includes bibliographical references (p.   ) and index.
  ISBN 978–0–520-25698-9 (cloth : alk. paper)
  ISBN 978–0–520-25699-6 (pbk. : alk. paper)
  1. Bolivia—Foreign economic relations.   2.
Globalization—Economic aspects—Bolivia.   3.
Investments, Foreign—Bolivia.   I. Shultz, Jim.   II.
Draper, Melissa.
HF1511.D54   2009
337.84—dc22   2008029117

Manufactured in the United States of America

17 16 15 14 13 12 11 10 09 08
10 9 8 7 6 5 4 3 2 1

This book is printed on Natures Book, which contains
30% post-consumer waste and meets the minimum
requirements of ANSI/NISO Z39.48–1992 (R 1997)
(*Permanence of Paper*).

To the people of Bolivia:
our teachers, friends, and neighbors

Contents

Acknowledgments

It would be difficult to imagine a book that had more people contribute to its publication than this one. We would like to offer our gratitude to as many of them as possible.

Many, many people, in Bolivia, the United States, and elsewhere, took time out to help with research, to share their stories, and to read and comment on drafts of the various chapters, making the book much stronger. They include Rob Albro, Carlos Arce, Carlos Arrien, Umair Badeeu, Adam Bauer, Marcelo Becerra, Pamela Calla, Aldo Cardoso, Jeff Carolin, Roberto Andrés Carvallo Arroyo, Mónica Castellón Barea, Ann Chaplin, Severina Barro, Nelson Chacón, Keiko Chisaka, Amparo Choqueribe, Carolyn Claridge, Eva Colque, Robert Conrad, Carlos Crespo, Lucy Draper, Matthew Draper, Thad Dunning, Raúl Escalera, Juan Luis Espada, Linda Farthing, Leonardo Fernández, William Finnegan, Douglas Flavio Rivero, María Eugenia Flores, Barbara Gagnat, Lesley Gill, Javier Gómez, Donna Gordon, Sara Grusky, Osvaldo Guachalla, Daniel Guzmán Landa, María Teresa Hosse, Smita Jassal, Annie Murphy, Tom Kruse, Kathryn Ledebur, Claudia López, Gustavo Luna, Gracia Luoma, Severina Mamani, Stephen Mandel, Mónica Mendizábal, Patricia Miranda, Jania Mueller, Juan Carlos Núñez, Carmen Peredo, Elizabeth Peredo, Valentín Pérez Mamani, Gary Rojas, Lawanda Sellan, Arminda Solíz, Pablo Solón, Yves Van Damme, Simona Velásquez, Nicholas Verbon, Medardo Villarroel, John Walsh, and David Zambrana.

We also want to thank our families, mentors, and friends in Bolivia and our respective home countries. They endured the book alongside each of us every step of the way. We would especially like to mention Juliette Beck, Eliana Abujder Chajtur, John Draper, Grace Goodell, Ben Kohl, Anabel Landa, David Lebow, Lynn Nesselbush, and Tom Pellens.

We owe a huge debt to many Bolivians who, over the years, have given us special insight into Bolivia and guided us in our learning process. They include Oscar Olivera, Casimira Rodríguez, Luís Gómez, Leonardo de la Torre Ávila, the people of the Desaguadero River, the people of the Yungas, Fundación Abril, the people of El Alto and the Asociación de Los Familiares Caídos en Defensa del Gas, Fundación Jubileo, the people of Guaqui, Saúl Escalera and the Yacimientos Petrolíferos Fiscales Bolivianos (YPFB) industrialization team, the people of Chuñu Chuñuni and the Asociación de Artesanos Andinos, the research teams of Centro de Estudios Superiores Universitarios (CESU) and Centro de Estudios para el Desarrollo Laboral y Agrario (CEDLA), and the Bolivian immigrants in Arlington, Barcelona, and Buenos Aires, especially Julia García.

We also wish to thank three funders who made this book possible with their financial and moral support: the Wallace Global Fund, the Open Society Institute, and the Oregon Shadow Fund. A special thanks to our indexer, Paula Pfoeffer, and to Yi-Ching Hwang, who helped us through final editing and promotion. In that same spirit we want to thank our publisher, the University of California Press, and our editors, Naomi Schneider and Mary Severance, for their patient guidance and support of this project.

Lastly, we agreed to let Jim Shultz thank his two dogs, Simone and Little Bear. Without their accompaniment on many, many walks into the Bolivian hills, where much of this book was edited, he might well have forgotten to come back down.

Melissa Crane Draper
Jim Shultz
Cochabamba, June 2008

Introduction

Melissa Crane Draper and Jim Shultz

Globalization (*glo · bal · i · za · tion*), noun: Process by which
the experience of everyday life, marked by the diffusion of
commodities and ideas, is becoming standardized around
the world.

Encyclopedia Britannica

We begin with a question: *What is globalization?* Historians might tell
us that globalization actually began fifty thousand years ago, when a
handful of our ancestors began a slow path out of Africa that ended
up populating the far corners of the world. For centuries, through
wars, commerce, migration, and religious proselytizing, the world has
become steadily more integrated. In short, globalization is nothing
new.

Today the word *globalization* has become a catchall that means
many different things all at once. On the lips of some, the word refers
to *economic* globalization—the movement of money, goods, business,
and migrant labor to foreign markets in search of higher profits and
wages. Others think more in terms of *political* globalization, the rise of
global rules and institutions that wield heavy influence over the choices
of sovereign nations. For others still, the term conjures up thoughts of
the *cultural* integration—Cuban salsa mixed with British rock, forming
something creative and new, or U.S. sitcoms supplanting local television
programming.

Globalization leaped into popular use even more in 1999, in the
aftermath of protests in the streets of Seattle outside a meeting of the
World Trade Organization. The movement that filled those streets was
quickly labeled *antiglobalization,* whereas the opposition was quickly
labeled *proglobalization.* Neither label actually catches the more complex story underneath.

Globalization is not so much an issue for debate as it is a force of nature. The peoples of the world are clearly intent on knitting themselves together. We travel to one another's lands. We trade with one another. We learn one another's languages. We migrate. We marry and we make children together. Draw whatever boundary lines on the earth's surface you wish; you aren't going to keep the world's people apart.

The issue is not globalization; rather, it is the rules that govern it, as well as who makes those rules and who benefits from them. For the past two decades, the path of economic globalization has become increasingly directed by a web of global regulations and agreements, from international trade accords to the lending conditions set down by international financial institutions such as the World Bank and International Monetary Fund (IMF). These rules have a substantial impact on all of us, as workers, investors, consumers, and inhabitants of a threatened environment. This is especially the case in low-income countries, where rules manufactured far away reach deeply into people's lives.

Dignity and Defiance examines what modern globalization means in a country that has become synonymous with conflicts over it—Bolivia. Our aim is to give readers a sense of the debate that goes beyond theory and rhetoric to the concrete, human stories on the ground.

The most indigenous nation in the Americas, Bolivia, has long been the target of attention from abroad. In the 1550s, as a Spanish conquest, Bolivia sat atop one of the most valuable deposits of mineral wealth the world has ever known—Cerro Rico (Rich Hill) in Potosí. That one small brown mountain was so filled with silver that the treasure the Spanish mined from it with slave labor virtually bankrolled their empire for two centuries. In exchange, Bolivia was left the most impoverished country in South America.

More recently, Bolivia has served for two decades as an unwilling test lab for a radical experiment in conservative economic reforms, most adopted under heavy pressure from abroad. These policies have come to be known by many different names—*structural adjustment, the neoliberal economic model, the Washington consensus,* and others. U.S.-dominated global institutions, led by the World Bank and the IMF, used conditions applied to lending and aid to assume the role of Bolivia's economic doctors, issuing a series of prescriptions implemented with the support of a small and wealthy national elite. These included privatizing state companies and the nation's natural resources, cutting back on labor protection, reducing government spending, and raising taxes to pay foreign debt.

This landlocked nation in the heart of the Andes was Washington's most obedient patient. John Williamson, the British economist who coined the term the "Washington consensus," has called Bolivia "the big bang" of the program's arrival in Latin America. Yet, while these reforms drew praise from foreign economists, they drew rage and resistance from large segments of the Bolivian people. Thousands of jobs disappeared overnight; the price of basics like water soared; economic power shifted to foreigners; and those economic impacts in turn had cultural and political impacts as well. Many Bolivians believed they were seeing a modern version of the gutting of Cerro Rico.

Since 2000, the Bolivian story of globalization has been marked by popular resistance to these policies. In wave after wave of popular protest, hundreds of thousands of people, across class lines, have taken to the streets to voice their discontent. In 2005 Bolivians took that discontent to the ballot box to elect the first indigenous president in their nation's history, Evo Morales, a leader who owes a good deal of his popularity to his attacks against the economic formulas imported from Washington.

While Bolivia's resistance to globalization has gained attention in headlines in recent years—from its rebellion over water privatization to the infamous U.S.-led war on coca—those headlines have not captured the complexities of Bolivia's tentative dance with global integration. A country that has fought to take back its natural resources from foreign corporations has also embraced the export of its textiles and weavings to foreign markets. While thousands have taken to the streets to protest foreign economic influence, thousands of others have migrated abroad in search of economic opportunity.

Bolivians are not rejecting globalization; they are challenging it to be something different. They are demanding that their integration into global economics and culture bring them something other than the exploitation that has been their national experience for five centuries. The eyes that stare out from the cover of this book capture the dignity and defiance with which a nation has sought to define its own course in a globalizing world.

In this book a team of writers has set out to bring readers an up-close look at what globalization means in the lives of real people—from water rebels and weavers to emigrants and coca growers. By joining those stories with analysis of the global forces and institutions involved, our aim has been to offer insight into the globalization debate, especially capturing the human stories so often ignored and yet so crucial to genuine understanding.

Dignity and Defiance opens in Chapter 1 with the story that made Bolivia synonymous with resistance to foreign recipes for globalization, the Cochabamba Water Revolt. It looks at why the revolt happened, the events as they unfolded, and importantly, the revolt's aftermath and its impacts in Bolivia and around the world.

The next two chapters explore Bolivia's handover of its gas and oil to foreign corporations and the efforts to take that resource back. Chapter 2 delves into the stark beauty of highland Bolivia, where indigenous communities were abruptly introduced to globalization in 2000 when an Enron-Shell oil pipeline burst, spewing toxic crude oil into the sacred river and fragile farmlands. Chapter 3 looks at the history and politics of Bolivia's struggle to control its oil and gas resources, including President Morales's efforts at reform and the potential that oil and gas reserves have for the country's future.

The next two chapters reveal how global institutions have intimately directed Bolivia's key economic decisions over the past two decades. Chapter 4 reports how IMF economic policy led to protests and violence that left thirty-four people dead in Bolivia's capital city. Chapter 5 examines Bolivia's long history with foreign debt and how that debt has shaped a culture of national dependency on foreign interests.

The book then turns to the issue of coca, one of the most intense and symbolic issues of Bolivia's resistance to global forces. Chapter 6 considers the U.S.-sponsored "war on drugs" through a kaleidoscope of culture and history, U.S. foreign policy, and personal interviews with Bolivians who have been affected by the drug war.

Chapter 7 takes up the issue of how globalization affects the lives of Bolivian women, looking at the stories of six women across Bolivia's spectrum of class and ethnic identities and how they have negotiated globalization in their lives and work. Through their stories we see how globalization creates a mix of new opportunity for some, new hardships for others, and has opened up new leadership opportunities for women of very different backgrounds.

Chapter 8 presents an in-depth analysis of Bolivian emigration. This is a form of globalization that is touching every Bolivian's life, as mothers, fathers, daughters, and sons are drawn to the demand for labor in countries like the United States, Spain, and Argentina.

Dignity and Defiance is the product of a team of people that went to great lengths to get Bolivia's story right. The authors are mostly foreigners, though some have lived in Bolivia for many years. These authors were joined throughout by a remarkable group of Bolivian researchers, advisers, and reviewers who helped craft the ideas and stories that make up this book. Their knowledge and insight was essential.

To collect our information, we reviewed a wide variety of documents, studies, news archives, and reports. Our interview subjects ranged from a Bolivian president and presidential cabinet members to coca growers, household workers, and members of indigenous communities. We also sought officials and spokespeople for the institutions that are often dealt with critically in the book—from the International Monetary Fund to foreign oil companies—to capture their point of view as well.

While each chapter is a self-contained story, the chapters are also clearly interrelated. The story of an oil spill sheds light on the politics of gas and oil. Women's labor issues impact the character of foreign emigration. Foreign pressures for discipline on debt spill into Bolivia's violent confrontations over new taxes. Bolivia's history is also a key element in many of these stories. Like the intricate weavings for which Bolivia is also famous, the book weaves together different threads to form a whole tapestry.

People knowledgeable about Bolivia, scanning through the table of contents, will quickly notice two topics vital to Bolivia and its recent experience that are not specifically the subject of any one chapter: social movements and indigenous peoples. The collective organizing of Bolivians for social change and the rise of communities that trace their Bolivian roots back beyond the Incas have not been left out of the book. Both of these themes are woven into virtually every chapter. They are defining factors of Bolivia's current history and the way Bolivia is making its way forward.

Finally, a word about a couple of words. *Poverty* (or *poor*) is a word that comes up frequently in the book. We use it here to mean material poverty, recognizing that spiritual, moral, and cultural wealth, which Bolivia has in abundance, is something very different. We use the term *American* from time to time, referring to people or institutions from the United States. We do this only because so many of our readers understand the term in that way. We are well aware, however, that *American* includes everyone in the Western Hemisphere.

In the end, *Dignity and Defiance* is not just the story of one country and its experiences with a globalizing world. Bolivia's story reveals themes and issues that are important in all countries, low-income and affluent alike. Bolivia's story is one of people looking at the larger forces shaping their lives and taking a stand, often with great courage, to demand what they believe to be right and to challenge what they believe to be wrong.

As Eduardo Galeano said with eloquence at the inauguration of Bolivia's first indigenous president in January 2006:

> Our countries were born condemned to a death from fear that keeps us from seeing who we are and who we can be. What has happened in Bolivia teaches us that the fear of being what we can be is not an invincible enemy. Racism is not a fatality of destiny. We are not condemned to repeat history. . . . [We are determined to] walk with our own legs, think with our own minds, and feel with our own hearts.

The lessons Bolivia offers are as individual as they are political. They are lessons that speak to us all.

A Bolivian woman holds back the advance of government forces with a single slingshot during the Water War on the streets of downtown Cochabamba. Photo: Thomas Kruse (2000).

CHAPTER I

The Cochabamba Water Revolt and Its Aftermath

Jim Shultz

In the opening months of the year 2000, the people of Cochabamba, Bolivia, took to the streets by the thousands. They were protesting the takeover of their city water system by a subsidiary of the U.S. corporate giant Bechtel and demanding the repeal of a new national water law that threatened to hand Bechtel control over rural water systems. On three separate occasions the people of Cochabamba and their rural neighbors shut down the city with general strikes and road blockades. Bolivia's president, a former dictator, responded with armed troops and a suspension of constitutional rights. More than one hundred people were wounded. A seventeen-year-old boy, Victor Hugo Daza, was killed.

On April 10, 2000, Bechtel officials finally fled the city, the water system was returned to public control, and the water law was repealed. The global legend of the great Cochabamba Water Revolt was born—a powerful modern-day tale of a corporate Goliath slain by a humble David of the Andes. In the years since, the story of the water revolt has been featured in so many international articles, books, and films that reporting about those events has become a phenomenon in itself. At the time of the revolt, the Democracy Center, based in Cochabamba, was the only ongoing source of reporting to audiences abroad. The center's coverage, which shared honors for top story of the year from Project Censored, became the basis of much of the reporting since.

In this chapter, Jim Shultz looks at the water revolt through seven years of hindsight, in a way that goes far deeper than any previous accounts by the Democracy Center. What motivated the people of Cochabamba to rise up? How did they organize themselves to fight and win against such a powerful foe? Of equal importance, however, is what happened after the revolt. How did it affect the global debate on putting water into corporate hands? What role has it had in Bolivia's subsequent political changes? And perhaps most important of all, what did the water revolt mean for the demand that sent the people of Cochabamba into the streets to begin with—the desire for clean, affordable water?

THE SEEDS OF A REVOLT

A two-and-a-half-gallon bucket of water weighs about twenty-two pounds, slightly more than the weight of five bricks. In Bolivia, that is just enough water to cook a family meal and clean up from it.

On the outskirts of Cochabamba, where water is scarce and taps in the home are merely a dream, young children, burdened mothers, and bent-over grandmothers carry such buckets of water over long distances from rivers or public spigots. For thousands here, gathering water in this way is a basic feature of their lives, in the way people in other parts of the world gather water by turning on a faucet.

But the demand for clean water is about something more than just the desire to shed heavy loads; it is also a matter of life and death. In Bolivia, more than one in twenty children die before starting kindergarten, and disease caused by the lack of clean water is among the most common causes.[1] It was this, the need for something essential to life, which was most truly the genesis of the now famous Cochabamba revolt.

Water Scarcity: Cochabamba's Perfect Storm

Water was an issue in Cochabamba long before any locals ever heard the words *Bechtel* or *privatization.* The city that sprawls across a large valley eight thousand feet high in the Andean foothills got its name from water: *Kucha Pampa,* from the indigenous language Quechua, meaning swampy land.

Cochabamba's roots can be traced to the mid-1500s, when it was the lush, green source of fruit and produce for the miners of Potosí, the silver-filled Bolivian mountain that bankrolled the Spanish empire for two centuries. In its early years, the small pueblo and the land around it were surrounded by small lakes and lagoons. By the mid-1900s that wealth of moisture was already becoming history—the result of a three-way collision of forces over which residents of the city had no control.

First, Cochabamba was growing—by a lot, and fast. In 1950, the city had a population of 75,000. By 1976 that number leaped to more than 200,000. In 2001 it topped half a million.[2] The once mighty silver and tin mines of the Bolivian highlands were in economic collapse; the small rural villages that had been the nation's heart were also becoming economically unsustainable; and families were headed to the temperate climates of Cochabamba by truck and busload.

A sprawl of new neighborhoods, often settled by whole mining communities that moved to the city together, sprang up across the hillsides of the city's southern and northern outskirts. Land that was long home to red-berried *molle* trees, sheep, pigs, cows, and farm crops was now dotted with small adobe houses with weak tin roofs held down by heavy rocks. And while the newly transplanted residents of those houses could live without electricity, without telephones, and without gas pipes running into their homes, they could not live without water.

Second, Cochabamba was running out of water, just as demand for it was starting to spike. Deforestation of the surrounding hills and years of drought left the once lush valley so dry for most of the year that light brown dust, the color of overcreamed coffee, became one of its most notable features. It filled the air during the August winds, blocking the view of the sun and sticking between Cochabambino teeth. To get water, neighborhoods drilled deep wells, exhausting the fragile water table underneath the city. Those who couldn't dig wells bought water at exorbitant prices from large dilapidated water trucks that traveled the new neighborhoods. Those who couldn't afford the prices charged by the trucks resorted to heavy buckets and long walks.

Cochabamba faced one more challenge that completed its water crisis—chronic poverty. Bolivia is the most impoverished nation in South America. The nation was falling deeper and deeper into debt. To get the people of Cochabamba the water they needed, huge investments were required in infrastructure—dams and pipelines to bring more water into the valley from the wet mountains above it, and tanks and underground pipes that could deliver that water to people's homes, or at least nearby. Neither the residents of Cochabamba, nor their city government, nor their national government, had the resources needed to get water to the people.

The Birth of a Water Company

In the mid-1960s Cochabamba's leaders began looking for assistance from abroad. In 1967, the city secured a $14 million water development loan from the Washington-based Inter-American Development Bank

(IDB). In exchange for that aid, the IDB also set conditions for how the city should go about the business of providing water for its people, the kind of strings-attached aid Bolivia would encounter with foreign assistance in greater and greater abundance down the road.[3]

The first requirement was that Cochabamba needed to set up a new public water company, SEMAPA (*Servicio Municipal de Agua Potable y Alcantarillado*) to manage the development of expanded water service. Run by a board headed by the city mayor, the company started building tanks and laying pipes. For years afterward, SEMAPA would be beset with charges of corruption and mismanagement and used as a source of cash and favors for the politicians who helped run it. A former director of SEMAPA described the corruption problem this way:

> Someone hoping to get a political job contributes funds to help a friend get elected mayor. His candidate wins and he is rewarded with a job at the water company, in charge of buying large water pumps. The guy goes out and prices pumps with companies who sell them. "The price is $10,000," the water company official is told. "No it's not," he replies. "It's $11,000. That's how much you will bill the water company. The extra $1,000 is a commission you pay to me directly."[4]

Side deals, payrolls padded with friends and relatives, and other acts of general mismanagement and inefficiency would plague the water company off and on for decades.

Nevertheless, throughout the 1970s, 1980s, and 1990s, SEMAPA continued to expand city water service—but it was never able to keep up with the rapid influx of new families, new neighborhoods, and the relentlessly growing need for water. The water service expansion that SEMAPA was able to achieve was also focused heavily in the city's wealthier neighborhoods in the center and north. The much poorer neighborhoods of the south—populated by ex-miners and people flowing in from the countryside—were left out almost entirely. A 1997 investigation concluded that in the more prosperous northern neighborhoods of the city (home to about one quarter of its population) 90 percent of the families had water hookups and indoor plumbing. In the poorer barrios of the south, less than half the families had these things.[5] Not only was Cochabamba failing to solve its water crisis; it was also creating an entrenched system of water haves and have-nots.

Faced with the public water company's failure to solve their growing water problems, the poor neighborhoods of the city's south began doing what Bolivians have done for centuries in indigenous communities and for decades in the mines—they organized to solve the problem themselves.

From the 1990s onward, more than a hundred "independent water committees" were formed, through which residents joined together to dig wells, lay pipes up to water sources in the hills, and look for other practical ways they could get water and manage that water collectively. But as with SEMAPA, these local water committees could not keep up with the demand for water and could not provide people with a long-term solution to the ever-growing water crisis.

Dams, Tunnels, and Wells

It was becoming a simple fact: Cochabamba had no real chance of solving its water problem if it relied simply on runoff from the Andean foothills surrounding it and the other sources that nature alone had provided. The city's quickly growing population required new sources for water, and city leaders aimed to fill that need with a combination of big projects, including dams, tunnels, and large-scale wells.

From 1967 to 1999, with financial support from foreign lenders such as the IDB, the water company dug more than sixty large-scale wells, enough to provide more than half of all the water it was distributing to Cochabamba water users. Many of these wells were dug not in the city itself, but in the rural areas that ring the far edges of the Cochabamba valley, and with each new deep hole dug under their land, farmers were getting more and more angry. The families of the countryside knew that draining the water underneath them would eventually take its toll on their land and their livelihoods. Valley farmers first tried to stop the well digging by persuasion. When that failed they shifted to resistance, triggering a series of confrontations that frequently became violent. Ultimately the War of the Wells was resolved through a combination of payments to the farmers and water-sharing arrangements with the city. The truce between the city and the countryside, however, was fragile at best. Real solidarity between the two would come only later, catalyzed by an unexpected source: a corporation headquartered a hemisphere away.

In the early 1990s, Cochabamba began debating two rival proposals for constructing huge new dams that would capture water from rivers far beyond the city, to be transported by pipe to the parched neighborhoods of the city. It was a debate as much about politics as engineering analysis. The cheaper and simpler plan was to bring water to the city via a new pipeline from Lake Corani, thirty-one miles to the city's east. The rival plan, one shrouded in rumors of behind-closed-doors sweetheart deals, was a $300 million proposal to build a huge dam at Misicuni, the convergent point of two rivers on a high plain far beyond the city, and to construct a twelve-mile tunnel through a mountain to bring the water to Cochabamba.[6] Backed by a coalition of city leaders and wealthy developers with an economic stake, Cochabamba opted for Misicuni. Construction began in 1998 and was expected to take more than a decade to complete.

Enter the World Bank and the Demand for Privatization

The IDB was not the only big institution in Washington lending Cochabamba's water company dollars for water development and getting more and more frustrated with SEMAPA's inefficiency and slow results. The World Bank, the giant global lender based in Washington, had spent much of the 1980s and 1990s lending poor countries money to build big, and hotly debated, infrastructure projects such as dams and highways. Along with those loans came an ever-lengthening list of conditions. One of the places that the World Bank lent funds for water expansion was Cochabamba.

Meanwhile, at the World Bank's U.S. headquarters, economists and analysts were developing a new strategy to solve the problem of access to water in poor nations. The plan was called privatization, and it meant encouraging governments in low-income countries to lease their public water systems over to private corporations, most of which were large global conglomerates with no previous relationships with or history in the countries where they would operate.

"Public sector utilities in developing countries have often not been efficient in providing access to reliable water and sanitation services," bank officials argued. "Evidence shows that the private sector, under contract with the public sector, has often yielded better results than public sector utilities alone."[7]

John Briscoe, the World Bank's senior water official, put the case for privatization more bluntly in an interview with PBS: "If you are genuinely concerned with them [poor communities] getting water, what is the best route to do that? It's a practical question, not a moral question. And a declaration that water is owned by the public to be managed by the public for the good of everybody—we've had decades of that, and it hasn't worked."[8]

World Bank officials, however, did far more than just argue the case for water privatization. In country after country, bank officials made the privatization of public water systems a requirement for getting water funds.[9] In Bolivia, the bank made its demand for privatization quite clear.

In February 1996, Cochabamba's mayor announced to the press that the World Bank was making privatization of SEMAPA a condition of an urgent $14 million loan to expand water service.[10] In June 1997, Bolivia's president returned from a meeting with bank officials in Washington and declared that $600 million in foreign debt relief, much of it from the bank, was also dependent on privatizing Cochabamba's water.[11] Bank officials would later dispute these declarations that they had forced Bolivia's hand, and they argued that they had opposed the Bechtel deal because it included the Misicuni dam project. But in 2002, in an internal report, the bank's own auditors confirmed it was, in fact, bank coercion that set the Cochabamba privatization in motion. Privatization of the water company had been, according to the report, "a bank condition" for extending water loans to Bolivia.[12]

Left with little choice, in 1999 the government of Bolivia put Cochabamba's public water system up for private bid. Only one company came forward, a mysterious new enterprise called Aguas del Tunari, named for the rugged peak overlooking Cochabamba and its thirsty valley.

Bechtel Comes to Bolivia

Bechtel Enterprises is one of the largest corporations in the world. With 2007 earnings of more than $27 billion, the engineering firm has been responsible for some of the biggest infrastructure projects of the last hundred years, including the Hoover Dam, Northern California's BART transit system, and the troubled Boston "Big Dig" project.[13]

Bechtel is also well connected politically. Caspar Weinberger, who later served as President Reagan's defense secretary, had been the company's general counsel and director. George Shultz, who served as Reagan's secretary of state, is a member of Bechtel's board of directors. In 2004, Bechtel's political clout was made even clearer when it was one of two U.S. companies selected by the Bush administration, with no competitive bidding, to receive contracts for rebuilding in Iraq, a deal worth nearly $1 billion.[14]

The San Francisco engineering giant was, however, a late arrival to the big international business of taking over public water systems. In 1996 it created a new London-based company, International Waters Limited (IWL), which moved swiftly to get into the global water game.

Like an aggressive player at a Monopoly board, gobbling up whatever properties come up for sale, Bechtel and IWL went after and won contracts to operate water systems in remote locations such as Estonia and Bulgaria—and Cochabamba.

To go after Cochabamba's water, Bechtel and IWL put together Aguas del Tunari, and in September 1999 signed a 214-page agreement with Bolivian officials. It was a deal negotiated behind closed doors and one that only a handful of Bolivians ever saw. The contract gave Bechtel and its co-investors control of the city's water company for forty years and guaranteed them an average profit of 16 percent for each one of those years, to be financed by the families of Cochabamba. No one at the negotiating table could have had any doubt what that would mean for Cochabamba water bills.

In the global scheme of things, Cochabamba was about as small a deal as Bechtel could have gone after. But for a company getting into water ownership late, a humble valley in the Andes was Baltic Avenue—that dark purple scrap of something to own just past "GO" that at least got you into the game. Cochabambinos, however, were getting ready to play by a set of rules that Bechtel and its associates probably never imagined.

REBELLION IN THE STREETS

The Cochabamba Water Revolt began in the countryside. It began over the rock and cement irrigation canals that snake across the rural areas outside the city, built by hand by farmers to bring water to their crops from nearby rivers. As part of its water privatization plans, the Bolivian government had approved a new water law to put those small trenches under its control, so that it could turn that control over to Bechtel. People in the countryside began mobilizing to stop the plan.

In November 1999, the Federation of Irrigators, furious about the new law, staged a one-day blockade of the highways leading in and out of Cochabamba. "Our objective was to test what capacity we had to fight," recalled Omar Fernández, leader of the irrigators' union. "We found out that [the people] wanted to move faster than even our leadership. In [the small town of] Vinto they blockaded the highway for forty-eight hours."[15]

Soon after, the irrigators paid a visit to Oscar Olivera, a former shoe factory worker who was president of the Cochabamba Federation of Factory Workers. In Olivera's office a group of farmers, factory workers, environmentalists, and others talked about the government's aim to seize control of rural irrigation canals and about the rate hikes headed toward water users in the city. Sitting around a table covered by a faded blue tablecloth pockmarked with cigarette burns, they decided to launch a unified rebellion—rural and urban—against the plan. They established an alliance—the Coalition for the Defense of Water and Life (Coordinadora)—and they started organizing.

The Coordinadora was a response to something more than just the fight over water. Its leaders saw it as a response to what they believed was the total failure of the local institutions that were supposed to look out for the public's interest. Cochabamba's then-mayor, Manfred Reyes Villa, as president of SEMAPA, had signed the agreement that authorized the handover to Bechtel. Cochabamba's Comité Cívico (Civic Committee), an institution representing a broad cross-section of organizations, had been taken over by city business elites and had also signed off on the Bechtel handover. The Coordinadora, with its roots in labor unions, farming communities, and neighborhoods, would represent the people in a very different way.

As 1999 ended and 2000 began, Coordinadora leaders spread out to neighborhoods and communities across the valley, armed with presentations on large paper notepads about the threat they saw coming. Key among them were Omar Fernández and Carmen Peredo of the irrigators, Olivera, environmental leader Gabriel Herbas, economist Samuel Soria, and a member of Congress, Gonzalo Maldonado. Some crowds were huge, others were small, but it made no difference. "Even if there were ten people they went," remembered one Coordinadora organizer.

On the edge of the colonial central plaza in the heart of Cochabamba, the Coordinadora set up its headquarters in the Factory Workers building, steps away from the offices of the city mayor and the regional governor. On a clear, crisp morning in January 2000, from the union's third-floor balcony, the Coordinadora unfurled a fifty-foot-long red cloth banner blaring out its new battle cry in huge hand-painted letters:¡El agua es nuestra, carajo! (The water is ours, damn it!). The banner and its defiant words would stare government officials in the face every day for the next four months.

"We fought to conserve the water systems that we built with our own hands—tanks, wells, pipes," explained Abraham Grandydier, a key organizer in the city's southern neighborhoods. Some of the most active people fighting the Bechtel contract weren't even hooked up to the city's water system. "But we knew that later we also would be affected by the rate increases."[16]

BOX 1.1 | Bechtel versus the Facts

The Bechtel Corporation has made a great effort to defend itself against charges related to its role in the Cochabamba Water Revolt. However, on two central issues, Bechtel has either fudged on the facts or lied about them directly.

1. What was Bechtel's role in Aguas del Tunari?
In the aftermath of the water revolt, Bechtel sought to distance itself from those events by claiming that the corporation was just one minority owner among many in Aguas del Tunari, with a stake of just 27.5 percent.[1] The corporation's statement was factually accurate at the time it was made, and also directly misleading.

The majority controlling owner in Aguas del Tunari throughout (55 percent of all shares), was a company called International Waters Limited (IWL). According to Bechtel's own records, IWL was founded in 1996 by Bechtel and remained owned and controlled by it until November 1999.[2] That means that during the entire time that the Bolivia contract was being negotiated and signed—setting the new rate hikes in motion—*Bechtel owned 55 percent of the Cochabamba company* and called the shots. It was only two months after the Cochabamba deal was completed that Bechtel sold 50 percent of IWL to another company, Edison of Italy, forming the basis of its claim that it owned just a minority stake in Cochabamba.[3]

2. How high were Bechtel's rate hikes?
Bechtel has long maintained that its average rate hikes were no more than 35 percent and the rate increase it imposed on the poorest families was just 10 percent.[4] After Bechtel was forced to leave, the Democracy Center asked managers at the new public company to use Bechtel's own rate data to compute the

---

The Revolt Begins: January and February 2000

If there remained any question whether residents of the city would rise up as people in the countryside had done, those doubts were swept away quickly in January 2000, thanks to Bechtel's Cochabamba subsidiary. Just weeks after taking over the city's water, Bechtel's company handed users their monthly bills, complete with a spiffy new Aguas del Tunari logo and rate increases that averaged more than 50 percent, and in some cases much higher. For years afterward, Bechtel officials would continue to lie about the extent of their rate increases, claiming that the price hikes on the poorest were at most 10 percent.[17] An analysis using Bechtel's own data shows that the increases for the poorest averaged 43 percent.[18]

Cochabamba water users reacted furiously to the Bechtel rate hikes, and through the Coordinadora, they found a voice and a vehicle to act

actual figures. In fact, the average increase for the poorest users was not 10 percent, but 43 percent, and the average increase for all users in Cochabamba was not 35 percent but 51 percent.[5]

In addition, Bechtel also sought to blame the water bill increases not on Bechtel's rates, but on a sudden and unexplained leap in water use among the people of Cochabamba, just as Bechtel took over.[6] In fact, Bechtel's alleged leap in water use never took place, and a comparison of water bills from before and after show that the rate hikes were not caused by increased use. Even customers who used less water after Bechtel's arrival were able to demonstrate increases of more than 50 percent.[7]

1. "Bechtel Perspective on the Aguas del Tunari Water Concession in Cochabamba, Bolivia," Bechtel Corporation, San Francisco, CA, March 16, 2005, www.bechtel.com/newsarticles/65.asp.

2. "Bechtel and Edison Reach Agreement on Edison's Acquisition of a 50% Stake in International Water Limited," Bechtel Corporation, San Francisco, CA, November 9, 1999, www.bechtel.com/newsarticles/162.asp.

3. Ibid.

4. "Cochabamba and the Aguas del Tunari Consortium," Bechtel Corporation, San Francisco, CA, March 2005, www.bechtel.com/pdf/cochabambafacts0305.pdf.

5. For a full analysis by the Democracy Center of Bechtel's Cochabamba water rate increases, including both systemwide figures and individual bills, see "Bechtel vs. Bolivia: Cochabamba's Water Bills from Bechtel," http://democracyctr.org/bolivia/investigations/water/waterbills_index.htm.

6. Ibid.; "Cochabamba and the Aguas del Tunari Consortium."

7. From the Democracy Center's analysis of Bechtel's Cochabamba water bills.

on that fury. On January 11, the Coordinadora launched a full blockade of the city, demanding a rollback in water rates and repeal of the new water law. The backbone of the January action was the irrigators, who blocked the two lone highways leading in and out of Cochabamba with tree trunks and huge rocks. People in the city shut down streets with ragtag assemblages of rocks, bricks, and strung wires. Cochabamba was closed.

Road blockades were not a new tactic in Bolivia by any means. They had been used long before by the miners' unions in their struggles. In Cochabamba, once or twice a year, local transportation workers or other groups would stage a one- or two-day protest in which buses stopped running, bridges and roads were blocked, and most businesses and schools closed. These blockades, however, usually had the feel of a brief citywide holiday. Families passed the day at home, or playing soccer, or biking the empty streets, as negotiators worked on a settlement over the demand of the day.

The January blockade over water privatization was something different entirely. For three days Cochabamba was shut down tight. The city's airport was closed. Bus service in and out of the valley was suspended. Thousands of protesters occupied the city's central plaza. Cochabamba was in the midst of something uncharted.

In January 2000, Bolivia's national government was headed by President Hugo Banzer Suárez. Elected with just 22 percent of the vote three years earlier, General Banzer had ruled the country once before, as its coup-installed dictator from 1971 to 1978. The people of Cochabamba, especially leaders of the Coordinadora, had very clear, often personal memories of the kind of serious human rights abuses Banzer was capable of committing. According to Coordinadora leaders, the factory workers' meeting room, from which their huge red banner now hung, had been used for a time as a makeshift torture center during the Banzer dictatorship.

Initially, the government declared that it would not deal with the Coordinadora, dismissing it as speaking for no one and hoping that the protests would collapse on their own. By the end of day two, government officials were sitting across a table from Coordinadora leaders and scrambling for a solution to get Cochabamba open for business again. At the end of day three an agreement was announced: the government pledged to take a hard look at both the rates and the new water law and come back with a proposal. The Coordinadora gave Banzer three weeks. In the meantime, residents of the city stopped paying their water bills. Bechtel's representatives announced that the company would start cutting off water to families that refused to pay the hiked rates.

At the start of February, Coordinadora leaders announced plans for a "takeover" of Cochabamba's symbolic central plaza. What they planned was a modest rally during the city's daily two-hour shutdown for lunch, involving a few hundred people. Those gathered would cheer on as a few fiery speeches were made reminding officials of their pledges. Then everyone would go back to work. "We told the minister of government, 'Nothing is going to happen,'" said Olivera. "It was going to be a takeover with white flags, with flowers and bands, like a party."[19]

Instead of letting the rally pass as a minor event, Cochabamba's regional governor, Hugo Galindo, a Banzer appointee, announced that the "takeover" of the tree-lined plaza was illegal and would not be allowed. Somewhere in the halls of power in Bolivia's political capital,

La Paz, Banzer and his senior advisers decided that it was time to offer the Coordinadora a show of force. Strategically, it could hardly have been a worse idea.

On Friday, February 4, Cochabambinos woke up to more than one thousand heavily armed police occupying the city center, all of them brought in from other cities across the country. Banzer and his aides understood that Cochabamba police could not be counted on to take such a hard line against their own neighbors and relatives.

For the people of Cochabamba, even those who may not have been sympathetic to the water revolt before that, the invasion of police was akin to a declaration of war against them by their own government. Not only were Bolivia's leaders refusing to roll back Bechtel's huge price hikes; now they were protecting those increases with tear gas and guns. Public support for the Coordinadora swelled.

For two days Cochabamba's graceful colonial center turned into a war zone. Every block leading to the plaza was converted into a battle-field. At one end police outfitted in full riot gear blocked the streets with tear gas cannons. At the other end, protestors—young people, old people, poor and middle class—held their ground with rocks and sling-shots. Many wore an impromptu uniform of vinegar-soaked bandanas over the mouth and nose and baking soda under the eyes to protect them from the gas. The doors of middle-class homes would suddenly open up and water and bowls of food would appear, an offering of sup-port to those standing up to the government in the streets.

It was in February that the water revolt was joined by an important new ally, the coca farmers of the Chapare and their leader, Evo Morales. The *cocaleros* brought with them years of experience in resistance tac-tics against troops sent in to destroy their crops. "It was the *cocaleros* who showed us how to use the bandanas and vinegar to fight the effects of the gas," said one Coordinadora activist. Morales himself was on the streets those days, standing down the police.

Almost all local radio programming was suddenly converted into all-day phone-in programs, as caller after caller condemned the government and the company. In two days, more than 175 people were wounded, most of them victims of flying tear gas canisters or police beatings. Whatever public legitimacy the government had on the water issue was gone. Faced with an unexpected and intense public rebellion, the government announced, over Bechtel's objections, a temporary rate rollback for six months. The Coordinadora had won its first victory. "This gave a lot of strength to the people, a lot of energy. They felt victorious," said Olivera.

A Change of Strategy

"The [Bechtel] contract was very hard to get hold of," remembered Omar Fernández of the Coordinadora. "It was like a state secret."[20] Through Congressman Maldonado, a Coordinadora leader, Coordinadora members were finally able to get a copy of the complex, inch-thick document. After the February confrontations, they began to examine the contract more closely, with the help of a team of Bolivian economists, lawyers, and other professionals who had joined the cause.

The team of professionals uncovered Bechtel's guaranteed profit of 16 percent per year and learned that the company had won the concession with virtually no up-front investment.[21] Coordinadora leaders became convinced that they needed to change strategies. Instead of demanding just a rollback in water rates, they began talking about canceling the contract outright and putting Cochabamba's water back under direct public control.

The demand for cancellation of a major international water contract was bold: nowhere else had popular protest succeeded in reversing such a major privatization deal. In March, Coordinadora leaders took the unusual step of organizing a *consulta popular*. For three days activists set up small tables in plazas and other public gathering places throughout the Cochabamba valley to survey residents about the rate increases and the water law. More than 60,000 people participated, nearly 10 percent of the valley's population, and 90 percent endorsed cancellation of Bechtel's contract. "The *consulta* made our movement much more participatory," said Olivera, and cancellation became the Coordinadora's official demand.

The Final Battle

At the start of April 2000, the Coordinadora announced what it called "La Última Batalla," the Final Battle. Coordinadora leaders warned that they would begin an indefinite general strike in the city and a blockade of the highways until the government met its two key demands: cancellation of the Bechtel contract and repeal of the national water law that threatened to seize control of rural well and irrigation systems. On Tuesday, April 4, the protests began and Cochabamba was shut down again for the third time in three months.

On Thursday, two days into the latest Cochabamba shutdown, officials led by the governor agreed to sit down to talk with Coordinadora leaders and other city groups in negotiations moderated by Cochabamba's

Catholic archbishop, Tito Solari. Late that night, the talks began in the regional governor's offices, with the governor, the city mayor, the archbishop, and other officials all present.

Just after ten o'clock at night, police—under orders from the national government in La Paz—burst into the room where the negotiations were taking place and put the Coordinadora leaders under arrest. None of the pubic officials present had any advance notice of Banzer's plan. "It was a trap by the government to have us all together, negotiating, so that we could be arrested," said Olivera, who was among those taken into custody that night. Archbishop Solari locked himself in his own office for the night, telling reporters that if the Coordinadora was under arrest, so was he. When word of the arrests spread, hundreds gathered outside the office where the leaders were being held. With the situation on the street growing more serious by the moment, Cochabamba's regional governor arranged for Olivera, Fernández, and the others to be released, just after three in the morning.

As the sun rose on Cochabamba the next day, the city could hardly have been more tense. Coordinadora leaders along with a good portion of other Cochabamba residents expected a military takeover of the city at any moment. The crowds in the city's main plaza grew to more than 10,000 people. Many of the people were from the city, but thousands of others had marched long distances from the countryside and had been there for days.

Community by community they arrived, to great cheers, each group carrying a banner bearing the name of their *pueblo*. One rural town official, who had marched forty miles to get to Cochabamba, said, "This is a struggle for justice, and for the removal of an international business that, even before offering us more water, has begun to charge people prices that are outrageously high."

A meeting was announced for four o'clock that afternoon between Governor Galindo and Coordinadora leaders, again to be mediated by Archbishop Solari, but held in the supposedly safe territory of his office in the Catholic archdiocese. By late afternoon, as word spread through the city that the governor had failed to show, people in the plaza feared the worst. A half dozen teenage boys climbed to the bell tower of the city's cathedral, tying ropes to the bells so that they could be rung as a warning when soldiers started to invade the city.

Just prior to the meeting's scheduled start, Galindo was in his central plaza office and could hear the angry crowd outside. Windows had already been broken on the front of the building. A fire was set against the giant wooden main door. He feared for the safety of the workers in the building. At the hour he was supposed to have met with Coordinadora leaders and the archbishop he telephoned his superiors in La Paz. He explained that he saw no alternative except cancellation of the contract or an all-out war between the people and the government. He recommended that the contract be canceled. His superiors in La Paz were noncommittal.

Galindo then called Archbishop Solari, who was still sitting in his office with Coordinadora leaders. The governor told the archbishop that he had urged Banzer to cancel the contract. When Archbishop Solari relayed that message to Olivera and other Coordinadora leaders, it was transformed into something different and more dramatic—that the company was leaving.[22] Minutes later, still wearing a vinegar-soaked red bandana around his neck and with white smudges of baking soda under his eyes, Olivera stepped out onto the third-floor balcony where the giant red banner still hung over the plaza.

"We have arrived at the moment of an important economic victory over neoliberalism," he yelled with a hoarse voice to the crowd, which erupted in a cheer that rivaled thunder. He thanked the neighborhoods, the transportation workers, people from the countryside, university students, and others who had made the battle and the victory possible. Cochabambinos celebrated in the streets. Archbishop Solari presided over a packed service of celebration in the cathedral.

However, just hours later, events in Cochabamba took a dark and unexpected turn. Asked for comment by journalists, Banzer's spokesman refused to confirm the company's departure. As the day ended, Bechtel's local representatives faxed notices to the local press declaring that they weren't leaving. At midnight, Governor Galindo went live on local television. In tears he announced his resignation, adding ominously that he didn't want to be responsible for a "blood bath." In Bolivia, under a president with a dictator's violent history, this was code for something frightening.

Coordinadora leaders scrambled to go into hiding. "At around midnight I was passing by the *Los Tiempos* [the daily newspaper] building and a reporter told me, 'The government is going to declare a state of emergency,'" recalled Omar Fernández, leader of the irrigators. "So I took off on my motorcycle and hid." Bands of police burst into the homes of Coordinadora leaders and their families, arresting all those they could find. Seventeen people were put on a plane in Cochabamba and flown off to a mosquito-infested jail in Bolivia's remote eastern jungle.

The next morning, Saturday, as panicked Cochabambinos scrambled to local markets to stock up on food, President Banzer formally declared a "state of siege." Constitutional rights were suspended; a curfew and a ban on meetings were imposed; and soldiers shut off radio broadcasts in midsentence. A whole section of the city, the hillside where antennas continued to broadcast news, had its power cut off.

The public response was quick and furious. From their clandestine locations, the Coordinadora leaders who remained free called for an immediate reinstitution of road blockades. In one neighborhood an elderly woman with a slanted back laid out rocks in the street to block it. Young people, dubbed "the water warriors," headed back downtown to challenge Banzer's troops. Women walked door-to-door to collect rice and other food to cook for the people who remained camped in the plaza. By Saturday afternoon the conflict exploded. Protesters set fire to a vacant government office building, sending a huge plume of black smoke into Cochabamba's clear blue sky. Soldiers switched from using just tear gas to live rounds.

Just past noon, Victor Hugo Daza, an unarmed seventeen-year-old, was in one of the clusters of protesters gathered on a side street near the central plaza. A local television station captured footage of an army captain, Robinson Iriarte de La Fuente, firing live rounds into the crowd. A bullet exploded into Victor Hugo's face, killing him on the spot. A stunned crowd led by his older brother brought his bloody body to the plaza and held an angry, emotional wake. Iriarte would later be tried in a Bolivian military court, acquitted, and promoted the same day to major.

The city had reached a bloody standoff. President Banzer, who now faced spreading protests on other issues in cities all across the nation, had made it clear that he was not about to cancel a contract with a major multinational corporation. His public relations staff told foreign reporters that the price increases had only been minor and that the protests were being orchestrated by narcotics traffickers intent on destabilizing the government.

The streets of Cochabamba, however, were only getting more crowded and the protests more resolute. Some began to speak of *hasta las últimas consecuencias,* until the final consequences. Ana Lara Durán, a member of the Cochabamba Human Rights Assembly, explained what that meant: "Once you have already paid a certain price, you don't back down; you don't back down for anything."

Then, on the afternoon of Monday, April 10, the government made an announcement. Officials of Bechtel's company, who sat out days of violence watching it on television in a five-star hotel and insisting they wouldn't leave, had fled to the airport and left the country. The Bolivian government declared the contract canceled, saying in a letter to Bechtel's people, "Given that the directors of your enterprise have left the city of Cochabamba and were not to be found . . . said contract is rescinded."

Cochabamba celebrated wildly. Cars paraded along Cochabamba's avenues with horns blaring. The Coordinadora's leaders came out of hiding. Those who had been arrested were flown back from jail in the jungle and were greeted as heroes. Facing down the government of a former dictator, overcoming the power of one of the world's largest corporations, and reversing a fundamental policy of one of the world's most powerful financial institutions, the humble people of a city virtually unknown outside the country had won a victory that would soon echo its way to Washington and to the world.

THE WATER REVOLT'S IMPACT ON POLITICS: GLOBAL AND BOLIVIAN

It did not take long for news of Cochabamba's victory against Bechtel to travel far. The Democracy Center's dispatches led the way. A PBS film on the revolt would later report: "Though a major American corporation was at the center of the Bolivian unrest, not a single U.S. newspaper had a reporter on the scene. And yet, news of the uprising was reaching a worldwide audience through the Internet. The source was an electronic newsletter with thousands of readers, written by the American who had uncovered the Bechtel connection, [Democracy Center executive director] Jim Shultz."[23] But those dispatches would end up magnified many times over because of a coincidence of timing.

During the same week that thousands filled the streets of Cochabamba to oust Bechtel, in the United States thousands were heading to the streets of Washington, D.C., to protest at the annual meeting of the World Bank and the International Monetary Fund (IMF). When Tom Kruse, a U.S. citizen living in Cochabamba, heard about the planned march in Washington, in the midst of the Cochabamba tensions, he arranged for groups organizing the event to fax invitations asking Olivera to come. The plan was never that he would actually go, but to use the invitations, released to the Bolivian media, as a way to scare off the government from arresting him again.

On the night that the water revolt ended, Olivera announced that he thought he should go to Washington to tell the story of Cochabamba's dramatic victory. Standing in his way, however, was his lack of a U.S.

entry visa, and it seemed unlikely that Olivera was high on the list of people the U.S. Embassy would like to let in. While he sat in the embassy in La Paz's waiting room for his visa interview, I received a call from a reporter for a U.S. newspaper chain asking my help to get an interview with Olivera. "How about an exchange?" I suggested that he call the ambassador directly and ask her if she planned to give Olivera a visa. Two days later, visa fresh in hand, Olivera was in the United States.

The Washington protests were the first major public actions since protests in Seattle six months earlier in response to a World Trade Organization meeting, and they had ignited a public debate over globalization. But the debate was still abstract. Into that abstraction and rhetoric flew a hot-off-the-streets drama with direct links to World Bank policy and one of the United States' largest corporations.

Olivera hadn't been off the plane for an hour before he was on a stage with Ralph Nader before thousands of activists. Maude Barlow, president of the Council of Canadians and one of the world's best-known water rights activists, announced to the crowd: "Our hero from Bolivia has arrived!" The short man in the black factory worker's cap was greeted with a three-minute standing ovation. Later that weekend, Olivera stood at the head of a huge procession making its way through Washington's streets. Standing beside him, I asked what he thought of his first visit to the United States. "It looks just like Cochabamba," he joked; "police and young people everywhere."

International media and researchers began cutting a path to Cochabamba in droves. *New Yorker* magazine came in early 2001, producing both a full-length magazine piece and, in coordination with PBS, a documentary aired nationally in the United States in 2002. On their heels came dozens of other filmmakers and academics from the United States, the United Kingdom, Europe, Latin America, and elsewhere. Long after the Cochabamba Water Revolt had become a distant memory for most of the people who actually lived it, writing about it and making films about it was becoming a global enterprise.

Impacts on the Global Water Debate

It was not just in the streets of Washington that the legacy of the water revolt was having an impact beyond Bolivia's borders. Around the world it was lifted up as an example and an inspiration in other public fights to keep water under public control, from Atlanta to Stockton and Uruguay to India. "The Coalition for the Defense of Water and Life was, without doubt, the clear example here for the struggle for dignity and the promise that 'another world is possible,'" said Uruguayan water activist Adriana Marquisio.[24] The noted Indian activist Vandana Shiva later wrote that the Bolivian water revolt "provides a political education for every community struggling to reclaim their common and public spaces in this age of corporate globalization."[25]

The impact of the water revolt also reached into the halls of global policy making. Officials at institutions such as the World Bank found themselves having to defend their policies in the aftermath of Cochabamba. During 2000, the World Bank's president, James Wolfensohn, found himself directly questioned about the water revolt before journalists in Washington. Defending bank policy, he argued that impoverished countries needed to apply "a proper system of charging" in order to keep the poor from wasting water.[26] The bank's chief water official, John Briscoe, was drawn into defending the bank's water privatization policies from the pages of Canada's daily newspaper *The Globe and Mail*, to PBS's Cochabamba film, to an international water summit in Japan.

Within some institutions, Cochabamba also seeded some internal reflection about the policies of privatization. In 2002, the Latin American water unit at the IDB asked me to visit its office in Washington. The conversation began with the question, "What is it that you think we can do to help public water companies function more efficiently?" While the Cochabamba Water Revolt and other water campaigns that followed afterward have not changed the fundamentals of the global water policies coming out of these Washington-based institutions, they have forced a more open debate.

Impacts on Bolivian Politics

In Bolivia, the water revolt ignited a chain of events that provoked historic political and social change. For almost two decades Bolivian economics had been dominated by the Washington consensus, market-driven policies pushed by the World Bank and the IMF and carried out by national leadership that was fiercely obedient to those policies. The water revolt shook those arrangements to their core.

"We have always repeated those slogans 'Death to the World Bank,' 'Death to the IMF,' 'Down with Yankee imperialism,'" said Olivera. "But I believe that it is the first time that the people understood in a direct way how the policies of the World Bank, free trade, free markets, [are] putting us at such a disadvantage among the most powerful countries."[27]

Álvaro García Linera, elected vice president in 2006, wrote as a political analyst in 2001 that the water revolt marked the rising of "the multitude." That multitude, he declared, "possesses an organizing force capable of challenging the relevance of the prevailing systems of government . . . and of erecting alternative systems for the exercise of political power and the conduct of legitimately democratic life."[28]

Where once Bolivian governments found themselves in de facto power-sharing arrangements with the military, after April 2000, a succession of weak governments—all elected with 25 percent or less support from voters—found themselves in a form of power sharing with a rising tide of Bolivian social movements, whose primary demands were to change the country's economic direction.

The first clear evidence that the water revolt had triggered something bigger in Bolivian politics came in 2002, when Evo Morales, leader of Bolivia's main coca grower unions, ran for the nation's presidency at the head of the MAS (Movement toward Socialism) party. Challenging Washington-made economic policies was at the forefront of Morales's platform and his rhetoric. Voting for Morales became the way to express at the ballot box what people had expressed on the streets in Cochabamba. That, and a public declaration against Morales by the U.S. ambassador at the time, helped propel him within a percentage point of finishing in first place.

In 2003, the challenge to foreign-pressured economic policies returned to the streets, in two huge explosions of public protest. The first came in February against economic belt-tightening policies demanded by the IMF. The second came that October, when word leaked out of a plan by President Gonzalo Sánchez de Lozada to export Bolivian gas at bargain prices through Chile to the United States. Eventually those protests would force Sánchez de Lozada's resignation and set up national elections in December 2005 in which Morales was elected in a landslide victory as Bolivia's first indigenous president. (For more on the gas issue, see chapter 3; for more on protests over IMF policy, see chapter 4.)

There is little doubt that the changes under way in Bolivia today owe greatly to the battle over water that took place in the streets of Cochabamba in the first months of 2000. As Morales told *Time* magazine in a May 2006 interview: "We needed to end that internal colonialism and return the land and its natural resources to those who have lived on it for so many hundreds of years, instead of putting our economy in the hands of the World Bank, the IMF and transnational corporations."[29]

BECHTEL STRIKES BACK

In November 2002, a year and a half after they were forced out of Bolivia, Bechtel and its co-investors struck back. In Washington, in a secretive international trade court run by the World Bank, Bechtel's water subsidiary filed a legal demand for $50 million—a prize equal to what it costs to run the Cochabamba water company for seven years.[30]

A Case Behind Closed Doors

Bechtel and its associates filed their demand with the International Centre for Settlement of Investment Disputes (ICSID), an arm of the World Bank created in 1966 to provide arbitration between countries and foreign investors. Since the 1970s, ICSID has received more than 330 cases with the number growing each year.[31] Cases are decided by three-member tribunals, one member picked by each party and another picked by mutual agreement.

For Bechtel, the World Bank trade court was an ideal forum, for both its secrecy and the long distance between it and the rebellious Bolivians who had caused them so much trouble. Hearings by ICSID tribunals are strictly closed-door. Neither members of the media nor the citizens who would ultimately pay a settlement are allowed to know when the tribunal meets, where it meets, who testifies, or what they say. The process assumes that the only representation that Bolivians needed was from the Washington law firm hired by the Bolivian government.

The other advantage ICSID offered Bechtel was that it eagerly enforced treaty accords allowing corporations to demand from governments not just their actual costs but lost profits as well. Bechtel's representative, Michael Curtin, told PBS, "We're not looking for a windfall from Bolivia. We're looking to recover our costs. Now, we can also claim lost profits. We may do so. That's a very large number."[32] In fact, a windfall, a massive one, is exactly what Bechtel and its associates were seeking. In a private communication between Bechtel's public relations department and the Democracy Center in January 2007, the company admitted that its investment in Cochabamba had been no more than $1 million. Bechtel was demanding $50 million.

But getting access to the World Bank trade court was not an easy task for Bechtel. In order for the company to bring its case to ICSID, its water subsidiary had to be headquartered in a country that had a trade agreement with Bolivia and that agreement had to name ICSID as arbiter. The United States and Bolivia don't have such an agreement, nor do Bolivia and the Cayman Islands, where Bechtel located its water subsidiary on paper for tax purposes. In the fall of 1999, with Bechtel officials fretting over the potential Cochabamba reaction to their yet-to-be-announced price hikes, the company quietly moved its paper headquarters from the Cayman Islands to a tiny office in Amsterdam.[33] The Netherlands did have a trade agreement with Bolivia that let companies take their grievances to the World Bank trade court. On the eve of its price hikes, Bechtel was legally prepared for the worst.

The Coordinadora and Its Allies Mount a Campaign

Very few people anywhere had ever heard of ICSID before Bechtel launched its Cochabamba case, and almost all of those who had were corporate lawyers. No ICSID case had ever faced a major challenge by citizens groups. Mounting an effective fight against Bechtel would be difficult. The Coordinadora, and its international allies, including the Democracy Center, launched a campaign based on a clear strategy—in a legal forum handpicked by Bechtel, the key to winning was not to beat the company legally but to undermine its willingness to wage the fight. The campaign targeted Bechtel and its leading officers.

The targeting of Bechtel began with its president and CEO, Riley Bechtel, the great-grandson of the corporation's founder, and started before the revolt ended. In April 2000, when the conflicts in Cochabamba were at their peak, the Democracy Center obtained the CEO's personal e-mail address and sent it to its two thousand readers worldwide, encouraging them to write and ask Bechtel to leave. Hundreds did, provoking the corporation's first public response to its Cochabamba debacle. Groups supporting the Cochabamba revolt also held a protest at the company's San Francisco headquarters. The public attack on Bechtel was resumed soon after the company filed its $50 million case in Washington with media work, international organizing, and direct action aimed at Bechtel and its officials.

The campaign tied Cochabamba around Bechtel's public neck like a heavy weight that would not go away. Google reports more than 127,000 Web pages linking Bechtel to the Cochabamba revolt, including stories by scores of major news organizations and by activist groups across every continent. Journalists and citizens who had never heard of Bechtel before knew the name first for its association with the water revolt and the company's attempt to squeeze $50 million from some of South America's most impoverished families.

In February 2002, Dutch activists scaled the outside of the building in Amsterdam where Bechtel had set up its paper-only headquarters and posted a large sign renaming the street for Victor Hugo Daza, the seventeen-year-old killed in Cochabamba. In July 2002, the city government in San Francisco, home to Bechtel's actual headquarters, passed a resolution calling on the company to drop the Bolivia case. That September in San Francisco, a public protest against the case blocked the entrance to the corporation's offices and ended in fifteen arrests. In February 2004, another protest, in Washington, D.C., brought opposition to the case directly to the house of Michael Curtin, head of the company's Bolivian subsidiary.

The campaign also took its demands directly to ICSID. In September 2002, with the legal support of Earth Justice, a public interest environmental law firm, water revolt leaders formally requested legal status to join the case. That demand was backed by an International Citizens Petition endorsed by more than three hundred organizations from forty-three countries, calling on the World Bank trade court to open the case to public scrutiny and participation. The case that Bechtel hoped would be quietly settled in its favor behind closed doors had become a major public story.

On January 19, 2006, representatives of Bechtel and its co-investors arrived in Bolivia. Sitting next to officials of the government, they signed a formal agreement in which they abandoned their $50 million demand for a token payment of two bolivianos (thirty cents). Bolivia's lead negotiator, Eduardo Valdivia, explained why Bechtel had finally decided to drop its case. "The CEO [Riley Bechtel] personally intervened," he said. "He told his lawyers that the case wasn't worth the damage to the company's reputation."[34] It was the first time that a major corporation had ever dropped an international investment case as a direct result of global public pressure. It was a major victory for Cochabamba, a major victory for global activism, and an important precedent for the politics of future privatization cases like it.

A LEGEND WITH MIXED RESULTS

But what happened in Cochabamba after David slew Goliath? What did the water revolt mean for the people and their thirst for clean, affordable water? On the ground, the water revolt is a legend with markedly mixed results.

The clearest victory was on the issue that first sparked the revolt—the resistance by irrigators and farmers against having the national government and potentially a foreign corporation take control of their rural water systems. On April 10, 2000, along with the government announcement that Bechtel's managers had left the country, Bolivian lawmakers also repealed the hotly contested water law. In the years since, the national irrigators' union and its allies have won adoption of new water laws that strengthen assurances that water will be treated as a common good rather than as a commodity to be sold. It has been in the city, however, and in the management of the public water company taken back from Bechtel that the results of the revolt have been much less than romantic.

The People Take Over—but Not Really

In the immediate aftermath of the water revolt, Coordinadora leaders joined with the city government and the water company union to take over management of the public company (named, again, SEMAPA). An interim board of directors was named and a water engineer who had been part of the professional team assisting Coordinadora, Jorge Alvarado, was appointed chief executive officer.

In its first few months, SEMAPA enjoyed a wave of public goodwill. It rolled back rates to their pre-Bechtel levels, and water customers quickly began paying their overdue water bills, refilling the company coffers that Bechtel's representatives had drained during their brief tenure. Bechtel's company left behind, among other things, an unpaid $90,000 electric bill. Coordinadora leaders also rode a wave of public popularity and received a stream of offers of technical assistance from public sector water managers across the United States and Canada. Public companies under privatization pressures there knew that SEMAPA's success or failure would have a significant impact on the global water privatization debate, and they wanted Cochabamba's public company to succeed.

Behind the scenes in Cochabamba, however, the management put in place after Bechtel left town suffered problems from the start. Coordinadora leaders were deeply suspicious of the role of Cochabamba's mayor in the company, given his part in approving the privatization. Leaders of the union representing SEMAPA workers, while mouthing the rhetoric of public service, seemed most interested in protecting their ability to add friends and relatives to the company's payrolls. "In reality the company wasn't retaken at all," said Olivera.

The Coordinadora leaders who had organized on the streets tried to dive into the company's practical challenges—management issues, rate structures, expansion projects, and dealings with foreign lenders. With glazed eyes and declining interest in the details, the leaders from the streets decided that the Coordinadora needed to turn those details over to a "technical support team." Put together in late 2000, the team included an academic, a former SEMAPA manager, and a pair of community organizers. They fanned back out to the rural communities and urban neighborhoods that had been the backbone of the revolt, assessing the challenges faced by the company and evaluating proposals for reform. Their goal was to set an agenda that could make SEMAPA genuinely representative of the people it was supposed to serve, and free of the corruption and mismanagement that had plagued it before.

The technical team proposed that company managers begin working directly with neighborhood committees to tap into community labor and skills and into local development funds to help get water to neighborhoods that lacked it.[35] "We did workshops with the employees and with communities across Cochabamba," recalled Carmen Peredo of the Association of Irrigators, a member of the team. "But the director [Alvarado] didn't want the changes that came out of them."[36] She also blames a lack of support from those who led the revolt. "The proposals were there, but the Coordinadora didn't fight for them."

The one major reform that the Coordinadora did take up and did win, partially at least, was having a portion of the company's board of directors elected directly from the community. But when the first elections were held in April 2002 to select those community members, less than 4 percent of eligible voters went to the polls. In a city where, just two years earlier, people had taken to the streets by the thousands and risked their lives to take back their water, there was virtually no public interest in the nuts and bolts of running the water company.

Soon afterward, the Coordinadora technical team disbanded, and Coordinadora leaders shifted their sights beyond SEMAPA. Some focused on working directly with neighborhoods on water development projects. Some ran for and won election to Congress. Others took up new national battles, such as the demand for taking back control of the nation's oil and gas. Over time, the water company's management and performance began to draw all the same complaints as it did before privatization—inefficiency, corruption, and the padding of the payroll by the union representing SEMAPA workers.

Unsolved Problems

The work of a water company is, as one technical expert said to me, "not rocket science." Water systems, be they public or private, need to find sources of water, buy pumps, lay pipes, connect users, and come up with a sustainable financing scheme to pay for it. SEMAPA's record in accomplishing those tasks is, once again, a mixed bag.

Cochabamba still faces the same intrinsic water challenges it always has. The city has continued to grow rapidly since April 2000, and Mother Nature hasn't added any new sources of water to help expand service. SEMAPA's area of responsibility encompasses just over 500,000 people, half of whom still have no water or sewage service hooked up to their home.[37] Most of those families live in the city's southern outskirts, still the center of immigration into the Cochabamba valley. Critics of SEMAPA (and of the water revolt) are quick to seize on that ongoing gap in service, but as usual with statistics, there is more to be said. The story of water in Cochabamba is most centrally about how fast the system can expand.

In the seven years since the water revolt, SEMAPA has more than tripled the size of its service area.[38] That expansion is based on a policy that, as a public company, SEMAPA has a responsibility to provide service to all residents of Cochabamba, not just those fortunate enough to live in areas where infrastructure is already in place. This policy of inclusion stands in contrast, for example, with the privatized water system in La Paz and El Alto, where a French-owned company, Suez, all but abandoned the growing and impoverished outskirts.

But the number of new hookups also doesn't tell the whole story. Most days the new tanks and pipes laid in the city's south deliver no water at all. "Their dream was to have water every day, twenty-four hours a day," says Coordinadora activist Gissel Gonzáles of the families in the city's south. "Six years after the water revolt they still have water three days a week for two hours per day."[39]

Water experts who know SEMAPA well say that the company has failed to address its two biggest problems. In a valley still deeply thirsty for water, SEMAPA loses about 55 percent of the water it has to leaks in the pipes and to clandestine hookups. And despite a steady flow of financial support from international donors and lenders, including the Japanese

---

BOX 1.2 | Public versus Private: SEMAPA and Suez

At the heart of the water revolt lies an important policy question: are people better off with a water system operated by a public company or a private one? A comparison between two Bolivian cities offers an interesting case. Since 2000, Cochabamba has operated under a public water company, SEMAPA, while the cities of La Paz and El Alto operated, until 2007, under a firm run by a large private water corporation, Suez of France.

In 2003 Suez's Bolivian water company (Aguas del Illimani) reported achieving "100 percent coverage" for its water service in La Paz and El Alto.[1] By contrast, SEMAPA reported in 2004 that in Cochabamba its water service coverage still hovered at a meager 46 percent and had remained virtually unchanged in the four years since its takeover from Bechtel.[2] On the face of it, private versus public seemed like no contest at all. But the real story lies beneath those numbers.

First, the two companies have radically different definitions of what it means to be "covered" in terms of water service. In Cochabamba, SEMAPA defines coverage to mean you have a water hookup to your house. In La Paz and El Alto, Suez claimed coverage if you had a water pipe running down your street, whether your home was actually hooked up to that pipe or not. And with hookups under Suez costing more than three and a half months of minimum-wage salary, many families can't afford them.

Second, the companies in La Paz and El Alto and Cochabamba also have radically different notions of who they are obligated to serve. Both areas are marked by established urban centers with developed infrastructure, surrounded by outskirts where water infrastructure has to be built from scratch. When Suez negotiated its contract with the Bolivian government in 1997 (another privatization demanded by the World Bank), it essentially took a map of the region, drew a line around the areas where water pipes were already in place, and established that as its "service area." It excluded the communities, most notably in rapidly growing

---

government and the IDB, the company still doesn't have a sustainable financing plan in place. One water expert familiar with SEMAPA's internal workings blames the problems on mismanagement: "It is an organization that is completely dysfunctional. They don't generate enough income to cover their costs, and they are letting the system deteriorate."

And the people paying the cost, the expert said, are the valley's most impoverished families. With the resources SEMAPA has been given "you ought to be able to provide water twenty-four hours per day, and the poor should actually pay less."[40] Luis Sánchez, who was a key leader in the water revolt and later served as the elected SEMAPA board representative for the city's southern neighborhoods, put it more bluntly: SEMAPA "is still a space for robbing money."[41]

El Alto, where infrastructure was absent and would be costly to provide. It was the water equivalent of a health insurance company carefully excluding people who might get sick. In contrast, in Cochabamba since the departure of Bechtel, SEMAPA has repeatedly expanded its service area, tripling its geographic obligations and increasing by 14 percent the number of families it needs to serve.[3]

Between 1997 and 2004, in a region surrounded by glacier melt and other abundant local water sources, Suez claims to have increased the number of homes connected to water service by 50 percent (78,000 connections).[4] SEMAPA, operating in a region where water has to be brought in from elsewhere, increased the number of homes connected by 16 percent (9,000 connections) during roughly half as many years.[5] In January 2005, citing Suez's policy of excluding more than 200,000 residents from its service area, angry residents of El Alto led Bolivia's second water revolt, resulting in a decision by the government to nullify the French company's contract and organize a new public utility to takeover.

1. Carlos Crespo F. and Omar Fernández, "Informe final: Estado, movimientos sociales y recursos hídricos. Presión social y negociación luego de la guerra del agua de Cochabamba" (Final report: State, social movements and water resources. Social pressure and negotiation after the water war of Cochabamba) (Programa Conflictos y Colaboración, Universidad de la Paz Costa Rica, CESU-UMSS, IDRC, 2004), 275. See http://idrinfo.idrc.ca/archive/corpdocs/121552/5-CESU_2.pdf.
2. "Informe de Gestión-Gerencia Comercial" (Commercial Management Report), SEMAPA, Cochabamba, 2004, 43.
3. Ibid.
4. "Aguas del Illimani le informa" (Auguas del Illimani informs you), Special newsletter from *Aguas del Illimani*, La Paz, Bolivia, 2004.
5. *Informe Gestión 2004, Gerencia Comercial Comparativo por Gestiones* (Management Report 2004, Comparative Comercial Management Report), SEMAPA, Cochabamba, Bolivia, 4.

In good part because of SEMAPA's failures, many outlying neighborhoods in the valley have stepped up their efforts to solve their water problems themselves, with the Coordinadora playing an active part. Gonzáles explained the experience of one neighborhood, Villa Pagador: "The community organized and dug a well 393 feet deep. That water is then pumped 7.5 miles to a tank that serves two hundred families. They decide themselves how much they will pay. If a pump breaks, they decide together how much each family will pay to help fix it. But 1,600 more people still lack water service. They need a bigger tank, more pipes. They need sewers."

This community approach to getting water is being repeated in many communities in the valley, often in cooperation with SEMAPA, with the company buying the pipe, for example, while the community provides the labor. Other communities leave SEMAPA out of the picture on purpose, arguing that by administering the water themselves they save having to pay the high administrative costs that SEMAPA would add if it controlled the water. Some communities are negotiating hybrid arrangements with SEMAPA, in which the public company gets water to the neighborhood and the neighborhood administers its distribution to residents.

This ad hoc system is not without problems, to be certain. It still subjects fragile groundwater supplies to overuse, and it can lose out on some of the efficiencies that a larger system can offer. It also only addresses the problem of access to water and not the parallel problem of sewage removal. But in many parts of Cochabamba, seven years after the water revolt, the spirit of public participation in water issues is most present in these projects. They are an example of the kind of collaboration between communities and the water company that many had hoped for when the water revolt was fought.

A Recipe for Repair

What will it take for the people of Cochabamba to realize, in a practical way, their dream of clean and affordable water for all the families that live in this high valley?

"It gives me some shame to talk about SEMAPA," said Carmen Peredo of the irrigators. "We have a historic responsibility to fix the company." That recognition has been slow to echo through the organizations that helped lead the water revolt. They know that public admissions of SEMAPA's many faults will be turned by their adversaries into claims that the water revolt itself was a mistake, that Cochabamba would be better off if Bechtel had stayed. The best way to defend the water revolt's legacy is to make sure SEMAPA, as a public company, is a success.

That work needs to begin with a clear analysis of SEMAPA's problems and a concrete set of proposals to address them. The Coordinadora and other citizens in Cochabamba have worked on these issues since the revolt, but that work has focused almost exclusively on process issues and almost never on the concrete nuts and bolts of company operations. Water activists in Cochabamba focus on how to build "social control" of SEMAPA—by having a board genuinely elected by communities, making its members and SEMAPA staff hold forums in neighborhoods, and engaging in joint planning with neighborhoods.

Social control of a public company is clearly important, but looking at process issues without looking at actual operational issues—such as the leak problem and SEMAPA's finances—has left the operational issues a mess. Not only do water activists in the valley lack clear positions on these matters; when the company has tried to undertake practical solutions, water activists have sometimes made it more difficult. For example, in 2006, when SEMAPA was pushed by the IDB to increase rates (unchanged in six years) just to account for inflation, activists attacked the proposal bitterly. But if costs are increasing and rates aren't keeping pace, how is the company supposed to keep up with the demand for expansion? Wading into the details of running a water company isn't romantic, but it is essential.

Luis Sánchez, the Coordinadora leader who later served in Bolivia's National Water Ministry, says that the only way to deal with the entrenched mismanagement that continues to plague SEMAPA is to combine pressure from the community with expert regulation by the national government. "We need intervention from above and below."

The "from below" part in Cochabamba has already begun. Neighborhood groups have marched to SEMAPA's headquarters the way they once marched to Bechtel's, demanding action. Pressure from the community led to a change in leadership of the union, when evidence surfaced of payroll padding and other corruption. The company's elected board members were scoured publicly when it was revealed that they were paying themselves expensive attendance bonuses for meetings that never even took place.

The national government, through the Water Ministry, has made some overtures toward regulation from above, but with little effect. The other source of pressure from above, one that has actually been a positive influence on efficiency at SEMAPA, is its chief lender, the IDB. But Bolivians shouldn't wait for pressure from Washington to make their water company work better, any more than they accepted pressure from Washington to make it private. The road to having an efficient public company that can provide water every day is still a long and winding one in Cochabamba.

CONCLUSION

Water privatization came to Bolivia as a theory, on the wings of foreign coercion. The World Bank officials who pushed the plan to bring in multinational corporations proclaimed that it would deliver three things that impoverished countries desperately needed—strong managers, skilled technical experts, and investment in expansion of service. That's how it looked on paper. In Cochabamba, however, the theory didn't work out quite the way its authors and proponents said it would.

The foreign managers sent in by Bechtel proved so unskilled that they got kicked out by a popular rebellion just a few months after they arrived. Further, when the government began shooting people in the streets to defend the company's interests, rather than try to help diffuse the conflict, Bechtel's people just poured gasoline on the flames with public announcements that they were in town to stay.

The technical expertise that Bechtel promised, and planned to charge a good deal for, proved to be available to Bolivia for free, from water experts all over the world eager to help. The much-needed capital that Bechtel was supposed to bring amounted to an up-front investment of just $1 million to acquire a forty-year lease worth vastly more. The cost of Bechtel's capital would be a guaranteed profit of 16 percent per year, and financing that high profit was one of the reasons for the big rate hikes that led to the rebellion.

Water privatization should not be held out as a matter of economic theology, something unchallengeable, by either its proponents or its critics. Privatization in general is not inherently good or evil. The debate is in the details. In Bolivia, there is a spiritual objection, among many, to ever putting water, the *blood of the earth,* into corporate hands. But in the case of water, that spiritual opposition to privatization also happens to be backed by experience and analysis. As a practical policy, water privatization suffers four huge problems.

The first is the natural way in which privatization prices water beyond what low-income people can afford. The World Bank is an advocate of "market pricing" of water, and in the Cochabamba case it directly argued against subsidies that might have made water affordable for the city's poorest families.[42] In nations both impoverished and wealthy, people with low incomes cannot afford the actual market cost for basic services. In the United States, states commonly provide "lifeline rates," subsidizing everything from electricity to basic phone service. In Cochabamba, privatization and Bechtel's profit demands priced water out of reach for many families.

The second problem is the distance that privatization puts between water users and those who make the real decisions. How is a teacher, or a seamstress, or a farmer in Cochabamba supposed to have any measure of influence on a major foreign corporation a hemisphere away? For all of the public company's faults, at least in Cochabamba today, when people want to complain, they know where to go and they get attention. Bechtel proved immune even to bloodshed.

Third, privatization opponents are justified in worrying about the protection of workers' rights. While there is certainly in Cochabamba a clear record of the water company union taking too much control, labor rights still matter and private companies are by nature far less interested in those rights than are public companies.

Last, it is important to note that while World Bank officials evidently deemed the Bolivian government insufficiently competent to run its public water systems, it acted as if that same government *was* sufficiently competent to negotiate a handover of its water to a huge foreign corporation and to capably regulate that corporation's work. This too proved false theory.

Privatizing a water system as a whole means handing over total control over a resource that is essential to life. That is the root of privatization's failures. But that doesn't mean that a public company cannot contract specific tasks out to private firms. Who lays pipe in the street is not a moral issue. In some cases it may well be good public policy, even in Bolivia, to contract out specific work, while keeping control of the system in public hands. "I think we need to rethink our critique of possible private participation in water. We've been too ideological," said René Orellana of Agua Sustentable, who served as a key Coordinadora adviser during the water revolt and later as vice minister of water in the government of Evo Morales.

In the end, Cochabamba's famous water revolt was really three separate battles. The first was fought and won in the streets of Cochabamba in 2000. It became an inspiration to so many because some of the most humble people in the world risked their lives to take on one of the most powerful corporations in the world, and they won. "The Bolivian water revolt has had an enormous impact on the global fight for water rights," said Maude Barlow, the water rights leader from Canada. "The personal stories of heroism and struggle of the Bolivian people are very powerful and have been recited over and over all around the world."

The second battle was the fight to block Bechtel from taking $50 million from the people who ousted it. That battle was won by building alliances that stretched from Sri Lanka to San Francisco and by having a clear, relentless strategy to make Bechtel bear, in public, the weight of its actions.

The third battle, the far less romantic one, is the one taking place in Cochabamba today. It is the struggle to match the dream of the water revolt with the reality of a solid public water system that serves everyone. On that one the jury is still out. "The thought that the people could simply recover the water company was an illusion," said Jenny Frías Alonzo, a resident of a Southern Cochabamba neighborhood and an activist in the revolt. "I don't think that the water revolt ended [in April 2000] but began then. Now the people are conscious that this is a process that continues."[43]

In the end, how *did* the people win the Cochabamba Water Revolt? Was it skilled organizing? Was it the foolishness of the company to raise rates so high and so fast, or the arrogance of the government to send out police to try to break the protests? Looking back on it now, it seems clear that what actually won the water revolt was heart. In a moment in history when so many people seem frozen by the complexity of things, the people of Cochabamba saw in the water revolt a simple issue of right and wrong and had the enormous courage to fight for what they believed to be right. It is an example that reverberates still.

Doña Ignacia herds her sheep and llamas through hillsides along the Desaguadero River, where an Enron-Shell oil spill in January 2000 unleashed an environmental catastrophe. Photo: Christina Haglund (2006).

CHAPTER 2

A River Turns Black

*Enron and Shell Spread Destruction across
Bolivia's Highlands*

Christina Haglund

*In January 2000, a Bolivian oil pipeline operated by a subsidiary of
Enron and Shell broke open in the Desaguadero River and spread
twenty-nine thousand barrels of toxic petroleum across nearly a million
acres of indigenous farm and grazing land. It was one of the gravest
environmental disasters in the nation's history, and yet it received virtually no attention outside of Bolivia. What foreign attention the spill did
receive was limited to accolades for the two companies for their postdis-
aster cleanup and relief efforts.*

*Six years later, Christina Haglund set about the task of looking
beyond the companies' public relations claims to what really happened
that January, and afterward, along the banks of the ancient highlands
river. First she reviewed nearly a thousand pages of legal documents,
environmental reports, and news stories. Then she set out to the river,
staying more than three months in the communities and homes of the
people who lived through the disaster. She gathered their stories and testimonies of an environmental catastrophe, the government that failed to
mediate it, and the corporations who escaped responsibility for it.*

THE MYSTICAL AND THE MACHINE

The Highlands

For the people of Bolivia's highlands, Lake Titicaca is a mystic place of
long memory. Here, they will tell you, is where the sun and the moon

were born. Here is the birthplace of the spirits of the Incas. Perched at an altitude almost three miles above the sea, this lake has only one vein, only one outlet that draws its water out onto the vast flatlands: the Desaguadero River. It is the river that, at the dawn of the millennium, would suddenly and mysteriously turn black.

The Desaguadero serves as the most important water source of the Bolivian altiplano, the high flatlands, where the river carves its route out of the hard earth down the western length of the country. Over the course of two hundred miles, the waters of the Desaguadero pass salty hillsides and swampy prairies, merge with lagoons, and finally settle to form the shallow muddy waters of Lake Poopó.

The men, women, and children who live within walking distance of the Desaguadero exist as echoes of centuries before. The farming and herding families of these highlands squeeze out a meager living where little or nothing grows. Trees are a rare find. Shade is a rare find. Fruit and green vegetables come in on trucks, if they do at all. Shrubs with wood never thicker than a child's wrist serve as the only available fire-wood, which is burned for cooking. Most homes are constructed of adobe mud walls, with roofs made of straw that was cut on the full moon.

Three different indigenous peoples make their life along the Desaguadero River. Their ethnicities and their languages are the same words. Urus speak Uru. Aymaras speak Aymara. Quechuas speak Quechua.

Women of the altiplano almost never wear pants. Instead, they wear heavy pleated skirts on top of wool petticoats, insulating their body from the cutting cold. These women spend at least five hours a day grazing sheep and llamas, animals whose meat is dried into jerky and whose wool is spun into clothes and textiles, braided into ropes, and even made into hats. With children wrapped tightly and strapped to their backs in woven blankets of bright colors, the women herders cover long stretches of community-shared land to fill their animals' bellies with wild plant life. They navigate in and out of the barren mountains of the Andes to quench the thirst of their animals in the waters of the Desaguadero. Their wealth is measured not in bank statements, but in sheep and llamas.

In fact, very little has changed along the Desaguadero River over the past five centuries. The cold continues to bite with sharp edges. Potatoes continue to be the most consistent food for a meal, whether boiled into a soup, baked in ovens made of pieces of earth, or freeze dried for the months to come. Children are born at home, and time is told by the movement of the sun and the moon. But not all aspects of rural Andean life are repetitions of generations past. People know about technology, and they want it.

Once a month, a plastic cassette is shoved into the community VCR at the high school in the village of Canuta. People from surrounding villages that have no electricity walk or bike as far as five miles to the makeshift movie theater. People want light for longer than the sun is up. Parents with more children than can be counted on one hand dream of plugging appliances into the wall. Women imagine how great it would be to have machines that could wash their clothes for them, saving them the long walk to the river and hours of washing by hand. Families can picture how much easier it would be to cook with the press of a button or the flip of a switch.

Don (Mr.) Pablo is a stout man who stands only as tall as my shoulders and who has permanently chapped red cheeks from the cold. In one of my long visits to the river, he demonstrated the essence of an ancient and profound bond between nature and human beings. He had a knife in his hand, and he whispered into the ear of a sheep. "La Pachamama (Mother Earth) is alive. And I am asking her for the life of this animal." With a controlled back-and-forth motion of the knife on the sheep's neck, the animal's blood spilled, and Don Pablo continued speaking in hushed Aymara. We watched life drain out of the sheep that his wife and daughters had so routinely pastured. This sheep would provide Don Pablo's family with meat for at least a week.

· · ·

For the people who live on these windy plains, Pachamama is alive in the same way that the sun and the moon were born. Nature and people cannot be separated. Survival depends on a family's efforts to plant and harvest, in combination with what the earth gives. Powers of the universe are personified, as well as respected, honored, and embraced. The Desaguadero River is one of these powers, and to the people who call the altiplano their home, this river is alive.

The Corporation and Its Pipeline

For four decades, Bolivia's state-owned oil company, Yacimientos Petrolíferos Fiscales Bolivianos (YPFB), ran the nation's vast oil and gas industry. With operations that covered exploration, industrialization, and commercialization, the YPFB brought in between $300 million and $400 million annually throughout the 1990s to Bolivia's impoverished public treasury.[1]

In the mid-1990s, the World Bank took new interest in Bolivia's oil industry. Its representatives agreed that South America's poorest country, in a state of economic crisis, could not fully tap its energy potential and take its resources to the global market. The bank commissioned a team of consultants to evaluate the extent of Bolivia's petroleum and ponder the possibilities for investment.[2] World Bank officials pressured Bolivia toward a path they deemed more modern, more lucrative: capitalization. Bolivian government officials bought into the new global economics and agreed to put Bolivia's gas and oil industry under primary ownership and control of foreign corporations. Bolivia's oil industry was broken up into three pieces, one for transport and two for exploration and development. Then the pieces were put into the hands of foreign corporations. (For more on oil and gas, see chapter 3.)

One of the foreign corporations that came shopping for a piece of Bolivia's oil industry was a new, relatively unknown firm from Texas—a company called Enron. Enron was one of the world's leading electricity companies, with energy operations from India to Mozambique. More than half of Enron's $6.5 billion overseas operations were located in South America.[3] *Fortune* magazine named Enron "America's Most Innovative Company" for six consecutive years. Enron found its true fame, however, at the end of 2001, when it was revealed that its financial miracle was based on creative and planned accounting fraud.

It was in 1994 in Miami when Enron first got involved. Bolivian government representatives took a break from their participation in the Summit of the Americas to sign the first of several secret agreements that would eventually make the company co-owner of Bolivia's oil and gas pipelines.[4] Even though the Bolivian Constitution clearly states that international contracts require congressional approval, the Bolivian Congress never laid eyes on the document, nor did the Bolivian public.

Three years later, in 1997, Enron joined with Shell of the Netherlands to form Transredes S.A., and the deal was finalized. The two foreign corporations now had a 50 percent controlling stake (with Bolivia owning the other half) in the steel snakes that transported Bolivia's valuable petroleum to foreign markets. To secure that ownership, a deal worth hundreds of millions of dollars, Enron and Shell never had to pay the Bolivian government anything. They paid, instead, with promises of future investment.

In 2004, an official Bolivian review concluded that, in fact, Enron and Shell had invested only about one-fourth of what they had agreed to.[5] Roberto Fernández Terán, a professor at Universidad Mayor de San Simón (the public university in the city of Cochabamba) who leads a national research project on oil and gas in Bolivia, said, "It is as if your family's farm were simply given to new owners for nothing. And the new owners began to profit off of what used to be your family's."[6]

Covering thousands of miles, gas and liquid hydrocarbon pipelines slither through jungles, creep up mountains, duck under roads, and dash across rivers. These tools of a modern economy sneak across flatlands without electricity and pass through remote countryside where Spanish is the second language, if it is spoken at all. The ancient Desaguadero River intersects with one of these pipelines, a 350-mile segment that moves Bolivia's oil onward to the Pacific coast at Arica, Chile.[7] On the last weekend of January 2000, a catastrophic event occurred at the intersection of that steel cylinder and that long path of water that originates at Lake Titicaca.

The Discovery

Why is our river black? This was the question in the minds and on the lips of the people living alongside the Desaguadero that would not be answered for another week.

Doña (Ms.) Porfiria's black braids reach down to the small of her back. I met her after having heard her incredibly high-pitched voice call for her daughter from a distance. Her village is south of Santiago de Callapa, located fifteen miles downstream from where the pipeline crosses the river. Doña Porfiria was one of the first to discover the strange black moving mirror that the Desaguadero had become.

On January 29, 2000, she was making her daily trek to the river accompanied by her family's herd of thirty-two sheep and fourteen llamas. But on this particular Saturday afternoon, when she arrived at the river, she did not recognize the waters she had known since her childhood. Her first reaction, she explained, was to think that the black was an omen of good luck.

"I laughed out loud. Whatever could this be? I was excited, and I wanted to tell my family about my discovery. The river flowed as it always does during the rainy season, but it was thicker. The water looked so different. It looked like it was in the shade, as if it was filled

with darkness. There was an odd smell, an unfamiliar smell, that made me think again about what this new river would actually bring us."[8]

. . .

For eight months of the year rain is only a memory on the altiplano. But in the four spring and summer months when water does fall from the open sky, it falls hard. In some stretches, the Desaguadero triples in size. The lakes and lagoons nourished by the river's waters can swell to double their dry season levels. The rainy season in 2000 was not unusual according to Bolivia's National Meteorology Service.[9] What was unusual was that a one-hundred-foot portion of the pipeline that was supposed to cross above the Desaguadero River was actually submerged beneath its fast-flowing waters.[10]

Where is our oil? This was the question operators at the Chilean end of the pipeline asked in an early Monday morning phone call, forty-eight hours after the spill began, to Transredes officials in Bolivia.[11] Just after dawn on that previous Saturday, Transredes officials in Cochabamba had opened up the giant valves that were supposed to send their petroleum on its usual journey out of the valley, over the hills, and on its 350-mile trek over the Andes to the Pacific coast. Just before noon that Saturday morning, the oil passed, as scheduled, through the Transredes Sica-Sica pumping station, about fifty miles shy of the pipeline's crossing at the Desaguadero. That was the last time Transredes could verify the oil in its system. Unfortunately, the machine used to measure the pressure of the oil moving through the pipeline at the Sica-Sica pumping station was not functioning properly at the time of the accident, one of the main reasons it took Transredes two days to find out about the spill.[12]

The thick black liquid making its way out of Bolivia to the Pacific coast was "residual petroleum," a particular mixture of crude oil with gasoline that is especially toxic to human and animal health. Exposure to it can result in leukemia, tumors, degenerative illnesses, as well as immune system deficiencies.[13]

After the frantic phone call from company officials in Chile, it took Transredes twelve more hours to locate the spill and choke the valves on both sides of the river.[14] By then, however, the irreversible damage had been done. The Desaguadero had been converted by the spill into a brutally efficient delivery system, sending the company's oil onto cherished prairies, into mazes of hand-dug irrigation canals and fragile bird sanctuaries. By the time Transredes acted, its toxic black mixture had been spreading across waterways and land for forty-eight hours. At least 29,000 barrels of oil—enough to fill over a million gallon-sized milk containers—spewed into the Desaguadero River and would eventually stretch across 155 miles.[15]

"The green plants turned into the color of ash. The sheep had on shoes of oil, and the water to clean them was not any cleaner. Life went away," Don Vidal, a resident of El Choro, explained. "And we had no idea that the worst was yet to come, that even after the black was gone we would still be suffering because of it."[16]

The Desaguadero River, which was swollen from the rainy season, carried the oil swiftly, spreading it though swampy lagoons that exist only during the rains, past natural salt hills, through the Andes, until reaching the shallow waters of Lake Poopó, which can cover up to 965 square miles during the rainy season.[17] Farmers who had made their own irrigation canals—some as long as three thousand feet—did not know to close their canals before the polluted waters began saturating their crops. In the end, Transredes's oil would contaminate almost a million acres of fertile grazing and growing grounds.[18]

Doña Lorenza wakes up before the sun does and cooks potatoes. She's got to pack lunch for a usual day of grazing—the same potatoes from breakfast and a bit of jerky will quiet her midday hunger. Cloths are wrapped and knotted around the food and serve as her lunchbox, which is bundled away with her two-year-old baby, Evita. Every day is spent with the sheep and llamas that are their compañeras. The little girl cried not once all day, not even when her mother left her alone with me and her fifty-some animals for hours. Off Doña Lorenza went to harvest potatoes out of sight, leaving us on the banks of the Desaguadero—the most fertile grazing grounds for most of the year.

• • •

In 2000, when the flooded waters and swampy lands dried up, these community-owned grazing lands were left contaminated. When the sparse pockets of green out of the river's reach were not sufficient, animals fed on contaminated lands. The people of the Desaguadero River tried to adapt to the contamination of their river—but how could they to adapt to a disaster that affected every aspect of their lives? The very water they used for cooking and bathing, for hand-washing clothes, for fishing and bird hunting was no longer safe. Though some families collected rainwater, it didn't come close to what was needed for livestock and basic family use.

Warnings Ignored

Negligence is a legal term that refers to "the failure to exercise that degree of care that the law requires for the protection of other people."[19] On three separate occasions, Transredes was alerted by Bolivian officials and the company's own technicians that their pipeline—at the precise place where it crosses the Desaguadero River—could be the site of a major spill. Transredes itself acknowledges that the company had been warned in advance that a disaster exactly like this was waiting to happen along the banks of the Desaguadero River.[20]

Enron and Shell's company knew that its inherited pipelines had long passed their expiration date by more than a dozen years, according to a document the company filed with Bolivian authorities the year before. In August 1999, months before the disaster, Transredes was told by one of its own employees that the pipeline crossing the Desaguadero River had fallen off of its H-shaped metal supports and was partially underwater.[21] Four months later, Transredes received another warning, a report from the Bolivian government's superintendent of hydrocarbons, telling the company that the duct that crosses the river was in need of maintenance.[22] That inspection, which also found corrosion in the metal tubing, was classified as "first priority."[23] When Transredes did not respond, the superintendent once again warned Transredes of the dangerous conditions of the company's pipeline.[24]

Yet, instead of taking preventive action, Transredes just kept pumping oil. According to a March 2007 memo prepared by Transredes officials in response to questions from the Democracy Center, the company made a deliberate decision to delay the repairs for two reasons. First, they were concerned that undertaking a repair during the rainy season might, in itself, provoke an accident. They also did not want to interrupt the flow of oil through the pipeline.[25] In essence, Transredes officials made a bet that the battered section of the pipeline could hold out just a few more months. It was, conveniently, a bet that avoided an interruption in Transredes's profits that ran through that pipeline. In the end, it was a bet that went horribly wrong, one that left the people of the Desaguadero to pay the real price.

HELICOPTERS AND PROMISES

A week after the spill, the silence of the altiplano was interrupted by noises from above. Doña Julia, an almost toothless woman who speaks Aymara and only a few words of Spanish, came out of her adobe home where she was peeling potatoes. She bent her neck to the sky. For the first time in her life, Doña Julia saw up close a machine that flies. Enron and Shell's representatives appeared out of the sky, arriving to villages not found on any map. The rural people were awed by the arrival of helicopters and anxious for answers to get their lives back to normal.

Six years later, Doña Julia kissed the banana that I handed her. She smiled wide and told me that she thinks her sheep are actually pigs. They never stop eating and never seem satisfied.

"They told us the petroleum was fertilizer," she said.

"Who?" I asked.

"The oil spill people."

• • •

Experts hired by Transredes told the people living by the river that the oil was fertilizer, and seven years later, the company still claims that some scientific research finds that petroleum can "accelerate the formation of nutrients in the soil."[26] That "scientific research" has little meaning for those who make a life off of the soils along the Desaguadero, where seven years later the plants don't grow as they once did.

During this first devastating week after the spill, Transredes officials in Bolivia spent their time making long-distance phone calls to the United States and Europe. The strategy that would emerge from those calls was a five-point plan. First, the company launched an aggressive public relations campaign that portrayed the spill as insignificant and under control. Second, it projected the appearance of a successful cleanup and adequate emergency relief. Third, the foreign company pressured individual communities into a unilateral compensation process defined by Transredes. Fourth, it took control of the scientific data to minimize the evidence of the environmental damage. Finally, Enron and Shell's subsidiary wrapped its compensation package in the respected image of the international aid organization CARE (Cooperative for Assistance and Relief Everywhere), to facilitate Transredes's repayment for the oil spill through community projects.

This strategy would eventually win both Enron and Shell accolades as a "model of corporate citizenship." Along the river, the story was very different.

An Aggressive Public Relations Campaign

Transredes's public relations efforts with the Bolivian media began by contracting with a British firm, Environmental Resource Management

(ERM), to manage the company's potential public relations disaster, or as ERM described it, "assisting Transredes to overcome community concerns."[27] Initially, the Bolivian press eagerly reported the company's account of the story: a manageable one thousand to five thousand barrels of petroleum had spilled out of a tiny hole the size of a Bolivian coin.[28] Transredes promised to "clean the affected zone so that it would be equal to or better than before the accident."[29]

On March 8, 2000, just a month after the incident, a Transredes spokeswoman appeared on local television stations saying, "Happily, the communities have not been affected."[30] The president of Transredes, Steven Hopper, proudly spoke of his company's success along the river: "We have done well this past month obtaining the participation of the affected communities who are the labor force for the clean-up, and are being attended by our brigade of medics and veterinarians, as well as our social operators, though there is still much to be done. We remain firm in our initial promise to continue working with affected communities and fairly compensate them for the impact of the spill."[31]

A few weeks after the spill, one of the biggest planes in the world came to Bolivia. Television cameras and journalists clustered at the Cochabamba airport to report the arrival of the Russian-made Antonov, which came filled with sophisticated oil remediation technology, all-terrain vehicles, and teams of foreigners to lead the cleanup.[32] The cost of getting this plane to Bolivia was $600,000—half of what the company would eventually award to 127 communities in the compensation process.[33] Transredes also boasted its setup of a toll-free information phone number for affected families, the vast majority of whom would have to walk as long as five hours just to reach a telephone.

The cleanup was highlighted in the national media with footage and photos of affected people of the region who were hired to do the cleanup. According to some of those whom Transredes employed, the protective gear, disposable sunglasses, gloves, and foot coverings billed as the cleanup's uniform had been donned only for the photos. In reality, the "sophisticated technology" that was used in the cleanup consisted of shovels, rakes, and plastic bags.[34]

A few news outlets presented a different version of the story. A La Paz newspaper denounced the spill as "the worst ecological tragedy in the history of Bolivia."[35] The regional governor, Carlos Börth, declared the region a disaster zone in the days after the spill.[36] In the end, however, nothing could match the well-oiled public relations campaign launched by the company.

The Corporation's Cleanup and Relief

In the spread-out village of Acopata, the Desaguadero flows just on the other side of the hill, less than half a mile away. The people of Acopata count their riches in llamas and sheep, not in currency. The only money pocketed with any sort of regularity is from a family member in the city or the rare sale of an animal not destined for their own consumption. Don Juan de Díos is a co-owner of a bakery in the capital of La Paz. Like many who grew up near the river, he returns to the place of his rural upbringing to support his family during the arduous harvest and planting seasons. Don Juan explained that his fellow community members who were lucky enough to get one of the highly coveted cleanup jobs thought they had won the lottery.[37]

Transredes recruited people who lived along the river—many who had never had a paying job—to be the labor force for cleaning up the oil that was supposed to go to Chile. Peasant farmers and animal herders worked long hours for thirty-five bolivianos a day, almost two-thirds more than a farmer's average daily income.[38] Over three thousand people were employed, managed by supervisors who didn't speak their language. None of them knew at the time the bitter price they would pay for their lottery winnings of temporary employment. Most of those who worked as the cleanup crew would end up sick from oil exposure or suffer from vision problems caused from the intense reflection of light off the company's spilled oil.[39] Despite an abundance of testimony to the contrary by those it hired, Transredes officials continue to claim that any health problems suffered by them could only have been temporary or were just the standard illnesses suffered in this highland region.[40]

Around forty community members from Ulloma had worked in the cleanup. Six years later, eleven members of this village of 250 families that sits fifteen miles south of the pipeline recounted their stories. They described how they met Texans with Cup-O-Noodles that only needed hot water to cook. They also said they felt they were "treated as dogs" during the cleanup by the company's imported specialists.[41] Unable to communicate with most of the cleanup technicians, the hired help of Ulloma also claimed they were not given adequate time to rest throughout the grueling work days.

The Emergency Plan That Didn't Exist

The Bolivian government and several public institutions repeatedly requested to see Transredes's legally required emergency plan, the specific

actions to be taken immediately following an environmental accident.[42]
The Vice Ministry of Energy and Hydrocarbons formally requested to
see Transredes's plan detailing the circumstances of the spill and the
immediate actions Transredes officials had planned in advance. The document was never presented to authorities.[43]

In order for Transredes, or any company, to operate legally in Bolivia,
it must obtain an environmental license. The process requires that the
company detail the environmental risks involved in its operations. Even
though the Desaguadero is the largest source of water in the altiplano,
Transredes never listed it as one of the waterways crossed by its
pipelines.[44] The cleanup was based not on any emergency plan devised
carefully in advance, but on improvisation two days after the emergency
took place.

The week after the spill, Transredes officially declared the river water
unsafe for human or animal consumption, and the company promised to
deliver emergency water supplies to the people of the Desaguadero.[45]
Later, 48 percent of the affected communities reported that they had consumed contaminated waters.[46] They simply had no other water to drink.

By February 19, 2000, less than a month after the spill, Enron and
Shell's pipelines were up and running again. Transredes had completed
the repairs that had been requested more than six months earlier. While
the people near the river still waited for clean water to be delivered, the
foreign corporation was back in the pumping business, ensuring there
would be no further disruption to its profits.

At the end of March, Transredes declared the massive cleanup to be
"80% finished."[47] Despite the company's public assurances that the
cleanup met international standards, a follow-up inspection by the
Bolivian Ministry of Sustainable Development concluded that the contamination remained and that the cleanup still required rigorous
efforts.[48] On July 31, 2000, six months after the spill, Transredes's
cleanup was officially concluded when the company deposited more
than 838,000 bags of contaminated materials in a cavern in the earth
near its Sica-Sica transport station.[49]

*Recess for the nineteen kids in the tiny village of Sica-Sica is in a little
park that sits adjacent to the schoolhouse. The children's playground—
equipped with a slide, monkey bars, and swings—had been funded by
Transredes. If children swing facing in one direction, they can see the
company's pumping station, a fenced-off area that is lit up twenty-four
hours a day. If they swing facing the opposite direction, they can see a*

football-sized field surrounded by tall fences, guarding a crevice in the earth filled with thousands of bags of contaminated waste.

• • •

On the Desaguadero in 2000, the fertile and lush season after the rain did not come as it had before. Despite cleanup efforts, land that Enron and Shell claimed to be cleaned was still spotted in black, and oil was found "sandwiched" in the earth according to the local community leaders.[50] There were no longer the normally abundant amounts of grasses and *totorales*—thick straw shoots nibbled by livestock—to provide the nutrition necessary for fattening sheep and llamas.

The Health Effects That Linger Still

When I first arrived in the village of Rancho Grande, the women told me that my *aguayo* was a fake. *Aguayos* are colorful rectangular cloths made of alpaca, llama, or sheep wool that are tied over the shoulders, an Andean version of a backpack. My *aguayo,* apparently, was made partially with synthetic yarn. Actually just the blue part. With keen and knowledgeable eyes, inauthentic *aguayos* can be spotted from a distance. Unfortunately for the women who weave and wear this cloth, damage that toxins can do to human and animal life years down the road is harder to see.

The most notable symptoms of exposure to toxic petroleum include skin irritations, headaches, nose and eye discomfort, and stomach problems.[51] The most dangerous health effects of residual oil are invisible. BTEX (benzene, toluene, ethylbenzene, and xylene) is a group of volatile organic compounds found in residual petroleum. Cancer- and deformity-causing, BTEX can be passed from grass and water to animals, from animals to people through meat, and from mothers to their unborn in the womb. These toxins can also be absorbed through the skin from clothes washed in contaminated waters or breathed into the respiratory system.[52]

Most of the families who live along the Desaguadero have very little or no access at all to basic health services.[53] Transredes's doctors set up temporary offices throughout the region to provide medical relief to the affected people in the aftermath of the spill. The thousands of people that saw the company's doctors reported suffering stomach pains, nausea, loss of appetite, headaches, and vision problems. Unfortunately, Transredes's medical help was limited. These health workers sent by the company had no special expertise in the effects of oil on human health.[54]

A Transredes press release from June 7, 2000, stated that more than five thousand people had been seen by the company's doctors—none of whom had symptoms related to the spill.[55] The only reference to petroleum in the company's medical report is the negation of any relationship between human health and the oil in the river. Possible future health risks were neither explored nor analyzed by the company's medical team.[56]

To treat the region's sick and dying animals, Transredes brought in veterinarians from Santa Cruz, the tropical city in eastern Bolivia where the company has its headquarters. The vets came, however, from a region where llamas live only in the small city zoo and had little expertise with the animals of the altiplano.

Don Teodosio, from the community of Acopata, is a cross-eyed man who can perfectly mimic the chirps of the native birds. He said that when veterinarians saw his ill sheep, they diagnosed the cause as consumption of poisonous plants. He explained that "the veterinarians did not help us, they simply blamed anything but the oil for the sickness of our animals. They took away our dead animals on trucks, and I never found out what happened to them."[57]

• • •

In the same June 7 release, Transredes declared that company veterinarians had seen more than 250,000 animals, none of which had symptoms related to the spill.[58] However, the company's private veterinary reports told a very different story, noting that animals indeed showed signs of petroleum consumption.[59]

The final failure of Transredes's emergency assistance was the company's inability to get food to the hungry animals that could no longer forage safely on contaminated lands. Hans Möeller, the former president of FOBOMADE (Oruro Forum of the Environment), an environmental organization in the regional capital, was present in a meeting when Transredes offered food for animals to a community: "I took out my calculator and discovered that the amount they offered was enough for each animal to eat four grams of straw—the equivalent of three matches—every day for a month, a ridiculous amount for sheep, considering they eat 1 to 2 percent of their body weight a day."[60]

Herding families had to choose between the lesser of two evils. They had to leave their livestock—their source of meat—to starve, or graze them on contaminated lands. Families chose to fill their animals' bellies.

The company's emergency assistance and relief fell far short of the communities' most basic needs. Though the company boasted about the medical and veterinary brigades it sent to the river region, as well as its distribution of emergency water supplies to thirsty people and animals, the reality was that sick families and animals received inadequate assistance and never received Transredes's promised emergency water supplies. The process of compensating communities for their losses proved to have its own set of problems.

The Transredes Compensation Package

The compensation process was always going to be problematic. Transredes, like any corporation, exists in a culture of documentation. Numbers must be assigned to assets in order to generate compensation amounts. Statistics and figures are needed to calculate market value. Into communities where books and pens are almost nonexistent and where literacy is a scarce luxury, Transredes dropped two piles of forms.

Communities, in the beginning, were glad to be involved in a process from which they could benefit financially. In the course of more than a hundred instances of environmental contamination in Bolivia, this would be the first time that affected people would be compensated by the company at fault.

The first document families were expected to complete required them to officially affiliate with a community. Transredes unilaterally decided that it would offer compensation only to communities, not to people as families or individuals. The second paper was a claims form, in which families were asked to document specific assets, quantifying and placing value on the livestock and crops of each affected family. This double-sided form made no sense to many people whose crops are not counted in kilograms or currency but are destined for consumption in their own household. Contaminated lands that are owned collectively by communities could not be claimed, nor could the damage done to the waters of the Desaguadero. The three lines designated for "needs" on the back of the form were hardly sufficient space to explain their need for clean water and food for animals or to make demands for fair compensation.

This compensation process actually began before the cleanup and was, in fact, a necessary prerequisite for it. Transredes told communities of the

Desaguadero that emergency relief would arrive and that the cleanup would start as soon as families associated themselves with a community and filled out a claims form.[61] With these forms, and the legal agreements that followed, the foreign company's compensation process began. It was a process that would eventually involve 127 villages.

The company promised an "open and honest compensation process."[62] The first step after the forms was the appointment of community "evaluators" to help quantify the damage caused by the spill. These community evaluators would then work with an evaluator representing Transredes to negotiate the compensation amount. The rural communities affected, however, did not have the resources to find or fund an evaluator. Instead communities had to resort to using professionals that Transredes paid for, and in some cases that the company hired themselves.[63] According to some residents, some of these "independent" evaluators worked justly for the communities they represented. In other cases communities claimed that their evaluator was more allied with the interests of Transredes. Together, the two evaluators agreed on a compensation amount for each community, which would include "all damage and harm, direct or indirect, present or future."[64] Due to the legal agreements signed earlier in the process, these settlement amounts could not be challenged by community members.

Even though the compensation amounts offered were minimal and fell well short of compensating the residents for the actual damage the company caused, tired and desperate communities signed the legal agreements anyway. Community members of Ulloma admitted their grim reality at the time. "We had no other option but to sign. Not signing meant we would receive nothing at all," one of them told me.[65] No one, not even the Bolivian government, was there to tell them what their rights were. The signatures of community leaders at the bottom of Transredes compensation contracts also gave the company something else its lawyers wanted dearly, a waiver of the community's right to bring later claims against Transredes for the damage caused by its oil.[66]

Don Vidal woke me up just after dawn. I had set up my tent just off of the road to El Choro as the rain began the night before. The broad-shouldered man with sculpted farming arms yelled to me inside my tent as if the walls were sound proof. "[Your tent] looks like a space-ship," he told me. Don Vidal told me that he did not understand the conditions of the contract. "We wanted to negotiate with Transredes

*and come to a fair conclusion, not to have imposed on us a contract we
did not understand."*[67]

•   •   •

The compensation received by the communities also failed to account
for the long-term effects of the spill. There would be no reimbursement
for the livestock stillbirths yet to come, the deformed animals yet to be
born, the reduced amount of milk yet to be produced, future health
problems, or the painfully slow recuperation of grazing pastures along
the river.

The agreements Transredes pressured communities to accept arrived
shortly after the spill, just as the people of the Desaguadero needed help
the most. In a number of cases the company held up emergency aid until
the paperwork was signed. Faced with the dire need for food for their
hungry livestock and clean water for their children, many communities
consented without asking any questions. People from the community of
Ulloma claimed that with the contract present and pen in hand, Transredes
said, "First sign, then you will have a veterinarian."[68] FOBOMADE, the
environmental institution that supported affected communities, claimed
that "poor rural people were blackmailed into signing agreements in
order to receive emergency assistance."[69]

Transredes's success in getting communities to sign its legal agreements and complete the paperwork owed itself not only to the desperation of the people along the river, but also to the work of Community
Liaison Officers (CLOs) hired by the company. This small contracted
team of Bolivian anthropologists, sociologists, and social workers spoke
the indigenous languages and understood the cultural complexities of
the social structures along the river. Twenty-five people were eventually
employed as CLOs under the direction of ERM, the British firm that
had also handled the Transredes public relations campaign.[70]

One Transredes CLO was a Bolivian anthropologist who hid under a
baseball cap. He refused to let me tape our conversation or use his name.
In a café in the regional capital of Oruro, he hushed the word Transredes
every time he spoke it. He said the Community Liaison Officers have a
bad reputation. They are accused of working for Transredes instead of
for Bolivia. He said that even six years later he is still haunted by a job
that he regrets having taken.[71]

Transredes's CLO reports documented that one of the greatest difficulties with getting people along the river to sign documents was the
result of "community leaders with an ideology contrary to that of the

company."[72] What the company labeled as difference in ideology was really about demands by communities for basic fairness. In the end, the CLOs proved to be very effective advocates on the company's behalf. Most of the affected families signed Transredes's legal contracts and were thereby officially locked in to the company's compensation plan.

The Company Takes Control of the Scientific Data

According to Transredes's lab samples, which were collected by scientists hired by the company and sent to the United States for analysis, the spill on the Desaguadero did not constitute an environmental disaster. Arthur D. Little Labs, based in Houston and Boston, concluded that most of the petroleum had evaporated. The company's water analysis showed very low levels of hydrocarbons, concluding that there was no ongoing risk to the population or to livestock.[73]

Independent analyses of water and soil, however, revealed very different results. The Civic Committee of Oruro refused to accept that the environmental destruction was so minimal and arranged for Patch Services of Canada to collect samples along the riverside to be analyzed by an independent lab in Alberta, Canada. Patch found significant quantities of petroleum in the samples collected.[74] According to their investigators, "If no positive action is undertaken, the residual oil will persist in the affected area for an extended period of time. The physical and chemical properties of the oil severely limit the extent to which the ecosystem can reasonably recover without treatment. Plant and animal life will be negatively impacted over the period the oil is allowed to remain untreated."[75]

The fact that the Desaguadero River does not have entrance or exit to the sea makes this body of water especially sensitive to contamination. Unfortunately for the people who make a living in the lands near the Desaguadero, Transredes's scientific results were used as the basis to quantify the damage done and thereby determine what was "fair" compensation.

Compensation Wrapped in a CARE Package

Getting compensation to communities would not be as easy as writing a check. Transredes addressed this challenge as one of its corporate parents, Shell, had done before in Nigeria.[76] It contracted the globally known international development organization CARE to handle the compensation process on the company's behalf. The contract signed between the two proclaimed that CARE would "turn a very simple process of compensation into a contribution to the sustainable development of a very poor region."[77]

The director of CARE Bolivia, Victor Rico, told me, even before I asked, that the dollar amounts for compensation were already determined before CARE got involved.[78] The aid organization stamped a humanitarian face on Transredes's process and was paid more than $800,000 for its services.

According to Transredes, the compensation program that CARE managed would return people's lives to equal to or better than conditions before the oil spill.[79] Compensation in cash was never an option, another decision made unilaterally by the company.[80] Instead, communities could opt for in-kind purchases, such as land, animals, or machinery. Or they could choose community projects, such as road building, electricity installment, or tourist development.

The communities of El Choro decided on a soil rehabilitation project, to improve the conditions of the earth for planting. Several communities put their compensation amounts together to buy a tractor. Their project also included training for the operation and maintenance of the machine. Six years later this tractor sits rusted and broken, the metal equipment worn down by the severe altiplano weather conditions.

Don Vidal, the man who thought my tent was a spaceship, took off his hat to wipe away his sweat. He shook his head and said that the parts to get the tractor fixed are too expensive and too far away.

The cold winter month that I spent in Acopata revealed how yet another of CARE's compensation projects proved better in theory than in reality. The aid organization awarded community members enough red bricks and cement to construct homes with a metal door, tin roof, and a window—a 250-square-foot dwelling. The people of the region themselves constructed the houses. In the frigid altiplano winter of 2006, I found many of those houses empty. Families opted instead to sleep in their adobe homes, which, according to them, provide far better insulation than brick and concrete.

Don Benedicto is an Uru fisherman who is missing his two front teeth and lives on Lake Poopó. He explained that his community's CARE project was the purchase of a used car—one that would ease the fishermen's long trek to the lake. This car lasted only a year. It broke down and the village didn't have the resources to repair it. This once-prized piece of the community's compensation now serves as play equipment for children.

·   ·   ·

Transredes officials claim that "there is no doubt that this was the compensation model that brought the best results and benefits to the population and local development."[81] The physical evidence and the testimonies of community after community, however, tell a story that does not trumpet the same level of success.

How did any of these projects repair environmental damage caused by the oil spill? How were pertinent issues such as water and food for animals addressed? While in theory, development projects and in-kind purchases were to be equivalent to damage done by the spill, this was far from the reality on the ground following the compensation process. New animals purchased as replacements for the ones that had died or fallen ill still grazed on contaminated lands and continued to drink contaminated water.

Ripped and faded CARE calendars were nailed into the adobe and brick walls of several homes in my travels along the Desaguadero. The top of the poster calendar read, "It is the hour to hold our hands together to get out of poverty." CARE distributed the equivalent of $1.2 million to just fewer than four thousand families through these various projects.[82] This works out to about sixty dollars per affected person, just short of the minimum wage in Bolivia for one month.[83] The $818,372 that CARE took home for its efforts was equal to 68 cents for every dollar it distributed in compensation.[84]

·   ·   ·

In the end, the total amount of direct compensation awarded to the communities accounted for less than 2.5 percent of the $48.2 million that the company claimed to have spent in the spill's aftermath.[85] According to the budget submitted to government officials by the company, the cost of planes and helicopters surpassed the amount awarded to communities. Evaluators were paid a total of $500,000, "security" cost $80,000, and over $70,000 was spent on long-distance phone calls.[86] Transredes also paid the equivalent of two-thirds of the compensation awarded to the communities to its own parent companies, Enron and Shell, for "professional services."[87]

COMMUNITIES SEEK JUSTICE

"Death to Transredes! Death to the contamination!" they cried.[88] The Bolivian farmers and families who live near the Desaguadero expressed their anger in the best way they knew how—they protested. After the spill, over and over again, communities affected by the disaster marched to the regional capital of Oruro and to the national capital of La Paz to demand action. Sometimes the protesters brought their animals—live ones walking by their sides or dead ones carried over their shoulders. On the same day that Transredes arrived at the Desaguadero in helicopters, more than 1,500 people had already abandoned their villages or homes to protest. Their message was simple: "We demand that the maximum authority of Transredes find the immediate solution to the damage caused, compensation for thousands of livestock at risk, and hectares of forage contaminated by petroleum."[89]

Among those who marched were members of the Uru Nation. The Urus are the original inhabitants of Lake Poopó and are considered one of the most marginalized indigenous groups in Bolivia. As fishing families, they often spend nights in their handmade boats on the lake, where they catch small *pejerrey* fish in 330-foot stretches of netting that they make themselves. The Urus also hunt the pink flamingos of the shallow lake and search for wild duck eggs hidden in straw shoots. The Urus are dependent on the life of the lake. Don Rufino, a man who always appears to be wearing green lipstick because of the ball of coca in his cheek, is an indigenous leader of the Urus. He said: "We have no official title that makes the lake our own. We are not recognized as the inhabitants of this land or this lake on paper, and this was our biggest struggle as we tried to claim damages against Transredes. The company knew that we did not have the papers, and Bolivian law was on the side of Transredes."[90]

The president of the Uru Nation during the time of the spill, Juan Condori Mamani, explained: "The fish and birds of the lake no longer exist. There are some flamingos, but not sufficient to hunt and dehydrate to sell. People say that our meat is contaminated. Children are not attending school because they are sick. . . . Nobody is helping us, we have no medicine or Transredes medics. They have not even given us the food that they promised."[91]

Transredes claimed that Poopó, the final resting place of the Desaguadero's waters, was not contaminated.[92] "We do not trust

Transredes," said the protesters.[93] After their efforts in Oruro failed, sixty of them marched onward to La Paz. Ultimately, Transredes and the Uru Nation finally did sign an agreement, adding the Urus of Poopó to the list of communities that would receive compensation.

Two Communities Resist Transredes's Process

The communities of Chuquiña and Japo chose another form of resistance: action in the Bolivian courts. Two months after the spill, the communities found an ally in CLAIP (Center for Public Interest Law), a group of young activists and lawyers in La Paz. On the two communities' behalf, CLAIP filed a civil suit against Transredes in July 2001, demanding $14 million. Japo and Chuquiña initially refused to let Transredes's cleanup crew onto their land, fearful that Transredes would remove the evidence of the spill.

In Oruro, Transredes's temporary offices had to be closed for security reasons due to threats by the angry communities. Mobs from Chuquiña broke windows, interrupted CLOs' meetings, and threw rocks at Transredes's vehicles. At one point, in response to the company's decision to reduce the number of cleanup workers by more than half, members of the community kidnapped Transredes officials and the four trucks they were driving. They vowed to continue their resistance "until the company cleans up the entire affected area to avoid the death of 12,000 animals."[94]

Don Saúl Apaza always wears his dark aviator sunglasses and a leather jacket. He is an irrigation farmer and leader from Japo who battled against the foreign company. "They were making a joke out of us. We knew that Transredes had caused significant damage to our land and our lives. We knew that signing on to their process would be giving them control. And we knew our rights," he said.[95]

· · ·

After two years of legal battling and protest, both Chuquiña and Japo settled with Transredes. The two communities were awarded more compensation than any of the others, though it still was only a small slice of their original $14 million demand. The people of Chuquiña settled for $450,000 and Japo received $476,000.[96] Both communities believe that the damage done to their livestock and land far surpassed the money that they received.

The Silence of the Bolivian Government

One would have expected the Bolivian government to be the first to respond to this disaster. But the initial response of Bolivia's executive branch, under President Hugo Banzer, can be described in one word: silence. According to Bolivia's Environmental Law of 1992, contamination of waterways constitutes an environmental crime and should automatically trigger criminal investigation and prosecution.[97] Although the spill clearly fit the law's language of serious environmental crimes, the Bolivian government initiated no criminal proceedings against Transredes. Neisa Roca, the minister of environment at the time, voiced her inability to act in a La Paz newspaper interview: "You know how many people work for me? One, two and three (she counted on her fingers). What else do you want me to do? Cut my veins? You think this is Switzerland? Or haven't you realized how this country works?"[98]

In May of 2003, a delegation of students and faculty from Fordham University Law School in New York City came to Bolivia to investigate and analyze the Desaguadero disaster from the perspective of international human rights law, documenting violations by both Transredes and the Bolivian government. Fordham's report suggests that the foreign company and even the U.S. Embassy pressured Bolivian government authorities to treat the company favorably.[99] According to the study, Bolivia's government did not properly enforce the law due to fear of scaring off foreign investment.[100] As a result, the one institution powerful enough to hold Transredes accountable, the Banzer government, stood quietly on the sidelines.

Bolivia's Congress, on the other hand, was vocal from the beginning. Congress members from the region accused Transredes of lying regarding the pipeline having a puncture the size of a tiny hole, when clearly the pipeline had ruptured entirely.[101] In August 2000, eight months after the spill, the national superintendent of hydrocarbons finally acted. The government agency fined Transredes $110,000 for its failure to maintain the pipeline that crosses the Desaguadero, an amount equal to less than one tenth of one percent of the company's 2005 net operating income.[102] Despite the insignificant amount, Transredes appealed the resolution to the Bolivian Supreme Court, but its appeal was overturned.[103] By comparison, when the Petrobras oil company in Brazil was responsible for a spill of about the same size in the Iguazu River in 2000, Brazilian authorities fined Petrobras $28 million.[104]

Nongovernmental Organizations Divide Rather Than Organize

In the absence of a strong response from the government, isolated communities turned to other allies. In the weeks and months following the spill, hundreds of community representatives joined civil and nonprofit institutions, including the Federation of Farmers of Oruro, the Civic Committee of Oruro, CISEP (Center for Popular Service Investigation), the Irrigation Farmers of Oruro, and FOBOMADE to organize a united effort to demand assistance and compensation. Throughout, the nongovernmental organizations' (NGOs) effort faced serious divisions, which some leaders blamed on Transredes' tactics, such as intimidation and payoffs.[105]

Felipe Coronado, president of LIDEMA (Environmental Defense League), claimed that Transredes "worried more about their media show than they did about the people suffering along the Desaguadero."[106] FOBOMADE, the regional environmental organization, was one of the institutions most intimately involved during the aftermath of the spill. It deemed Transredes's stream of press releases following the spill to be propaganda.[107] Former president of FOBOMADE Hans Möeller explained the constant struggle to open the process to more than just the two private parties: "The conflict was totally asymmetrical. On the one hand there was the company, who manages important resources and has the support of silence of the government. On the other side there were the communities, without support, without resources. I knew that the communities needed outside support, and I found out very quickly that this company was filled with lies, lies, and lies. Communities were eventually pressured by Transredes to disassociate themselves from entities such as FOBOMADE. Our duty is to serve as an ally, and we could not do that properly."[108]

According to Möeller, much more than five thousand barrels of oil—Transredes's initial claim—had spilled into the river. He estimated that at least eighteen thousand barrels had gushed out of the pipeline—a number that would be later documented officially at twenty-nine thousand barrels.[109] Möeller, who has spent more than forty years working on environmental justice issues, claimed that he received threatening phone calls from Transredes and that intimidating people staked out his office and followed him when he ate lunch.[110] Möeller's fellow FOBOMADE colleagues, all of whom were volunteers, chose to stop working on the project out of fear of the company and over doubts that Transredes could be so mistaken about their spill estimates. Möeller said: "My colleagues were nervous; they were afraid. People left in the middle of the meeting. They said, 'How are great energy companies like Enron or Shell going to mistake the amount of petroleum by 1,500%? They can not have been so mistaken.' These people thought they were going to lose everything and did not want to fight against such a power. . . . Transredes was very successful in scaring off or paying off the very ones whose responsibility was to defend the people of the river region."[111]

When the government failed to represent the people, nongovernmental groups were the only other logical allies. Yet even they were unable to adequately represent the interests of the affected people and communities of the Desaguadero.

THE AFTERMATH: TRANSREDES'S CLAIMS VERSUS REALITY

On October 5, 2005, the Inter-American Development Bank (IDB) put the icing on the cake of Enron and Shell's public relations victory in *IDB America,* its monthly magazine. In an article titled "How an Oil Spill Helped a Bolivian Energy Company to Become a Model of Corporate Citizenship," the IDB applauded Transredes's swift response to the disaster:

> It was the kind of accident that gives the oil industry a bad name. . . . Just as the 1989 Valdez oil spill in Alaska left a permanent stain on the corporate image of Exxon Corp., the Desaguadero incident could have ruined Transredes' reputation in Bolivia. . . . Within hours of detecting the rupture, Transredes hired a team of specialists. . . . Transredes also purchased and delivered tons of supplemental forage to areas where grasslands had been contaminated, and it hired 11 full-time licensed veterinarians who assisted affected communities in treating any livestock that became sick. Six months after the spill, Transredes announced that toxic quantities of oil were no longer in the area. The small traces of oil that did remain were repeatedly tested to ensure that they were not dangerous to people or animals. Thanks to treatment offered by the veterinarians, no sheep or cattle died as a result of the spill, and virtually all of the affected vegetation recovered.[112]

From a distance, in an office in Washington, D.C., it would be easy to believe Transredes's many claims and to conclude that Enron and Shell's company really had done what was needed to fix what it had broken. But the closer one gets to the river itself, the more the IDB and Transredes's happy reporting gives way to the realities facing those who still live, years later, with the disaster's aftermath.

An Environmental Audit Surfaces New Facts

Some of those realities would be revealed two years after the spill, in the conclusions of an environmental audit that finally broke the silence of Bolivia's executive branch. In response to pressures from institutions such as FOBOMADE, affected communities, and the Bolivian media, the Ministry of Sustainable Development ordered this audit, the first of its kind to be completed in Bolivia. The government did not have the resources to pay for the $1.3 million investigation. Transredes was ordered to pay for it, and it hired Environmental Services (ENSR), head-quartered in Westford, Massachusetts, to carry it out. ENSR's local Bolivian subsidiary, located in Santa Cruz, also assisted in the process. According to the firm's Web page, it "assessed the environmental and socio-economic impacts of the spill."[113]

The report, released in June 2001, a year and a half after the spill, is hundreds of pages long and thick with annexes. The audit based much of its scientific results on the controversial initial lab results of Transredes's imported scientists—the same environmental conclusions used to quantify the compensation amounts. Siding with the company, the audit concluded that water, soil, and sediment samples did not contain dangerous levels of contamination.

However, buried deep in the audit's annexes is another study that looked even deeper into the long-term damage Transredes left behind. It was carried out by a Bolivian, Roger Carvajal, a biochemist and post-graduate professor at Universidad Mayor de San Andrés, the public university in La Paz. Carvajal highlighted a long list of inconsistencies and manipulated scientific conclusions in Transredes's findings. For example, the Transredes report concluded that the damage revealed in sediment samples was within accepted international limits; it wasn't.[114] Carvajal also detailed how the company made dangerous results appear unthreatening—by altering measurement formulas.[115] He came to very different conclusions than did Transredes's hired experts from abroad regarding the health consequences of the disaster. He wrote: "It is reasonable to expect significant effects in the health of human, animal, and plant life as a consequence of the spill."[116] He referenced potential long-term problems such as tumors, leukemia, immune system deficiencies, and other degenerative illnesses.[117]

ENSR's audit did highlight the warnings contained in Transredes's inspection documents from before the spill, and how the company chose to ignore those warnings. It declared Transredes's response efforts to be insufficient and uncoordinated. It criticized the company's emergency

water donation program, which resulted in almost half of the affected
people consuming contaminated waters. It denounced the medical and
veterinary assistance for disregarding the spill's health impacts. It condemned Transredes for not addressing the harm caused to wildlife such
as fish, the dozens of species of wild birds native to the region, or
vicuñas—a deerlike animal that is on the endangered species list of the
U.S. Fish and Wildlife Service. It also criticized the company's failure to
confront the issue of stillborn or deformed animals, which had been
reported repeatedly in Bolivian media.[118]

Finally, ENSR's audit deemed Transredes' compensation package to
have been overly complex, unilaterally defined, and not proportionate
to the damage caused.[119] Afterward, the Ministry of Sustainable
Development ordered that the company pay almost double of what communities had originally received—$3.7 million more for the damage
caused by Transredes's oil, as well as $2.2 million for destruction to the
native prairies.[120] Based on the results of the audit, the Bolivian government fined Transredes $1.9 million, a sum that has since been reduced
to $1.3 million, and as of 2007, has still not been paid. According to
one U.S. newspaper, a visit from the former U.S. ambassador Donna
Hrinak to Bolivia's Minister of Sustainable Development, Luis Carvajal,
effectively prevented this fine from being enforced.[121]

The Company's False Claims

*Tomás of Acopata had a story to tell. "I was rejected from the compen-
sation process. I live a twenty-minute walk from the river. My sheep—
though few—feed off the foliage of the river and drink from the river. I
could not prove I was affected. I had no evidence that my sheep would
get sick." Tomás has kind eyes, rough hands, and a dirt-colored hat that
he made himself. He was more motivated to speak with me about methods of getting money from Transredes today than he was to speak of his
story of rejection in 2000. "I have traveled to Oruro, even to Santa
Cruz, in an attempt to get the money that I deserve from the oil company. They did not even reimburse the cost of my bus ticket. I have lost
money because of Transredes, and my surroundings have lost life."[122]*

• • •

Though Transredes claims to have compensated the affected peoples of
the Desaguadero, stories such as Tomás's beg to differ. No issue better
highlights the broad gap between the corporation's claims and the IDB's

applause versus what actually happened along the river than the issue of animal sickness and death as a direct result of the spill.

Repeatedly, Transredes asserted that not a single animal was made ill or died as a result of the million-acre oil spill. In a March 8, 2000, press release, Transredes claimed that the eleven veterinarians who were traveling through the region found *no evidence* of ill animals as a result of oil intoxication. The press release detailed that "in all reported cases to date . . . domestic animals are affected by illnesses not related to the oil spill."[123] In June, a full five months after the spill, the company claimed to have visited over 250,000 animals in the region and reported that company veterinarians "tended to 10,000 animals for illnesses not related to the oil spill."[124] The environmental audit, published two years later, confirmed the communities' claims that their animals' health was indeed affected by the oil spill. The audit declared that "approximately 40% of the diagnoses of the [sick or dead] animals are related to consumption of oil toxins."[125]

How many animals died as a result of the spill is impossible to calculate. Doña Ignacia lost two llamas and five sheep. Doña Porfiria lost eight sheep. Don Saúl Apaza claims that hundreds of animals of the community of Japo fell ill or died as a result of the spill. If the numbers reported by the sample of families interviewed are consistent across the almost four thousand families compensated, the number of dead animals would easily reach into the thousands.

Don Saúl Apaza showed me a photo of a two-headed cow born at his neighbor's house. In the aftermath of the spill, baby sheep were stillborn with tongues that reached the ground, with only one eye, or with legs of different lengths.

Deformed and stillborn animals have meant great losses to the people who count their assets in livestock. Even today, people of the river complain that stillbirths and unhealthy animals are more common as a result of the spill, something for which they never received compensation. Despite all the evidence, like the animal carcasses carried by families for miles to prove their losses, and the photographs of animal autopsies where oil was indeed found inside of sheep and llamas, Transredes officials refuse to acknowledge even a single animal death as a result of the company's spill. Instead, Transredes relies on theoretic assertions based on the amount of oil that an animal must consume according to its weight in order for its health to be affected.[126] Seven years later, the company stated again that "not one case is attributed to consumption of the crude oil."[127]

THE DISASTER'S LEGACY: LESSONS LEARNED

Don Santiago Castillo Ramos was born just on the other side of the river, in front of the village of Ulloma. He left the countryside for La Paz two dozen years ago, but his parents still occupy the very house where he was born. His mother and father speak only Aymara and no Spanish, but they constantly communicated with me through generosity and smiles. Though they have lived on the banks of the Desaguadero River for more than fifty years, and the black from the oil spill "became our backyard," according to Don Santiago, this family was not included in the compensation process. "It was not enough proof for Transredes that our house is right here, that we live right here, that our animals are right here. We did not have any papers saying that we did. The company used the law where it was convenient and dismissed it when it was inconvenient."[128]

Rural life in the countryside usually conjures up images of the riches of the earth. In the Bolivian altiplano, however, the unaccustomed observer will see barren monotony: repetitive plant life, bright sun, burning cold, and continuous flatness that finally leads to mountains. The truth is that few if any of those not born in these high flatlands would ever choose such a difficult life for themselves.

On these high flatlands along the river, I found human stories not included in any report by Transredes, CARE, or the IDB. I found the stories that have been silenced, ones that beg for the grass that lived before the spill and that scream for the end of animal stillbirths. People here now recall, with bittersweet nostalgia, how much easier it used to be to find wild duck eggs with yolks more orange than the sun. People here now fearfully wonder what mysterious sickness could come their way.

The Desaguadero River is filled with faces: barely five-foot-tall women who tote their babies on their backs, men with leathered toes peeking out of sandals made of recycled tires, and children who walk miles to get to schools that don't even have books. Enron and Shell never saw these faces.

At an IDB conference in 2003, a Transredes official, Tony Henshaw, claimed that "a company must measure and manage not only its impact on the environment, but also the health and safety risks to its employees and neighbors, and indeed its impact on society as a whole."[129] If only Transredes had truly held itself to those standards, perhaps the disaster on the Desaguadero could have been avoided.

If there is one thing that can be done in the name of the people whose livelihoods were destroyed by the oil spill, it is that the rest of us carefully consider the lessons to be learned from this story on the altiplano. What can be taken away from this tale of an environmental disaster and its aftermath?

The spill and its aftermath resulted in a clash of cultures. Transredes operates in a corporate world of global enterprise, an environment in which numbers and legal papers are essential to systems of measurement, management, and control. Its objectives are about investment and return, about profit and, in the event of a disaster like that in Bolivia in January 2000, about minimizing cost. It knows well how to use the tools of public relations, legal maneuvering, and subtle political pressure to defend itself when it makes an error, especially a huge one like that along the banks of the Desaguadero. In the confines of their corporate headquarters in Santa Cruz, studying the spill on paper, Transredes officials still believe, or pretend to, that not a single animal died from its million-acre disaster, that no one got sick for more than a week, and that the soil along the Desaguadero is better off now for having been soaked in petroleum.

The people along the river, however, who were forced to endure the results of the company's disaster, live in a world that is vastly different. What people own is not recorded. Their assets are not quantified, nor is Pachamama. They know little of lawyers, accounting procedures, or how to stand up against the powers of two giant foreign corporations. When the clash came in the form of a strange black river, the communities never had a chance.

It is precisely these situations in which government is most needed to serve as a protector of the people. Only governments have the resources and the power to counterbalance the formidable clout of a modern multinational corporation. Only a committed government can intervene to prevent such an environmental calamity, and only a committed government can act to ensure justice in its aftermath.

In the United States or the Netherlands—the home countries of the two corporations involved—one would expect the government to have done just that. But the Bolivian government, with few resources and under clear pressures from foreign interests, was both unable and unwilling to act forcefully in defense of its people. In the face of powers as strong and strategic as Enron and Shell, the government, too, stood little chance of forcing them to justice.

The people of Bolivia, however, are well aware of the struggle for power and justice amid the growing role of foreign corporations and foreign economic institutions in their country. They take power in these situations in the way Bolivians have long taken power—they organize, they make demands, they stand together with great courage.

If observers from abroad want to better understand why foreign corporations such as Enron and Shell engender such deep mistrust in Bolivia, they can look to the banks of Bolivia's ancient and mystic river. Six years after Transredes's pipeline broke open and left a million-acre stain across the highlands, Evo Morales, an Aymara Indian and former llama herder who grew up there, was sworn in as Bolivia's president. One of his earliest acts was an executive decree to nationalize his country's gas and oil reserves. He also vowed to take back control of the pipelines given over to Enron and Shell.

Doña Ignacia has a permanent smile. All but one of her nine children have sought out a better life in the city. She jokes that pretty soon she will be the only one left on these grounds, and she remains firm that she will die exactly where she was born, in the home she generously opened up to a strange foreigner one cold winter night.

"Life in these parts is no longer what it used to be. We even encourage our family to leave. We tell them, there is nothing more for you here. This life is no office job, and unfortunately there is no insurance for our workplace. This company was allowed to destroy our place of work and act like they fixed it. We know that our lives have been made harder. Transredes broke something without fixing it."

More than a hundred thousand people marched on the city of La Paz in October 2003 to protest a plan by the government to export the nation's gas to the United States and Mexico at reduced prices. Photo: Noah Friedman-Rudovsky (2003).

CHAPTER 3

Oil and Gas: The Elusive Wealth beneath Their Feet

Gretchen Gordon and Aaron Luoma

The issue of gas and oil and who controls those resources has been at the center of Bolivia's recent political upheavals. Mass protests, demanding that Bolivia's government take back control of the hydro-carbon industry, privatized in the 1990s, have toppled two presidents since 2003. Bolivian history for more than seventy years has been an ongoing struggle over whether its precious oil and gas wealth should be developed by foreign corporations or by Bolivia itself. In this chapter, Gretchen Gordon and Aaron Luoma dive into both the history of Bolivia's gas and oil battles and the complex questions that drive that debate today.[1]

On May 1, 2006, banners reading "Nationalized: Property of the Bolivian people" were hung over filling station entrances and strung across the gates of refineries and gas and oil fields across Bolivia. From the San Alberto gas field in the eastern region of Tarija, President Evo Morales stood flanked by his ministers and military before a crowd of television cameras. In a carefully orchestrated public relations event, Morales made the surprise announcement that the military was at that moment securing the country's oil and gas fields. "It's the solution to the social and economic problems of our country," Morales proclaimed. "Once we have recovered these natural resources, they will generate work; this is the end of the looting of our natural resources by multinational oil companies."[2]

By the time Evo Morales won his unprecedented landslide electoral victory in December 2005, nationalization of Bolivia's oil and gas reserves had become a widespread popular demand. In 2003, resentment over the unfulfilled promises of the mid-1990s radical privatization of Bolivia's oil and gas resources erupted in massive protests against a proposed sale of cheap gas through Chile to the United States, ending with over sixty dead and the ousting of Bolivia's president.

From a historical perspective, Morales's May 2006 "nationalization" decree was only Bolivia's most recent salvo in a long battle with foreign companies over control of its oil and gas resources. The call for change draws from the collective memory of a people who believe their country has never benefited from the exploitation of its natural resources. Morales's reform, while more conservative than a traditional nationalization, reflects an effort to regain some measure of control over an industry that after privatization generated extraordinary profits for foreign oil and gas companies, even while Bolivia has remained the poorest country in South America.

With the second-largest gas reserves in South America—valued at over $200 billion[3]—Bolivia is looking to this resource as a way out of poverty and as the foundation for broader economic development. However, turning natural resource wealth into improvements in people's daily lives has proved unattainable for most countries throughout the world. Bolivia's chance at bucking this trend will require not only withstanding the pressure of powerful political and economic interests, but also breaking out of a mold that dates back to colonial times.

FROM SILVER TO GAS: ELUSIVE WEALTH

For nearly five centuries Bolivia has seen its valuable and finite natural resources siphoned off one by one to create wealth abroad while a majority of its citizens live in poverty. Bolivia is emblematic of countries that become dependent on a single export commodity, leaving their economies vulnerable to the volatility of international markets. In the 1500s and 1600s, Bolivia's economic fate was symbolized by *Cerro Rico,* the silver-filled mountain outside the city of Potosí that was emptied by the Spanish and that virtually bankrolled the Spanish empire for two centuries. In the late nineteenth century, rubber and guano—dried bird dung coveted by the British for gunpowder and fertilizer—joined silver as resources that were exploited by foreign interests in collusion with wealthy Bolivian elites.

At the turn of the twentieth century, the invention of tin cans for food preservation along with the prewar armament buildup in Europe and the United States led to a boom when huge tin deposits were discovered in Bolivia's highlands. Backed initially by foreign investors, three Bolivian families eventually controlled 80 percent of the tin industry.[4] In an economy dominated by tin exports, these tin barons consolidated their economic and political power. Simón Patiño, known as the "Bolivian Rockefeller," became one of the world's richest men, controlling half of the country's tin production. In a remarkable feat for a land-locked, mountainous country, Bolivia supplied nearly half of the tin for the allied effort in World War II.[5]

Not surprisingly, like silver, this untold tin wealth was accumulated at the expense of poorly paid workers laboring in miserable conditions. A 1945 report determined that the average age of miners suffering from severe lung disease was just thirty-two years old.[6] Protests by miners for better working conditions met violent repression by private security forces and government troops. Those protests laid the foundation for later social resistance.

Throughout most of the twentieth century—until the tin market collapsed in 1985—tin provided the majority of Bolivia's export income, and its volatile price swings created repeated boom and bust cycles in the Bolivian economy.[7] Sergio Almaráz Paz, a Bolivian historian, reflects on tin's legacy: "Bolivia finds itself at the end of a familiar road: a half-century of exploiting tin has left in its wake a backward and impoverished country, with an economy essentially the same as fifty years ago. What does this experience tell us? Bolivia was tin. Bolivians lived off the crumbs tin left behind. In this perpetual reality, the economic and political system was developed—was deformed—from the impact of tin."[8]

The Hope of Gas

After the crash of the tin industry, gas became the country's most important natural resource. The giant gas fields of Bolivia's temperate eastern Chaco region soon emerged as the modern-day *Cerro Rico*.

Until the end of the twentieth century, natural gas was regarded by many oil developers as a waste product in the process of extracting the global economy's black gold. "The notion that gas might be a money-maker would have struck most oil executives as absurd," writes Paul Roberts in *The End of Oil*.[9] In the last six years, however, with oil becoming increasingly scarce, natural gas prices have doubled, leaving oil companies "racing to attain a stronger position in gas," writes Roberts.[10] Global consumption of natural gas now matches that of coal, and by as early as 2025, gas could surpass oil as the world's most dominant energy source.[11]

In light of mounting concerns over climate change, natural gas is an increasingly popular alternative to its more polluting cousins—oil and coal. While natural gas is a fossil fuel and its extraction process comes with significant environmental costs, it is often seen as a convenient "bridge" fuel—one that will help ease global demand for oil. As analysts continue to debate when oil supplies will peak, the dash for gas is already in full swing.

Gas is prized for its versatility. In the more industrialized countries of Brazil, Argentina, and Chile, the need for energy to power industry is driving demand for natural gas. Gas is also a cheap fuel for cars, heating, and cooking. In Bolivia alone, in less than three years, the number of cars fueled by natural gas has tripled, approaching sixty thousand vehicles.[12] Natural gas for cars in Bolivia is one-third the price of gasoline, a boon to taxi drivers struggling to make ends meet. According to industry expectations in 2006, Bolivia was poised to have nearly 20 percent of its cars—one hundred thousand in total—running on gas by 2008, which would be the highest percentage in South America.[13]

Bolivians are keenly aware of the legacy of their vast mineral wealth disappearing beneath their feet and are determined to ensure that gas does not meet the same fate as silver and tin. Carlos Rojas, a representative of the Federation of Neighborhoods (FEJUVE) in the city of El Alto, laments: "After the looting of our gold, silver, tin, of all the minerals we've had . . . the last resource we have left is gas. . . . What future can we hope for—for our children? . . . There is no other resource in Bolivia that can be our future economic support."[14]

Struggle for Control

Since the 1930s, Bolivia's oil and gas resources have been subject to an ongoing tug-of-war between the Bolivian state and international oil and gas companies. Some Bolivian governments have granted private companies generous exploration and development rights and vast influence in policy making. At other times, the pendulum has swung back toward greater government control, such as during the nationalization of the oil and gas industry in 1937 and 1969.

BOX 3.1 | ## The ABCs of Gas

Natural gas, oil, and other hydrocarbons come from the same geologic process: decaying organic matter found deep beneath the earth's surface. Reservoirs of these carbon-based fossil fuels normally also contain water, which sinks to the bottom because it is heavier than either gas or oil. Oil lies above the water, while natural gas lies closest to the surface, pushing up against the earth, pressurizing the reservoir like a shaken bottle of champagne.

Deposits that primarily contain oil are called oil fields, and those richest in gas, gas fields. Gas found in oil fields is called associated gas. Because gas is expensive to separate and process, many oil developers flare, or burn off, natural gas in the process of extracting oil. This process releases harmful pollutants and is illegal in most of the industrialized world, though it is still practiced in many countries. The majority of Bolivia's gas is free gas—meaning it is found with little or no oil—and is therefore less expensive to extract and process. Venezuela's gas reserves, on the other hand, while exceeding Bolivia's reserves by more than three to one, are predominantly associated gas, which complicates Venezuela's ability to profitably exploit them.

In its purest form, natural gas is colorless and odorless. It is actually a mix of a variety of gases including ethane, butane, propane, and natural gas' largest component: methane. Bolivia is fortunate in that its gas is over 90 percent methane, a valuable gas that can be converted into electricity or processed into derivative products such as plastics, fertilizers, synthetic diesel, and gasoline.[1]

Though natural gas has many uses, because it is a gas, transporting it is complicated and time-consuming. To export natural gas overseas, it must be liquefied in expensive processing plants and then shipped in large tankers that are more costly to build than traditional oil tankers. Only recently—in tandem with rising natural gas prices—has exporting natural gas longer distances become economically viable.

Because it is difficult to market globally, natural gas, unlike oil, does not have an established international reference price. Prices are therefore determined based on regional demand and bargaining between producing countries and purchasing companies.

1. Saúl J. Escalera, PowerPoint presentation: *Industrialización del gas natural boliviano* (Industrialization of Bolivia's natural gas), Universidad Mayor de San Simón, Escuela Universitaria de Postgrado (July 2002).

This struggle for control of Bolivia's oil and gas reserves began in 1896, when Manuel Cuellar, on an expedition in the remote Chaco area of eastern Bolivia, noticed the local Guaraní people using a black and greasy liquid to cure the wounds of their animals. He later confirmed this substance to be high-grade petroleum and, after securing investment, formed Bolivia's first oil company, which was sold to U.S. corporate giant Standard Oil in 1921.[15]

For fifteen years, Standard Oil, then the world's largest oil company, founded by John D. Rockefeller, was able to operate virtually unregulated and without competition in the sparsely populated eastern fringes of Bolivia near its border with Paraguay and Argentina. For several years Standard illegally exported oil via a secret pipeline to Argentina, evaded taxes, and failed to adequately supply Bolivia's domestic fuel market. Standard was also charged with sabotaging the Bolivian army's fuel supply during the unsuccessful Chaco War with Paraguay in 1932–35, in which more than fifty thousand Bolivians—in a country of just 2 million—died.[16]

The trauma of the Chaco War brought the nation together for the first time and created a wave of nationalist sentiment and new political ideas. Among these was a realization of the importance of the state's role in developing the country's hydrocarbon resources, 85 percent of which today are located in the Chaco region. The Bolivian people, increasingly indignant about Standard Oil's actions during the Chaco War, took to the streets in protest.[17] In response to popular demand, the government founded Yacimientos Petrolíferos Fiscales Bolivianos (YPFB)—Bolivia's state-owned oil company. The 1936 law that created YPFB states that "the importance of oil in the world, its economic significance and value to the state, demands more and more each day that these resources be placed under the direct control of the nation."[18]

Nationalization, Privatization, and Nationalization Again

A year later, in 1937, Bolivia became the first country in Latin America to nationalize its oil industry, a historic event that paved the way for Mexico to do the same the following year. The nationalization seized all Standard Oil's assets and operations, handing them over to Bolivia's state oil company while paying compensation to Standard of $1.7 million. Bolivian writer Carlos Montenegro wrote: "For the first time in world history, the most powerful company on the planet [Standard Oil] was morally rebuked by a state."[19] The nationalization of the country's oil industry would be the opening act in a decades-long struggle between the state and foreign companies for control of Bolivia's oil and gas.

Within five years, the Bolivian state oil company produced more barrels of crude oil than Standard Oil had in its fifteen years in Bolivia, and

---

BOX 3.2 | Nationalization in a Nutshell

The term *nationalization* can mean several different things. Technically, nationalization means expropriation, or the government seizure of privately held assets. This can be done either with or without some payment of compensation by the government to the owner of the assets. A government's decision to expropriate privately held goods or property in order to better serve the public interest, while providing compensation, is a right of sovereign nations recognized by the United Nations. While nationalization can involve goods or services, such as the 2001 nationalization of airport security by the U.S. government, the most well-known nationalizations have involved the recovery of natural resources that had previously been privatized. While the term *nationalization* has become politically popular in Bolivia recently, the Morales government's reform of Bolivia's oil and gas sector is not a nationalization in the traditional sense because it hasn't involved the seizure of private assets.

---

in 1954 YPFB achieved its principal goal of producing enough fuel to meet all domestic demand.[20]

Just three short years after the 1952 revolution that brought dramatic changes for the Bolivian people, including the nationalization of the mining industry, YPFB's monopoly of Bolivia's oil industry ironically came to an end. The pendulum swung back toward private foreign control of Bolivia's oil resources when President Víctor Paz Estenssoro opened Bolivia's doors to outside investment, citing budget shortfalls and slow economic growth.[21]

The U.S. government made it clear that any new investment from U.S. companies was contingent on Bolivia reforming its petroleum sector. The result was Paz Estenssoro's 1955 Davenport Code, which allowed U.S. oil companies to exploit Bolivia's oil under extremely generous terms, paying just a 20 percent share of profits to the state.[22] By the 1960s, ten U.S. oil companies had begun operations in Bolivia, with Gulf Oil emerging as the dominant player in Bolivia's oil industry.[23] Bolivia's policy changes were rewarded with a fivefold increase in U.S. aid.[24]

Throughout the 1950s and 1960s, YPFB continued its activities in oil exploration and development. The low government share of oil revenues, however, severely limited reinvestment in new development and technology, as did the diverting of revenues by successive Bolivian governments.[25] YPFB's influence and importance steadily began to wane in the shadow of Gulf Oil.

In the early 1960s, Gulf discovered Bolivia's first significant natural gas reserves.[26] In 1964, Bolivia's dictator, General René Barrientos, a staunch U.S. ally, gave Gulf rights to exploit these reserves, taking advantage of the Davenport Code's imprecise language on whether gas discovered by foreign companies belonged to the state or to the companies.[27] Bolivia's first gas export deal was signed with Argentina in 1968, with Gulf as the primary beneficiary.[28]

By 1968, Gulf had been able to reinvest its lucrative earnings and increase its oil reserves to five times those of cash-poor YPFB and extend its control to 80 percent of Bolivia's oil and 90 percent of its gas.[29] Augusto Céspedes, a Bolivian writer and former diplomat, urged resistance to Gulf's powerful presence in Bolivia, arguing that "sovereignty is merely theoretical" when a weak state confronts a company backed by powerful international economic and political forces.[30]

In September 1969, after General Barrientos's death, a left-wing military government formed under Alfredo Ovando annulled the Davenport Code. The Ovando administration argued that the code "was not drafted by Bolivians, included provisions that violated the independence of the state, and that the Bolivian people had repeatedly and categorically repudiated it."[31] Gulf countered with an offer to split oil and gas revenues fifty-fifty, but the government wasn't negotiating.

On October 17, 1969, on the government-declared "Day of National Dignity," Bolivia's minister of oil and mines, Marcelo Quiroga Santa Cruz, signed a decree that nationalized Gulf Oil's assets. Quiroga later wrote that previous administrations had given Gulf control of national oil policy and that the highest public officials were "at the service of the interests [of Gulf]."[32] General Ovando called Gulf "an enterprise that has acquired an economic and political dominance similar to that of the tin barons."[33]

Foreign oil and gas companies responded by staging a boycott of Bolivian oil that cost the government $14.4 million in export revenues. Meanwhile, the U.S. government successfully pressured the Ovando government to pay limited compensation of $78 million for the property, machinery, and vehicles Gulf left behind.[34]

YPFB: Bolivia's Breadwinner

In the 1970s, under the dictatorship of General Hugo Banzer Suárez, YPFB expanded operations thanks to increased revenues from a tripling of global oil prices. A new oil and gas law passed in 1972 provided generous investment opportunities for foreign companies but gave the government 50 percent of all revenues. Deals struck with two U.S. oil and gas companies in 1972 provided the investment to begin exporting gas to Argentina, fulfilling the contract originally signed in 1968.[35]

With the collapse of Bolivia's tin industry in 1985, YPFB became the government's main breadwinner, occupying a place among the largest Latin American companies and employing 9,150 people.[36] During the 1980s and early 1990s, Bolivia's state company participated directly— as well as through contracts with private companies—in exploration and production and held a monopoly on transportation and commercialization of oil and gas and its derivatives.

In addition to the Argentine gas export deal, YPFB began exporting oil to Chile and Argentina, and both oil and gas to Brazil.[37] Though YPFB was criticized for inefficiency and corruption, it was a highly profitable company, generating $3.57 billion between 1985 and 1995, roughly half of total government revenues in that period.[38]

Starting in the mid-1980s, however, conservative policy makers and business interests began a campaign to discredit YPFB's image and implemented policy measures that stunted its growth.[39] Part of this effort was a law passed in 1985 that siphoned off 65 percent of YPFB's revenues to the national treasury each year, leaving little for investment in exploration and development of new fields.[40] An artificially low export price negotiated with Argentina in 1986 also limited its revenues, and YPFB couldn't expand capacity. "They de-capitalized the company," explained Bolivian academic Carlos Villegas Quiroga, who later became Evo Morales's energy minister in 2006. "It didn't have funds to invest in exploration, development, production, or other types of activities."[41] These moves laid the groundwork for the eventual dismantling of YPFB a few years later.

CAPITALIZATION: PRIVATIZATION BY A NEW NAME

On the night of October 17, 2003, the entire nation sat glued to television news channels and radios as Gonzalo Sánchez de Lozada resigned as president of Bolivia and boarded a plane for Miami, fleeing a country in chaos.

For months, increasing social unrest over Sánchez de Lozada's economic policies had exploded onto the streets in cities across Bolivia in what became known as the Gas War of 2003. After the government's crackdown on protests against a proposed gas export deal left more than sixty people dead and four hundred wounded, a social upheaval was set in motion that eventually brought down two governments and dramatically changed the country's political course.

Ten years earlier, in 1993, Sánchez de Lozada was the country's wealthiest mine owner and had set his sights on winning Bolivia's presidential election. The economy was in disrepair and the U.S.-educated Sánchez de Lozada offered a solution. As economic planning minister in 1985, he had ushered in the country's first wave of neoliberal economic reform. Teaming up with a group of World Bank and International Monetary Fund (IMF) economic planners, Sánchez de Lozada now proposed to take those reforms to an unprecedented level.[42] The World Bank and the IMF called it "the Bolivia Model." Sánchez de Lozada called it "capitalization."

Sánchez de Lozada's capitalization program promised to bring half a million new jobs in four years, double the economy in ten years, and fund an ambitious new pension plan for Bolivia's elderly.[43] The plan helped propel Sánchez de Lozada to his first term as president (1993–97). It also delivered Bolivia's most strategic state industries, among them oil and gas, into foreign corporate hands.

The overhaul of Bolivia's oil and gas sector rested on a basic neoliberal economic belief: development requires foreign investment, and to entice foreign investment, you need to offer an attractive deal. In many countries in Latin America the "attractive deal" was the privatization of state enterprises at bargain prices and the easing of government regulations on foreign companies. But Bolivians had had negative experiences with privatization in the past and were adamant about not losing control over their most important resources and public services. So Sánchez de Lozada's capitalization proposed something different: the transformation of Bolivia's state companies into joint public-private partnerships that would generate both increased investment and ongoing revenues for the state.

YPFB's assets were divided up into three new capitalized companies: Transredes, Chaco, and Andina. Sánchez de Lozada promised Bolivians they would maintain control of 51 percent of the new companies, while the foreign corporations would be given a 49 percent stake.[44] Rather than paying the government for their share in the new businesses, foreign companies would pledge to invest that same cash value in the new company over the next seven years.

In addition to dividing up YPFB, as part of a new oil and gas law written in close coordination with the IMF and the World Bank, Bolivia gave away drilling rights for oil and gas reserves that would later be valued at over $100 billion.[45] And to make the deal even more enticing for investors, the government slashed the taxes and royalties those companies would have to pay on their production from 50 percent down to 18 percent.

Capitalization's Promises versus Its Results

Bolivians were sold capitalization on bold promises: public-private partnerships would allow the government to maintain control of its oil and gas resources, while increased foreign investment would double the industry's economic potential; new technology and increased efficiency would bring new revenues, jobs, and economic growth. The actual results of the capitalization experiment, however, paint a very different picture.

The Myth of Retaining Control

With capitalization, the Bolivian government and its people lost control of both their most profitable state company, YPFB, as well as their ability to regulate the oil and gas industry as a whole. In an effort to sweeten the deal for foreign investors, instead of Bolivia maintaining a majority stake in the new capitalized firms, the 51 percent–49 percent public-private split promised by Sánchez de Lozada was turned on its head and private interests gained majority control.

A consortium of Enron and Shell was awarded the Transredes company, which took over YPFB's pipelines and distribution infrastructure. British Petroleum and Spain's Repsol were given control of the new exploration and production companies, Chaco and Andina, and were given YPFB's equipment, infrastructure, and geological studies free of charge. They also gained control of oil and gas reserves valued at approximately $12 billion.[46] Even Bolivia's minority shareholding in these firms was not its own. Bolivia's shares were handed over to two foreign companies to manage as a pension fund for the country's elderly, and the administrators of those funds were named by the foreign oil and gas companies. As one analyst explained it: "Under this scheme, [the foreign investors] not only are owners of 51 percent, but rather 100 percent, since they control and administer the totality of the [capitalized] companies, with no participation of the minor partner: Bolivians."[47]

Not only did the government give up decision-making ability over the capitalized firms, but it also gave up its role as regulator of the entire industry. The government's regulatory authority was replaced with "independent" third-party entities that relied on the foreign companies to self-report how much oil and gas they extracted and exported, determining tax and royalty payments from the companies' own calculations. It was the equivalent of leaving a note on the door: "Come on in, take what you want and leave the money on the counter." Though decreasing corruption and improving environmental practices were given as motives for capitalization, gas smuggling and tax evasion continued or even increased, as did spills and other environmental accidents.[48] (For more on the Shell-Enron oil spill in January 2000, see chapter 2.)

The Myth of What New Foreign Investment Would Bring

Bolivia did see a dramatic increase in foreign investment during capitalization, but that investment didn't lead to a modernization of the industry or the generation of new job-creating industries. The foreign companies that took over Bolivia's oil and gas industry found it more profitable to export the country's natural gas as a cheap raw material, processed by their own affiliates in Argentina or Brazil. Also, because they weren't obligated to do so by their contracts, they never invested in improving domestic infrastructure or technical capacity. The country's two main refineries in operation today, for example, were both built by YPFB before capitalization and have not been significantly upgraded since that time.[49]

Capitalization's defenders frequently argue that increased foreign investment boosted Bolivia's certified oil and gas reserves by twelve times. However, in reality, most of those "new" reserves had already been discovered before capitalization but had not yet been certified by international agencies.[50]

Oil and gas companies operating in Bolivia during the capitalization era received an average investment return of ten to one, benefiting from some of the lowest production costs in the world.[51] Those profits, however, never trickled down to fulfill the promises of growth and development. Rather than creating half a million new jobs, 50 percent to 70 percent of YPFB's staff was laid off, joining thousands of unemployed workers from other capitalized industries and from the light manufacturing and technology firms that had supplied those industries.[52] The formal unemployment rate of 3 percent before capitalization in 1994 had climbed to 11.7 percent in 2003, while the gap between rich and poor also grew sharply during the 1990s.[53]

The Myth of Increased Public Revenue

Sánchez de Lozada's promise that capitalization would lead to increased government revenues also never played out. The capitalized companies that acquired YPFB's assets generated less than half the government revenue that YPFB had.[54] While Bolivia was producing 135 percent more oil and gas after the first seven years of capitalization, government oil and gas revenues grew by only 10 percent.[55] Even though more of Bolivia's finite natural resources were being depleted, the government's revenues essentially remained flat.

Also, because the capitalization process eliminated the state's ability to set domestic prices for oil and gas products, such as cooking fuel and diesel, prices for common fuels increased between 70 and 100 percent.[56] The government responded by implementing fuel subsidies to keep prices accessible for consumers, putting an even greater stress on government resources.

The Privatization of Corruption

In the end, the capitalization process not only was bad economic policy, but was riddled with corruption as well. One of the most egregious cases involved Enron, more than four years before the company's name became synonymous with corporate corruption. Without putting forth a cent of investment, Enron successfully lobbied Sánchez de Lozada for control of the country's most important energy project—the Bolivia-Brazil pipeline.[57] Later investigations revealed that the finished pipeline included a side branch that supplied gas directly to Sánchez de Lozada's mine on Bolivia's eastern border.[58]

The crafting of Bolivia's capitalization plan and new oil and gas law involved laborious consultations with foreign investors and international lenders. The Bolivian people and Congress, however, were kept in the dark. Oil and gas contracts, as well as the operations and finances of the capitalized companies, were deemed confidential information. For the majority of Bolivians—including most of the country's own business community—capitalization left a bitter taste.

"Personally, I feel swindled," said Enrique Menacho Roca, former president of Bolivia's Hydrocarbon Chamber, which represents both foreign and domestic oil and gas companies operating in Bolivia: "I saw capitalization as a better way to operate and produce, where 50 percent was the capitalized company and 50 percent Bolivian, but later came the big scam. . . . There was no real Bolivian participation. For me it was . . . a big deception."[59]

A decade after capitalization was invented as a campaign slogan, the stage was set for a major civic rebellion against it.

THE GAS WAR IGNITES

On October 11, 2003, twenty-nine-year-old David Salinas Malléa was shot by the Bolivian military in the sprawling highland city of El Alto. On any other day, David could be found working as a mason, or in his free time playing soccer with his younger brother, Néstor, in the city that sits high on a ridge overlooking La Paz, Bolivia's seat of government. But on October 11, 2003, Néstor and David's neighborhood became a war zone. Thousands of Alteños (residents of El Alto) had taken to the streets in protest of President Sánchez de Lozada's plan to export cheap gas to the United States through Bolivia's historic rival, Chile. El Alto residents erected blockades, cutting off supplies of food and fuel to the capital below. The president called out the military to break up the protests.

Six days later, El Alto's protest had spread throughout the country, demanding both the nationalization and industrialization of the country's oil and gas resources and the resignation of the nation's president. When Sánchez de Lozada finally fled, he left behind more than sixty people dead, among them, David Salinas.

Sánchez de Lozada's Gas Plan

The gas export deal that sparked the Gas War of 2003 had been in negotiation since 2001, when then-president Jorge "Tuto" Quiroga (2001–2) began talks with two companies regarding the export of liquefied Bolivian gas to California: Pacific LNG, a consortium of Repsol, British Gas, British Petroleum, and France's Total; and Prisma, the company that took over Enron's assets after its collapse. But the plan was no simple deal. Because Bolivia is landlocked, the gas needed to be transported to the Pacific, and Chile was the closest and therefore cheapest route.

Exporting gas through Chile, however, was guaranteed to meet significant opposition. Historical animosity with Chile over the century-old seizing of Bolivia's seacoast in 1879 still runs strong among the Bolivian people. When news of the deal broke, it became the lightning rod for Bolivians' growing economic discontent. After centuries of losing the benefits of their resources to outsiders, Bolivians saw the sale of gas through Chile as another Cerro Rico.

Under pressure from the U.S. ambassador to accept a low selling price, Sánchez de Lozada agreed to charge only half of what Brazil was paying for Bolivian gas.[60] According to one estimate, although corporate profits were projected at almost $1.9 billion annually, Bolivia would receive only $190 million.[61] The foreign company that would transport Bolivia's gas from Chile to Mexico would make $1 billion a year.[62] Many Bolivians viewed the country's gas resources as their bargaining chip for regaining sea access from energy-scarce Chile. They were incensed at the idea of handing over their gas without getting port access in exchange.[63]

The Gas War

In early September 2003, civil unrest grew over a variety of social and economic issues, and miners, factory workers, transport workers, university students, coca growers, and others took to the streets. Demonstrations spread to El Alto, Oruro, Sucre, Potosí, and other cities across Bolivia.[64] In response, Sánchez de Lozada relied increasingly on the heavy-handed approach pushed by his defense minister, Carlos Sánchez Berzaín.[65]

On September 20, the government launched a military mission to clear road blockades that had been erected in the rural altiplano to protest the imprisonment of a local indigenous leader. The blockades had also stranded a large number of Bolivian and foreign tourists. The military action left five people dead and twenty-nine wounded. Among those killed was eight-year-old Nancy Rojas, shot in the chest by army bullets fired into the window of her home.[66]

The repression by the government only solidified and emboldened the mounting protests, and the proposed gas sale emerged as a symbol of discontent with Sánchez de Lozada and his failed economic promises. Social-movement groups settled on four main gas demands: government control of the industry, a program of industrialization, the overhaul of Sánchez de Lozada's hydrocarbons law, and a referendum on exporting gas. El Alto launched a general strike. Hundreds of miners began a march to the capital, and nearly all routes into La Paz were blocked. Food and gas supplies began to run short.

On Saturday, October 11, Sánchez de Lozada decided to clear the main roads to La Paz by force. The president issued an executive decree declaring a national emergency "to guarantee the normal provision of fuel" to La Paz.[67] Sánchez Berzaín declared the militarization of El Alto.

With their city under siege, Alteños began to mobilize neighborhood by neighborhood, through FEJUVE, the association of neighborhoods.

Residents dug ditches to prevent the passage of military vehicles. Neighbors took shifts keeping vigil at night. As the convoy of military tanks, cisterns of gas, and trucks full of soldiers pushed through makeshift blockades of rocks and burning tires toward La Paz, El Alto residents, wielding slingshots and sticks, stood in the way. The army responded with tear gas and rubber bullets, and then with live rounds. "They began to shoot at houses, shooting at any human being," remembered Néstor Salinas. "Imagine children just five years old, eight-year-old girls, pregnant women, men, brothers, fathers, teenagers," he continued. "They all died."[68]

In an El Alto neighborhood, Néstor's brother David raced to find their younger brother, Raúl, who had been seen playing near the protests. When David stopped to help a wounded person lying in the street, a soldier's bullet entered his abdomen and exited just above his leg. Néstor was helping to transport wounded people to the local hospital when he heard that his brother David had been shot. When Néstor found his brother, he was told there wasn't an anesthesiologist and that overburdened hospital staff couldn't keep up with the incoming wounded. Outside the hospital, Néstor could hear gunshots. He pleaded with staff for something to be done. After two unsuccessful surgeries, David died a week later.[69]

Following the deaths on October 11, the demand for gas nationalization became a call for the president's resignation. Vice President Carlos Mesa broke ranks with Sánchez de Lozada over the use of force and declared, "They asked me if I have the courage to kill. And my response is no, no I don't have the courage to kill, nor tomorrow will I have the courage to kill. For this reason it is impossible for me to consider returning to the government."[70]

By Sunday, October 12, twenty-six more people were dead.[71] Discipline among exhausted military and police forces began breaking down. The Bolivian middle class, and increasingly the elite, joined in the demand for the president's resignation. Hundreds of intellectuals, artists, and public officials began hunger strikes across the country.

On Monday, October 13, U.S. ambassador David Greenlee reaffirmed the Bush administration's backing of embattled Sánchez de Lozada. "We are very concerned by the attack on democracy and constitutional order in Bolivia," the ambassador declared. "Poles and rocks are not a form of peaceful protest." The Organization of American States also offered its "plain and decided" support of Sánchez de Lozada.[72] By the end of Monday, another twenty-eight people were reported dead.[73] On Tuesday, with cities across the country shut down

---

BOX 3.3 | Fighting Impunity:
Another Legacy of the Gas War

For those who lost family members in the Gas War of 2003, the fighting in the streets was just the beginning. Like many other Latin American nations, Bolivia has had a painful history of governments escaping responsibility for human rights abuses. The Association of Families of Those Fallen in Defense of Gas is working with Bolivian human rights groups to ensure that impunity, in the case of the deaths of 2003, does not continue.

Of the more than sixty people killed in September and October 2003 at the hands of government forces, the vast majority were shot in the head, chest, or abdominal region, demonstrating that the aim of soldiers and police was not to minimize fatalities.[1] Many of the more than four hundred wounded were severely injured, lost limbs, or were otherwise incapacitated to the extent of no longer being able to provide for themselves or their families. "They say 'Gas War.' I say, what *war*?" challenged Néstor Salinas. "It was a massacre."[2]

The Bolivian government and the families of the victims of October 2003 are working to extradite Sánchez de Lozada and his ministers Sánchez Berzaín and Jorge Berindoague Alcocer, who currently reside in the United States, to stand trial for the human rights abuses committed in September and October 2003.

"We are seeking the incarceration of Gonzalo Sánchez de Lozada [and his ministers] in order to set a precedent in the country that these types of crimes must be punished and not remain in impunity," said Néstor.[3]

1. Legal archive of the Comité Impulsor del Juicio de Responsabilidades, La Paz.
2. Néstor Salinas Malléa, e-mail interview with authors, May 2007.
3. Ibid.

---

by protests, the Bush administration escalated its support for Sánchez de Lozada, praising his "efforts to construct a more prosperous and just future for Bolivians," warning that any other government would not be recognized by the United States.[74]

On Thursday, October 16, three hundred thousand people marched on La Paz's colonial Plaza San Francisco.[75] Hundreds more joined in hunger strikes. Representatives of the Argentine and Brazilian embassies urged Sánchez de Lozada to resign.[76] Solidarity protests were held outside Bolivian embassies and consulates in Europe, the United States, and Latin America. The country was at a crossroads; either the president would heed the demand for his resignation, or the country would be consumed by violent conflict.

On Friday, October 17, Sánchez de Lozada faxed his resignation to the Bolivian Congress and then boarded a plane for Miami. The death toll for the last two months of Sánchez de Lozada's presidency eventually reached sixty-seven people.[77]

On Bolivian television that evening, a split screen showed on one side the taxiing plane taking Sánchez de Lozada to eventual political refuge in the suburbs of Washington, D.C., while on the other, in the Legislative Palace in La Paz, a solemn Carlos Mesa was sworn in as Bolivia's sixty-fourth president. Drawing a stark contrast with his predecessor, Mesa asked the assembled Congress members to stand in a moment of silence for those who "gave their lives for their country, democracy, the future, and life."[78]

The Gas War of 2003 that brought down the government was about much more than the country's gas. It was the rejection of a political system that had been transformed into the welcome mat for economic policies written elsewhere for the benefit of others. As the old economic and political system was being stripped of its last legitimacy, the social movements that had led the protests put forth an agenda of their own. It became known as the October Agenda and included the nationalization and industrialization of gas, a constituent assembly to rewrite the nation's constitution, and bringing Sánchez de Lozada to trial for the deaths in September and October 2003.

THE MIDDLE ROAD

On October 19, 2003, thousands rallied in La Paz's Plaza San Francisco following the departure of Sánchez de Lozada. The former television news analyst and respected historian Carlos Mesa arrived unannounced and asked to address the crowd. Facing a sea of people who just two days before had brought down the country's government, Bolivia's new president asked for their support. Mesa committed to seeing through four initiatives: a national referendum on the gas sale, the modification of Sánchez de Lozada's oil and gas law, a revision of the capitalization process, and the convocation of a constituent assembly.

While Mesa split decisively from Sánchez de Lozada over his use of lethal force, on the gas issue Mesa wasn't looking for a radical departure from existing policy. Bolivia's new president wanted to secure more revenue for the state through legislative reform but was opposed to nationalization and wary of meddling with existing contracts for fear of scaring off foreign investment.

Though Mesa enjoyed approval ratings of 60 percent to 70 percent during his first few months as president, he quickly found himself constrained by powerful opposing forces.[79] El Alto's FEJUVE, labor unions, and a growing indigenous movement continued to hold demonstrations and strikes demanding the fulfillment of the October Agenda and the nationalization of gas. A powerful movement led by the business community and political elite from the center of Bolivia's oil and gas industry, Santa Cruz, began demanding autonomy and greater control over local resources.

Carlos Villegas described a conservative political bloc made up of the oil and gas companies and their home-country embassies, international financial institutions such as the World Bank and the IMF, the civic committees of gas-rich Santa Cruz and Tarija, and Bolivia's Chamber of Commerce: "They all formed a bloc with an important presence that said . . . 'We won't accept changes in the gas contracts.' . . . Rodrigo de Rato [managing director] of the IMF arrived and said that the multilateral organizations wouldn't accept changes to the rules of the game and that if this happened they were going to cut off all aid to Bolivia."[80]

In the midst of these competing forces, Mesa chose the middle road. He rejected the traditional political parties and attempted to govern from his broad base of public support. But those parties still wielded a congressional majority, leaving Mesa without allies to push his agenda. Mesa made an alliance with Congressman Evo Morales, the coca growers' leader who had played a role in the protests against Sánchez de Lozada. Morales was now seeking to distance himself from the most radical protesters in order to gain mainstream support for his Movement toward Socialism (MAS) party in upcoming municipal elections. Mesa, however, found that that alliance would soon fail him.

The Referendum

The president's first act on the gas issue was to hold a national referendum. Mesa's aim was to establish a political mandate for his new oil and gas policy. The national vote in July 2004 would concern the repeal of the capitalization law, a proposal to rebuild the state oil and gas company, recovering state ownership of oil and gas, and whether Bolivia should export its gas.

The La Paz–based Center for Development, Labor, and Agricultural Studies (CEDLA) contends that the referendum questions were intentionally crafted to ensure a positive response, but also so ambiguous that "to vote yes didn't necessarily signify to change a policy or to continue with it."[81] Several groups, including unions, El Alto's FEJUVE, and the Coordinating Committee for the Defense and Recuperation of Gas, boycotted the vote.[82]

Four months before the referendum vote, the IMF announced that a much-needed $150 million loan would depend on the referendum results, warning that a negative response to the gas export question "would not be understood by the governments" that support Bolivia.[83]

On July 18, 2004, the final vote tally achieved exactly what Mesa had hoped. All five questions passed with a clear majority in favor; 92 percent of voters voted to recover state ownership over oil and gas, 87 percent voted to repeal Sánchez de Lozada's oil and gas law, and 62 percent voted yes on exporting gas.[84] But Mesa's victory was short-lived. When it came time to translate the referendum into a new law, neither the conservative majority in Congress nor MAS supported Mesa's draft proposal, and a yearlong struggle began over new legislation.

A New Oil and Gas Law

Mesa's proposal for a new oil and gas law essentially left all the existing foreign oil and gas contracts alone. The president proposed, instead, a complex formula that would increase oil and gas taxes for certain fields, depending on their size, but leave others unchanged. MAS's counterproposal sought the renegotiation of contracts and an across-the-board 50 percent royalty on oil and gas development. The traditional parties in Congress clamored that both proposals went too far, while FEJUVE and other social movements criticized both as inadequate.

After months of political impasse, on March 6, 2005, Mesa surprised the nation by offering his resignation to Congress. Spontaneous protests broke out urging the president to stay. It turned out to be a savvy public relations ploy, as Congress rejected the resignation and promised to pass oil and gas legislation. But while Mesa tried to fortify his public support, in terms of policy options he had already tied his hands. That same month, in order to secure approval for Bolivia's annual loan package from the IMF, Mesa promised IMF officials he would not renegotiate oil and gas contracts.[85]

On May 7, after months of tense negotiations, Congress finally passed new oil and gas legislation, largely on traditional party lines, despite significant opposition from MAS and other minority parties.[86] The new legislation would require the renegotiation of all existing contracts within 180 days and added a 32 percent tax—in addition to the existing 18 percent royalty—which would be divided up between Bolivia's regional departments, municipalities, universities, indigenous communities, police and military, and the national treasury.

Immediately the World Bank and the IMF warned that the new law would scare off foreign investment, warnings echoed by protests from the Santa Cruz autonomy movement. Multinational oil and gas companies threatened to initiate legal suits. Mesa scrambled to find a way to have the legislation redrafted. Eventually he refused to either sign or veto the bill, throwing the decision back to Senate president Hormando Vaca Díez, who approved the new oil and gas law on May 17 without the president's support.

Bolivia's social movements loudly rejected the new legislation from the start as a distortion of the referendum results and a betrayal of the October Agenda. They criticized the oil and gas law for falling short of both nationalization and the rebuilding of the state company. Although the law allowed YPFB to participate in each step of the chain of production, it didn't give the state company the authority or resources to do so. Also, because of a loophole inserted in the new law, the new tax and royalty scheme would actually fall well short of the 50 percent royalty that had been in place before capitalization.[87] Though MAS had supplied the original draft of the new hydrocarbons law, the party opposed the final version's tax structure.[88]

By the end of May 2005, despite the passage of the new oil and gas law, the wave of support for nationalization had taken on a powerful momentum. While other leaders on the left were calling for a complete government takeover of the industry and the expulsion of foreign companies, Morales was still talking about tax reforms. Morales and MAS quickly found themselves left behind while more radical social movements staged massive protests demanding nationalization and criticizing Morales as a compromiser. By late May, MAS played political catch-up by adopting the nationalization call and mobilizing the MAS constituency around it, though the party's policy position remained basically unchanged.

The Fallout

The middle road approach of both Mesa's referendum and the oil and gas law sparked renewed civil unrest, and La Paz was once again paralyzed by protests. Rumors circulated of a possible military coup or a civil war. Carlos Rojas, executive committee member of FEJUVE, explained the frustration felt by those in the streets: "It's not as though we merely said, 'we want nationalization.' It wasn't just a discourse; we put forth a draft law, but it was ignored. For this reason, in April, when we saw that the Congress was still going forward and passing yet another hydrocarbons law that favored the multinationals, we began this fight."[89]

On June 6, amid the mounting crisis, Mesa offered his resignation to Congress for the second time, telling the nation, "This is as far as I can go."[90] Mesa's move set in motion a chaotic power struggle. The next officials constitutionally in line for the presidency—Senate president Hormando Vaca Díez and lower house president Mario Cossío Cortéz—were members of Sánchez de Lozada's traditional party ruling coalition. Faced with the possibility of a return to politics as usual, Bolivians from all walks of life joined in the protests to demand that neither assume the presidency. Protest numbers surged. Congress couldn't meet to determine a presidential transition because once again La Paz was locked down by protests. El Alto was in an indefinite general strike. The Guaraní people of eastern Bolivia took over seven gas fields.[91] Road blockades shut down eight of Bolivia's nine departments.[92] Mesa publicly pleaded with Vaca Díez to step aside to prevent major civil conflict. The middle class joined in the call, while mayors from every major city entered into hunger strikes along with university presidents and other professionals.

Historians Forrest Hylton and Sinclair Thomson describe the scene in La Paz during those days of crisis: "On June 6, between 400,000 and 500,000 protesters, largely of Aymara decent, poured down from El Alto into the heart of the capital. Some twenty truckloads of community peasants from Aroma arrived with clubs, stones and slings. They were accompanied by tens of thousands of *paceños* [residents of La Paz]. . . . Miners announced their presence by setting off dynamite charges. Crowds overflowed the Plaza San Francisco, and then headed off to the Plaza Murillo vowing to take over parliament and occupy the presidential palace."[93]

Lower house leader Cossío Cortéz announced he had no intention of assuming the presidency, but Vaca Díez, next in line after Mesa, was set on receiving his political due. On June 9, he moved the Congress to the judicial capital of Sucre in a last-ditch attempt to hold a session, but social movements converged on that city as well. Protesting miners arrived from Potosí and striking airport workers shut down the city's airport, stranding Congress members. As violent conflict seemed certain, it became clear that a Bolivia led by Vaca Díez would be ungovernable, and calls from national leaders mounted against a Vaca Díez presidency. Finally, the ruling coalition in Congress fell apart. As Vaca Díez stepped aside, the presidency was left to Supreme Court president Eduardo Rodriguez Veltzé, who was next in the line of succession. This also triggered a constitutional requirement for new elections to be held within six months.

The uprisings of May and June 2005 were a clear continuation of the Gas War of 2003: a reassertion of the unfulfilled demand for nationalization and a rejection of the middle-road reforms put forth by Mesa and the Congress. The message was clear: social movements demanded profound changes in the political and economic order. The presidential transition in June allowed the country to step back from the edge but failed to put it on solid ground.

The Presidential Election of 2005

The presidential election of December 2005 centered on the gas issue. Each candidate sought to distance himself from the delegitimized politics of the past and proposed some degree of recovering the role of the state in the economy. The term *nationalization* became a common catchphrase, but with interpretations that differed greatly from one candidate to the next.

On the conservative end of the spectrum, former president Jorge "Tuto" Quiroga ran under the flag of the Social Democratic Power (PODEMOS) party. He promised to "nationalize the benefits of gas" by increasing exports but warned of scaring off foreign investment by infringing on investors' legal security.[94] In the center, Samuel Doria Medina, a prominent businessman and owner of Bolivia's Burger King franchise, ran with the National Unity (UN) party. Doria Medina proposed regaining control of the capitalized firms by purchasing back shares, stating that what the people understand as nationalization is "to have more resources for Bolivians," but "not expropriation."[95]

On the left, Evo Morales, who had finished just less than two percentage points behind Gonzalo Sánchez de Lozada in the 2002 elections, ran at the head of the MAS party. Morales promised "nationalization and industrialization without confiscation" by rebuilding YPFB and changing the country's contractual relationships with foreign firms.[96] While using strong rhetoric about ending the neoliberal model and the sacking of Bolivia's natural resources, Morales intentionally distanced himself from candidates and leaders further to the left who proposed a "nationalization without compensation" and the expulsion of foreign oil and gas companies.

On Election Day, December 19, 2005, with a record turnout of 84 percent, Morales surprised even his own supporters by securing the largest vote margin in Bolivia's modern democratic history. With just under 54 percent of the vote, he became the country's first indigenous president. Morales's support went beyond his *campesino* and social movement base to include a strong showing from the middle class, and even 33 percent in historically conservative Santa Cruz. For the first time in twenty years, Bolivia's president had an indisputable popular mandate and could govern without needing to form a formal coalition with other political parties.

The election had been an unequivocal vote against the traditional parties and in support of a new way of conducting politics. In an emotional inaugural address, President Morales spoke of a new "democratic revolution" that would reverse the country's neoliberal history: "Capitalization has only decapitalized the country. Capitalization as I understand it means that you have to import capital rather than export capital. But . . . now as a product of these policies the only thing that we export is people. It must be recognized that these mistaken, failed, self-serving policies of depleting natural resources and privatizing basic services require a new consciousness in the Bolivian people. We have the obligation to change these policies."[97]

NATIONALIZATION BY NEGOTIATION

On May 1, 2006, the smell of gas hung strongly in the air as a crowd of cheering Bolivians celebrated in front of the Brazilian Petrobras oil and gas refinery just outside Cochabamba. A state worker clad in tan coveralls and a hardhat propped a wooden ladder against the front wall of the refinery just beneath the blue metal letters reading "Petrobras" and ascended the ladder as the crowd looked on. As he attached a YPFB banner over the Petrobras sign, a voice called out, "Long live Bolivia! Long live the nationalization!"

One of Morales's first acts as president was to announce the "nationalization" of the country's oil and gas reserves through presidential decree. The media show surrounding the May 1 decree (Supreme Decree #28701, "Heroes of the Chaco"), complete with Bolivian flags and armed soldiers, provided ample fodder for a slew of foreign media reports that Morales was seizing private assets and militarizing the country's gas fields. But soon after the cameras left, so did the military, and the oil and gas companies continued operations as before.

The government's "nationalization" policy was in reality much more moderate than a classic nationalization scheme. The Morales government has maintained an explicit commitment to a "nationalization without confiscation or expropriation." The result is a mix of policies to reinsert the state company in the industry and the negotiation of more favorable contract terms with foreign companies. The government's approach centers on four main objectives: first, to reassert the state's ownership over oil and gas resources as stated in the Constitution through a reconstituted YPFB; second, to increase the government's income from oil and gas by renegotiating exploration and development contracts; third, to find new export markets and negotiate higher export prices with Brazil and Argentina; and last, to implement an industrialization policy to allow Bolivia to use its gas to develop value-added products such as electricity or plastics.

Reactions to the May 1 decree were mixed. Shouts of protest came from Santa Cruz and the IMF, predicting capital flight and political isolation. U.S. president George Bush warned of an "erosion of democracy."[98] Most reactions, however, were more tempered. Regional neighbors, including Bolivian gas importers Argentina and Brazil, gave their tacit support of Bolivia's right to regain control of its natural resources while they waited to see what the full policy would look like. Foreign oil and gas companies announced the freezing of investments in Bolivia but continued operating. Bolivian social movements called the decree a good first step but voiced concern that the government's policy wasn't going far enough. The general Bolivian public received the decree favorably, and Morales's approval rating climbed to 81 percent.[99] In the months following the decree announcement, however, criticism mounted as the government suffered logistical and political setbacks in implementing its policy.

In October 2006, the government signed new contracts with ten oil and gas companies, changing their tax obligations and solidifying their stay in Bolivia for at least twenty to thirty more years. Morales declared the negotiations a success. "Mission accomplished," stated Morales in a press statement at the contract signing. "We're consolidating the nationalization of oil and gas . . . without expelling anyone and without confiscation [of property]. . . . Within ten to fifteen years, Bolivia will no longer be 'this little poor country, this beggar country.'"[100]

Some analysts warn, however, that the Morales government isn't striking as good a deal for Bolivia as it may seem. University of San Simón economics professor Roberto Fernández Terán described the Morales approach this way: "Evo is playing a political game where he doesn't want to make enemies with the foreign companies. [Morales] says, 'We're going to nationalize in a responsible manner, we're not going to expropriate, we're not going to affect the companies.' This is a strange form of nationalization—a nationalization that doesn't affect companies, that doesn't expropriate, where the companies are happy. It's a little suspect."

Others criticized the government's continued focus on exportation of raw materials. One key social movement leader from the oil-rich Chaco region called the new arrangements "contrary to the nationalization that the people demanded."[101] Social movements in the Chaco have periodically clashed with government forces over their demands for real nationalization.[102] Many Bolivians, however, including many in the business community, take a more pragmatic approach. They feel the government is striking the best balance within the established playing field—recovering more control and revenue while not scaring off foreign capital.

According to Juan Patricio Quispe, president of the Association of Family Members of those Fallen in Defense of Gas during the Gas War of 2003, the Morales government's approach is the most "sound" way to go about the nationalization: "What we want as Bolivians is to be able to count on . . . a greater quantity of resources in order to be able to develop the country. They're doing this, and this is very important to us. I believe that they're completing the objectives that were outlined in the October Agenda as we understand it, but we hope that this continues in the same way that it's going now and that it continues deepening even more."[103]

Key Challenges

In February 2007, Evo Morales described the "nationalization" as being half completed.[104] In turning its policy into reality, the government faces major challenges. Among those are rebuilding the state company, capturing more revenues from oil and gas development, negotiating better export deals, and securing investment for industrializing its gas into value-added products.

Rebuilding Bolivia's State Oil and Gas Company

On paper, the May 1 decree "recovers the property, the possession, and the total and absolute control" over Bolivia's oil and gas resources.[105]

However, the more important question remains: will YPFB have the resources and infrastructure necessary to effectively exercise ownership of the nation's oil and gas?

The crux of the government's plan to reconstitute the state oil and gas company is to recover control over the three capitalized firms that took over YPFB's exploration and transportation duties, as well as the two private firms that purchased Bolivia's other privatized oil and gas facilities in 1999. The nationalization decree requires that these five firms sell the government enough shares to give it a majority holding in each firm. In the three capitalized companies, the government already controlled between 31 and 45 percent.[106] In June 2007 the government bought back two privately held refineries for $112 million, but as of early 2008 majority control had not yet been recovered in the other four companies.[107]

Bolivia's move to recover a majority interest in the remaining four previously state-owned firms falls far short of the oil nationalizations of 1937 and 1969. On those two occasions, the government took over—with compensation—entire foreign companies. In fact, Morales's program is, ironically, much closer to what President Sánchez de Lozada originally proposed as the blueprint for privatization in 1992—public-private joint ventures in which the state maintains majority ownership. Some analysts question why the government does not instead cancel its concession contracts where cases of gas smuggling, tax evasion, or failure to meet contractual obligations have been demonstrated. This would allow the government full control of the capitalized companies without having to buy back shares.

Recovering majority ownership would give the government the means to participate once again in the entire chain of production. But that doesn't mean the government would have actual *control* over those companies. As Robert Conrad of Duke University points out, "If you own 51 percent of the company you may make the tacit decisions but you may in fact be dependent on the foreign investors approving decisions" if the state company lacks the technical capacity to make those decisions itself. "Either you have the expertise to monitor the investments and to make the investments yourself . . . or the ownership may not have much practical meaning in terms of investment decisions or the cash flow the government receives."[108]

Even if the government is able to gain control over the five companies, it would only be involved in exploration and development of a small fraction of the country's total reserves. Repsol, Total, and Petrobras would still manage operations in 83 percent of Bolivia's gas

and 86 percent of its petroleum reserves.[109] Without regaining monopoly control of the industry, it is questionable whether YPFB can compete
with the economic resources and political influence of already established multinational oil and gas companies.

Capturing More Revenues

With the new exploration and development contracts signed in October
2006, the government also instituted a new tax and royalty scheme that
establishes the government's take at 50 percent to 80 percent of oil and
gas revenues. According to official calculations, the new contracts will
bring in $1.3 billion in hydrocarbon revenues annually beginning in
2007, nearly triple those of 2004.[110]

In the new contracts, the foreign companies extract Bolivia's gas
and oil, but then hand it over to YPFB. Then YPFB handles all the foreign and domestic sales of that gas and oil and pays the taxes and royalties to the government, dividing the remaining profit with the
companies. That is the plan on paper. But as part of the new contracts
the government agreed to compensate the private companies for
"recoverable costs," including personnel, legal, and marketing
expenses, and even costs incurred by the company's international headquarters. While the government theoretically reviews those costs, they
remain within the decision-making authority of the companies, raising
the possibility of a huge bite being taken out of the government's potential revenue.[111] So, in effect, actual levels of new revenue remain a matter
of projection.

Securing Better Export Deals

Bolivia's location in the heart of South America provides it with several
potential export markets. Argentina and Brazil currently import $5.4
million of Bolivian gas daily, and demand for gas is expected to double
in Brazil by 2015.[112] Paraguay and Uruguay have also expressed interest
in importing Bolivian gas. Chile may be the best potential market for
Bolivian gas given its relative isolation and lack of domestic energy
sources. However, long-standing animosity between the two countries
remains an obstacle to a potential deal.

In October 2006, Argentina and Bolivia signed a deal to build a
second, $1.5 billion pipeline that was slated to quadruple gas exports to
Argentina by 2010. As of March 2008, however, pipeline construction
was on hold and the government stated it might need until 2013 to meet
export commitments to Argentina.[113]

Another of the government's first challenges was to increase export prices for its existing markets. In June 2006, it succeeded in negotiating a 48 percent increase in the gas price with Argentina, bringing an additional $110 million into government coffers per year.[114] After drawn-out, intense negotiations with Petrobras that ended in early 2007, the government was unable to significantly increase its export price to Brazil under the existing contract, which ends in 2019.

Here again, some social movements and analysts criticize the Morales government's focus on exporting gas as a raw material, a development model that has failed the country for centuries. Prioritizing the export of Bolivia's raw gas, they say, could come at the expense of servicing the country's internal market, domestic industrial development, and the greater revenues available from the production of value-added products. This issue became particularly salient for the Bolivian public in mid-2007, when shortages in home heating and cooking fuel led to the need to import gas from Venezuela.

Industrializing Bolivia's Gas

The Morales government has announced ambitious plans to industrialize Bolivia's gas through the construction of several gas separation and processing plants, asserting that Bolivia's days as a raw resource exporter have ended. These investments would allow for the production of value-added products including electricity, synthetic diesel, plastics, and fertilizers that could generate increased revenue.

Many of the investors keen to get a foothold in the Bolivian gas market are not the predictable Western players. Gazprom, the Russian state energy giant, has expressed interest in investing more than $2 billion in Bolivia, while inquiries have also come from Asian powers India and China.[115] In December 2006, Evo Morales and Venezuelan president Hugo Chávez inaugurated the first Bolivian projects of Petroandina, a joint venture between PDVSA (Venezuela's state-owned oil company) and YPFB. The plan includes new service stations and the construction of two gas separation plants, which would provide cooking fuel for domestic consumers as well as for export to Paraguay, Argentina, and Chile. The company also has plans to invest in exploration and development.[116]

Securing new investment, however, is only part of the solution to industrialization. Bolivia's ability to break from its history of being an exporter of raw resources depends on YPFB having the strength and resources to lead that industrialization. Multinational companies maximize profit in countries like Bolivia by extracting raw materials for the lowest price possible, and not by building processing plants or improving services for domestic consumers. This arrangement may be highly profitable for companies like Repsol, but it hasn't been good for Bolivia. YPFB will need to be economically and politically strong enough to change that equation. There are concerns, however, that once again the government is not sufficiently prioritizing investment in a YPFB-led industrialization program.

Morales's Rocky Road

The Morales government has encountered a string of political and institutional obstacles in its efforts to implement a reform of the oil and gas industry. Shortly after the May 2006 decree announcement, YPFB announced it was unable to assume fuel distribution duties as mandated by the decree. The following August, the government declared the nationalization process temporarily suspended due to "a lack of economic resources."[117] That same month, YPFB president Jorge Alvarado resigned, accused of signing a diesel contract that violated the nationalization decree. All of this created further unease and fueled critics' concerns that YPFB lacks the capacity, competence, and cash to carry out its new role.

Also in August 2006, Bolivian police and prosecutors searched the offices of the largest foreign investor in oil and gas in Latin America, Spain's Repsol. The move followed the issuing of an arrest warrant in February for Repsol's top executive in Bolivia as part of separate smuggling and malfeasance investigations. The company expressed outrage, warning that the investigations were jeopardizing the company's continued investment.[118] In this instance, as in others, the government is often pursuing a difficult good cop/bad cop strategy with foreign energy companies: negotiating for continued investment while wielding strong rhetoric to expose corporate malfeasance, though repeatedly stopping short of canceling any contracts.

The Morales government has also faced stiff opposition in the Bolivian Congress from conservative party members from the hydrocarbon-rich eastern lowlands of Santa Cruz and Tarija, who are looking to gain more control over local oil and gas profits. In the region of Tarija, local government officials are looking to cut their own gas deals with foreign oil and gas companies, hoping that the recent decentralization process and the autonomy movement being promoted by the eastern states will clearly establish such rights.[119] Critics, however, point out that Santa Cruz and Tarija already receive a disproportionate share of oil and gas revenues due to their position as producing departments.

In addition to the inability of the government to regain control of the capitalized companies, shortages in fuel supplies for the domestic market have brought further questioning of the government's competence. YPFB president Manuel Morales Olivera noted the government's deficit of experience. Reflecting on Bolivia's negotiations with foreign firms, he said, "On one side of the negotiating table sat professionals with thirty years of experience [in oil and gas], and on our side, people just thirty years old."[120]

In just over two years, the Evo Morales administration experienced excessive turnover of key staff in its oil and gas team, including one hydrocarbons minister, three heads of the oil and gas industry's regulatory agency, and four YPFB presidents. This constant instability has generated continuing concerns about the state company's operational capacity and the government's ability to complete its nationalization process.

TURNING GAS INTO DEVELOPMENT

Throughout its history, Bolivia has been unable to turn its abundant natural resource wealth into improvements in the lives of its people. "The final result," explained Carlos Villegas, "is what you see: a country with a lot of misery . . . inequality, concentration of wealth, and a lot of exclusion."[121] Bolivia is not alone; countries throughout the world have struggled, and more often than not, failed in the difficult task of leveraging natural resources to increase social and economic development. Frequently resource-rich countries experience stark underdevelopment, falling victim to a perplexing phenomenon economists call "the resource curse."

Whether Bolivia can convert its oil and gas wealth into development is largely based on a set of political questions: Can it determine and implement effective strategies to invest new oil and gas revenues to create opportunity and employment? Can it build strong institutions to root out corruption and regulate the oil and gas industry? Can it mitigate the social and environmental impacts of energy development? And can it think long-term and diversify its economy, knowing that one day those resources underfoot will be gone?

BOX 3.4 | The Resource Curse

All in all, I wish we had found water.[1]
—*Sheik Ahmed Yamani, Saudi Arabia's oil minister, 1962–1986*

"If we hadn't discovered oil, we would have been better off today," lamented a former Nigerian finance minister.[2] Since oil production began more than forty years ago, more than $340 billion in oil money has passed through Nigerian government coffers, while living standards have fallen precipitously. Today, 70 percent of Nigerians live on less than $1 a day.[3] Many residents in the oil-rich Nigerian delta region live in squalor, some just a few feet away from oil wells that pollute their air and drinking water. Military personnel patrol the area to protect the interests of foreign oil companies, putting many communities in a near state of siege.[4]

Lessons from the last half-century of natural resource development are sobering: countries endowed with an abundance of oil and gas have not experienced improved living standards and rising incomes, but paradoxically suffer from high levels of poverty and inequality, poor governance, corruption, environmental damage, and civil unrest.[5] The curious paradox of the resource curse is largely political in nature.

Because natural resources are potentially a highly lucrative business, they have the ability to manipulate and corrupt political processes. Governments often succumb to pressure to accept nontransparent contractual relationships— relinquishing control over resource development and often a fair share of revenues. In this climate leaders are also likely to turn a blind eye to the negative environmental and social impacts incurred in natural resource extraction and production. Revenues are also mismanaged when governments, suddenly awash in oil and gas money, become honey pots, with different political factions and other interested parties vying to convince government officials to channel funds in their direction.[6]

Another reason for the resource curse is that overdependence on one resource or industry causes economic instability and stymies broader development. Even if a country is able to achieve increasing and abundant revenues, that influx of

---

Investing New Revenues and Building Strong Institutions

Growing Bolivia's oil and gas industry will not on its own generate employment or improve public welfare. Determining the most effective way to spend new oil and gas revenues is a critical task for Bolivia. Some advocate distributing revenues directly to citizens, as is done in Alaska, but in a country lacking basic public goods like clean water and schools, public investment is an obvious and urgent priority. Bolivia has several options. It could use oil and gas revenues to improve

resources can tend to make governments complacent and shield them from the difficult task of long-term planning. A country's heavy reliance on one natural resource can leave it vulnerable to volatile swings in international prices. Additionally, natural resource development provides extremely limited employment for host country populations.[7]

"Non-renewable natural resources are the bread of today and the hunger of tomorrow," declared the intellectual architect of Bolivia's 1969 nationalization of Gulf Oil, Marcelo Quiroga Santa Cruz.[8] With natural resources growing scarcer and prices rising, if a country is not able to capture and wisely invest its resource wealth to benefit future generations, it can actually be more advantageous to just leave it in the ground.

1. Michael L. Ross, "The Political Economy of the Resource Curse," *World Politics* (January 1999), www.polisci.ucla.edu/faculty/ross/paper.pdf.

2. Jonathan Power, "The Gift that Corrupts: Nigeria Struggles against the Curse of Oil," *International Herald Tribune*, January 8, 2004.

3. Jim Shultz, *Follow the Money: A Guide to Monitoring Budgets and Oil and Gas Revenues* (New York: Open Society Institute, 2005), 32.

4. Emira Woods, "Oil Trip," *Foreign Policy in Focus*, September 26, 2006, www.fpif.org/pdf/gac/0609oiltrip.pdf.

5. Terry Lynn Karl, "Understanding the Resource Curse," in *Lifting the Resource Curse,* vol. 2, *Covering Oil: A Reporter's Guide to Energy and Development* (New York: Open Society Institute, 2005), 22.

6. Ibid, 25.

7. David Waskow and Carol Welch, "The Environmental, Social, and Human Rights Impacts of Oil Development," in *Lifting the Resource Curse,* vol. 2, *Covering Oil: A Reporter's Guide to Energy and Development* (New York: Open Society Institute, 2005), 102.

8. Roberto Gonzáles Palaez, "Evaluación del Sector Hidrocarburos" (Evaluation of the Gas and Oil Sector), *Informe Económico No. 4* (Economic Report No. 4), *Estructura Actual Resultante de la Capitalización/Privatización de YPFB* (Current Structure as a Result of the Capitalization/Privatization of YPFB) (Santa Cruz, Bolivia), 5. Translation by authors.

the country's struggling social services, which it has begun to do through the expansion of public health coverage. The government could also give priority to public works such as roads or sanitation projects, which have the immediate capacity to create employment. Another investment option is to funnel revenues into microenterprise loans or agricultural assistance that could spur local development. The challenge is balancing immediate economic and social needs with investments that provide more profound development results over the long run.

Thus far, the most publicized destinations for new hydrocarbon revenues have been a modest annual scholarship distributed to over 1 million primary school students and funding an expanded pension program for Bolivian senior citizens. On the one hand, proponents of the program praise the direct distribution of funds as more efficient than distribution through a bueareaucracy often prone to corruption. Others, however, call the program a political tactic to shore up Morales's popular base.

Since the 2005 oil and gas law, much of Bolivia's oil and gas revenues are channeled to regional and municipal governments rather than the central government. In many instances, local authorities have failed to put those resources to good use. While hydrocarbon revenues accumulate in regional and municipal government coffers, the Morales administration has been eager to work on legislation to change how oil and gas revenues are distributed. In November 2007, legislation passed by the Bolivian Congress took revenues from regional governments to pay for the new pension plan, exacerbating tensions between the Morales administration and opposition party governors.

If Bolivia is to use oil and gas revenue to spur development, ensuring transparency and building effective regulatory capacity must be priorities. Robert Conrad is concerned that in oil and gas nationalization in other countries, state companies have lacked transparency. He warns that "incentives for corruption could increase."[122] Breaking that corruption cycle means building a strong and independent regulatory body capable of effectively monitoring financial transactions.

As part of that effort, the government has increased the transparency of oil and gas contracts, which during the capitalization years had been kept secret. Nobel laureate and former chief economist for the World Bank Joseph Stiglitz said: "Without transparency, it is easy for citizens to feel that they are being cheated—and they often are. When foreign companies get a deal that is too good to be true, there is often something underhanded going on."[123] In Bolivia there has still been little talk to date of mechanisms to ensure that civil society has a strong role in oversight of YPFB and how hydrocarbon revenues are spent.

Mitigating Environmental and Social Impacts

Another crucial challenge for Bolivia is to mitigate the environmental degradation that accompanies oil and gas extraction, transportation, and industrialization. Bolivia is recognized among the ten most biodiverse countries in the world, and oil and gas development is located in some of the country's most sensitive areas.[124]

Bolivia's gas development has caused significant environmental damage. Industrialization projects such as refining and the production of plastics and fertilizers would bring with them additional negative impacts on the natural environment and the health of surrounding communities. To manage these impacts, Bolivia must greatly improve its environmental laws and regulations over oil and gas operations, including environmental impact assessments, stringent monitoring of ongoing projects, and effective enforcement.

Another challenge for Bolivia will be adequately ensuring a just relationship with indigenous communities living in oil and gas exploitation areas. Historically, in Bolivia and globally, these largely impoverished communities have never benefited from the resources taken from their lands, and they have borne the brunt of the negative environmental and social impacts of extraction and production. Mechanisms to allow for consultation with native communities before oil and gas extraction, and compensation for damages, have been gravely inadequate. A MAS-supported draft of the 2005 gas law would have given indigenous communities veto rights over oil and gas development in their territories, but it was stripped from the bill's final version. That veto mechanism was also not included in Morales's 2006 nationalization decree.

Guadalupe Montenegro of the Santa Cruz-based Center for Legal Studies and Social Research (CEJIS) explained that in the past, many isolated communities negotiated alone with wealthy companies without support from the Bolivian government: "When [people] demand nationalization or control by the state, they also want the state to assume its role of society's defender. The state needs to have the information and the capable entities and experts in this. They should be the ones who are in the relationship between the companies and the communities."[125] Government control of gas development by no means ensures less harm to the environment and surrounding communities. Affected communities need to be meaningfully involved in policy making at all levels—from development decisions to revenue spending decisions—so that informed decisions can be made as to whether the benefits of development outweigh the costs.

Diversifying the Economy

With oil and gas constituting approximately 50 percent of all Bolivian export revenue in 2005 and 2006, the government has a long way to go to wean itself from its dependence on this one sector, a dependence that leaves the economy vulnerable to international market swings as well as to the eventual depletion of this nonrenewable resource.[126] Bolivia's gas revenues could be used to spur development of renewable energy sources such as the country's ample wind and solar potential, or to develop other sectors such as agriculture, manufacturing, and service industries.

Carlos Villegas, while serving as President Morales's minister of planning and development, said public funds would be invested in rural and urban programs aimed at helping "micro, small, and medium-size businesses," part of an economic plan which aims to create one hundred thousand jobs a year for the next five years.[127] From Villegas's viewpoint, a core reason why Bolivia remains South America's most impoverished country is because of the exclusion of Bolivia's small private sector in favor of foreign firms: The small business sector "has been excluded during the last twenty-two years of deregulation and liberal economic policies. . . . [But] what we're doing now is to invite Bolivian businesses to participate in services and processes related to the industrialization of natural gas."[128]

History has shown that the exploitation of nonrenewable resources is not a viable long-term development strategy. In the coming years Bolivia will need to reinvest its resource wealth in other, more sustainable industries and projects that will translate into an improved quality of life for future generations.

CONCLUSION

In May 2005, when President Evo Morales announced his nationalization decree, he pledged to use Bolivia's abundant gas reserves to bring an end to the country's chronic poverty. Across the world, however, history has shown time and again that possessing great resource wealth alone does not bring development. Reversing Bolivia's fortunes will require a diverse set of economic strategies and profound political and institutional changes. But while gas can't be the fuel that ignites an economic transformation in Bolivia, it could be a crucial spark—providing financial resources to make other political and economic changes possible. For Bolivia to fundamentally reshape its oil and gas industry, the government needs three things it currently lacks: a long-term vision, the capital to fund it, and the capacity to carry it out.

First and foremost, the government needs a cohesive long-term vision—reaching years beyond the Morales administration—for how the oil and gas sector will be run, how raw gas will be industrialized and used to develop other sustainable industries, how Bolivia will use its resources to meet domestic demand, and how finite revenues will be invested to provide future resources. That vision, in turn, needs to be developed with and carry the long-term support of a wide consensus among the Bolivian people.

Second, to rebuild its state oil and gas industry and to develop domestic industrialization capacity, Bolivia needs investment capital. Part of that capital could come from new investment or development deals with foreign investors or lenders. If so, it needs to come under terms that don't hand over control of planning and regulation to outsiders—a repeat of the mistakes of the past. Investment capital could also come from Bolivia's own growing domestic revenues from gas. But that will require tough political decisions and a careful balancing of long-term development goals and short-term spending needs.

Perhaps Bolivia's greatest challenge will be developing the necessary human resources and technical capacity to run a state industry, to negotiate with foreign players, and to regulate private investors. Bolivia's lack of capacity has become the bottleneck to real change and has caused significant problems in actually implementing policy. In the long-term, Bolivia needs to look at how its own educational system can start training the petroleum and environmental engineers, chemists, lawyers, industry analysts, and tax auditors the country will need. In the short-term Bolivia will need to find, and in many cases pay for, outside experts.

For Bolivians, the legacy of their natural resource wealth disappearing beneath their feet is indelible. Nearly five centuries ago, armor-clad conquistadors rode in on horses and emptied Bolivia of one of the largest mineral deposits history has known. In the 1980s and 1990s, modern-day conquistadors in suits and ties preached a theory that private business alone is best-suited to develop the country's natural resources.

But Bolivia's most recent experience could have been very different. How would Bolivia be economically positioned today if it had followed the lead of its neighbor Chile, ironically often held up as Latin America's neoliberal poster child, and had excluded its oil and gas from capitalization reforms as Chile did with its state mining sector? What if Bolivia had privatized its state oil and gas company but maintained the government's regulatory role and preexisting tax and royalty levels? Bolivia had a range of options in reforming its economy, and in most cases, under clear foreign pressure, it chose the most extreme, and it chose poorly.

Morales's policy approach, politically speaking, is clearly middle of the road—choosing to reform rather than rewrite the existing rulebook. A part of that policy aims to give the state a stronger direct role in how its oil and gas are developed, but the extent of this role remains an open question. The risk is that limiting YPFB's role may stunt the company's potential from the start, leaving it unable to grow in the shadow of much more powerful private foreign companies, and once again failing to take advantage of Bolivia's full potential.

Foreign companies and the international financial institutions that back them have fiercely resisted new changes to Bolivia's oil and gas rules. It is essential to note, however, that the economic approach championed by foreign companies, international lenders, and a chain of conservative governments, only left Bolivia mired in deficits and unable to lift itself from its chronic poverty. It was only pressure from the country's social movements and political left—both before Morales took office and after—that led to policies that have made government revenue soar and have contributed to Bolivia's first fiscal surplus in thirty years. The new contracts signed in October 2006, tripling the companies' taxes, show that there was a good deal of "crying wolf" in the conservative warnings about change.

After two decades of failed theories, the global state-versus-private-market struggle is swinging the other way, especially with regard to oil and gas, where 80 percent of global reserves are currently in public control.[129] The Morales government has said that reversing twenty years of neoliberal economic policy in Bolivia won't happen overnight, and that assessment is right. A state oil and gas company reduced to rubber-stamping contracts with foreign companies will take years to rebuild.

Evo Morales has made big promises that gas will bring change for Bolivia's 9 million citizens, and the people have shown they will hold him accountable if he does not fulfill those promises. The hope for Bolivia is that its real fuel for change is not gas or government, but the Bolivian people themselves. In the words of Néstor Salinas, who lost his brother in the Gas War of 2003, "Governments come and go, but the memory of the people is constant."[130]

The Bolivian Congress seen through a bullet-shattered window, the legacy of two days of violence set in motion by the International Monetary Fund's demand for economic belt-tightening in February 2003. Photo: Kathryn Cook (2005).

CHAPTER 4

Lessons in Blood and Fire

The Deadly Consequences of IMF Economics

Jim Shultz

In February 2003, Bolivia's capital city, La Paz, exploded in two days of violent protest and conflict over a tax increase on the country's working poor.[1] The increase was a direct product of demands by the International Monetary Fund (IMF) that the government take action to reduce its budget deficit.

To understand what went on behind the scenes that led to a conflict that left thirty-four people dead and almost two hundred others injured, Jim Shultz reviewed archives of agreements between Bolivia and the IMF to trace the trajectory of demands the fund has placed on the nation's leaders. He spoke with Carlos Mesa, Bolivia's vice president at the time, with the key government economic advisers, with IMF officials, and also with leaders of the protests in the streets and the mother of the conflict's most well-known victim.

The following account of Bolivia's Febrero Negro offers an on-the-ground view of what happens when impoverished countries scramble to meet the economic demands of powerful multinational economic institutions. It offers lessons that reach well beyond the borders of Bolivia.

Through the panoramic windows of the International Monetary Fund's office in La Paz you can see down to the rooftop where Ana Colque, a twenty-four-year-old student nurse and single mother, was shot and killed in February 2003. Army sharpshooters sent a bullet through her chest when she climbed to the roof to come to the aid of a twenty-five-year old repairman who had also been shot and killed by sharpshooters just an hour earlier. Both of them died during a violent military assault intended to quell public protests against an economic belt-tightening package imposed on Bolivia by the IMF.

The day before, the conflict had converted La Paz's city center into a war zone, with the country's army and a unit of the national police firing upon one another on the steps of the National Congress and the Presidential Palace. Before it was over, the two days that became known in Bolivia as Febrero Negro (Black February) would leave thirty-four people dead and nearly two hundred others wounded.

The story of Bolivia's Febrero Negro is not just the story of two tragic days in La Paz, but also of the global economic system that set that violence in motion. All of the major actors in that system are present in this drama: the IMF, the World Bank, and their economic policies toward poor countries; a government caught between those policies and the demands of its people; international corporations pressing their interests; workers and social movements taking to the streets; and individuals mortally caught in the crossfire.

THE IMF AND THE POLITICS OF ECONOMIC BELT-TIGHTENING

In 1944, with the end of World War II visible on the horizon, the powers of Europe and the Americas set out to develop a group of global institutions through which they hoped to bring peace and economic prosperity to the community of nations. To protect the peace, the victors of the war established a new United Nations (UN). To chart a course toward global economic prosperity, delegates from forty-four nations gathered that June in the small New Hampshire town of Bretton Woods.

In forming the UN, it was the failed aftermath of World War I and the Treaty of Versailles that was on the minds of its founders. At Bretton Woods, the ghost in the shadows was the memory of the Great Depression, and delegates hoped to create a world economic order that could avoid the kind of global economic collapse suffered just a decade before.[2]

Out of these negotiations two global institutions were born. One was the World Bank, which was given the responsibility of financing large-scale infrastructure projects, beginning with the reconstruction of postwar Europe. The other institution born that summer in New Hampshire was the International Monetary Fund. The role given to the IMF was to promote a stable international demand for goods. The fund would do this by stabilizing international currency exchange rates and by making short-term loans to governments that would otherwise have trouble meeting their international payments, for trade or debt, to other countries.[3]

While today both the IMF and the World Bank suffer a blizzard of criticisms, it is important to remember that, in the eyes of their founders, the establishment of the IMF and the World Bank was equally impor-tant as the establishment of the UN that same year. "The IMF was founded on the belief that there was a need for collective action on a global level for economic stability, just as the United Nations had been founded on the belief that there was a need for collective action at the global level for political stability," writes economic Nobel laureate Joseph Stiglitz.[4]

John Maynard Keynes, the British economist who led the U.K. dele-gation to Bretton Woods and is credited as a chief architect of the insti-tutions born there, said at the conference's end: "We have shown that a concourse of 44 nations are actually able to work together at a con-structive task in amity and unbroken concord. Few believed it possible. If we can continue in a larger task as we have begun in this limited task, there is hope for the world. The brotherhood of man will have become more than a phrase."[5] The IMF boasts a series of important successes over its history, among the more recent: buttressing South Korea with $21 billion in loans during the 1997–98 Asian financial crisis; helping Kenya with a $52 million loan to combat the effects of a national drought in 2000; and helping set up treasury systems in the countries of the former Soviet Union after its political collapse in the 1990s.[6]

Six decades after its birth, the IMF has a staff of twenty-eight hun-dred and a global mission that goes far beyond the one given to it by Keynes and the other founders who gathered at Bretton Woods. Headquartered in Washington, the IMF describes its role this way: "It aims to prevent crises in the system by encouraging countries to adopt sound economic policies; it is also—as its name suggests—a fund that can be tapped by members needing temporary financing to address bal-ance of payments problems."[7] The fund declares, "By working to strengthen the international financial system and to accelerate progress toward reducing poverty, as well as promoting sound economic policies among all its member countries, the IMF is helping to make globaliza-tion work for the benefit of all."[8]

How did the IMF evolve from a limited mission dealing with cur-rency exchange and balance of trade payments to become a key setter of global economic policy? First, the fund's original work became largely obsolete. When the IMF was born, global currency exchange was based on the gold standard. When the gold standard was abandoned in 1971, the IMF lost its core function and soon began hunting for another.[9] It found that new purpose in the 1980s in the conservative economic movements led by U.S. president Ronald Reagan and British prime minister Margaret Thatcher.

In their respective countries, Reagan and Thatcher were leading battles to remake the economic rules, aimed at creating more freedom for corporations and more limits on the role of government. The IMF became a main vehicle for exporting those policies to the rest of the world, with conditions on lending being the fund's chief tool. "The IMF and the World Bank became the reluctant missionary institutions, through which these policies were pushed on the reluctant poor countries that often badly needed their loans and grants," writes Stiglitz.[10]

The resulting package of IMF-pressed economic reforms became known by a variety of names—Structural Adjustment, the Neoliberal Economic Model, the Washington Consensus. As a condition of IMF, World Bank, and other international aid, countries were required to privatize their natural resources. They were coerced to sell off state-owned enterprises, from airlines to telephone companies. Labor protections needed to be scaled back. Public spending had to be cut and taxes raised to reduce public budget deficits.

Today the IMF is no longer a simple economic adviser sitting on the sidelines. It is a political power that, in many countries, wields more influence over economic policy than elected governments.

The IMF in the Eyes of Its Critics

To its critics, especially those looking at the fund and its activities from the perspective of low-income countries, the IMF was designed from its start to protect the economic interests of the wealthiest nations, often at the expense of poor ones. Officially, the fund's highest authority is its board of governors, composed of representatives of all 184 member countries. In reality, however, the IMF is run by a much smaller executive board dominated by its permanent members: the United States, Japan, Germany, France, the United Kingdom, China, Russia, and Saudi Arabia, plus a handful of other wealthy countries that hold the largest shares: Canada, Italy, Sweden, Belgium, and the Netherlands.[11]

Moreover, IMF governing power is not based on "one nation, one vote," as the UN General Assembly is, but a "one dollar, one vote" scheme based on the size of each country's economy. The United States' voting power, for example, is two hundred times Bolivia's.[12] IMF rules also give the United States unique control over the fund's most important choices. The IMF's Articles of Agreement require an 85 percent supermajority to make major decisions. Not coincidentally, the United States holds a voting share of 17.6 percent. As a result, it can effectively veto key fund decisions, the only single nation in the world to wield such control.[13]

Not surprisingly, the promarket policies imposed by the IMF and the World Bank also directly benefit the economic interests of the wealthy countries who control those institutions. Privatization of public resources has opened up new markets for corporations such as Bechtel and Enron of the United States, British Petroleum of the United Kingdom, Shell of the Netherlands, and Suez of France. Pressure to hold down public spending to free up funds for loan repayment also benefits wealthy nations and their major banks, which have made billions of dollars in loans to poor countries.

U.S. officials openly admit that IMF and World Bank policies offer a direct benefit to U.S. corporations. As the writer William Finnegan observed: "Testifying before Congress in 1995, Lawrence Summers, then of the Treasury Department, disclosed that American corporations received $1.35 in procurement contracts for each dollar the American government contributed to the World Bank and other multilateral development banks."[14] For the United States and other wealthy nations, support for the IMF and the World Bank is not simply an act of charity, or an extension of conservative economic ideology. That support is also a calculated and lucrative opportunity for return on investment. Bolivian economist Roberto Fernández Terán writes, "Through its own constitution and the distribution of internal power since its birth in Bretton Woods in 1944, the fund has always favored the economic and political interests of the United States and the countries of the current European Union."[15]

Critics also charge that the IMF is either unable to understand the impact that its policies have on poor countries or is deliberately unconcerned. This includes, critics note, the narrow makeup of the IMF staff, a full two-thirds of which are economists. More than 90 percent of the IMF's staff is based in the fund's headquarters in Washington. Typically the IMF's permanent staff in a country is limited to a single person.[16]

In Latin America, Asia, and Africa, the IMF finds itself and its policies under attack, both in intellectual circles and on the streets. The models that promise economic prosperity when presented in PowerPoint in Washington have, time after time, failed to deliver the goods when actually implemented on the ground. Among IMF policies, one that has often resulted in the deepest damage and provoked the most bitter protest is the IMF's insistence that poor governments reduce public spending and increase taxes in the name of reducing public deficits.

The Demand for Deficit Reduction

The IMF's interventions related to debt and deficit reduction have their roots in the Latin American debt crisis of the 1980s. As a result of heavy borrowing and the skyrocketing interest rates at the time, many countries found themselves so overburdened by debt and so incapable of paying their lenders that a number of major international banks veered close to bankruptcy.[17]

The IMF describes its role in the debt crisis this way: "The IMF helped debtor countries design medium-term stabilization programs, provided substantial financing from its own resources, and arranged financing packages from creditor governments, commercial banks, and international organizations."[18] Translating the jargon, this means that the IMF loaned countries emergency aid so that they could keep up with their payments to banks and other lenders. Roberto Fernández adds, "Of equal importance, [the IMF] took advantage of the circumstances to apply longer-term policies on poor countries, aimed at making them more subordinate to the larger economies and their political power."[19]

A public deficit, simply put, is the amount that a government spends in a year over and above what it will take in as taxes, foreign donations, and other revenue. Deficits are the part of the budget that must be borrowed and paid back with interest. Poor nations borrow money from many sources, including international financial institutions like the World Bank and the IMF, private banks, and other governments.

Deficit spending is common practice among many governments, not just those of poor countries. The United States has run budget deficits, from small to gargantuan, for all but five of the past forty-three years.[20] In 2006, the U.S. budget deficit reached nearly $250 billion, which amounted to almost 10 percent of all federal government expenditures.[21]

Reducing public deficits is a cornerstone of IMF policy and a central condition that governments must meet in order to receive IMF loans and other aid. The IMF argues that deficit reduction is essential to help poor countries achieve economic stability. It writes: "One of the central insights from past research on developing countries is that prudent fiscal policy—that is, low budget deficits and low levels of public debt—is a key ingredient for economic growth, which in turn is essential for reducing poverty and improving social outcomes."[22]

IMF officials argue that their real concern is not about helping lenders but about helping poor countries obtain the resources they need from abroad in order to develop their economies. The fund says that heavily indebted countries are like a family that repeatedly borrows from the bank or the local store, until one day it is told that it is too far in debt to receive any more credit. Fiscal discipline, the IMF says, is about making tough choices now in order to avoid tougher choices down the road and, ultimately, about ensuring long-term economic sustainability.[23]

By definition, reducing budget deficits means that governments must either cut public spending or raise taxes, or both. While the IMF touts such action as important to supporting long-term economic growth, many researchers and poor governments argue that the economic squeezing forced on already fragile economies pushes them over the edge. As Arthur MacEwan, an economist at the University of Massachusetts, writes:

> The IMF mania for reductions of government spending in times of crisis has been rationalized by the claim that balanced budgets are the foundation of long term economic stability and growth. The IMF officially laments the fact that these policies have a severe negative impact on low-income groups (because they both generate high rates of unemployment and eviscerate social programs). Yet, fund officials claim these policies are necessary to assure long-term stability. Nonsense. In recessions, moderate government deficits (like those in recent years in Argentina) are a desirable counter-cyclical policy, and balanced budgets only exacerbate downturns. Also, curtailing social spending—on education, health care, physical infrastructure projects—cuts the legs out from under long-term economic progress.[24]

Joseph Stiglitz goes further, saying that the IMF's strict rules about deficit reduction go directly against its original mission, to foster economic expansion: "Today the IMF typically provides funds only if countries engage in policies like cutting deficits, raising taxes, or raising interest rates that lead to contraction of the economy. Keynes would be rolling over in his grave were he to see what has happened to his child."[25]

What does the IMF policy of deficit reduction mean in practical terms for the people who must live with the results? In the African republic of Cameroon, Oxfam reports, the IMF required the government to achieve a fiscal surplus by 2005. The cuts in public spending required to accomplish that goal would be enough to double the country's health budget in a country where infant mortality remains a profound problem.[26] Failure to agree to the IMF's terms can also cost a country dearly. When Honduras had a dispute with the IMF over teacher salary increases, it cost the Honduran government $194 million in delayed debt relief and donor aid. That assistance was more than three times what the country needed to fill the gap in providing universal education to all the nation's children.[27] In Bolivia in 2003, the IMF's demands for deficit reduction not only meant higher taxes for the country's poor, but also set in motion a chain of events that left thirty-four families burying their dead.

THE IMF IN BOLIVIA

For two decades the IMF and the World Bank have been primary architects of Bolivia's economic policies. Many would argue that the IMF has been more influential than the Bolivian government itself. From 1986 to 2001 Bolivia received $350 million in IMF loans in exchange for adopting a specific prescription for its economic policies.[28]

The IMF's deep involvement in Bolivian economic policy can be traced back to the country's battle with hyperinflation in the mid-1980s. The late 1970s and early 1980s were years of extraordinary political instability in Bolivia; from 1978 to 1982, Bolivia had nine different presidents—some elected, some brutal dictators.[29] This instability, combined with a collapse of world prices for tin—the base of the Bolivian economy at the time—took a huge economic toll.[30] From 1970 to 1980, Bolivia's foreign debt exploded by more than sixfold, to over $3 billion. The national economy was collapsing on itself.[31]

Blacklisted for aid from the IMF and the World Bank, the Bolivian government stopped servicing its foreign debt and started printing money to keep up with its commitments for public spending.[32] It also allowed its currency to float in value against the dollar, sparking inflation that, for a time in 1985, hit levels equal to an annualized rate of 25,000 percent per year.[33]

In 1985, a newly elected government led by President Víctor Paz Estenssoro implemented a series of extreme measures to bring inflation under control. These included the devaluation of the Bolivian currency, elimination of producer subsidies, deregulation of interest rates, and repressive actions against labor unions to prevent demands for higher wages.[34] Two years later, inflation was under 20 percent and Bolivia's economic growth had climbed back to a rate of 2.4 percent per year.

A year after Bolivia's self-imposed shock therapy, the IMF offered the country limited aid, support for a Social Emergency Fund to help generate employment for some of those hardest hit.[35] Through that door the IMF and the World Bank would enter Bolivia and over the next two decades bring with them the full array of structural adjustment programs as conditions of economic assistance. IMF and World Bank policies would become the Bolivian government's economic blueprint, through administration after administration.

IMF and World Bank Predictions versus Bolivian Reality

In August 1998, the IMF, the World Bank, and the Bolivian government unveiled a joint policy framework paper that laid out a comprehensive plan for overhauling the nation's economy.[36] Policy papers and letters of intent such as these are the mechanism by which IMF officials secure promises from governments about the reforms they will implement in exchange for aid. They are also the only public paper trail of the closed-door negotiations between the IMF, the World Bank, and governments.

The 1998 paper laid out the specifics of the overhaul—widespread privatization, labor reform, deficit reduction—and then predicted a rosy picture of the economic results that Bolivia could expect: "Against this background, a key objective . . . is to achieve a significant reduction in poverty by 2002 through faster economic growth and stronger social programs. Specifically, the program aims to raise economic growth from 4.5 percent in 1998 to 5.5 to 6 percent by 2001, reduce inflation gradually to 5 percent in 2001, achieve moderate gains in reserves, and keep the external current account deficit on a sustainable path."[37]

Bolivia implemented virtually the entire program. But instead of it making the Bolivian economy more prosperous, the program made Bolivia's economy even worse. Four years later the Bolivian government reported gloomily to the IMF: "The government that took office in August 2002 inherited a situation of prolonged economic stagnation. Economic growth averaged only 1.5 percent a year in 1999–2002. The resulting fall in per capita income and employment, and the contraction of the informal economy . . . have contributed to rising social tensions that erupted recently. Moreover, the weak economy has undermined government revenues, raised the fiscal deficit, and placed a heavy financing burden on the public sector. The prolonged economic stagnation has also weakened the financial and corporate sectors."[38]

The gap between what the IMF and the World Bank predicted and what actually happened on the ground could hardly be wider. Two decades into the IMF and World Bank Bolivian economic experiment, the results have been dismal. In 2005, the poverty rate was at 64 percent of the nation and climbing.[39] The unemployment rate was 14 percent of all workers, higher than at any time in fifteen years; it had more than quadrupled over the last decade.[40] Nearly two-thirds of the nation's budget was financed from debt and donations.[41] Economic growth, when it did come, mostly benefited a few specific industries owned mainly by foreign corporations.[42] What has been true for the Bolivian economy as a whole has also been true with specific reforms required by the IMF and the World Bank, among them privatization of public water systems and the gas and oil industry.

Bolivia's experiment with water privatization ended up a good deal worse than predicted. In the mid-1990s, the World Bank made privatization of public water systems in two of Bolivia's largest cities, Cochabamba and El Alto/La Paz, a condition of assistance for water development.[43] The World Bank argued that handing water over to foreign corporations was essential in order to open the door to needed investment and skilled management.[44]

In Cochabamba, that demand for privatization led to a forty-year contract with a consortium led by the Bechtel Corporation of California. Upon taking over, the corporation immediately forced rate increases averaging more than 50 percent, and in many cases much higher.[45] Citywide protests ultimately led to the company's ouster in April 2000, but only after a declaration of martial law by the government, aimed at protecting the companies' contract, left one teenage boy dead and more than one hundred people wounded. A similar uprising in 2005 led to the cancellation of another privatization deal in El Alto/La Paz with the Suez Corporation of France. (For more on the water revolts, see chapter 1.)

Privatization of the oil and gas sector was also part of the IMF and World Bank master plan for Bolivia, which called for "privatizing all remaining public enterprises."[46] The theory behind it was that if Bolivia severely limited state involvement in the oil and gas sector and reduced its share of profits for oil and gas fields from 50 percent down to 18 percent—and increased the share of the foreign oil companies accordingly—investment and production would expand dramatically and Bolivia would actually make significantly more money than if it retained higher royalties.[47] Unfortunately, that prediction, like many others from the IMF and the World Bank, did not turn out as promised. While Bolivia was producing 135 percent more oil and gas—and producing big profits for the private companies that took over—government oil and gas revenues only grew by an anemic 10 percent.[48] (For more on the Bolivia gas issue, see chapter 3.)

By complying with the IMF's demands for privatization, Bolivia ended up reducing its public revenue and started acquiring higher public deficits. Later the IMF would return to Bolivia and pressure it to reduce those deficits, not at the expense of foreign corporations but of Bolivia's working poor.

The IMF Tells Bolivia to Reduce Its Budget Deficit

Bolivia, like many poor countries and a good many rich ones, relies on borrowing to finance its annual public budget. In the years leading up to Febrero Negro, however, Bolivia's budget deficit had shot through the roof. In 1997 Bolivia's budget borrowing equaled 3.3 percent of the country's gross domestic product (GDP). By 2002 it had leapt to 8.7 percent.[49] That borrowing meant that each year a larger portion of the budget had to be spent on financing debt instead of providing services like heath care and schools. In 2002 Bolivia owed a debt payment of more than $496 million, 16 percent of the nation's total budget.[50]

For years the IMF had been pressuring Bolivia to take drastic action to reduce its deficit, a demand reflected in the formal memoranda exchanged between Bolivia and the fund. In 1999 the IMF and the government agreed to a target. By 2002 Bolivia would bring down its deficit to just 2 percent of GDP.[51] Bolivia missed that target by more than $400 million.

How did Bolivia's deficit grow so much so fast, and how much of a problem was that deficit growth? In many ways, Bolivia's ballooning deficit was an Andean echo of the deficit explosion under way just around the corner from the IMF headquarters in Washington, in the Bush White House. In 2000, the year before George W. Bush took office, the United States had a healthy budget surplus of 2.4 percent of GDP. By 2004 that surplus had disappeared and become a deficit of 3.7 percent, a fiscal nosedive more drastic than Bolivia's.[52]

President Bush justified the mounting U.S. deficit this way: "I remember campaigning in Chicago, and one of the reporters said, would you ever deficit spend? I said only—only in times of war, in times of economic insecurity as a result of a recession, or in times of national emergency."[53] Vice President Dick Cheney went further: "Reagan proved deficits don't matter."[54]

During the same period, Bolivia's economy was also in trouble, in part because of forces coming directly from the United States. One was a U.S.-backed program to eradicate Bolivia's coca leaf crop, a base ingredient for cocaine. The other was the U.S. economic slowdown and its negative impact on U.S. trade and investment throughout Latin America. As 2003 began, Bolivia's economic growth lagged at just 1.5 percent, and the informal sector, where the poor find much of their employment, was actually contracting.[55]

In the years running up to Febrero Negro, Bolivia was in almost exactly the same kind of economic situation used to justify high deficits in the United States. Serious economic experts were counseling that running deficits instead of cutting spending was exactly the economic medicine needed to jump-start the Bolivian economy. During an October 2001 visit to Bolivia, Joseph Stiglitz told government leaders: "Now Bolivia is in a recession. . . . That is why I believe that there are ways to use the resources of the future to help resolve current problems . . . one of the most common methods for attacking a recession is to increase public spending."[56]

IMF officials would not take the same generous view toward Bolivia's deficit problems that the United States reserved for itself. As 2003 began, IMF officials decided that it was time for Bolivia to get tough and tackle its deficit with serious action. They demanded that the budget shortfall be cut in a single year, by almost a third, down to a target of 5.5 percent of GDP. Reaching that target would be a condition of receiving long-term support from the IMF. To comply, the government would have to come up with a combination of budget cuts and tax increases totaling more than $250 million, 8 percent of the country's total budget.[57]

After the February 2003 fiasco, IMF officials insisted that the Bolivian government had been in full agreement with the 5.5 percent deficit target. An IMF spokesman in Washington said, "The fiscal deficit target of 5.5 percent of GDP was mutually agreed between the government and fund staff as a way to restore sustainability."[58] Yet high-level Bolivian officials, from the vice president on down, reported that the fund insisted on the 5.5 percent target, despite government warnings that it was both economically and politically impossible. Government officials also warned the IMF that forcing such a cut could lead to exactly the kind of violent social upheaval that struck Bolivia that February.

Bolivia's former president Carlos Mesa, who was vice president at the beginning of 2003, said that the government was explicit in its conversations with IMF officials: "The minister of finance, who met [with IMF officials,] explained to the International Monetary Fund the impossibility of making so large a leap." The government proposed an alternative deficit target of 6.5 percent, still a substantial decrease from the previous year's deficit of 8.7 percent.[59] Bolivia's national budget director, Edwin Aldunate, who also negotiated with the fund, said that IMF officials were unrelenting. "The IMF insisted on 5.5 percent. We explained that 5.5 percent wasn't viable. I told them right here in this office that [the spending cuts and tax increases required] could provoke serious social problems."[60]

Exactly how obligated is Bolivia, or any poor country, to follow the IMF's suggestions? Fund officials say that they only give countries advice, not orders. Countries are sovereign, says the fund, and it is the country, they claim, that makes the actual decision to accept or reject an IMF recommendation. But in reality Bolivian officials had little choice but to follow the IMF's suggestions. Not doing so, fund officials warned, could cost dearly in international aid that the government needs in order to survive.

George Gray Molina, as a senior staff member at the Bolivian government's research office on economic issues, UDAPE, was involved in negotiations with the fund both in Washington and in Bolivia. He reported that in meetings with IMF officials the fund made it clear that if the government didn't meet the 5.5 percent target, the IMF would refuse Bolivia a long-term lending agreement (known in IMF jargon as a poverty reduction and growth facility, PRGF). Without such an agreement, Gray says, the government risked not only assistance from the fund but also budget assistance from key donor governments such as Germany, Denmark, and Sweden.[61]

Molina explained the IMF's approach this way: IMF officials "tell you that we own the agenda. Strictly speaking that is true. But if we don't close a deal, we can't pay the salaries for education. Are they going to help us? No, no, they are not going to give us one more bridge [of economic aid]. We are up against the wall every month."

The Politics of Developing a Tax Package

Up against that wall and looking for a way to cut Bolivia's deficit by a quarter of a billion dollars, UDAPE, the tax and treasury departments, and others began drawing up some options for the government to consider. The first alternative they developed was for new taxes on Bolivia's gas and oil industry. This made sense from a variety of perspectives. First, it was the privatization of oil and gas in the 1990s that helped plunge Bolivia into deep deficits. Second, by applying those new taxes to exported gas and oil products, the cost would be passed on to foreign companies rather than Bolivian consumers. The proposals developed would have generated as much as $160 million per year, more than half of what was needed to meet the IMF's demands.[62]

The second alternative that UDAPE and the Vice Ministry of Tax Policy proposed to the president was a new progressive income tax, which would be paid by the wealthiest 4 percent of the population.[63] The tax would apply only to incomes of ten times the minimum wage and higher, with graduated rates rising along with income. Because it affected so few people, the new tax was not a big revenue generator, however. Estimates were that it would generate only about $20 million each year. Advocates for the tax, which included UDAPE, Vice President Mesa, and others, saw it as a way to begin to make Bolivia's overall tax system more progressive—placing the tax burden on those most able to pay. Over time they also hoped it could begin to replace the country's regressive value-added tax (similar to a sales tax).

Plans for the new gas and oil tax were soon upended. That same month, Bolivia's oil and gas minister flew to Mexico City to meet with an international consortium, Pacific LNG, to discuss a plan to export Bolivian gas to California. When he returned and heard about plans for the new gas and oil tax, Molina says the minister told the president and his budget advisers: "This is impossible; this is crazy." He warned that the tax would make closing a gas export deal even harder.

The vice president at the time, Carlos Mesa, explained the argument made by foreign oil companies and their Bolivian allies against raising the taxes: "The great alibi, the great argument of the multinational corporations, is legal security. The moment that you change your tax rules, you are changing the rules of the game that establish the possibility that those companies will come and invest in Bolivia. With another set of rules that are less predictable, they say, we wouldn't have risked coming here. This would demonstrate that this isn't a serious country [in which agreements are respected] and would send a signal—Don't come and invest in Bolivia because they say one thing and do another."[64] In Mesa's view and others', the demand for higher taxes on foreign oil companies was a legitimate one. In the United States and elsewhere, raising corporate taxes is always considered a legitimate issue for discussion in making budget and tax policy. President Sánchez de Lozada, however, sided with his minister and quickly took oil and gas taxes off the table. It is worth noting that, if projecting an image of stability to foreign investors was Sánchez de Lozada's goal, it is unlikely that he accomplished it by setting off the international spectacle of the nation's army and police firing at one another in front of the Presidential Palace.

Looking for an alternative way to bridge the deficit, Sánchez de Lozada cast his eye toward the progressive income tax proposal developed by the analysts at UDAPE. Molina said that when they brought the proposal to the president, he wanted to see how much the government could earn under a variety of tax alternatives, including expansion of the tax to people earning two times the minimum wage, salaries equal to about $110 per month: "When we went to discuss this with the president, he was very interested in seeing the whole range, that is, all the possibilities. The tax plan that we proposed from UDAPE raised very little money, less than $20 million. In contrast, the simulation [extending the tax down to people earning twice the minimum wage] went from $20 million up to $80 million, $90 million."

In early February, President Sánchez de Lozada and his chief political and economic advisers engaged in an intense debate over whether to move forward with the broader income tax plan. Those against it argued that it would create a new burden on the poor and could set off fierce public resistance, an opinion backed by polls commissioned by the government. UDAPE prepared charts for the president showing who would be affected by the new tax—teachers, police, nurses, and other low-income workers.

Then, remembered Molina, the president asked about the impact of the tax on various groups, including teachers and nurses. According to UDAPE's analysis, people with the lowest incomes would have to pay an added fourteen bolivianos per month, about two dollars. For people like the president and his advisers, that was pocket change. For many other Bolivians it was enough to buy a two-course midday meal in the market for three days.

Sánchez de Lozada made his decision to back the tax and on the evening of Sunday, February 9 announced it in a speech to the nation. To the Bolivian people it seemed like the government was trying to balance the budget on the backs of the working poor. "Ninety percent of the population was still exempt from the tax," said Molina, "but it was a terrible error, an error of politics and of economics." How grave that error was would soon be demonstrated in blood and violence.

TWO BLOODY DAYS IN FEBRUARY

Imagine the Washington, D.C., police and the U.S. Army firing at one another from across Lafayette Park in front of the White House. In the heart of La Paz, Bolivia, on the steps of the Presidential Palace and the National Congress, the two main armed forces, the army and the security unit of the national police, were engaged in open warfare. How did the announcement of a tax increase by the nation's president spark a chain of violent events that would end with the deaths of thirty-four people?

Opposition from Almost All Quarters, Including the National Police

Popular reaction to the government's proposal to tax the working poor was as swift as it was negative. The following morning the country's main opposition leader, Evo Morales—who finished just two points behind Sánchez de Lozada in the presidential elections seven months earlier and who led the second-largest voting block in the Congress—called on the Bolivian people to reject the tax proposal. He also called for national protests, including marches and acts of civil disobedience.[65] Over the course of the next twenty-four hours, that call for resistance was joined by the country's main national labor organization, Central Obrera Boliviana, labor and civic groups in Cochabamba, and a key unit of the national police force, Grupo Especial de Seguridad (GES).[66]

The police force was also already locked in battle with the government over not having received its January salaries and over the president's rejection of its demand for a 40 percent salary increase.[67] "The proposed tax law was the last straw," said David Vargas, the GES major who led the police protests.[68]

According to Vargas, the police—taking into account the large number of uncompensated overtime hours they were expected to work—ended up earning the equivalent of fifteen cents ($US) per hour. Even though many low-ranking police earned less than twice the minimum wage and would not be immediately affected by the tax, he said police believed that the tax would someday affect them and that it would have an immediate effect on other members of their family. "The police have brothers and sisters who are teachers, brothers and sisters who are factory workers, brothers and sisters in different areas of the social sector, and obviously they were also going to be affected."

As soon as the president made his tax announcement, it became the main topic of discussion at police stations throughout La Paz. Vargas recalled that the reaction among the rank-and-file officers reflected the indigenous Aymara culture to which many belonged. In Aymara pueblos, community decision making is deeply respected, closed to outsiders, and given the final word. "They remained silent, waiting for those who weren't part of their social class to leave. They told me, 'Thank you, Major. We will call you if we need you.' I left and they began to meet." Emerging from their discussions, the rank-and-file cops announced that they would oppose the government's tax proposal and immediately demanded a meeting with the minister of government, Alberto Gasser.

That Tuesday, February 11, Gasser declared that he would not hold talks under pressure from police and that the government's tax proposal was "nonnegotiable."[69] But at six o'clock the next morning, Wednesday, February 12, Gasser entered the GES police headquarters to begin negotiations. The GES headquarters, a building painted in fading green, sits just across the capital's central square, Plaza Murillo, from the Presidential Palace and the National Congress building. As the minister of government entered, he encountered a police force fully armed with pistols, tear gas, rifles, and a variety of assault weapons. Major Vargas and other police leaders laid out thirty specific demands, leading with a rejection of the proposed tax increase but also including a salary raise and other issues.[70]

President Mesa and others charge the police with blatant opportunism. "The police looked for the moment in which the government was weakest, as a way to pressure the government to give them a positive response," he said.[71] From this point forward, the government referred to their actions as "a police insurrection."

Said Vargas, "The other points were born when we said, 'We are going to talk with the minister.' We said, 'Since we are going to talk with the minister, let's take advantage [of the opportunity]. Let's talk about other things that affect us.'" Vargas insisted, however, that there was never any question that the central demand of the police was the withdrawal of the tax proposal, which the police suggested be modified to affect only those earning five thousand bolivianos—at the time, the equivalent of $660 per month—and higher. If the government had said yes to that, he claimed, the police would have ended their protests.

Vargas said that the minister's response to each of their demands, most notably the withdrawal of the new tax, was to repeat over and over, "No se puede" (It isn't possible). Vargas said that the minister told them: "It can't be withdrawn. The president can't do that. We have a commitment with the International Monetary Fund. We can't go back on this because it would say that the government isn't serious."

Wednesday in the Seat of Government: An Unintended Spiral toward Bloodshed

With the failure of the sunrise negotiations, events in Plaza Murillo began to spiral out of control in a way that neither the government, headquartered on one side of that plaza, nor the police, headquartered on the other, had ever intended.[72] Throughout the morning, police around La Paz abandoned their posts and headed for the headquarters at the plaza. At least two hundred of them would fill the building, just steps from the president's office. At ten o'clock about one hundred police, some dressed in uniform and others in civilian clothing, began to march into the plaza itself, chanting their demands at the windows of the Presidential Palace where Sánchez de Lozada and his cabinet were meeting to discuss how to resolve the growing crisis. At this point the protests, while angry, remained nonviolent.

At noon, students from a nearby high school, Colegio Ayacucho, entered the plaza to join the protests. Approaching the Presidential Palace, they began to throw rocks at the windows, drawing cheers and applause from the police. Military guards from inside ran out onto the palace balconies and began firing tear gas at the students in the plaza and in the direction of the police headquarters. The students ran to the other side of the plaza and called on the police to protect them. "The firing [of the tear gas] reached the police headquarters and was taken as an act of provocation, and [the police] fired tear gas back," said Vargas.

Moments later, as many as a thousand military troops, armed with M-16 rifles, rocket launchers, and other sophisticated assault weapons, began to occupy the half of Plaza Murillo closest to the Presidential Place. Police and civilian protesters, who filled the half of the plaza nearest to the police headquarters, began to shout obscenities at the soldiers. In the chaos a soldier positioned in front of the National Congress fired a rubber bullet into the crowd, hitting a policeman in the face.

As the afternoon began, each side occupied half of the plaza. Police families, retired police, and other supporters streamed in from other parts of La Paz. Shortly after one o'clock the leaders of Bolivia's National Permanent Assembly on Human Rights mediated a meeting between the government and the GES police, held nearby in the offices of the defense minister. Political leaders, including Evo Morales, went on television to reiterate their demand that the government's tax proposal be withdrawn. Some leaders, including Manfred Reyes Villa, leader of the third-largest political party in the Congress, called for the president's resignation.

At two o'clock, as the negotiations continued, the tense situation in the plaza finally reached a flashpoint. Police and soldiers again began launching tear gas at one another, and then tear gas turned to live rounds. A subsequent report by the Organization of American States claims that it was the police who fired bullets first. The police claim it was the army. By the end of the day eighteen people would be dead from the exchange of fire—police, military, and civilians.[73] Among them was a sixteen-year-old boy killed by an army sharpshooter.

Just after four o'clock President Gonzalo Sánchez de Lozada went on television and radio to announce that he was withdrawing his tax plan. By this time it was too late. The combination of public rage at the killings in the plaza and the absence of police throughout the city triggered a wave of rioting and vandalism. Sánchez de Lozada and Vice President Mesa left their offices for more secure locations. Rioters entered the vice presidential offices, throwing computers and other equipment out windows. The headquarters of the two major political parties in Sánchez de Lozada's coalition government were sacked and burned. Other incidents occurred at the Ministry of Labor and at targets including a Burger King outlet owned by one of the president's key political allies.

Thursday: A Militarized City and Death on a Rooftop

On the morning of Thursday, February 13, the residents of Bolivia's capital awoke to streets filled with soldiers and a swirl of public protests demanding the president's resignation. Plaza Murillo was now guarded with army tanks on its four corners. Protests calling for Sánchez de Lozada's departure were also under way in the cities of Santa Cruz, Cochabamba, and Oruro.[74] Many of the protests targeted the symbols of international power in Bolivia. Above La Paz, in the city of El Alto, a huge march sought to occupy a Coca-Cola bottling plant. Soldiers were brought in by helicopter, opened fire on the crowd, and killed four people. Ten others would be killed before the day was over, as the military repressed the protests with tear gas and live rounds. "On the thirteenth not a single police officer was killed, not a single soldier. All of the victims were civilians, a product of the government's repression," said Sacha Llorenti, then the president of the National Permanent Assembly on Human Rights, who also played a key mediating role between the government and the protesters.[75]

In La Paz another crowd of protesters assembled outside the doors of a sixteenth-century Catholic church in Plaza San Francisco. Throughout the morning military police sought to break up the gathering with tear gas and rubber bullets. Just across the street from the church sits a three-story building covered in crumbling green stucco. Its bottom floor houses a photo-developing store, its second floor offices, and its top floor a gymnasium also used as a dance studio. Just after noon a twenty-five-year-old handyman, Ronald Collanqui, climbed to the roof, where he had been doing repair work, to recover his tools. He was shot and killed by army sharpshooters firing from a window across the street. As Collanqui lay dying on the roof, the building's doorman called for an ambulance.

Ana Colque was a twenty-four-year-old student nurse. A single mother with a twenty-two-month-old son named Luis, she lived with her mother and father. The whole day before, according to her mother, Ana had been dispensing first aid to the wounded. On Thursday morning she told her family she was going out again. Her mother recalled that Ana had been involved just before in a special medical project and because of it had a batch of hard-to-get medical supplies on hand. "She had tweezers, bandages, equipment to apply intravenous tubes, injections, pain killers. The day before she said that the wounded didn't have painkillers; they suffered and cried, she said." Her family asked her not to go out, but Colque left early, telling her mother to take good care of her baby son.[76]

At 1:20 P.M. that Thursday Colque arrived at the building where the handyman's body lay on the roof. She pulled up in an ambulance marked with a red cross and was wearing a white nurse's uniform. She climbed up the stairs to the roof, accompanied by a doctor, Carla Espinosa. As Colque approached the handyman's body a military sharp-shooter fired from a small window of a building just a short distance away. The shot pierced her chest. Ten minutes later she left in the same ambulance in which she arrived and died shortly afterward in the hospital. The soldiers responsible for both deaths would later claim that they had mistaken both the repairman and the uniformed nurse as sharpshooters and had shot in self-defense.[77]

IMF officials from Washington were in La Paz during the days of violence sparked by their demands for deficit reduction. According to several people who met with the IMF mission, as violence overtook the streets the officials checked out of their rooms at the five-star Plaza Hotel, headed for the La Paz airport, and left Bolivia. Their route to the airport would have taken them right by the building where Ana Colque was shot and killed.[78] The next day the IMF issued a public statement saying that it "regretted the tragic events in Bolivia" and expressing its interest in continuing to negotiate with the Bolivian government.[79]

THE AFTERMATH

By Friday morning both the violence and the protests had ceased. President Sánchez de Lozada took out full-page ads in the nation's major newspapers to declare, "Happily I can report that peace and calm have been restored."[80] With its tax package so soundly rejected, the government withdrew both the package and the targets for deficit reduction for the year. It opted instead for a series of symbolic gestures aimed at assuaging the public's anger. Sánchez de Lozada announced that he would start donating his $3,900 monthly salary to an orphanage. He eliminated a collection of minister and subminister positions in the government, proclaiming the cuts part of a new commitment to public efficiency.[81] He fired the members of his cabinet most closely associated with the government's repression. Finally, the president declared to the nation, "Our budget will not be a budget of the International Monetary Fund."[82]

Bolivia's Budget Deficit

Bolivia's public deficit for 2003 ended up being 7.9 percent of the GDP. This was a percentage point lower than the year before but a full 2.5 percent and $195 million higher than the IMF's intended target. It was also almost 1.5 percent higher that what government analysts thought they could have achieved with their original plans for a gas and oil tax and an income tax targeted toward the wealthiest 4 percent of the population.

Two years after Febrero Negro, in February 2005, Sánchez de Lozada's successor, Carlos Mesa, announced that the nation had reached a deficit, coincidently, exactly in line with the IMF's original target, 5.5 percent.[83] The government credited the reduction to a new tax it had imposed on dollar transfers into Bolivia from abroad and a modest increase in national economic growth.

In the aftermath of the February 2003 bloodshed, the IMF moved quickly to deny that it bore any responsibility for the violence. "The fund mission strongly supported the government's efforts to reduce the fiscal deficit from unsustainable levels. However, the choice of fiscal measures to be included in the government's policy package was determined by the government," said the IMF in a written statement.[84] Less than two weeks after the shootings, the IMF publicly announced that it had agreed to a stand-by support program for the government that apparently jettisoned all the deficit reduction targets that it had previously demanded.[85]

In February 2005, two years almost to the day after the Febrero Negro killings, the IMF's top officer, Managing Director Rodrigo de Rato, paid a visit to Bolivia and met with its senior politicians and others. He made no mention of the deadly events of two years before and offered no apology. He did, however, demand that Bolivia continue to reduce its deficit even further. And, once again, the fund cast the issue not as an IMF command, but as something jointly agreed to by the fund and the government: "We agreed that, in light of Bolivia's still high debt burden, the government's fiscal program must aim at bringing down Bolivia's fiscal deficit and debt so as to entrench macroeconomic and financial stability, and sustain the current economic recovery."[86]

In December 2005, the IMF announced the cancellation of debt owed to it by nineteen low-income countries, including $251 million owed by Bolivia.[87] In March 2006, two months after he took office, President Evo Morales let the country's current IMF agreement expire and declined to enter into a new one. Bolivia joined a growing trend, alongside its neighbors Argentina and Brazil, of Latin American countries ending their borrowing relationship with the fund and its economic conditions.

In May 2006, President Morales issued a presidential decree that began a process of recovering state control of the country's gas and oil reserves and that implemented steep new increases in the taxes paid by foreign oil companies. As a result, annual state revenue from oil and gas was expected to leap by more than $1 billion in 2007.[88] Bolivia went from having a budget deficit to having a budget surplus by enacting the very reforms, increased taxes on foreign oil companies, that the IMF had directly warned against.

The Government of Gonzalo Sánchez de Lozada and the Search for Justice

Despite President Sánchez de Lozada's offer to give away his salary to an orphanage, and despite the U.S. government's immediate proclamations of support for him, the February 2003 killings left a residue of public anger and mistrust from which he was never able to recover. Just eight months later, in October, Bolivia was engulfed in public protest once again, this time over Sánchez de Lozada's plan to export a portion of the country's vast gas reserves through Chile to Mexico and on to California. This was the same deal that led Sánchez de Lozada to push new oil and gas taxes off the table the previous February. Widespread public mistrust led many to believe that Sánchez de Lozada was preparing a deal that would enrich the foreign corporations involved and a few lucky politicians, but that would produce no real benefits for average Bolivians. Bolivians also harbor a deep historical antagonism toward Chile, their neighbor to the west, which seized Bolivia's last access to the sea in 1879.

Once again the president met protest with the gun, leaving at least sixty-seven people dead and hundreds of others injured. In the wake of those killings, calls from the streets for Sánchez de Lozada's resignation took hold. Many of the country's most prominent intellectuals and human rights leaders joined in a national hunger strike to press the demand. Even his own vice president, Carlos Mesa, broke with Sánchez de Lozada over the violence. On October 17, 2003, he resigned the presidency and fled to the United States. In February 2005, the Bolivian government announced its intentions to prosecute the former president for murder, for the killings of February and October 2003. As of mid-2008, Sánchez de Lozada continues to live in a self-imposed exile in suburban Maryland, and the United States has refused demands by the Bolivian government that he be returned for trial.

Bolivia's Febrero Negro left 34 people dead and another 182 seriously wounded.[89] They included civilians, soldiers, and police. They ranged in age from eleven to eighty-six. Some were combatants in the conflict. Others, like Ana Colque, were dragged into it by fatal circumstance. What has been done to bring justice for those killed and wounded?

In the immediate aftermath of Febrero Negro, President Sánchez de Lozada made a formal request to the Organization of American States (OAS) to lead an investigation into those events. The OAS agreed and in May 2003 issued its findings. The OAS report blamed the February violence on the "unconstitutional actions" and "insubordination" of the police. It defended the actions of the military, calling them "proportional" and "contained." Then, the OAS pledged its support to the government of President Sánchez de Lozada.[90]

Amnesty International, which conducted its own investigation of the same events, along with Bolivian human rights groups, contested the

OAS's finding that the Bolivian government and military bore no responsibility for their actions: "Amnesty International believes that, in light of the testimonies and reports gathered by the organisation's delegation, press information, court documents and the high number of victims, the behaviour of the military forces in action on 12 and 13 February, would appear to have been neither 'restrained' nor 'proportional.'"[91]

Judicial efforts to bring those responsible to trial have been stymied by army resistance, prosecutors say.[92] In May 2003, Ana Colque's mother, with support from Bolivian human rights groups, initiated a criminal case against four members of the army identified as her daughter's killers. The case has been buried in legal disputes over whether members of the military can be tried in the civil courts. The army insists that its members may be tried only in army courts, where they are typically acquitted even of crimes demonstrated by clear evidence. Five years later, no one has been convicted or held accountable for any of them.

Ana Colque's mother lives every day with the memory of her daughter's killing and with her anger over the impunity with which her daughter's killers remain free: "I will always demand justice, to recognize who is who. This is what hurts me so. There is no reason to kill a nurse. An ambulance is respected even in a war. Knowing this, they fired at my daughter. This is what makes me furious, that in cold blood they killed a young woman."[93] Ana Colque's father is a soldier, a musician in the army band. Ana's mother says he has never mentioned the case in army ranks. "He hasn't said anything, not even that it was his daughter. He says, 'What am I going to do to them? Am I going to kill them? They are captains, they are generals.'" The family worries that without his army salary, they won't be able to support their other children and Ana's son, Luis.

CONCLUSION

February 2003 was a national tragedy for Bolivia. Thirty-four families buried loved ones. Nearly two hundred others had their bodies broken. A country watched in horror as its two armed forces—the police and the army—fought a war with one another in the very heart of its government. For two days, Bolivian democracy itself seemed on the verge of a total meltdown. A tragedy like this demands that those who were involved seek out the lessons that can be learned from it because, in the absence of that reflection, more tragedies just like it are sure to follow. The lessons of Febrero Negro are, as Carlos Mesa said, lessons "learned in blood and fire."

Sacha Llorenti, the former president of Bolivia's Asamblea Permanente de Derechos Humanos, who played an important mediating role during the conflict, calls Febrero Negro "the moment in which the crisis of the country was stripped down to the point where you could see its bones." It was a moment in which the politics of the International Monetary Fund and the global economic system were stripped to the bone as well.

The IMF and the World Bank operate in a world of theory. Ideas of how the world works are laid out neatly on sheets of white paper. Economic formulas and findings are shared with other economists in well-appointed conference rooms. None of the officials who work for these institutions live in poverty. None must live with the practical results of what they propose. The staff and leaders of these institutions believe not only that they are right in their assessments of what is best for poor countries, but that they know better than the people who live there.

Former Bolivian president Carlos Mesa said: "It is clear that there is a standard line, strictly macroeconomic, without a vision that represents how to apply it in the context of each country. I believe that the examples of Latin America are extremely illustrative. I won't add to the issue of Argentina [where IMF pressures helped spin the nation into political chaos in 2001], which is a dramatic example of how a policy that is blind in one direction produces results that are catastrophic."[94]

So what happens if the IMF and the World Bank get it wrong? What if the theories that look so good on paper turn out not to look so good once they are implemented in the real world? What then? John Maynard Keynes, godfather to both institutions, once said, "When the facts change, I change my mind. What do you do, sir?"[95] If we were to ask that same question of officials of the IMF and the World Bank, their answers would more likely be, "Defend the theory and blame the implementation."

Over and over again, when confronted with realities on the ground that fall short of their theories and predictions, IMF and World Bank officials place the blame not on the theory but on faulty implementation by poor governments. It is the governments, they say, that make the real decisions. They can raise gas taxes, impose a new income tax, or cut the deficit by cutting spending. The fund says that poor governments have all kinds of practical options.

Yet in the real world, those options end up being much more difficult than the IMF is willing or able to admit. An income tax on the wealthiest only comes up with a fraction of the revenue that the IMF demands. A proposal to tax foreign oil companies gets slammed down as a barrier to gas export, another demand of the fund. Cutting public expenditures by any large degree cannot be done without affecting the poor, who rely on public services, or provoking huge rebellions.

This approach—we just set the general parameters, the governments make the real choices—is a convenient one for the IMF and the World Bank. It allows them to deny responsibility when those policies go wrong. It relieves them of accountability when people suffer and when blood is spilled. It is a position that brings to mind a lyric from the satirist Tom Leherer, in a song about the inventor of the nuclear bomb, Wernher von Braun: "Once the rockets are up, who cares where they come down? 'That's not my department,' says Wernher von Braun."

All people, and therefore all institutions run by people, are capable of being convinced that they are right when, in fact, their blind spots make them wrong. The great wisdom of democracy is that authority is held accountable. The people who must live with a decision have an inalienable right to choose and influence the people who will exercise that authority. The great curse of global economic institutions such as the IMF and the World Bank is that, by their very nature, they are antidemocratic. The people who run them are in no way accountable to the people whose lives they affect, and as a result, officials are allowed to escape from feeling any sense of the pain they cause. How does a Bolivian teacher, or police officer, or nurse earning $120 per month influence the actions of the International Monetary Fund that end up making them pay a tax beyond what they can afford? By what means are economists in Washington held accountable for the pressures they bring to bear on impoverished countries?

Reduced to its most basic elements, the IMF's worldwide policies of deficit reduction are about forcing governments to adopt a certain discipline, to implement an economic squeeze. To be sure, governments, like individuals, should reasonably strive to live within their means. But few governments in the world, including rich ones like the United States, actually do. Squeezing is something we do all the time in life. We squeeze a piece of fruit to see if it is ripe. We squeeze our daughter's arm to get her attention as we cross the street. We also know that we can squeeze too hard. We can damage the fruit. We can hurt our child. How does the IMF know, in the absence of any real accountability to the people whose lives are affected, when it is squeezing too hard? February 2003 in Bolivia, like so many other examples before and after, give clear evidence that the IMF is shockingly numb to the pressures and the pains it inflicts on poor countries.

The IMF and its supporters can point to a dozen events which, had they happened differently, would have produced a result different than the deaths in La Paz, including that of a nurse on a rooftop visible from the fund's own window. If only the government had taken a different approach to the tax question. If only the police had not led a protest against the government's plan. If only the military and the police had shown more restraint that afternoon in the plaza at the center of government. If only the government had shown more restraint in its action to quell the protests.

Yet it is clear that each of these events was set in motion by the decision of IMF officials. They chose to squeeze Bolivia, to squeeze it through the instrument of economic coercion, to squeeze it to reduce its budget deficit faster and further than the government said was possible without provoking social upheaval, the very kind that erupted with such a bitter end during those two days in February. Despite warning after warning, the IMF did not listen. It kept on squeezing until events spiraled to a bloody, yet predictable, tragic end. Bolivia is not the first country where the IMF squeezed to the point of tragedy. Regrettably, it is not likely to be the last.

A young child, representing Bolivia's foreign debt, offers up a piggy bank in a demonstration in front of the UK Treasury in London, England. Photo: Richard Hanson/Tearfund—used by permission (www.tearfund.org) (1999).

CHAPTER 5

Economic Strings

The Politics of Foreign Debt

Nick Buxton

One of the most significant and consistent things about Bolivia's economic relationship with the rest of the world is that for its entire postcolonial history Bolivia has been deeply in debt to foreign lenders. More recently, Bolivia has been one of the world's major recipients of debt cancellation—the first of four countries in Latin America to be targeted for such relief. What does it mean for a nation to be in debt? What does it mean in terms of economic impact and in the loss of sovereignty and power to those it owes? Who are the winners and losers when a country borrows? Does debt relief make a real difference?

As Bolivia finally moves toward more sustainable debt levels, the big question is whether Bolivia can avoid a future debt crisis and assert its economic and political independence. As global trade agreements expand worldwide, might Bolivia find itself enmeshed in new economic strings? Is trade replacing debt as the means by which countries find their economic choices influenced and affected by powers abroad? Few countries offer a better example than Bolivia about the issues of debt. In this chapter, Nick Buxton looks at Bolivia's experiences as a debtor nation.

María Luisa Ramos had been in meetings with government officials before, but this was different. This time she was in the driving seat. The policy researcher and activist of the party Movement toward Socialism (MAS) had been invited, along with representatives of Bolivian social movements, to participate in the transition commissions preparing for the installation of the new MAS government in January 2006. "It was brilliant. We had indigenous community leaders and campesinos [small-scale farmers] asking government functionaries for information, and these officials were unable to refuse, because we were now the ones in power," she said, her face lighting up as she recalled the meetings.

What Ramos and the other activists discovered, though, shocked them. "We suddenly realized that it wasn't the authorities that made decisions, but the international institutions, consultants, other countries." They found out, for example, that entire ministry work teams were paid for by international aid and even run by foreign consultants. A few weeks later, María Luisa Ramos was confirmed as Vice Minister for Economic Relations and External Trade. "The biggest challenge I faced was to break relations of dependence," she said, "because previous governments had built a model of government highly dependent on outside interests."[1]

The intricate way foreign interests had woven their way into Bolivian political and economic decision making was through debt. For decades Bolivia had become more and more financially indebted to international financial institutions such as the World Bank and the International Monetary Fund (IMF). Those institutions and the wealthy nations that controlled them gained increasing influence over the nation's destiny. The MAS government arrived in power promising to deliver political and economic sovereignty. Yet undoing the web of dependence would first require a clear understanding of how Bolivia's indebtedness created a system and culture of control that may take years to unravel.

What Is Debt?

What does it mean for a nation to be in debt? Debt is not about complex financial tables, fluctuating interest rates, or restructuring schemes. It is about something much more basic—power. And debt creates a relationship that involves those who lend as much as those who borrow. There is nothing inherently bad about borrowing. Individuals and families borrow for all kinds of good reasons—to buy a house or finance a college education, for example. These are responsible expenditures that can genuinely improve one's standard of living and that make sense to pay over time. Governments can also borrow for good reasons, such as to finance public projects like highway or school construction—projects that produce important public benefits but which make sense to finance over time and require a large injection of funds that the country does not have immediately at hand. They might also borrow to invest in productive activities, such as gas exploration, that can help generate more public income in the long term.

In both cases, be it with a family or a country, the issue of whether to borrow and how much depends on the same basic considerations. Is the purpose for which we are borrowing something worth paying for and worth the price to be paid? How much will it cost all together, after expensive interest payments are added? Will we have the money to pay what we owe and, in order to set aside that money, what sacrifices will we have to make? Are we becoming dependent on debt, or do we have realistic plans about generating our own income in the longer term?

These questions suggest three key problems with going into debt. The first is when the borrowed money is foolishly spent: a family buys a fancy new car that is beyond their means, or a country finances dubious and corrupt "public" works. The second is when the borrower realistically has no ability to pay back what has been borrowed. The third, and perhaps most important, problem is that the lender has power over the borrower. A bank can take away an individual borrower's home, or a tax agency can garnish wages. A foreign lender can start directing an indebted nation's economic policy. The deeper in debt, the less power the borrower has. And, for a low-income country like Bolivia, this loss of power translates into a substantial loss of both political and economic sovereignty.

In the case of indebted nations, there are other issues to consider. Often, the political decision makers who put the country into debt benefit personally from the borrowing, or have close allies who do. Those who benefit are not usually the people who bear the burden of repayment. In the face of corruption and limited public accountability, debt becomes a tool by which the wealthy become wealthier, and pass the burden on to the poorest.

Countries, including Bolivia, borrow in a variety of different ways. They can issue bonds to their own citizens (internal debt). They can also borrow from sources abroad, such as other governments (bilateral debt) or international private banks (commercial debt). Perhaps the most controversial, especially in the case of Bolivia and other low-income countries, is the borrowing that governments do from international financial institutions (IFIs) such as the International Monetary Fund (IMF) and the World Bank (multilateral debt).

What Is a Debt Crisis?

A debt crisis occurs, first, when there is more money going out than coming in and, second, when the lender will not lend the borrower any more money. This happens when a government is consistently spending more money than it has (called a deficit) because it is paying back the multiplying interest on the loans it has contracted. More money is leaving the country's economy in debt payments or as deposits in foreign banks than is being generated internally through taxes or exports or being received in aid and loans.

In practice, many countries borrow more money than generate—in taxes, for instance—but do not find themselves in this kind of crisis. The trigger point usually lies in creditors' confidence, or lack of it, that they will ever get paid at all. The U.S. government, for example, currently runs annual budget deficits of hundreds of billions of dollars and has the largest public debt of any nation in the world. Yet, the United States has never encountered a debt crisis. Too much of the world is invested in the U.S. economy and the U.S. dollar to let such a crisis occur.

A small country like Bolivia, though, is not so fortunate. If its creditors decide to cut or reduce lending when the government is spending more than it can generate internally, the country has three choices: it can stop paying and default on its debts; it can print more money to pay the debt, triggering sharp inflation; or it can come to some form of agreement with its creditors to restructure its payment obligations. At various points in its history, Bolivia has done all three.

Nations do not have the option, as individuals and corporations do in most countries, of declaring "bankruptcy." This is a legal process administered by an independent arbitrator who looks at a person's or company's debt situation and decides on a compromise arrangement that involves sacrifices from both sides—the lender and the debtor. But countries are not allowed to go bankrupt, so their debt continues to rise while the country keeps borrowing. And if countries like Bolivia do end up negotiating a "restructuring" of their debt, to pay off less or to pay it over a longer period, there are no neutral arbitrators to broker a compromise. Instead, it is the lending institutions like the IMF that govern the restructuring. They cannot serve as neutral arbitrators. They are lenders.

The world's chief IFIs are dominated by wealthy lending nations, which are their major contributors. In the IMF, for example, the ten wealthiest nations control 50 percent of the voting power, and the United States maintains veto power over key decisions.[2] The president of the World Bank is appointed directly by the U.S. president. These wealthy lender nations clearly have self-interest in ensuring that debt repayment is a priority in any debt restructuring plan and have traditionally used IFIs to protect that interest. Consequently, when a debt crisis hits, the costs for a country and its people can be devastating. First, it means that earnings are increasingly dedicated to paying debts. This "debt service" often redirects resources away from other public investments, notably social spending on health and education. Second, the long-term policies enforced by lenders, known as structural adjustment policies, are more directed to the interests of the creditor nations than the debtor nation.

Debt has serious costs for a country like Bolivia, both politically and economically. As the Inter-American Development Bank notes, it was Bolivia, more than any country in Latin America, that most closely applied the economic structural reforms suggested by the IMF to resolve its debt crisis.[3] Its story has lessons for indebted countries everywhere.

BOLIVIA: THE HISTORY OF AN ADDICT BORROWER

Bolivia was born into debt. On August 6, 1825, the day it awoke as a free republic, Bolivia already owed its neighbor Peru for military costs from the War of Independence from Spain.[4] One of its first acts as a nation was to issue government bonds to pay off Spanish debts and to award compensation for those who had suffered fighting for independence. For almost two hundred years since, Bolivia has continued on that same road, repeating the pattern of borrowing, indebtedness, and economic crisis.

In 1872, Bolivia took on the biggest financial loan in the world at the time, £1.7 million, equivalent to three years of total government revenue, for a scheme to construct a railway linking Bolivia with the Atlantic Ocean. Even by today's standards, it was a highly complex construction project based on inflated estimates of customs duties that would help pay it back. Within a year, the British firm hired to undertake the project admitted that "even with all the capital of the world and half its population it would be impossible to construct the railway." The plan collapsed, but the debt remained. Servicing the loan for the failed railroad accounted for 70 percent of all of the country's debt payments at the time.[5] Three years later, in 1875, Bolivia had its first debt default.

In 1931 Bolivia confronted its second major debt crisis in the after-math of several decades of bad borrowing by a series of dictatorships. The crisis was set off when the global price of the country's primary commodity—tin—plummeted. The plunge in tin prices occurred at the same time as a halt in lending by Bolivia's northern creditors, a result of the worldwide economic depression. With substantially more money flowing out of the country than flowing in, the government announced that it could no longer pay its debts.

In each of its debt crises, Bolivia received some form of debt relief, always accompanied by government proclamations that the nation would set its economic house in order. In 1875, private bank and lending institutions (bondholders) agreed to reduce interest payments and extend the timetable for repaying the debt. In 1950, Bolivia received relief that the U.S. bondholders complained was "more generous than we could have anticipated."[6] In the 1980s Bolivia was offered relief under no fewer than five initiatives before it was eventually included in the Highly Indebted Poor Country Initiative (HIPC) in 1996, heralded by the leading creditor nations as providing a "sustainable exit from debt."[7]

Despite these breaks from lenders, Bolivia's debt has just kept rising: $2.4 million in 1909; $147 million in 1950; $3.3 billion in 1985; over $5 billion in 2003, seven years after the HIPC initiative.[8] For almost two centuries, Bolivian governments and elites have acted, with the encouragement of the international community, like credit card addicts, borrowing more and more with the illusive hope that they can pay off their debts and become solvent—but all the while falling deeper and deeper into debt.

That indebtedness and relief has come at a high price for Bolivia. In 1904, as part of a peace treaty with Chile, Bolivia received debt relief partly in exchange for agreeing to give up its claim to its lost access to the sea, taken in its war with Chile that ended in 1884. In 1922, a loan from U.S. bondholders was conditioned on the establishment of a commission that gave the lenders responsibility for Bolivia's taxes during the life of the loan.[9] The latter turned out to be the opening act of the much more intricate foreign economic supervision that would follow. In 1957, backed by a U.S. threat to cut aid, the IMF imposed its first conditionalities on Bolivia, including restrictions on government spending, cuts on public subsidies, and price controls on key goods. Bolivia had received its first taste of the neoliberal medicine that it would digest in larger quantities thirty years later.

BOX 5.1 Portrait of a Loan: The Dangerous Road

"Cycle down the most dangerous road in the world!!" scream the posters from almost every travel agency in La Paz. Death, it seems, is now the latest tourist attraction. The adventure trip the agencies are keen to promote is a dramatic, plummeting descent by mountain bike on a muddy track that clings impossibly to mist-cloaked cliffs. The car-width, snaking dirt road has also been the main transport route from Bolivia's two-and-a-half-mile high city of La Paz to the subtropical lowlands known as Los Yungas. The road got its name from the Inter-American Development Bank (IDB) in 1995, because two hundred to three hundred people died each year as buses and other vehicles careened off its treacherous slopes.[1]

What most tourists do not notice in their adrenaline-fueled descent is a road branching off near the start. That ribbon of new, comfortably wide pavement was supposed to be the safe new route, one that should have opened in 1999. It finally opened, partially, in December 2006, but the Bolivian government admits that ongoing geological instability could mean frequent closures.

Bolivia's troubled replacement for the "road of death" is more than a cautionary tale of the perils of highway engineering. It is also a story about the perils of taking on foreign debt for a project that is poorly conceived and where there are strong commercial interests in seeing its costs spiral out of control. The proposal for a safe alternative to the dangerous road was put forward by an international consortium in 1989, which charged the Bolivian government $5.5 million dollars to do the feasibility study. The original budget was estimated at $87 million dollars with three international development banks: the IDB, the Andean Corporation Fund, and the German bank Kreditanstalt für Wiederaufbau (KfW) jointly agreeing to lend two-thirds of the money. By the time the road opened, the costs of constructing it had more than doubled. Moreover, Bolivia agreed to take on another $100 million in debt from the IDB to pay for ongoing work on the road.[2]

While the Bolivian, Brazilian, and German companies that built the road have benefited handsomely from the delays and the international banks are guaranteed repayment, it is regular Bolivians who pay the price. Some paid with their lives, going over the edge. The rest of the country continues to pay with high costs for principle and interest.[3]

1. Mark Whitaker, "The World's Most Dangerous Road," BBC News, November 11, 2006, http://news.bbc.co.uk/1/hi/programmes/from_our_own_correspondent/6136268.stm.

2. "BID dona recursos para Cotapata" (IDB donates funds for Cotapata) *La Prensa*, November 28, 2006, 4b.

3. Statistics were provided by the Servicio Nacional de Caminos (National Road Service). The original project estimate was for $86,796,806 and should have been completed within fifty-four months. The total cost as of November 2006 was $175,974,881. On November 28, 2006, *La Prensa* announced the latest IDB loan.

The 1980s Debt Crisis

"We were all billionaires then," joked mining union leader José Pimentel Castillo, recalling the 1980s. It is a darkly ironic joke. He was referring to the depths of the gravest economic crisis in Bolivia's history. Inflation soared to the kind of levels that made economists check to see whether they had used too many zeros. In June 1983, a dollar was worth five thousand Bolivian pesos, the national currency of the time. In July 1985, when the crisis reached its peak, one dollar equaled 2 million pesos.

José recalled taking handfuls of money just to buy a loaf of bread and at times carrying money in sacks.[10] Across Bolivia, it was the people with the lowest incomes who suffered the most from constant price increases. Meanwhile, banks and others with access to U.S. dollars on the official exchange market—where the dollar was frequently undervalued—would lend and resell dollars at their real value for exorbitant markups.

The crisis had been prompted by a mix of bad economic news: an unsustainable rise in debt payments due in part to a sharp rise in U.S. interest rates, a collapse in export income, and a fall in lending from creditors.[11] All of that meant that there was far more money leaving the country than coming in. It was a crisis replicated across the continent. The Bolivian government, led by President Hernán Siles Zuazo, responded by printing money. That, in turn, provoked a calamitous fall in the value of Bolivia's currency and sparked the hyperinflation that made José Castillo Pimentel and his fellow citizens wealthy in currency and poorer in everything else.

Bolivia's mid-1980s debt crisis and its accompanying economic meltdown were blamed on the government at the time, led by the left-leaning Democratic and Popular Unity (UDP) party. The leaders' actions certainly failed to resolve the crisis. However, the causes really dated back to a spate of lending in the early 1970s by some of the world's largest commercial banks.

Banking giants like Citibank and Bank of America were flooded with so-called petrodollars, the huge flows of new cash invested by Middle Eastern states as a result of a big spike in oil prices. The banks were desperate to lend, and in Bolivia they found an eager borrower, the military dictator Hugo Banzer Suárez, who held office from 1971 to 1978. In less than a decade, Banzer managed to triple Bolivia's foreign debt, to a total of $1.8 billion.[12] In a country stripped of all regular systems of democratic accountability and oversight, a great deal of that money was invested in poorly planned projects and skimmed off by corruption.

One all-too-typical project was the establishment of the Agricultural Bank of Bolivia, which lent at rates of interest that were lower than those of commercial banks. As a result, many more affluent farmers, including political allies of Banzer, borrowed not to grow crops but to deposit in banks in order to make a quick profit. The farmers then failed to pay the bank back, and the government had to absorb the losses. Foreign borrowing also financed the building of an oil factory in Villamontes in the south of the country, which never functioned beyond 16 percent of its capacity.[13]

While a good deal of the borrowing benefited Bolivia's economic elite, very little was aimed at the country's impoverished majority or small-scale producers. Inocencio Apaza, a farmer in Guaqui near the Peruvian border, recalled applying for a loan in the Agricultural Bank of Bolivia. "I wanted some money to help set up a small business, but they refused to lend to me because my collateral of five hectares was not enough. It was those who least needed the money, with lots of land, who got loans and then called for cancellation of the debts."[14]

Bolivia's rapid accumulation of debts soon became unsustainable. Over half of the loans President Banzer borrowed, largely at high-interest commercial rates and for short-term periods, were used to pay off former debts.[15] Bolivia was then confronted with more bad news: falling prices for its key mineral exports. The Andean nation was caught in a squeeze between falling income from exports on the one hand and rising debt payments on the other. By the time democracy was restored and a weak divided government—the UDP—was elected in 1982, the seeds of the crisis were already planted and ready to sprout.

The crisis demanded radical solutions. In 1985, the breach was filled by a new government led by Víctor Paz Estenssoro, the former president who helped lead the nation's 1952 revolution. He failed to challenge the legitimacy of paying off dictators' debts. Instead, he offered the country a radical agenda that promised not only to deliver Bolivia from debt and inflation but also to lay the groundwork for long-term economic growth. It was an agenda that would shape Bolivia's economic path for the next two decades.

The Arrival of Neoliberal Doctors

On July 9, 1985, a U.S. economist and Harvard professor barely thirty years old stepped off the plane at the La Paz airport intrigued to witness Bolivia's economic crisis and hyperinflation, something that until then he had only read about in history books. He came with the aim of curing Bolivia's hyperinflation and setting the country on the path to economic growth. His name was Jeffrey Sachs and Bolivia was to be his first patient.[16]

Sachs set to work immediately with the new government of Víctor Paz Estenssoro, and in particular the planning minister, Gonzalo Sánchez de Lozada, to bring an end to hyperinflation. Sachs argued that a rapid, short, and massive increase in oil prices would fill the Central Bank coffers and end the spiral of inflation caused by printing and spending money the government did not have. The plan was incredibly successful, ending hyperinflation within one week. For much of the Bolivian population, the new government offered a new sense of order and authority.

This short-term fix to hyperinflation was accompanied by a whole series of longer-term extreme measures to restrict money supply in the economy in order to keep inflation low. This primarily meant cutting government spending and increasing revenue. That meant the elimination of subsidies for food and agriculture, cuts in social spending such as health services and education, repression of labor unions to prevent demands for higher wages, and a rise in interest rates to encourage saving. At the same time, a focus was given to stimulating exports.[17] Two years later, inflation was under 20 percent and in more recent years has remained in single figures.

The government's proposals to deal with the debt crisis, however, went much further than just making the budget figures balance. Sachs, together with officials in the Bolivian government, believed that the underlying reasons for the debt crisis lay not just in bad economic management but in the failure of an entire economic model in which government played a central role. In their view, state dominance was a recipe for distorting the market and for corruption and inefficiency.

According to Juan Carlos Águilar, Bolivia's vice minister for public investment and external finance in 1995–97 and a former World Bank official, the economic policies implemented following the crisis were "tough measures that needed to be taken." Echoing the view that would dominate Bolivia's governments for twenty years, he noted: "State capitalism, strong public companies and powerful unions had led to hyperinflation, low economic growth, and companies not able to produce because they couldn't save or invest."[18]

With the 1985 crisis as its justification, the Bolivian government set out on a radical new economic course, known in Bolivia by the number of the decree that proclaimed it: 21–0–60. The new recipe included all the main ingredients of the market-first policies called Reaganism and Thatcherism in the wealthy countries to the north, and what were called structural adjustment programs in low-income countries.

The promise was that the free market–driven economic prescription for the country's debt crisis would deliver economic growth and lift the Bolivian people out of extreme poverty. Exports would increase. Foreign investment would increase. Jobs would be created. Incomes would rise. The government would be in a more fiscally sound position to invest in public goods and public works. Bolivia would extract itself from the debt crisis. The results, however, never managed to match the promised debt solutions.

What the Medicine Wrought

The dark-red rusting cranes stand looking out across vast blue Lake Titicaca. At their feet, overgrown railway tracks stretch between collapsing warehouses into the distance of the altiplano, or highland plain. The scenery is stunning as the horizon is framed by the snow-white mountain peaks of the Cordillera that stand out against the relentless blue sky. Yet, at Guaqui, the dominant feeling is one of neglect and abandonment. In the early 1980s, this was a small but busy port, one of the major routes for exporting minerals brought by train from mining areas like Oruro and then ferried across to Peru and onwards to international markets. Today Guaqui is a ghost town that had its death sentence signed in 1985 in the aftermath of the debt crisis.

One reason for the port's demise is simple market economics, in particular, the collapse in tin prices that same year. But it was also related to specific debt-driven government policies that were determined to cut back state companies and to keep wage costs and social spending down. One union leader explained that the government had decided to start shutting down the state mining company, Corporación Minera de Bolivia (COMIBOL) well before the collapse in tin prices: "Decree 21-0-60 [issued in August 1985 three months before the fall of tin prices] ended overnight benefits that miners had fought for, over decades, such as the right to subsidized food, health, and educational support. There was no negotiation; it was just imposed. When two thousand of us went on strike, they arrested us for ten days."

COMIBOL went from having thirty thousand workers in the 1980s to three thousand in 1993. The railway and port that exported minerals struggled on after 1985 but eventually closed in the early 1990s. Out of work, the miners were forced to migrate to other parts of Bolivia or to neighboring countries like Argentina. (For more on Bolivian emigration, see chapter 8.) A few stayed behind, working for private companies that employed them in precarious and dangerous conditions with few rights.

Debt-driven economic reforms affected far more than just state companies. Rural agricultural communities were hit when price controls ended and tariffs were cut on foreign imports with the idea of improving efficiency and competition. Lower prices were better for low-income consumers, but they devastated rural communities. Farmer Martín Nina, his sun-browned face shadowed by a Bolívar soccer team cap, explained that he now produces potatoes, chilies, and onions only to eat and not to sell. He can no longer compete with Peruvian imports. An extensive study of the Bolivia campesino [small-scale farmer] economy in 2003 concluded that structural adjustment had led to a "systematic reduction in the real agricultural incomes of campesinos."[19]

In manufacturing, the story was the same when products like cheap clothing flooded local markets and pushed out Bolivia's small but vibrant textile industry. Inocencio Apaza explains how he had to close his small textile company as a result of "free trade" policies. "My life changed overnight when they opened the borders and allowed in used clothes. I clung on until the early nineties but eventually was forced to close."[20]

Debt-driven reforms even affected the tax system, further deepening inequalities. A new regressive tax on consumer goods fell harder on people with the lowest incomes. A study in 2001 showed that the poorest fifth of the nation was paying 25 percent of its income in taxes, while the wealthiest fifth of the nation paid out 14 percent of its income in taxes. Private companies benefited even more. In 2001, consumers paid 80 percent of the nation's taxes, while taxes on companies brought in just 20 percent.[21]

The closure of state companies meant that many jobs were lost in the formal sector and very few new ones were created. The focus on attracting foreign investment may have created added profits for a few, but it did not create jobs for very many.[22] As a result, Bolivia has seen a huge explosion in the informal sector, visible on the streets of every major city, where 64 percent of the population—primarily indigenous—eke out a meager living, selling an oversupply of cheap imported manufactured goods, from battery chargers and shoelaces to shoes and television antennae.[23] At the same time, the new discipline by conservative governments to keep up with foreign debt payments was also diverting resources from essential public services. Between 1981 and 1993,

Bolivian government investment in education fell by 39.7 percent, in health services by 28.3 percent, and in housing assistance by 77 percent[24] as debt payments reached an average $270 million a year.[25]

As incomes collapsed and public services dwindled, more than two-thirds of the population stayed stuck at or fell below the official "poverty line," the income level required to cover basic needs such as housing, food, and education.[26] Even during periods of economic growth, the overall number of impoverished people increased by an average of 130,000 a year.[27] As a result, the effects of Bolivia's worsening impoverishment were expressed not only in numbers but in lives as well. Ana María Aguilar, a physician working in La Paz Children's Hospital in 1995, expressed her anguish at treating rising malnutrition: "I've seen far more serious malnutrition in children since 1985."[28]

Yet not everyone in Bolivia was doing badly. In the aftermath of Bolivia's privatization program in the late 1990s, multinational companies, in particular in the hydrocarbons sector, were especially strong winners. Companies like Repsol and Petrobras were granted assets worth an estimated $10 billion dollars, scoring almost $4 billion in revenue between 1999 and 2004 while contributing only $1.2 billion in taxes to Bolivia.[29] Some Bolivians, especially those associated with these changes, also benefited during a time of growing impoverishment. In 2002, a review of the heads and representatives of the newly capitalized hydrocarbons companies revealed that many had previously been ministers in the post-1985 governments.[30] By that same year, the most impoverished 10 percent of the population was earning 0.2 percent of all the country's income, compared to 47 percent earned by the richest 10 percent, a significant deterioration since 1986.[31] In essence, the reforms adopted to tackle debt made the wealthy richer and the poor more impoverished.

Juan Carlos Carranza, an economist in the Bolivian Central Bank in the 1980s who participated in the Bolivian government's negotiations with the World Bank in the aftermath of the debt crisis, is unequivocal when he describes what the debt crisis delivered in Bolivia: "While we redid the financial framework and changed the state, the group in power used this just to enrich themselves. We managed to privatize the gains and 'state-ize' the losses."[32]

Overcoming economic and debt crises could be expected to have human costs, but the argument by the IFIs was that their recommended harsh treatment would provide the cure in the long term because it would create the context for economic growth, debt reduction, and greater financial independence. Yet even these promises have failed to materialize.

The foreign and Bolivian economic doctors had prescribed "a medium-term economic strategy to achieve high rates of sustainable economic growth with a steady reduction in poverty."[33] Yet year after year, the IMF was forced to revise its growth projections. Per capita income growth remained at an average of only 2 percent over the last twenty-five years.[34] While some of this was due to external factors, it was clear that the IMF prescription was not working.[35]

In the end, rather than helping Bolivia to escape its debt crisis, IMF reforms were making Bolivia more indebted than ever. Bolivia's creditors became the real winners. Between 1985 and 2005, Bolivia paid its creditors a total of $5.4 billion dollars, an average of $270 million per year.[36] As a result, debt relief initiatives hardly made a dent. For example, Bolivia received debt relief of $813 million between 1998 and 2004 but took on $3.25 billion of new debt during that same period and paid out $1.97 billion to service its debt. Eight years after it had been promised an escape from the debt crisis, Bolivia was still running just to stand still.[37]

THE DISAPPEARING LINE BETWEEN BOLIVIA'S GOVERNMENT AND ITS FOREIGN LENDERS

Most of the international institutions, NGOs, development banks, and think tanks in La Paz can be found in the south of the city, a twenty-minute drive from the city's center, which houses the Presidential Palace, government ministries, and legislature. The Zona Sur (Southern Zone) has the advantage of being downhill, which at the Andean mountain altitudes of La Paz means it is several degrees warmer. There, most local representatives of the international community nestle comfortably among the city's wealthier neighborhoods.[38]

The IMF, however, is different. Not only is it headquartered in the center of town; its panoramic offices sit on the seventeenth floor of the headquarters of Bolivia's Central Bank. The IMF's relationship with Bolivia's monetary powers could hardly be tighter. In fact, it is often difficult to see exactly where the line begins and ends that separates the Bolivia government from the IMF and its key partner, the World Bank.

Bolivia's debt crisis in the mid-1980s opened the door to the direct involvement of institutions such as the IMF and the World Bank in the country's economic decisions. In the decades since, those institutions have woven themselves deeper and deeper into the nation's decision-making structures. Their rationale is not hard to understand. Both the IMF and the World Bank are convinced that their expertise, in addition to their cash, is a valuable resource for low-income countries.

BOX 5.2 | Portrait of a Borrower:
Gonzalo Sánchez de Lozada

Gonzalo Sánchez de Lozada, who served as Bolivia's president twice (1993–97 and 2002–3), and his brother Antonio Sánchez de Lozada were co-owners of a prominent Bolivian mining company, Compañía Minera del Sur (COMSUR). In the 1970s, during Bolivia's great borrowing boom, COMSUR received more than a third of its financing from New York–based First National City Bank (later known as Citibank).[1]

In 1985, Sánchez de Lozada (known as Goni in Bolivia) took up a key post in the nation's government. As planning minister, alongside U.S. economist Jeffrey Sachs, Sánchez de Lozada helped design and implement the plan that delivered Bolivia from its hyperinflation, a plan that also began the transfer of increasing amounts from the national treasury as debt payments to the IMF and the World Bank.

While Sánchez de Lozada worked with the IMF and the World Bank as planning minister, his company continued to receive loans from the International Finance Corporation, an arm of the World Bank. In the 1990s, as president, Sánchez de Lozada was praised by World Bank and IMF officials for his radical privatization plans, which turned control of key state companies and resources (gas and oil, the train system, electricity) to private, mostly multinational corporations.[2]

In 2003, during his second term as president, Sánchez de Lozada was responsible for the highest level of Bolivian borrowing since the Banzer dictatorship—more than $700 million dollars in just one year.[3] His borrowing failed to save his government at a time of economic crisis and rising opposition to the impacts of the policies he had played such a crucial role in developing since 1985. This opposition came to a head later in 2003, when a popular revolt against his proposed plan to export gas to California forced him to flee to the United States.

1. Fernández Terán: *FMI*, 60.

2. Sánchez de Lozada's company, COMSUR, also got financing from the International Finance Corporation (IFC) in 1988, and he acted as a joint shareholder with the World Bank's IFC in the Banco Industrial S. A. (BISA). Fernández Terán, *FMI*, 60, 85.

3. Gerencia de Operaciones Internacionales (International Operations Management), Departamento Deuda Externa (Department of External Debt), "Bolivia, Estado de la deuda publica al 31 de Diciembre 2003" (Bolivia, the State of public debt through December 31, 2003) (La Paz, Bolivian Central Bank), 1.

Alongside their ideological stake, however, IFIs also have a direct financial one. As lenders themselves, they need to show that their policies are successful in facilitating the payment of the debt owed to them. On the other side of that relationship, governing elites in countries like Bolivia also have an interest in close connections with lenders. They depend on a continual flow of resources to maintain power. Many of the national political leaders in the 1980s had become successful and wealthy businessmen during Banzer's dictatorship and now were commissioned to resolve the debt crisis they had played a part in creating. Some, like Gonzalo Sánchez de Lozada, continued to depend personally on these institutions.

The current IMF representative in Bolivia, Esteban Vesperoni, described the relationship between Bolivia and the IMF as "intense." He went on to explain: "We can't impose a program. It is up to the country. . . . Our role is only policy advice, nothing more."[39] Waldo Gutiérrez, the Bolivian finance minister in 2005 and a long-term official in the Finance Ministry, agreed. "The IMF doesn't provide solutions, just references on where we should go." His views reflected those of other ex-ministers, who when interviewed, talked about a relationship of negotiation and cooperation that helped to extract Bolivia from hyperinflation and lead it to macroeconomic stability.

However, the relationship between Bolivia and its foreign lenders is not one of equals, any more than is the relationship between a mortgage seeker and a bank. Former World Bank chief economist Joseph Stiglitz explained the imbalance this way: "Officially, of course, the IMF does not 'impose' anything: it negotiates conditions in order to offer help. However, all the power during the negotiations is one-sided, that of the IMF, and the fund rarely gives enough time in order to achieve a wide consensus or to carry out diverse consultations whether with parliament or civil society."[40]

The IMF's influence goes beyond its own lending; it has acted as well as a gatekeeper for other bilateral funders. Until recently, European governments and partners like the World Bank have looked to the IMF to determine whether a government is suitable to receive loans or development assistance. Countries that break ranks with the IMF do so at substantial risk. (For more on the IMF and the World Bank, see chapter 4.)

The Sources of Influence: Ideology, Opportunity, and Cash

The specific sources of influence wielded by IFIs in a country like Bolivia are many and varied. To be sure, one is the natural leverage of

lending. Bolivian officials know that if the IFIs are going to keep lending, they need to be kept confident and happy with the economic course
chosen by the government. But there are other, less obvious sources of
influence by IFIs.

Officials at institutions such as the IMF and the World Bank and
Bolivia's traditional economic elite share a common ideological view
about how national economies should be run. It is a view that aligns
closely with the free market and limited government principles, which
are the heart of IMF and World Bank doctrine, as well as the heart of
Bolivian economic policy since the debt crisis. Many of President
Estenssoro's key economic chiefs serving during the crisis, including
Gonzalo Sánchez de Lozada, had been educated at universities in the
United States, which in the late 1970s played a key part in fostering free
market ideas. Political leaders were also able to convince many Bolivians
that free market reforms would help end government corruption.

Another source of the IMF's and the World Bank's influence has been
their considerable capacity to do research and to develop information
that support the institutions' ideologically driven views.[41] When this
capacity is coupled by the Bolivian government's inability—for lack of
human and financial resources—to provide other perspectives based on
its own independent research and analysis, the IMF and the World Bank
create a monopoly on the information decisions can be based on. One
finance ministry official recalled that in the late 1990s many of her colleagues traveled to Washington to participate in courses organized by
the IMF. "They came back utterly convinced and fanatic about applying
neoliberal policies."[42]

Juan Carlos Carranza, who also served as a finance ministry official
from 1980 to 1992, concurred: "It was only the 'yes men' that they took
to Washington. They came back implementing plans that looked great
on paper but would never work in practice because they bore no relation
to reality."

The line between the government and the IFIs becomes even less clear
with the apparent revolving door through which officials move seamlessly
from one side to the other. Two former World Bank employees, Javier
Nogales and Jacques Trigo, became presidents of the Bolivian Central
Bank.[43] Several ex-ministers went on to work for the World Bank, including Alfonso Revollo, former minister of capitalization appointed to over-
see Bolivia's privatization program between 1993 and 1997.

The line between the institutions and the government was erased altogether with the invention of a controversial system of "plus payments"

that put hundreds of Bolivian government officials on World Bank, IMF, and creditor government payrolls. In the mid-1980s, key institutions including the World Bank, the U.S. Agency for International Development (USAID), the Inter-American Development Bank (IDB), and the United Nations all began making direct bonus payments to Bolivian officials. A local paper reported that 265 state functionaries, spread across important state ministries, were receiving salaries or supplementary payments from these and other institutions.[44] Alfonso Revollo was typical of many. While he was in charge of implementing the controversial program of selling off state enterprises to foreign corporations, he was also receiving a salary from the IDB, which gave strong backing to the plan.[45]

Bolivian analyst Javier Gómez called the "plus" payments to officials "the most important instrument to embed the IMF and the interests of the international community within state policies." A confidential 1990 World Bank report admitted that paying Bolivia's officials "motivates the professional staff to follow directives of agencies more than the official ministerial policies (if these exist). . . . These supplements at times reach absurd levels . . . several times higher than the official government salary."[46] This system still exists. María Luisa Ramos, Vice Minister for Economic Relations and External Trade, reported that her first year in government (2006) led to several conflicts with the international aid community, whose members were used to a system of effectively managing their own projects within the foreign ministry. "They seemed surprised that we wanted to make decisions," she said.[47]

DEBT CANCELLATION: WHAT DID IT MEAN FOR BOLIVIA?

The plan seemed incredibly far-fetched: to link people in a human chain along six miles of busy streets, badly lit canal walkways, and urban neighborhoods to surround the corporate conference center that was the venue of the Group of 8 (G8) summit, a meeting of the world's eight most powerful nations, in Birmingham, England. Yet at three o'clock on a sunny afternoon in May 1998, a great roar went up as seventy thousand people linked hands in a chain of solidarity, calling for an end to the chains of international debt. The symbol of human chains sprung up in cities as far-flung as Seattle, Kampala, Chennai, Melbourne, and Prague.

The Campaign for Jubilee

Jubilee 2000, the debt cancellation campaign, officially started in the United Kingdom in 1996. The campaign had its roots in calls for a "Jubilee" year of debt cancellation led by African churches in the early 1990s. It was inspired by the Jewish principle of Jubilee, outlined in the Torah and the Old Testament, which calls on the Jews to mark every fifty years with the cancellation of debts, the restoration of land, and a radical redistribution of power and wealth to end accumulated inequalities between peoples. Linked to the idea of celebrating the millennium with a profound act of justice by canceling impoverished countries' debts, the campaign inspired participation by thousands of organizations and millions of people.

As more citizen antidebt campaigns in the debtor nations of the global south collaborated, the movement questioned the very legitimacy of the debt. Indeed, most of the debt had been built up under dictatorships, paid back several times over due to rising interest rates, and had never actually benefited most of the people who bore the burden of paying it. By the end of 1998, more than a hundred civil society organizations were active in the UK campaign, including trade unions, women's organizations, immigrant and refugee groups, and faith groups. Groups in more than sixty countries had launched campaigns by the start of 2000, collecting a record 24 million signatures calling for world leaders to cancel the debt of low-income countries.

The cancel-the-debt campaign in Bolivia was launched in 1998 by the national Catholic Church under the slogan "Yes to life, No to debt." A strong public awareness campaign drew broad support, and within a year Bolivian activists had collected four hundred thousand signatures calling for debt cancellation, which they presented at the next G8 summit in Cologne, Germany, in July 1999. In the international Jubilee campaign, "globalization" found an expression that was very different from the game of moving global capital to where it could earn the most profit. Globalization also came to mean global activism and the promotion of grassroots democracy.

Campaigning for debt cancellation proved to be a starting point for campaigning for a change in economic policies. In 2000, Jubilee Bolivia organized an unprecedented series of civil society discussions that involved four thousand people in nine regional workshops on how debt relief resources should be effectively used, as well as how to develop proposals for tackling poverty. Juan Carlos Nuñez, director of Bolivia's

Jubilee Foundation, explained: "We started thinking about where public resources should go, how they should be used, and what measures could be taken to increase civil society participation . . . because the demands were no longer focused on the fight against poverty but were structural demands of institutional changes to the state."[48]

The debt cancellation campaign showed the power of global activism and helped contribute to an upsurge of global involvement in justice issues. Momentum continued to build with the massive demonstrations in Seattle that disrupted the meetings of the World Trade Organization in 1999, the presence of an estimated 250,000 activists at the G8 meeting in Genoa, Italy, in July 2001, and the worldwide campaign under the banner of "Make Poverty History" in 2005.

The mobilization of so many people worldwide against debt put the creditors, in particular the richest eight nations, as well as the World Bank and the IMF, under an intense spotlight. In 1999 Anthony Gaeta of the World Bank said, Jubilee 2000 "has managed to put a relatively arcane issue—that of international finance and development—on the negotiating table throughout the world. . . . [It] is one of the most effective global lobbying campaigns I have ever seen."[49]

The Lenders Discover Poverty Eradication

Debt relief measures are not new. In the 1980s, it became obvious that many low-income countries were unable to pay for debts built up in the lending boom of the 1970s. Rather than let countries default on their loans, since that could have serious implications for the international financial system, lenders chose to negotiate a series of debt relief agreements to provide the low-income countries with some support. Global lenders also believed structural adjustment programs would resolve the underlying problem. Bolivia received debt relief under five separate agreements before the launch of the Highly Indebted Poor Country Initiative in 1996.

HIPC was a new type of debt relief because it brought together cancellation of debts by commercial banks, governments, and IFIs. However HIPC, and later initiatives, was limited in its impact due to the small amount of relief offered, the limited number of countries included, and the conditions that continued to be required of countries in order to qualify. In the absence of an independent arbitrator, the agreements were ultimately based more on what creditors determined was in their self-interest to give or a simple economic calculation of what they could expect to get, rather than what was needed to help countries find relief

BOX 5.3 | Debt Relief Initiatives since 1985

1986–1995: Bolivia became involved in a series of five separate debt relief negotiations with commercial banks and governments, which reduced total debt by $3.2 billion. Interest rates and new loans, however, meant that debt in 1995 was still $4.5 billion dollars.[1]

1996: The Highly Indebted Poor Country initiative (HIPC) was launched with the support of G8 nations. Forty-two countries, including Bolivia, were eligible if they completed a program of economic reforms approved by the IMF. Bolivia qualified in September for debt relief of $760 million. In 1999, Bolivia still owed $4.6 billion.

1999: The launch of the Enhanced HIPC initiative (HIPC II) was announced at the G8 Summit in Cologne. This initiative promised additional debt relief and a shift in focus toward tackling poverty. Countries were required to produce a Poverty Reduction Strategy Paper (PRSP) to demonstrate how resources released by debt relief would benefit those who needed it most. Bolivia qualified in June 2001 for debt relief of up to $1.2 billion dollars, a cancellation of 40 percent of its total debt. By 2002, Bolivia still owed $4.4 billion dollars.

2002: Chief bilateral creditors, such as Germany, Spain, Italy, France, Japan, and the United States agreed to an additional 100 percent cancellation of government-to-government debts that promised Bolivia a further $630 million of debt relief. Yet in 2003, with high levels of new borrowing, Bolivia's debt reached new heights of just over $5 billion dollars.[2]

2005–2007: G8 nations agreed to 100 percent cancellation of multilateral debts owed by HIPC-qualified countries to the IMF and the World Bank. In January 2007, the IDB cancelled half of Bolivia's debt, which dropped the country's debt significantly, to $2.5 billion.[3]

1. Abendroth et al., *La deuda externa de Bolivia* (Bolivia's external debt), 302–10.

2. Statistics for 1998–2005 from Gerencia de Operaciones Internacionales, Departamento Deuda Externa, Bolivian Central Bank, www.bcb.gov.bo/deudaexterna. The total amount of debt relief predicted for each initiative is spread out over many years—in the case of HIPC, up to 2045—so it is cancelled in much smaller proportions each year.

3. Fundación Jubileo, "Después de la condonación del BID, el desafió es el endeudamiento responsable" (After forgiveness by the IDB, the challenge is responsible indebtedness) (La Paz, January 23, 2007).

from unsustainable indebtedness. The Jubilee movement continued to apply pressure on the creditors to improve on the HIPC initiative. However, it would still be a long time before Bolivia would see a significant decrease in its debts.

Debt-cancellation efforts were key in bringing about a shift in language. The IFIs increasingly acknowledged that structural adjustment policies had adversely impacted people with low incomes. Suddenly phrases like "poverty eradication," "country ownership," and "civil society participation" slipped into the operating vocabulary of the institutions. Even the IMF, with its well-known narrow focus on conservative fiscal and monetary policy, joined in the new rhetoric about combating poverty. The IMF's managing director, Michel Camdessus, sounded more like a priest than an economist in 1999 when he declared, "It is the honor of the IMF, even if it is not a development institution, to try continuously to help governments to be responsive to the cries of the poor. The cries of the poor! The time has come for a new and more decisive start."[50]

Under the new debt relief initiatives, eligible countries would be required to develop Poverty Reduction Strategy Papers (PRSPs). This, it was announced, would be a process led by the debtor countries themselves, in which citizens and civil society would play a direct role in deciding how the resources freed by debt relief could be best allocated to fight chronic poverty in their countries. As a country with an almost-perfect track record of meeting IMF conditions, Bolivia was always one of the first countries slated to receive debt relief. Moreover, the Bolivian government was quick to pick up on the new rhetoric of "poverty reduction" and "civil society participation"—launching the first ever preliminary Poverty Reduction Strategy Paper in 1999, which was heralded as a model by the international community worldwide.

The Theatrics of Civil Society Participation

In April 2000, President Hugo Banzer—the former dictator later elected president in 1997—convened a National Dialogue with civil society leaders to develop a Poverty Reduction Strategy Paper. Jorge "Tuto" Quiroga, Banzer's vice president, in an announcement to the World Bank, said the dialogue "committed the whole nation in a common effort to reduce poverty and was the best way to respond to international confidence in Bolivia and appropriately use the resources of an amplified HIPC initiative."[51]

Key community and social movement leaders in Bolivia were not as enthusiastic. That same April, while Banzer and Quiroga were trumpeting their dialogue with Bolivia's citizens, they also declared a national suspension of constitutional rights and sent the Bolivian army to the city of Cochabamba to combat massive protests against the government's handover of the city's public water system to the U.S.'s Bechtel Corporation—privatization that had originally been coerced by the World Bank. (For more on the Cochabamba Water Revolt, see chapter 1.) In addition, it had been Banzer who, just two decades before, as Bolivia's dictator, had been responsible for the accumulation of the majority of the nation's heavy debt.

A World Bank study in the city of El Alto in 2000 reported that a large majority of residents thought the National Dialogue was a barely veiled "political maneuver."[52] Oscar Olivera, the Cochabamba union leader who helped lead the anti-Bechtel revolt, called the dialogue "a show," with "the people being the main absentee." Some of those who did attend describe a process so tightly controlled by the government that any substantive discussions about poverty eradication were left off the table. One participant, Kati Murillo, from the Bolivian Jubilee Campaign and a former economist in the Finance Ministry, said facilitators posed questions as though they had a predetermined plan. "They would say things like 'You do want roads, don't you? . . . Right . . . roads it is then.'"[53]

In the end, Bolivia's antipoverty plan reflected few of the popular demands that did arise in the National Dialogue. The consultant appointed to write the PRSP, according to one member of the technical team, "was chosen in large part because he had the experience and ability necessary to write a plan that would be acceptable by the World Bank and IMF."[54] That December, before social movements were allowed to see it, the plan was presented by the government to donors. For Nuñez, the 350-page paper was just a "montage of what the government and international donor community wanted."

The development of a national antipoverty strategy excluded any real debate about Bolivia's deeper structural issues and dominant economic policies. It was a strategy that focused on increased spending on health, education, and infrastructure, which, while worthwhile, gave little emphasis to other popular demands for investment in technical training, microcredits, microindustry, and small-scale farmers. As the United Nations Development Program has noted, the IMF and the World Bank continued to focus their economic policy toward the companies that employed only 7 percent of the labor force because they created 65 percent of the wealth, thereby ignoring the small microproducers, which employ 83 percent of Bolivians.[55] The strategy also failed to address issues such as the privatization of the nation's natural resources, land redistribution, and national labor and tax policies. Instead, the focus remained on keeping government expenditure and wages low in order to prevent inflation, increasing exports, limiting the role of government, and encouraging private investment.

The real national dialogue about poverty reduction, instead, took place on the streets and in other forums, convened not by the government but by civil society groups themselves. These forums helped articulate a new set of priorities.[56] Union leader José Pimentel Castillo, who participated in the forums, explained: "By talking about poverty, we naturally looked at the causes and . . . we came to the same conclusion: that neoliberalism, destruction of the state, and imposition of the international financial institutions were the fundamental problems." These agendas would soon gather significant political force, providing a basis for growing opposition to prescriptions put forth by the IMF, the World Bank, and their allies among the Bolivian elites and the relationships of control and dependence they had constructed.

The Dilemma of Money That Isn't Really There

To be clear, debt relief did not mean that the Bolivian government suddenly had new money. The average $81 million a year released by the HIPC initiatives looks good on paper, but it was never actually new revenue for Bolivia.[57] It was money the government theoretically would have paid in debt repayments, and therefore it was largely an illusion. As Javier Comboni, Bolivia's finance minister from 2002 to 2003, explained: "If we can't pay our debt, why is it assumed we can spend it on social services?"[58]

At the same time that lenders like the World Bank were canceling a part of Bolivia's debt, they were also cutting back on the low-interest lending ("concessional" lending) to Bolivia. It was "giving with one hand and taking with the other," noted Juan Carlos Nuñez.

At the same time, high expectations for the use of debt relief dollars vastly exceeded what debt relief could actually deliver. The budget laid out in Bolivia's PRSP was $1.2 billion, an amount that exceeded actual funds available from debt relief by ten times.[59] This, in part, explains why the country's budget deficit started to explode. Bolivia was taking on new spending commitments at a time when government income was falling. By the end of 2002, the budget deficit had shot up to nearly 9 percent, almost a threefold increase in five years. In fact, that increase in deficit prompted another round of heavy pressure by the IMF for fiscal constraint. In February 2003, public protests against an IMF-induced tax hike on the working poor left thirty-four people dead. (For more on Bolivia's deficits and IMF pressures, see chapter 4.)

What Relief Accomplished

"There are twenty-five new staff in this hospital, thanks to debt relief," said Alfredo Mendoza, head of emergency services at La Paz's Children's Hospital. The relief allowed for a 10 percent increase in staff, including, for the first time, an epidemiologist and an allergist. Debt relief resources also paid for some building work in the hospital and helped to cover costs for Bolivia's Universal Mother and Infant Insurance (Seguro Universal Materno Infantil, SUMI). "Children's access to health care has definitely improved," he said.

Bolivia's Poverty Reduction Strategy allocated $406.5 million dollars to social programs between August 2001 and July 2006. This was a redirection of the government's debt servicing to social purposes, an average of $81 million a year. Twenty-seven million dollars a year went to the central government for spending on education and public health, with the rest divided among municipalities for spending on infrastructure development, education, and health.

Determining the overall impact of public spending is difficult in all situations. However, it is possible to note some specific examples. The Children's Hospital is among many programs that received a share of those new funds. La Paz's head of education reported that, using debt relief funds, the schools had been able to improve and expand student breakfast programs, build fifty new educational buildings, and buy enough new furniture so that every child could have his or her own desk.[60] At a national level, the funds have gone toward employing 2,400 health workers and 4,300 teachers since 2001.[61]

Nationally, access to basic services like health, drinking water, housing, and education has improved. Some of these improvements can be dated to government programs prior to HIPC, such as the Law of Popular Participation of 1994. Nevertheless, during this period of increased debt relief and attention to poverty issues, child mortality fell by 24 percent, and at the same time (1998–2004) institutional support for child birth increased by 40 percent.[62] Since 2000, Bolivia has doubled the amount earmarked for various social welfare programs to almost

23 percent of social expenditure, which is higher than the average in Latin America.[63]

In the end, however, the impact of funds linked to debt relief in Bolivia has been consistently limited by three basic factors. First, Bolivia's current need for increased investment in public services and public goods requires more than debt relief can offer. The IMF/World Bank formula for debt relief is not about complete cancellation of the country's debt, but a partial cancellation, to reduce the debt to what the IMF considered a "sustainable level."[64] Debt relief of an average of $81 million is paltry compared to Bolivia's budget in 2006 of $5.8 billion dollars.[65] The second limitation has been the legal restrictions and administrative problems that have kept many municipalities from spending available funds.[66] Educational authorities in La Paz reported frustration that they could only spend money on infrastructure rather than urgently needed teacher training, which remains a responsibility of central government. Between 2002 and 2005, the country's 327 municipalities managed to spend only half of the money they received.

Finally, mechanisms for public oversight have not been properly funded. As a result, it is very difficult to get a complete picture of whether the resources stipulated in public budgets have actually reached those who most need the resources.[67] Daniel Cáceres, president of the National Mechanism for Social Control said that he fears many "HIPC resources have not been used well because of lack of knowledge and information."[68]

Deep Poverty and Dependence Remains

In the La Paz Children's Hospital, Teresa, an Aymara indigenous woman, clung to her crutches as she looked anxiously at her sleeping son, Isaac. In a very soft voice, she said she was twenty, although she looked almost forty. Isaac, who was fourteen months old, had come into the hospital after being listless and weak for days. He suffered from severe malnourishment. "We didn't have any money for food. All I could give him was breast milk," she whispered. "But he is eating now." She explained that she had had to borrow money just to get to the hospital, that she hadn't eaten anything in the last two days, and that she didn't know what she would do during the scheduled two weeks' treatment. While her son was now eating, she was starving.[69]

Teresa and Isaac's story speaks to a stark reality in Bolivia. While access to basic services such as health care have improved modestly since the HIPC debt relief initiative was launched, it has not changed Bolivia's deep levels of impoverishment. In 2003, six years after the first

HIPC initiative was launched, reports showed that poverty had increased from 63 percent to 65 percent. Extreme poverty, defined by the inability to earn enough to afford basic food, rose from 38 percent to 41 percent. That means that almost two-thirds of Bolivians live on less than ten bolivianos a day ($1.25), which is considered the minimum income required to satisfy basic needs in Bolivia. An economic recession from 2001 to 2003 amplified the problem, but even so, real per capita income in Bolivia in 2005 was lower than it was in 1978.[70] With the drop in income levels, inequality has also increased. In 2001, Bolivia surpassed its neighbor Brazil for being the most economically unequal country in Latin America.[71]

Just as debt relief has had little impact on structural poverty, it has also done little to reduce Bolivia's financial dependence on foreign lenders. To meet that challenge, Bolivia must develop its own sources of revenue, independent of international lenders. In Bolivia, these efforts have focused on raising taxes on the foreign oil corporations, which were given control over the country's most valuable natural resource in the 1990s under privatization programs encouraged by the IMF and the World Bank. In response to public demands in 2005, the Bolivian Congress approved a major tax hike on the corporations. In 2006, that generated nearly a billion dollars in new revenue for Bolivia—a home-grown revenue source that overshadowed the average $81 million from debt relief. Rather than supporting these efforts, the IMF opposed these changes claiming that Bolivia failed the IMF-imposed target of creating an "appropriate framework for developing large hydrocarbons resources."[72] (For more on Bolivia's gas and oil, see chapter 3.)

Debt Reborn

The question remains: following the many rounds of debt cancellation, has the nation so long addicted to debt entered some form of recovery? Has Bolivia decreased dependence on debt so that it can shake the long-standing economic pressures of its global lenders? On the surface, Bolivia's situation looks healthier than it has for several decades. Following the cancellation of almost 100 percent of its debt to the IMF and the World Bank in 2006, and a subsequent cancellation announcement by the IDB in January 2007, Bolivia's total foreign debt fell from a high of $5 billion in 2003 to $2.5 billion in 2007.[73] Most significantly, it meant that Bolivia was able to end a twenty-year string of agreements with the IMF, giving it more freedom to make its own economic choices, such as the increased taxes on oil and gas multinationals.

However, the fact remains that if the country's remaining debt were divided among its people, the average Bolivian still owes $260 in external debt, equivalent to almost seven months' income for two-thirds of the population.[74] The money is now primarily owed to the Andean Corporation Fund (CAF) and IDB. Moreover, external debt service, defined as how much the government pays out per year was projected to fall only to roughly $170 million in 2007, as opposed to the average of $250 million paid out between 1999 and 2005.[75]

The reason that payments on its debt have not fallen significantly is that Bolivia's debt is being reborn in a more expensive form. As the government reduces or severs its borrowing relationship with lower-interest "concessional" lenders, such as the IMF and the IDB, it is shifting more and more to lenders who charge higher market rate interest. These are loans which are quick, easy, and flexible to take out and have fewer conditions attached, but they do carry a significant cost in higher interest rates and shorter payback periods. As a result, Bolivia's debt costs may even rise in coming years.

Internal debt is also rising rapidly. In 2007, it was expected to hit almost $3 billion and overtake external debt.[76] This is money that the Bolivian government is borrowing within the economy by issuing bonds, and unlike external debt, it cannot be cancelled. In Bolivia's situation, the government owes this money to the national pension funds. There are growing concerns that the pension funds may be insufficient to pay retirees beyond 2012.

The combination of rising internal debt and higher interest rates is a "matter of great worry," admitted Raúl Mendoza, a senior economist in Bolivia's Central Bank.[77] The debt situation at the moment still looks manageable and doesn't include conditionalities that accompanied IMF loans. However, the new issue with Bolivia's borrowing will be not only how much it owes, but whether this time the revenue is used effectively to invest in education, job creation, and sustainable production in order to increase Bolivia's own revenues and extricate itself from continued dependency.

GLOBAL TRADE AGREEMENTS: THE NEW STRINGS
OF INFLUENCE

In November 2002, Bolivian president Gonzalo Sánchez de Lozada visited the White House in Washington, D.C. Bolivia was suffering a recession and its budget deficit was deepening. Sánchez de Lozada, facing a growing political crisis as a result, asked the Bush administration for $150 million in emergency loans to help with growing discontent at home. "I asked them to help us build bridges over turbulent waters," he later explained. In exchange for that assistance, Sánchez de Lozada pledged to keep Bolivia in line with U.S. objectives in the region, in particular to continue supporting U.S.-backed coca eradication and to promote a deal to export Bolivian gas and oil to the energy-hungry country in the north. Sánchez de Lozada returned to Bolivia with U.S. pledges totaling no more than $10 million.

Less than a year later, Sánchez de Lozada was on a plane to Washington once more, this time as a former president ousted by his people and headed into effective U.S. exile, a direct result of his proposals to export Bolivian gas at bargain prices to the United States. He later blamed his fall in popularity on his failure to win loans and aid in Washington, funds that could have helped him weather the nation's economic storm. "We lost that moment," lamented Sánchez de Lozada.[78]

Fast-forward three years to September 2006. Another Bolivian leader in a very different government, Vice President Álvaro García Linera, arrived in Washington—for the second visit in three months. On behalf of the new socialist government of Evo Morales, who came into power in January 2006, the vice president was not seeking aid or loans; he was looking for a trade deal.

Bolivia's government faced the imminent expiration of the Andean Trade Preferences and Drug Eradication Act, an agreement that gave Bolivian textile manufacturers preferential entry to the U.S. market. Tens of thousands of jobs were at stake, and Linera warned that the end of those preferences would be a "serious blow" to the Bolivian economy.[79] Like Sánchez de Lozada, Linera promised Bolivian cooperation on the U.S. War on Drugs, though he stopped short of pledging support for other U.S. desires, such as a full "free trade" agreement. Weeks later the Bush administration announced its backing for an extension of six months, which was later approved by the Republican-controlled U.S. Congress. Linera had at least bought Bolivia a little time.

Where once the governments of low-income countries like Bolivia visited their wealthy neighbors in search of loans and debt relief, today they are increasingly boarding northbound flights looking for something else: trade deals and access to markets. As one foreign debt after another is being cancelled, trade is quickly replacing debt as one of the key instruments that nations like the United States are using to exert influence over their low-income counterparts.[80]

Trade as a Tool for Influence

One of the biggest challenges that Bolivia faces now in preserving its ability to set its own economic course is in the area of so-called free trade agreements. "Free trade" pacts are not new. In fact, the liberalizing of markets was a central principle of structural adjustment programs that have been at the heart of World Bank, IMF, and other IFI lending. Based on that ideology, indebted countries were required to lower tariffs on imported goods and to concentrate on exports of cash crops in order to facilitate foreign investment, create currency to pay debts, and allow the market rather than public policy to allocate goods. Backers of "free trade" policies argue that tariffs only serve to protect inefficient industries and increase prices for consumers.

However, since the mid-1990s, wealthy industrialized countries including the United States and European Union nations have pushed a trade agenda that goes well beyond simply lowering tariffs. They have pushed for "free trade" and investment agreements between countries whose requirements included the privatization of essential services such as water, extraordinary protections for foreign investors, and intellectual property rights that included restrictions on the production of low-cost medicines. The government's role in terms of regulation of the economy was to be kept to the minimum. Under "free trade" rules, even the purchase of military uniforms by the government would be required to be subject to foreign bidding. The trade deals were promoted to low-income countries with the promise of ensuring increased investment, growth in exports, and improved economic development. Instead of the threat of withholding loans, trade agreements are enforced by a set of special international tribunals that can fine a country for huge sums, or cut off markets.

One of the best-known cases of this type involved Bolivia in the aftermath of the Cochabamba Water Revolt. The Bechtel Corporation sought a minimum of $50 million in damages against local water users, despite the fact that Bechtel had invested less than $1 million. Bechtel brought the case, under an investment treaty, in a closed-door trade court operated by the same institution that had forced the privatization from the beginning: the World Bank. Eventually an international uproar against the case led Bechtel to abandon it. (For more on the Bechtel case, see chapter 1.) A typical "free trade" treaty usually includes terms similar to those in the investment treaty Bechtel used to sue Bolivia.

Pablo Solón, Bolivia's chief trade negotiator for the Morales administration, observed the relationship between "free trade" agreements and debt: They "are two sides of the same coin. Debt was used to impose structural adjustment programs that sought to privatize and generate benefits for multinational companies. Free trade agreements are used to lock in the rules to benefit multinationals. In some ways it is easier to get out of debt by paying it off, as Argentina has done, than it is to extract yourself from commitments within free trade agreements."[81]

In a conference on international arbitration in June 2006, top legal officials within the Morales administration talked openly about being hamstrung by trade agreements signed by previous administrations, frustrated that the broad rights assigned to foreign investors in the past often trumped national law in practice.

"Free trade" agreements have been pushed at an international level through the World Trade Organization and through regional and bilateral agreements. More recent trade agreements have aimed to go even further in imposing economic conditions that restrict government sovereignty. The United States initially promoted a continent-wide Free Trade Area of the Americas. When that failed, it shifted its focus to winning a collection of regional agreements modeled after the North American Free Trade Agreement (NAFTA) with Mexico and Canada. While the United States succeeded in signing the Central American Free Trade Agreement, it has not been able to complete an Andean Free Trade Agreement, which would have included Bolivia. The trade mosaic that U.S. trade negotiators had originally hoped to create as a hemispheric whole is now being built piece by piece. In each case, the carrot held out to Latin American countries is the promise of greater access to the U.S. market.

Critics of these agreements argue that the profits they promise mainly go to small, privileged parties on both sides, such as multinational corporations, at the expense of workers, those with low incomes, and the environment. Instead of promoting "free trade," they lock in and exacerbate the inequalities among trading partners. They protect the unfair advantage of the largest corporations, who often have significant government support. They also restrict competition in essential areas such as medicines and agriculture, while requiring disadvantaged countries to open their most vulnerable industries to foreign competition. The U.S. economy, for example, is nearly five hundred times larger than Bolivia's and provides $20 billion in subsidies to its farmers.[82] Bolivia's national budget of $5.8 billion in 2006 is dwarfed by the profits of many large U.S. multinational companies. Bolivian small firms and producers, who receive little support or protection, are simply not positioned to compete against counterparts abroad.

The experience of the North American Free Trade Agreement in Mexico, twelve years after it was signed, is a warning of the potential costs for Bolivia to sign a template U.S. free trade agreement. Despite promises of growth and jobs, NAFTA has led to the loss of 2 million agricultural jobs in rural areas, a high increase in environmental pollution in factories in the "free trade zones" on the border between Mexico and the United States, and increased inequality and poverty.[83] Nevertheless, trips by Bolivia's vice president to Washington seeking an extension of trade preferences are likely to be just the first in a string of many to northern capitals and Latin American neighbors.

People's Trade Agreements

When Bolivia's MAS government took power in January 2006, it did so with a self-proclaimed mandate to "end neoliberalism" and, in the words of María Luisa Ramos, to "break relations of dependency." MAS and Morales probably have more potential to do this than has any previous government. Not only is Bolivia's foreign debt at an all-time low, but also the economy is strong and, against many predictions, Bolivia has managed to negotiate better deals with foreign oil companies in order to increase state revenue. All of this puts Bolivia in a completely new position to reduce its dependence on external creditors and chart its own economic course.

A part of that course is what the government and key allies call People's Trade Agreements, accords that stress not just opening of markets but also shared commitments to buy products. They clearly assert the right of Bolivia's government to protect and support small-scale industries and producers by, for example, restricting imports. They establish the country's right to strengthen rather than privatize public services, such as water, and they reject patents on medicines and biodiversity. They look for complementary relationships between economies rather than naked competition. People's Trade Agreements, advocates argue, are those that recognize that the global economic playing field is not level and that the rules need to benefit smaller, economically poorer nations.

In April 2006, Bolivia signed such an agreement with Cuba and Venezuela. Venezuela agreed, for example, to buy soy and other agricultural goods from Bolivia at a zero import tariff. As a smaller economy, Bolivia is not required to offer the same to Venezuela. The agreement provided funds to small businesses and producers to help them export and create jobs. The agreement also included a large social program as well, starting with a Cuban commitment to offer free eye surgeries and training for a nationwide literacy campaign.[84]

Bolivia also signed an agreement with Uruguay in 2006 in which it agreed to export gas in exchange for support in building thermoelectric plants and developing liquefied gas. A June 2006 agreement between Bolivia and Argentina approved a 57 percent increase in the price of Bolivian gas.[85] While the short-term total impact on Bolivia's nonhydrocarbons exports from these agreements remains marginal, they do signal an important new economic approach.

To be sure, Bolivia's chosen path is a risky one. Failure to sign a standard free trade agreement with the United States, for example, could mean the end of the current trade preferences under the Andean Trade Preferences and Drug Eradication Act. That fear is represented in a call by the powerful Bolivian Institute for Foreign Trade (made up of Bolivian exporters) to sign an agreement with the United States. The institute argues that People's Trade Agreements are nothing more than rhetoric. Nevertheless, the MAS government is committed to seeking trade accords of a different nature. The ability to do so and to prevent trade from replacing debt as the new tool of foreign economic control presents a huge challenge, not just for Bolivia, but for low-income countries across Latin America.

CONCLUSION

On January 3, 2006, Evo Morales returned to the community where he was born, Orinoca, in the department of Oruro. It was an event he probably never could have imagined. More than forty years earlier, Morales spent his childhood in Orinoca in an impoverished mining family, forced to eat orange peels thrown out of buses and, he has said, wishing he could one day travel on a bus. In 2006, he was returning as a man about to be inaugurated as the country's president.

In his speech to a joyful community, Morales addressed the issue of external debt: "Bolivia will not pay an external debt because indigenous people, Aymaras, Quechuas, and Chiquitanos, have no debt. If [the international community] want[s], we can renegotiate the debt, but there is no reason why we should pay it. In fact, they owe us for the looting of our natural resources. . . . We are not asking that they repair all the damage, but they must understand the economic situation of the country and cancel the external debt."[86]

For many Bolivians, including President Morales, the debt crisis is viewed as the modern-day incarnation of a cycle of foreign exploitation that started in colonial times, beginning most starkly with Spain's extraction of Bolivia's mountain of silver at Potosí. Three and a half centuries later, Bolivia's economic transfers abroad took the form, not of silver, but of debt payments.

In fact, the debt crises in low-income nations over the past two decades bear a striking resemblance to the dynamics of dependency and empire. Where once kings, viceroys, and Spanish aristocrats sent economic edicts to their colonies, G8 economic officials and their allies in international financial institutions use debt to coerce independent states to approve economic arrangements to their liking. Economic elites in Bolivia and abroad helped develop these arrangements and also benefited richly from them, while Bolivia's majority bore an ever-increasing burden. The relationships of power and dependency that the new order established seemed so natural that even today the IFIs and many former Bolivian officials rarely question them.

The failure of the debt-driven economic model is told in both numbers and stories—people like Teresa, whose children suffer from malnutrition in a country rich with fertile soil and natural resources; the fact that after twenty years of neoliberalism 41 percent of Bolivians live without enough money to buy sufficient food, while the country continues to pay almost $200 million a year to wealthy creditors.

The unacknowledged debt owed from wealthier countries to low-income countries is not just measured in minerals and cash. Indigenous communities talk also about the deep "ecological debt" that wealthier countries owe, from the trees sacked from the Amazon forests to the devastating damage of global climate change. How will the wealthy nations of the world, who bear the chief responsibility for climate change, compensate Bolivia for that damage, including its millennia-old glaciers predicted to disappear within three decades?

While debt relief failed to break the chains of dependency in a way that many campaigners had hoped, in Bolivia it did accomplish some important things. It redirected investments into the crucial areas of health and education; it improved access to essential services for previously excluded communities; it even helped save lives. But perhaps more important, it also opened up space for the voices of the marginalized majority in Bolivia—the indigenous, small-scale farmers, women, workers, and other social movements that were ready to challenge an economic model that had failed them. They used debates about debt relief resources to raise bigger questions about how all the country's resources should be distributed, about the elites who had ruled Bolivia for their benefit, and about a development model that served the interests of multinationals more than local citizens. Many of the social movements in Bolivia that helped champion debt relief are still in the fray, holding their government accountable and pushing for alternative visions of the country's economy and society, often drawing on indigenous visions based on solidarity, reciprocity, and living in harmony with nature.

Bolivia still faces a formidable challenge in undoing a culture of dependence created under twenty years of neoliberalism. Learning from its experience, Bolivia needs to sort out how the nation should limit its borrowing to loans that are genuinely productive, agreed upon transparently and with open knowledge of civil society, and that can be paid back without putting a burden on future generations. Bolivia needs to open up the doors of economic decision making so that its people are engaged in the nation's choices and its political leaders are held accountable to the public interest. Bolivia will have the difficult challenge of negotiating trade deals that support rather than do further harm to those who have been excluded by the "free market" economic model.

For the international community, the experience of Bolivia raises troubling questions about how international financial institutions set out on their presumed missions. Institutions like the IMF, with creditor government backing, were directed to resolve the debt crisis but clearly failed to do so. Instead they oversaw a vast transfer of resources from Bolivia to its far wealthier lenders. They aligned themselves with wealthy local elites, who both enriched themselves and ushered in policies that left the majority worse off. In Bolivia, and in many other low-income nations in Latin America, the broad political rejection of the IFIs's model is clear evidence that the people have not seen the promised results.

In the end, the most important story about debt is the one this chapter began with: debt between nations is less about cash than it is about power. Millions worldwide campaigned for debt relief. Yet canceling debt is not enough if changes are not made to the systems of financial power that created the debt crisis and built a Bolivia dependent on external resources and decisions. Trade could be a tool for Bolivia to help promote the well-being of its people. It should not be a tool to impose a foreign model that benefits only a few. Building a more just and dignified society, in Bolivia and elsewhere, requires directly challenging the institutions and governments that constrain Bolivia. It involves standing alongside Bolivians who have a vision to free themselves from the relationships of dependency, collusion, and control imposed from abroad.

Local farmers, shielding their faces from the hot afternoon sun, harvest coca leaf on a steep hillside in Los Yungas, near La Paz. Photo: Kathryn Cook (2006).

CHAPTER 6

Coca: The Leaf at the Center of the War on Drugs

No issue has dominated Bolivia's recent struggle with powers from abroad more than coca. This small green leaf embodies the clash between Bolivian tradition and identity and the international policies that call for its eradication. It is a leaf that has been used in ceremonies, consumed as a medicine, and traded as a valuable commodity by Andean civilizations for over four thousand years. But the leaf is also the raw ingredient to manufacture cocaine, a drug that plagues communities and feeds violence on the streets of Brazil, Europe, and the United States.

Here, a series of writers lay out the many aspects of the controversial and complex coca issue. The chapter begins with a historical description of coca's place in Andean culture and society and how it became an object of interest to Spanish conquistadors and an international commodity. It goes on to examine how outside forces continue to play a role in Bolivia with the imposition of the "war on drugs," an international effort initiated by the United States to eradicate coca due to its connection to cocaine. Following that are the stories from Bolivians who have been intimately affected by that war—an innocent mother punished by the country's antidrug law and the families who depend on coca cultivation for their monthly income. The chapter ends with an analysis of the alternatives to coca production and considers the viability of alternative crops as well as alternative uses of coca.

ANCIENT SYMBOL, TRADITION, AND COMMODITY

CAROLINE S. CONZELMAN

When Doña Corina harvests her coca bushes, each leaf makes a soft *snap*, indicating that she has picked it off whole, not torn or crushed. With all the women working together in her field, the air is filled with these snaps, a rhythm that decorates the women's conversation like the sequins embroidered on their festival skirts at home. At the end of the day they will have accumulated a large cloth bag of the leaves that Corina can carry on her back along the winding paths to her adobe home. There she has a slate patio called a *kachi*, where she will spread out the leaves the next morning in the sun to dry. This is all the processing that coca needs before it is put into bags to sell at the legal market or stored for her family to use for tea, medicine, and ceremonies.

The leaf is regularly chewed by people in her community because of its many beneficial properties and because it is a potent symbol of their indigenous heritage. "Coca is our life," said Doña Corina, quite literally, for coca sustains her community's health, economy, and spirituality. However, for centuries coca has been despised, misunderstood, and controlled by colonial and elite powers, or maligned for its notorious derivative, cocaine. Its popular image has veered from one extreme to the other, perceived as either the sacred leaf or the devil's leaf. All the while, indigenous people in Bolivia have considered coca a fundamental aspect of their livelihoods, politics, and traditions.

If you travel over the mountain pass from the city of La Paz and the altiplano highlands down into the steep eastern slope of the Bolivian Andes—where you can simultaneously see the snowy peaks of the Cordillera to the south and the rivers deep in their valleys flowing north toward the Amazon—you arrive at the legendary coca fields of the Yungas region. The Yungas is one of two major coca-growing regions in Bolivia and is recognized as the main traditional coca-growing zone. The Chapare, in central Bolivia, is another important coca-growing area that gained notoriety beginning in the 1960s due to the influx of migrants who moved in from the highland regions and began growing coca, much of which, in the 1980s, became destined for the burgeoning cocaine market abroad.

The telltale signature of a Yungas coca field, or *cocal*, is the row upon row of low earthen terraces stacked up in vertical columns until they cover the hillside, radiating a brilliant emerald green. The old Inca stone terraces are even still visible in some places. Because coca leaf has been grown here for many centuries by Aymara and Quechua people, its cultivation is legal in the Yungas for domestic markets. The sweet coca grown here is preferred over the leaf grown at lower altitudes, like that found in the Chapare, and is thus sold around the country for chewing and making herbal tea, its most common and ancient uses.

Coca leaf is used this way as a mild stimulant—comparable to how people in other parts of the world use coffee and tea—and offers significant nutritional value for daily life in the fields, mines, meeting halls, and markets. Compared with fifty other native plants consumed in Latin America—including a variety of nuts, vegetables, cereals, and fruits—coca ranks higher than average in protein, carbohydrate, calcium, iron, and vitamins A and E.[1] Coca is an important source of nourishment for rural and urban indigenous laborers who often have only limited means to sustain a balanced diet. The leaf is also a remedy for a variety of physiological ailments, including altitude sickness, gastrointestinal inflammation, and hypoglycemia.[2]

It makes sense that coca cultivation evolved together with potatoes in the Andes because chewing the leaf after a meal helps regulate the blood sugar produced by potato starch. Local communities also benefit from the leaf's high calcium content.[3] Coca can be used as a healing agent for minor wounds and as a mild topical anesthetic owing to the presence of the leaf's fourteen alkaloids, one of which is the cocaine alkaloid. The minute amount of the cocaine alkaloid ingested by chewing the leaf or drinking coca tea is not in any way similar to the effect of consuming the drug cocaine. Nor is coca leaf addictive, as pure cocaine can be.[4]

It is not difficult to understand why coca has been a sacred and central component of life in the Andes and parts of the Amazon for more than four thousand years.[5] One Aymara myth says that coca leaf was a gift from Pachamama (Mother Earth) long ago when her people needed sustenance during a food crisis in the Yungas.[6] She guided them to a simple shrub that was able to survive under these conditions and told the people to suck on the small flat leaves. Thus the Aymara began to discover the nutritional and medicinal properties of coca. They continue to offer coca leaves in their ceremonies to honor their connection to the land and the divine realm of the spirits, especially Pachamama.

Coca is a hardy crop. It can grow in acidic or rocky soil and remain productive for thirty years. The Aymara developed a method of terracing, which they still use today, to take advantage of the extreme topography and mild climate of the high-altitude, subtropical forests. The hard work of building these terraces, primarily the men's work, is punctuated by breaks to chew coca. Coca is also shared by the sisters, daughters, aunts, and other women who spend their days picking coca surrounded by swirling mist, warm sunshine, and stunning mountain vistas.

In the Yungas, coca is the principal export crop within a diversified subsistence agriculture system, with each coca field harvested three to four times a year. The labor involved is a shared enterprise, in which extended families and neighbors join together to plant and to harvest. This practice of reciprocity, which has a long history in the Andes, is called *ayni* in Aymara.

The principle of *ayni* is at the heart of the ancient Aymara political economic system called the *ayllu*, created to take advantage of the tremendous ecological diversity of the region. Each of the three primary climate zones produces certain goods that are essential to people's survival—potatoes, quinoa, and llamas from the altiplano; root vegetables, maize, medicinal herbs, and coca from the lowlands; fish and salt from the Pacific coast. All families of an *ayllu* took turns holding positions of authority, overseeing the distribution of resources, like food and land, for the benefit of the entire *ayllu*.[7] The philosophy and practices of *ayllu* live on in many Bolivian communities, where coca leaf continues to be shared at social and political gatherings to represent their essential bonds of reciprocity.

Coca as Commodity

Tata José (*tata* is an Aymara term of respect for an older man) has many stories to tell about the *nayra pacha*, the old times of the Aymara culture, which he learned from the oral history passed down through generations of his indigenous ancestors in the Yungas. He explains that long ago, coca leaf was the most valuable product the Andean people had, next to their fine wool textiles, so it was often used to trade for other goods or to compensate someone for labor.[8] This use of coca was only one component of a comprehensive system of barter exchange called *trueque,* in which products and labor, not money, were the basis of trade. This type of bartering and exchange remains common today in Bolivia among people who live outside the formal cash economy.

When the conquistadors destroyed the Inca Empire in the 1500s and replaced it with a Spanish Catholic empire, they viewed the sacred leaf as the devil's leaf. The Spaniards were appalled at the pervasive practice among the indigenous people of chewing coca leaf, and they called for its elimination. Their perception was that coca "was used extensively in heathen rites, and was almost worshipped for its magical power as a stimulant. It formed a bond among the natives and was an important obstacle to the spread of Christianity. Because of this, coca was condemned and attacked with passion [by Catholic priests, who] declared that 'Coca is a plant that the devil invented for the total destruction of the natives.'"[9]

It did not take long, however, for the Spanish to realize how coca could be useful to them. Obsessed with acquiring wealth by any means, the Spanish had established a repressive feudal system of estates called haciendas that gave enormous tracts of land—along with the indigenous inhabitants—to the conquistadors and their descendents. They realized that coca could support the indigenous field workers and silver miners to work longer and harder.[10] They took control of the production and commercialization of coca throughout the Andean region.[11] Aymara and Quechua miners were able to endure the interminable shifts that lasted for weeks deep inside the mountain of Potosí by chewing the leaf. Coca staved off hunger, thirst, and fatigue and also signified protection by the god of the underground, called Tío.[12]

Coca also became an important symbol for the Aymara and their strength in resisting Spanish control. During the rebellion of 1780–81, led by Tupac Katari and his wife, Bartolina Sisa, La Paz was cut off by the Aymara rebels for seven months. Chewing coca and carrying out rituals with coca was the way the indigenous men and women surrounding the capital endured the rain and harsh temperatures. Coca, a Bolivian historian wrote, "raised their spirits, and gave them strength and bravery in combat."[13] The rebellion was eventually defeated, and Katari was brutally killed by Spanish forces. According to legend his last words were, "You kill me now, but I will return, and then I will be millions."[14]

After Bolivia gained its independence from Spain in 1825, the ruling elite continued its control over coca, using it to sustain the exploited workforces in the mines that were key to increasing their profitable mineral exports. Tata José explained what it was like to pick coca as an indigenous peón before the Revolution of 1952 brought agrarian reform: "Aymara children did not go to school, or even learn to speak Spanish, but worked in the cocales with their parents. That was our education, learning how to pick coca."

Coca and Cocaine

In 1860, a German chemist was the first to isolate coca leaf's cocaine alkaloid and concentrate it into a white crystalline powder. Cocaine soon became a popular bourgeois recreational drug in Europe and the United States and was also considered a medical panacea, endorsed by figures such as the Pope, Sigmund Freud, and Ulysses Grant.[15] Coca-Cola was created in the 1880s as an elixir of cocaine and caffeine and became an international sensation. By the early 1900s, however, cocaine's deleterious effects were becoming clear. In 1914, the United States passed the Harrison Narcotics Act, which prohibited the possession and use of cocaine. In 1929, Coca-Cola eliminated cocaine from its popular soda but retained the unique flavoring of the leaf in its recipe.[16]

Records from the 1920s show that 87 percent of Yungas coca was consumed in Bolivia—primarily in the mines—and of the 13 percent exported, most supplied laborers in Argentina and Chile, while the rest was sent to Europe to be used in pharmaceuticals.[17] Yungas hacienda owners fiercely defended their right to grow the leaf as a mainstay of the national economy and a crucial source of public tax revenue. They also stressed that coca did not pose health risks.[18] These voices were initially honored in international agreements, but coca leaf was becoming increasingly confused with the drug cocaine. As one researcher described it, "A mild stimulant that had been used with no evidence of toxicity for at least two thousand years before Europeans discovered cocaine came to be viewed as an addictive drug."[19]

The link between coca and cocaine became the basis for international law in 1961 with the approval of the United Nations Single Convention on Narcotic Drugs, which classified coca leaf as a narcotic, alongside heroin and cocaine.[20] The accord prohibits Bolivia from exporting coca leaf or other products such as tea that are made from it. It also set into motion a plan to eradicate all illicit coca cultivation in Bolivia and Peru within twenty-five years and to eliminate the practice of coca chewing altogether within that same time period. Backers of the plan argued that coca was a root cause of underdevelopment and poverty in the region.[21]

In the two decades following the passage of the UN convention, the fear that Bolivia's coca leaf would become broadly used for cocaine production persisted. In the mid-1980s, however, two phenomena would lead to a surge in coca cultivation in Bolivia that would turn that fear into a reality. At the international level, the cocaine boom in the United

---

BOX 6.1 | Coca and Cocaine: What Is the Difference?

Coca leaf is to cocaine what grapes are to wine—it is a raw material that must be altered significantly in order to turn it into a drug. Coca leaf contains a small concentration of the cocaine alkaloid, which is what is extracted to make pure cocaine. Chewing coca leaf is the traditional way of consuming coca in the Andean culture and produces none of the euphoria or paranoia that occur with cocaine use, because the alkaloid is ingested as a component of the whole leaf and is absorbed slowly by the body through the digestive system.[1] The World Health Organization (WHO) reported in 1995 that even long-term users of coca leaf experience no detrimental health effects and do not suffer from addiction.[2]

Turning coca leaf into cocaine requires an elaborate process involving a set of specific chemicals. First, the dried coca leaf is turned into coca paste using sodium carbonate and kerosene.[3] Coca paste is then elaborated into cocaine through an even more sophisticated process using special equipment and more noxious chemicals. It takes about 390 pounds of coca leaf to make one pound of cocaine.[4] Although the numbers are highly contested, the director of Bolivia's antinarcotic force, FELCN, claimed in early 2007 that as much as 50 percent of coca leaf produced in Bolivia eventually goes to making cocaine.[5]

1. Andrew Weil, "Letter from the Andes: The New Politics of Coca," *New Yorker*, May 15, 1995, 77.

2. Roberto Laserna, *Veinte juicios y prejuicios sobre coca-cocaína* (Twenty judgments and prejudices about coca-cocaine) (La Paz: Edición Clave, 1996), 14.

3. "Coca Cultivation and Cocaine Processing: An Overview," Drug Enforcement Administration, Intelligence Division, September 2003, www.druglibrary.org/Schaffer/GovPubs/cocccp.htm (accessed March 30, 2007).

4. Kevin Riley, "Snow Job? The Efficacy of Source Country Cocaine Policies," Rand Graduate School Dissertation series, RGSD-102, 1993, 78.

5. "EEUU exige 'resultados' en reducción de coca" (The U.S. demands "results" on coca eradication), *Los Tiempos* (Cochabamba), March 30, 2007.

States and Europe spiked demand for the coca leaf. In Bolivia, economic crisis and radical changes in national economic policy left thirty thousand people without jobs practically overnight. Scrambling to find a new income, these Bolivians turned to their best option: to become coca farmers in the Chapare. Ironically, the Chapare was precisely where government programs were encouraging the newly unemployed to migrate. Soon after, the United States and its international partners would launch the massive initiative that came to be known as the "war on drugs" in the Andes.

A BRIEF HISTORY OF THE U.S. "WAR ON DRUGS" IN BOLIVIA

COLETTA A. YOUNGERS

In September 2006, Bolivian president Evo Morales stood before the United Nations General Assembly and held up a small coca leaf. The nation's first indigenous president declared: "This is the green coca leaf; it is not white like cocaine. It represents Andean culture." A leader of the Bolivian coca growers, Morales had been denied a U.S. visa to attend a UN Special Session on Drug Policy a decade earlier. As president, he has had access to an international platform to defend the historic, religious, and cultural uses of the coca leaf and to distinguish it from the illicit substance cocaine with which it had become indelibly linked. He also has had a historic opportunity to put an end to the U.S. "war on drugs" in Bolivia.

Bolivians have paid a high price waging Washington's war. U.S.-backed coca eradication efforts have long been characterized by human rights violations in the Chapare coca-growing region. Although abuses have not reached the level of the executions and disappearances carried out by some of Bolivia's military dictators in past years, a disturbing pattern of killings, mistreatment, and abuse of the local population has prevailed. The primary victims are not drug traffickers but poor farmers who support their families through the production of coca and other agricultural products. Coca crop eradication has plunged communities and families deeper into poverty, generating social unrest, violence, and political instability. That discontent ultimately led to the creation of the political party MAS (Movement toward Socialism), that later elected the country's most visible coca grower leader to its highest office.

Garnering 54 percent of the vote in the December 2005 elections, Morales earned an unprecedented mandate for change. Well aware of the negative consequences and failures of past policy, his government adopted a radically different approach to the drug issue, best characterized by its slogan "coca yes, cocaine no." Other coca grower leaders began directing the government agencies responsible for carrying out the new policy, giving it greater credibility and legitimacy in Bolivia. The new strategy offered the possibility for the long-term success in limiting coca production that had eluded past governments by promoting economic development in poor rural areas and cooperative coca crop reduction.

The U.S. "War on Drugs"

The explosion of the crack cocaine epidemic in the United States in the mid-1980s led the U.S. Congress to pass increasingly draconian legislation intended to thwart both illicit drug abuse and the violence and other social problems associated with the drug trade at home. U.S. officials placed blame on the foreign countries where illicit drugs were produced—primarily the Andean region of South America and Mexico. Policies were developed to decrease the supply of illicit drugs by eradicating the production of coca, curbing cocaine production in overseas laboratories, and seizing shipments en route.

For the past two decades, approximately two-thirds of federal funding for drug control programs has gone to programs to limit supply, with only one-third designated for treatment and education to reduce demand. The premise for the policy was that limiting supply would drive up the price of illicit substances and lead to decreased consumption. Both the premise and the policy would prove to be a failure.

The U.S. appetite for drugs was also cast in national security terms. In 1986, President Reagan first declared illicit drugs a national security threat. In 1989, President George H. W. Bush launched the Andean Initiative, which led to a dramatic increase in U.S. involvement in the so-called source countries of Bolivia, Colombia, and Peru, where coca is grown. At the same time, the U.S. Congress designated the Defense Department as the single lead agency for the detection and monitoring of illicit drugs. Latin American militaries and police forces were provided with U.S. economic assistance, training, and intelligence and logistical support to carry out counterdrug initiatives.

The expanded role of the United States and Latin American security forces in domestic counterdrug efforts is commonly referred to as the militarization of U.S. drug policy. Since September 11, 2001, coca grower leaders have been included on U.S. terrorist lists, targeted as "narco-terrorists." Within this policy framework, economic development and democratic institution building were usually minimized.

Governments in the Andean region initially resisted the forced eradication at the heart of the U.S. approach—particularly the nascent civilian government in Bolivia, where the military had only recently returned to the barracks after decades of violent dictatorships. (Bolivia has notoriously suffered 182 military coups since gaining independence in 1825—a regional record.) While U.S. officials considered coca farmers to be the first link in the chain leading to drug abuse in the United States,

Bolivian and other Andean officials saw poor farmers who were trying to eke out a subsistence-level living. Forced coca eradication pitted government forces against one of the most vulnerable segments of the population; conflict and violence resulted.

Despite this initial resistance, Washington used its political muscle to ensure compliance. In 1986, the U.S. Congress passed legislation mandating the president to annually "certify" that major drug-producing and transit countries were cooperating fully with U.S. antidrug programs. Countries that were not certified faced a range of sanctions, including a cutoff in U.S. financial assistance, *no* votes on loans from multilateral development banks, and discretionary trade sanctions.[22] In Bolivia's case, annual coca eradication targets had to be met to receive U.S. certification.

Bolivia is particularly susceptible to such pressure. As one of the most impoverished countries in Latin America, it is heavily dependent on U.S. foreign aid and on aid from international lending institutions closely tied to the U.S. government. As a result, Bolivia has long followed Washington's marching orders on drug control policies. U.S. lawyers reportedly drafted the Bolivian "Law to Regulate Coca and Controlled Substances," commonly referred to as Law 1008, while the U.S. Embassy lobbied heavily for its approval by the Bolivian Congress in 1988. Ultimately, the U.S. government made approval of the law a condition for releasing U.S. aid.[23]

Until the election of President Morales, Law 1008 provided the legal framework for repressive coca eradication efforts. The draconian statute, among other features, set up a special U.S.-funded team of antidrug prosecutors and required that all Bolivians accused of a drug offense be held in jail, with no option for bail or release, until the process of trial was completed. Given that these trials often took years to complete, the effect was that those arrested were treated as guilty until proven innocent.

In May 1990, the Bolivian government also capitulated to U.S. pressure and signed a secret agreement that formalized a role for the Bolivian armed forces, including the army, in counterdrug operations. As it was a wildly unpopular move, the Paz Zamora government repeatedly denied the existence of the agreement. Despite the public outcry after news of the accord finally leaked out, the Bolivian armed forces had already gained a growing foothold in the drug war, with little if any oversight by civilian officials.

The Bolivian military and police forces dedicated to counterdrug efforts have been funded almost solely by Washington, creating even greater dependency and further skewing bilateral relations. The U.S. government has provided antidrug forces with everything from uniforms to weapons and the cost of feeding the arrested, as well as the special U.S. bonuses paid directly to Law 1008 prosecutors. Critics have complained that the country's judiciary has become directly subservient to the United States and that prosecutors have jailed innocent people by the thousands to satisfy U.S. officials. Because the U.S. government has held the purse strings and accounting has been far from transparent, the Bolivian government has been unable to calculate the budget for its counterdrug program. "We don't even know the cost of a basic antidrug operation," complained one former Bolivian official, "as it is all paid for by the U.S. Embassy."[24]

Throughout the 1990s, the Chapare coca-growing region experienced cyclical patterns of dialogue and conflict. Wanting to avoid social unrest among the powerful coca grower movement, successive governments offered economic compensation in exchange for voluntary eradication, even while forced coca eradication continued. However, such promises were rarely fulfilled, and minimum eradication goals had to be met to keep the U.S. aid spigot open. Inevitably, as the annual deadline neared, periods of relative calm were followed by conflict and violence.

Plan Dignidad and the High Cost of Eradication

The cycle was interrupted by the election of former dictator Hugo Banzer Suárez to the presidency in 1997, which eliminated dialogue and made conflict the norm. Banzer declared that Bolivia would achieve "zero coca" in five years and launched a massive eradication offensive as part of Plan Dignidad, or "Plan Dignity." Coca in the Chapare was the primary target of this initiative; the traditional growing zone of the Yungas was not. The armed forces were used for on-the-ground operations, and approximately five thousand troops were moved into the Chapare, greatly increasing tensions. Young military conscripts guarded by antidrug police made their way across the region, pulling out coca plants as distraught families watched their primary source of cash income going up in fire and smoke.

Initially, the program produced impressive gains in decreasing coca production. By 2000, the government said it had almost met its goal of zero coca. The gains, however, proved to be short-lived. By 2001, coca production was on the rise and had increased by 23 percent in 2002.[25] The reason that the policy was not sustainable in the long run was simple: eradication far outpaced the provision of economic alternatives. "Alternative Development," which was intended to offer coca growers other cash crops, was one of Plan Dignidad's primary pillars and showed little success. Poor peasants had no choice but to replant coca—which they did at a rapid rate.

The economic, social, and political costs of the U.S.-backed "war on drugs" in Bolivia, and Plan Dignidad in particular, were extremely high. Forced eradication efforts led to human rights violations including executions, illegal detentions, and torture. Massive sweeps of the coca-growing region led to hundreds of arbitrary detentions where those arrested were presumed guilty until proved innocent. Though ultimately released, most detainees were never presented before judicial authorities or allowed to notify family members of their arrest. Reports of mistreatment and even the torture of detainees became disturbingly common.

As coca production plummeted, so did the incomes and hence the health and nutrition standards of local residents. As income levels fell, families had less to spend on health needs and children were taken out of school so they could work in order to supplement the household income. Though hard data are not available, local health care and education officials repeatedly complained of a surge in malnutrition-related illnesses and declining school attendance.[26] Social discontent resulted in violent confrontations and blockades of highways that shut down regions of the country for months at a time. During these protests, food supplies rotted on trucks and commerce ceased, with a significant negative impact on the Bolivian economy.

Many lives were lost during these years. Dozens of coca growers were killed during eradication campaigns or during protests that turned violent. Police and military officials were also killed. In some cases, circumstances were murky; however, even clear-cut murders have not been investigated or sanctioned.

The killing of coca grower Casimiro Huanca presents a particularly disturbing case. It began in December 2001, when a small protest took place in the town of Chimoré.[27] Coca growers had stacked boxes of fruit on the side of the road to protest lack of markets for alternative crops. At one point, soldiers followed coca growers, including Huanca, as they headed toward a union office. According to those present, Huanca was shot twice at close range. He bled to death from the wounds. His killer was identified as Juan Eladio Bora, a member of the Expeditionary Task Force (ETF), a paramilitary antidrug force funded by the U.S. government. The Bolivian military tribunal determined that Bora acted in self-defense, despite the evidence indicating that neither Huanca nor any of his colleagues threatened him or other ETF members at any time.[28]

As in other cases, the U.S. Embassy defended the military's action. In a 2002 interview with U.S. Embassy officials, the "human rights" officer said that the shooting of Huanca could not be considered a human rights violation, because he was shot in the groin. He even went so far as to accuse local human rights activists of his death, saying they did not get him adequate medical attention. However, the health facilities necessary to treat him did not exist in the region.[29]

Angry farmers, sometimes armed with machetes, have also posed a threat to the police and soldiers called out to quash protests. Between 1997 and 2004, 35 coca growers and 27 police and military personnel were killed; nearly 600 coca growers and 140 military and police were injured.[30] Impunity became the norm for human rights violations attributed to members of the Bolivian security forces, as well as for farmers accused of killing soldiers or police.

Eventually Bolivians' patience with outspoken U.S. ambassadors and repeated U.S. meddling in domestic politics wore thin. During the 2002 presidential elections, U.S. ambassador Manuel Rocha spoke out directly against Morales, who was a candidate, warning that Bolivia would lose U.S. economic support and become an international pariah if the electorate "played footsie with coca growers."[31] Morales shot up in the polls and lost by only 1.5 percent of the vote. Morales's stunning presidential victory in 2005 was in part due to Washington's relentless—and ultimately unsuccessful—antidrug crusade. The conflict, violence, and economic hardship caused by coca eradication policies, among other issues, helped propel Morales into the national spotlight and generated popular support for his anti-U.S. rhetoric.

Coca Yes, Cocaine No

As a coca grower himself, President Morales has had an unprecedented opportunity to put into place an antidrug strategy that could win broad Bolivian support.[32] The new government's goal was to limit coca production that fuels the cocaine market but avoid the conflict and violence that have characterized previous policy. Morales also made clear his intention to continue combating the illicit drug business, stating in his inaugural address, "We are convinced that drug trafficking is a disease afflicting humanity."[33]

The basis of Morales's plan was to carry out cooperative coca reduction and extend it into other coca-producing areas previously unaffected by forced eradication. Based on an agreement signed in October 2004 by the then president Carlos Mesa, the Morales government continued to allow each coca-growing family to maintain one *cato* of coca (1,600 square meters, or a little more than one-third of an acre). The agreement required that any coca grown beyond that be subject to eradication. In addition, coca farmers accepted eradication in the two major national parks in the region. Initially with a one-year mandate, the October 2004 agreement put an end to forced eradication. If cooperative coca eradication is going to have long-term success, it will require that effective monitoring systems be put in place.[34]

In the Chapare, the strategy to limit coca production appears to be working, and the lack of conflict and violence has contributed to an environment that is conducive to economic development. According to local journalist Juan Alanoca, "In economic terms, the situation has improved. People are now assured that they will have some money from coca."[35] This allows them greater flexibility to experiment with other agricultural products and seek out other income-generating opportunities—key elements of a long-term coca reduction strategy (discussed in more detail later in this chapter). In both its first and second years in office the Morales government met its goal of eliminating 5,000 hectares (12,350 acres) of coca but without the violence characteristic of previous administrations.

"Popular participation and cooperation has increased with this government," says Col. Miguel Vásquez, former director of the country's antidrug police.[36] With that participation comes cooperative regulation that is far more effective than the heavy hand of unilateral forced eradication and interdiction. However, the continued use of the Bolivian military in coca reduction efforts and U.S. pressure to meet eradication targets have led to violence in other coca-growing regions. In September 2006, two coca growers were killed in a confrontation with members of a joint military-police eradication force in the Vandiola Yungas. The tragedy illustrates the difficulties the government faces in implementing its coca strategy in areas where coca has traditionally been grown and where farmers are largely dependent on the cultivation of coca as their principal crop.

Challenges for the Future

Despite skepticism and resistance to some aspects of the new Bolivian government's approach, the U.S. government has continued its antidrug

---

BOX 6.2 | Who's Who in Bolivia's "War on Drugs"

Some of the key players in the drug war include:[1]

Coca grower unions: Local grassroots organizations in the coca-growing regions that have been the basis for resistance for coca farmers against "war on drugs" initiatives.

The Expeditionary Task Force (ETF): A paramilitary antidrug force funded by the U.S. government, which was disbanded after repeated accusations of serious human rights violations in the Chapare.

The Joint Task Force (JTF): A combined military and police unit in charge of eradication until 2006 and then voluntary coca eradication under the Morales government.

The Bolivian Special Antinarcotic Police (FELCN): A special branch of the national police that oversees interdiction of illicit drugs and precursor chemicals used to make drugs.

The U.S. State Department's Bureau of International Narcotics and Law Enforcement Affairs (INL): Through its Narcotic Affairs Section (NAS) and Air Wing, the INL supports and assists all interdiction and eradication forces.

The Narcotic Affairs Section (NAS): A section of the U.S. State Department that oversees drug war policy on the ground.

The Mobile Rural Patrol Unit (UMOPAR): The rural arm of the FELCN, whose members have special training in antinarcotics intervention.

The U.S. Embassy, La Paz: Meets routinely with Bolivian government officials to coordinate policy and implement programs and operations.

The U.S. Agency for International Development (USAID): Represents the largest of all international donors in efforts of alternative development.

1. U.S. Department of State, International Narcotics Control Strategy Report 2007, Bolivia section: www.state.gov/p/inl/rls/nrcrpt/2007/

---

programs in Bolivia and collaborates closely on drug interdiction efforts in particular. While tensions often run high and the uneasy truce could easily dissipate, both governments point out that a rupture in bilateral relations would not benefit either country.

The key to the potential success of the new government's approach on eradication will be its ability to prevent the replanting of destroyed crops, a problem that has thwarted long-term success in the past. To date, initial results are promising. In 2006 and 2007, government efforts to work collaboratively with coca grower federations and individual communities to reduce cultivation met with success. At the time of this writing, violence and conflict have, for the most part, been avoided, creating a climate more propitious for rural economic growth.

The future challenge, however, will be to provide economic opportunities to improve overall quality of life for those traditionally dependent on coca cultivation. To the extent that drug crop eradication efforts have succeeded, it has been in Asia—most notably Thailand—where the government put into place comprehensive development programs to increase both the income levels and the standards of living of local farmers, which were then weaned from opium poppy production. Eradication efforts were carried out in collaboration with the local community and within a framework of respect for the rule of law and human rights. Development and law enforcement efforts were kept separate in order to ensure the continued support of the local population. In adopting a similar approach, the Bolivian government could be the first Latin American country to repeat this Asian success story.

PORTRAITS FROM THE BOLIVIAN DRUG WAR

Beyond the debate over the public policies involved in Bolivia's U.S.-backed "war on drugs" lie the stories of the people affected. The chief victims of that war are the thousands of innocent people sent to jail to beef up arrest statistics and the subsistence farmers trying to eke out a living by growing the small, green leaf.[37]

A Baby Turns One in Jail Courtesy of the "War on Drugs"
JIM SHULTZ

If it hadn't been her mother's birthday that day, Lourdes Mamani probably wouldn't have spent twenty-two months in a Cochabamba jail. Her son Marcos wouldn't have spent his first birthday, on the fourth of July, in that same jail with her, courtesy of the U.S. "war on drugs."

On June 23, 1999, Lourdes was in her mother's kitchen baking her a cake when a distant cousin, Eduardo, showed up at the front door. He said he had come to pick up two small sealed opaque plastic bags, which Lourdes's older brother had stored in their father's small tool room. The bags were filled with *q'owa,* he told her, a common plant burned like incense during the first-Friday-of-each-month rituals by the same name. She helped him carry the bags to a waiting taxi. He declined an invitation to join them for cake, and he left.

Two hours later there was another knock at the door. This time it was two uniformed officers from the FELCN, Bolivia's special antinarcotics police. Lourdes's cousin, they told her, had been arrested with two bags of marijuana and had given the police a false name. The officers had traced the cousin back to the house where he picked up the bags and demanded that Lourdes or her mother come with them to the jail to identify him.

With a promise that they would drive her to the jail and promptly return her to her mother's house, Lourdes swept her baby into her arms and got into the backseat of the officers' car. At the jail she gave them the identification of her cousin that they asked for, but instead of being driven home, Lourdes and Marcos were locked in a ten-by-fifteen-foot concrete cell with a dozen other women and their children and infants. "I've always accepted that I am poor, that I wear old clothes," she explained. "I never chose to do anything illegal to change that. Never in my life did I think I would be here."[38]

Law 1008 Claims a New Victim

Like all those accused of a drug-related crime in Bolivia, Lourdes was prosecuted under Bolivia's notorious Law 1008, the draconian statute under which all those accused are held in jail, with no option for bail or release. In 1999, the year Lourdes was jailed, more than 1,000 of the nearly 1,400 prisoners in Cochabamba had never been sentenced, never had the chance to defend themselves at a trial. The situation became so desperate that women prisoners went on hunger strikes—sewing their mouths shut with heavy needles and thread, or crucifying themselves to a jail balcony—in a desperate move to call public attention to their situation.

In 2001, a new penal code was passed with the intention of lessening the wait period for cases. While that may provide better treatment for some, it still makes little difference to those who can't afford an able lawyer. In 2007, Cochabamba's six prisons still confined 1,315 inmates, half of whom were sent to jail under Law 1008. In the San Sebastian women's prison, three-quarters of the 122 women were there as a result of the drug law.[39] Most of those women live in the prison with their young children.

The prosecutor who put Lourdes behind bars was one of those receiving a special salary bonus directly from the U.S. Embassy. A former member of the prosecution team explained at the time: "If I heard it once, I heard it a hundred times, 'we have to justify the bonuses.'"[40] What that meant was clear, ever-increasing arrest statistics that U.S. officials could use as evidence of success. In 1999, the year Lourdes was one of those statistics, the number of arrests boasted by the U.S. Embassy was 2,050. That also included the twenty-two-year-old taxi driver who had the misfortune of picking up Lourdes's cousin as a passenger that June day. For that turn of fate, he also spent twenty-two months locked in jail. By 2005, the number arrested had more than doubled, to 4,376.[41]

It is clear when you enter any of the Cochabamba jails that the people most often caught in the drug war's net are Bolivia's poor. Those with resources can often buy their way out, or at least hire a capable lawyer to argue their case. Those who can't, end up in the frustrating and frightening maze of the Bolivian drug courts.

In Cuffs in Front of Her Daughters

A month after her arrest, and after Marcos's first birthday, Lourdes was allowed to transfer from the special drug jail, where she and her cellmates slept on rotation for lack of floor space, to the San Sebastian jail for women. Set off a quiet plaza near the center of town, the decaying brick building was constructed to house a hundred prisoners. When Lourdes—for a two-hundred-dollar fee—was allowed to move there, more than two hundred women occupied the jail, plus their children.

Lourdes's trial could hardly have been more different from the stuff of a television drama. The process dribbled out in bits and pieces over nearly two years. Each piece—the reading of charges by the prosecutor, the response by the defendants, the offering of testimony—took place separately, often with months passing in between. Lourdes would wait nervously for each new hearing date to be set. Each trip to court meant hope that the case might slowly be inching forward to a conclusion. Each also meant the humiliation of being escorted into the courtroom in handcuffs before the downcast eyes of her four young daughters. On a number of occasions the lawyers, the witnesses, the families, and the cuffed defendants, all crowded anxiously into the hallway outside the courtroom, would just be sent away because the three-judge panel hearing the case hadn't managed to make it back from lunch.

During the course of her time in jail, Lourdes missed the birth of her first grandchild, had to send her baby son off to the doctor in the hands of her teenage daughters, and missed the high school graduation of her eldest daughter. The graduation ceremony, it turns out, was just across the street from the jail. As a family friend remembered, "I will never forget the silhouette of a girl in cap and gown making her way through the entrance of the jail to see her mother."

By the start of 2001, Lourdes had been in jail for eighteen months and, because her trial had still not delivered a verdict, she became eligible for provisional release. Four months later, after spending twenty-two months in jail, Lourdes walked out the doors of San Sebastian and went home with her children.

But Lourdes's name still had not been cleared. As her trial was ending, two of the judges sitting on the panel abruptly resigned and were replaced. The new panel pulled the names of each defendant out of a hat to decide who would rule on which case.[42] The judge who drew Lourdes's name had been on the court for only a few weeks, hadn't been present for any of the testimony by any of the witnesses, had never set eyes on Lourdes or her family. He found her guilty and sentenced her to five years in jail. Her conviction was sent for appeal to the Bolivian Supreme Court in Sucre, where it sits along with thousands of others, lost in a maze of paperwork that will probably never be looked at again. Every month, as she awaits a final verdict, Lourdes has to take a bus downtown to the courthouse in Cochabamba to sign a book verifying that she still lives in the city and hasn't fled.

Cocaleros: *Stories from the Chapare*
CAITLIN ESCH AND LENY OLIVERA ROJAS

A curvy mountain road connects the dry, high valley city of Cochabamba to the steamy jungle town of Villa Tunari. The air thickens and oppresses the lungs throughout the four-hour descent. The small town sits on the main highway that connects Cochabamba with Santa Cruz and serves as the political center of the Chapare, the coca-growing region most associated with export of the leaf for the drug market. The town's dirt roads are puddled from the region's frequent cloudbursts. Palm trees line the streets, and a handful of hotels and restaurants cater to the town's seasonal surge in tourism. Peasant farmers with wheelbarrows full of bananas, oranges, and tropical fruit sell their crops along the main road. Verdant mountains loom in the background.

The Transplanted Farmer
Forty minutes by car outside of Villa Tunari, the main road passes through a military drug checkpoint, then turns from pavement to cobblestone to dirt. Marina, a thirty-six-year old *cocalera,* lives deep in the

green overgrowth, beyond the town of Eterazama. A few houses, elevated on stilts, peek out through the thick greenery. Women wash colorful clothing where the river crosses the road, while children splash and take cold baths.

A light rain sounds on the tin roof of the small structure that Marina uses as her kitchen. The dirt floor is freshly swept and the space is tidy. Marina sits on a stool, leaning over the three large stones and flaming kindling wood that serve as her stove. She is stirring a large pot of broth, talking to herself quietly in her native Quechua. Two long black braids twisted skillfully over her head are tied tightly with hair ornaments common in the region.

In 1982, at the age of twelve, Marina moved to the Chapare from Tarabuco, an arid region near the highland city of Sucre, where her family farmed.[43] She said that the droughts forced her family of ten to relocate. Marina spent the remainder of her childhood in the Chapare and eventually was able to rent a *chaco*, a small plot of land, on which to grow coca. Half of her crop went to the landlord and half she kept, either to sell or for personal use. By the time Marina was eighteen, she had saved up enough money to buy her own *chaco* with her husband. Today, Marina grows her crop on a little bit more than half an acre. "It isn't enough," she asserted. Abandoned nine years ago by her husband, Marina continues to work her land alone, "which," she said, "is extremely difficult." Living at a subsistence level, Marina supports herself, her two teenage daughters, and a grandchild on eight hundred bolivianos (about one hundred U.S. dollars) a month earned from the coca she grows and sells.[44]

The Miner's Daughter

Cintia, twenty-eight years old, is also a *cocalera* from the Chapare. But unlike Marina, Cintia has temporarily exchanged life in the Chapare for a life in the city of Cochabamba.[45] The daughter of a Cochabambino father, the dusty-eyed Cintia spent her early years in the mountain town of Potosí, where her father worked in the mines. Along the way her father contracted *mal de minas,* a colloquialism used to refer to the serious lung infection, silicosis, that commonly afflicts miners. No longer able to work in the mines, Cintia's father decided to pursue an agricultural life in the lowlands. While his family (his wife and eight children) stayed in Cochabamba, her father went to the Chapare in hopes of establishing himself as a *cocalero*. In 1990, after five years of renting land on which to grow his crop, Cintia's father was able to buy his own *chaco* deep in the jungle of Ivirgarzama—a half hour by car from the highway.

Cintia said her father chose to grow coca because it was the most lucrative crop available to him in 1985. He was eventually able to move Cintia and her siblings to live with him in the Chapare. Since 1990, the family *chaco* has grown, enabling the family to produce three hundred pounds of coca leaf every three months, which amounts to a little less than four hundred dollars in income.

Coca Growing as a Family Tradition

Juan, now forty-six, was born and raised in the Chapare into a family where the tradition of growing coca goes back generations.[46] In 1952, his grandparents were among the first coca growers to come from Yungas de Vandiola, a small pocket of traditional coca farms near the Chapare, to settle in Paracti, a town just a few miles outside of Villa Tunari.

"All my life I have been a *cocalero* like my grandparents." Juan said that he grows coca because "the plant has been cultivated in this zone for centuries and is the sustenance of my family. There used to be ancient trees [of coca] here that you could pick from. But these trees disappeared during the forced eradication." He described the ancestral techniques of coca cultivation, passed down through generations, but noted, "The miners who migrated here do not know of these practices." Juan, his wife, and the three children who still live with them (two of his sons have emigrated to Spain) cultivate the family's land. "We earn, more or less, 2,500 bolivianos ($300) every three months. This is our salary; this is our sustenance."

Facing the Drug War

Coca grower unions are an important part of life in the Chapare. Before the drug war, the unions assigned land, resolved disputes, and undertook community projects such as building schools or roads. After the U.S.-backed forced eradications began in the 1990s, the unions became the forefront of *cocalero* organizing to protect their crops. "Huge numbers of men would come in trucks. Hundreds of them," Marina recounted, "and they would beat me and my daughter." The eradication soldiers would smash cooking ware and steal leftover food so that Marina would have nothing left to feed her family. Then they would destroy her crops. She knows several women, she said, who were raped. It was in response to experiences like these that the *cocaleros* became one of the most radical and politicized forces among Bolivia's impoverished, a trajectory that would eventually make their leader, Evo Morales, the nation's president.

Both Marina and Cintia said that things are getting better for coca growers. When asked about the current MAS government, which took office in January 2006, Marina said she unequivocally supported President Morales. "Evo used to come to my *chaco* and we would dance. But now that he's president, he doesn't come anymore." For many coca growers, Morales is still a local personality, and it has taken time for them to adjust their vision of his new responsibilities as president of the country.

The challenges confronting *cocaleros* in the Chapare region are still significant. Single mothers, common in the Chapare, are faced with the task of raising children and maintaining *chacos* entirely on their own. "Who is going to help me on my *chaco*?" Marina asks rhetorically with an exasperated sigh. But Cintia, five months pregnant and engaged to a military official, looks forward to moving her immediate family back to the Chapare after having been in Cochabamba to study. Thanks to coca, she said, she was able to save enough money to go to college in Cochabamba in 1996. Now she wants to return to the Chapare and buy her own *chaco* and grow coca with her father and siblings. Despite the challenges of farming in this tropical region, Cintia, like many other coca farmers, chooses to make her life in the Chapare.

COCA AND THE SEARCH FOR ALTERNATIVES

LINDA FARTHING

"Coca substitution completely failed under past governments," Bolivia's vice minister in charge of drug control, Felipe Cáceres, told reporters in August 2006. "But our government's plan has an important innovation: the focus is on the struggle against poverty. We will work on health, education, roads, electrification and . . . opening markets. . . . The best way that countries can help us in the struggle against drugs is to open up their markets to us."[47]

Offering a viable alternative to coca cultivation has long been the Holy Grail to reducing production and ensuring that coca is not going into the drug trade. Throughout the long "war on drugs" in Bolivia, its architects have promised that alternative development is the best option for coca farmers to earn their income in other ways. Coca growers, however, have always questioned whether alternative development is a real strategy for crop replacement or merely a fig leaf to distract attention from harsh eradication measures. Evidence of alternative development's failure to deliver on its promises can be seen in the empty buildings—optimistically constructed over the last two decades to process crops such as palm hearts or milk products—that are now rapidly deteriorating in the hot and steamy Chapare lowlands.

Part of the problem is that coca is an almost perfect crop. It generates four harvests per year and weighs much less than alternatives such as fruit, important in regions where products have to be hand-carried partway to market. Despite sometimes sharp fluctuations in prices, coca has consistently provided a relatively stable income to farmers. What, then, can provide enough security to farmers to convince them to take the risk to switch to a new crop? This is a particularly difficult task given an economic environment that is more often than not in crisis, and in a country with one of the highest rates of rural poverty in the world.

Alternative Development and the Flawed U.S. Approach

Alternative development refers to a spectrum of development strategies that aim to provide income to farmers so that they no longer have to depend economically on the cultivation of coca. Since the Chapare region has long been pegged as the largest source of the country's illicit coca production, it has been the primary focus of such programs. Since 1982, the U.S. Agency for International Development (USAID) has relied on two basic approaches—first, try to stem migration into the Chapare, and second, promote direct crop replacement among the families already there and growing coca. Reliable figures on how much has been spent by the United States to pursue these objectives are extremely hard to come by, but estimates are approximately $300 million over the course of two decades.[48]

The USAID approach to crop substitution tried to entice coca growers into shifting to banana, pineapple, passion fruit, palm hearts, and black pepper. But all of the U.S. projects centered around alternative crops have failed for four basic reasons. First, alternative crops can rarely compete economically with coca. Second, alternative development was poorly planned and executed with the focus on reducing coca instead of reducing poverty. The United States promoted crops without serious market analysis and without adequate thought to transportation, infrastructure, and adequate technical support. Third, participation in these development programs was consistently conditioned on total eradication of coca, which is unrealistic considering that without coca, most farmers would have no income at all beyond the crops they grow for their own consumption. Finally, the United States refused any cooperation with existing coca-growing unions and municipal governments in implementing its projects.

When asked about her experience with alternative development, Chapare coca grower Marina scoffed softly: "It doesn't work."[49] "You can't make enough money growing palm hearts and pineapples when you only get forty centavos [$0.05] for a palm heart and three to four pineapples for one boliviano [$0.13]." Compared to the one thousand bolivianos ($125) reaped for one hundred pounds of coca, alternative development crops face stiff competition.

Juan explained that "the price of fruit is so low that it doesn't even cover the cost of renting a truck to transport it."[50] He noted that one hundred mandarin oranges in the Chapare can be sold by small-scale farmers for between three and six bolivianos ($0.40 and $0.80). Cintia concurred: "Growing fruit is difficult because it can only be harvested once a year and [in some cases] needs to be replanted after every harvest. It is time-consuming and expensive." Juan explained how he tried to grow pineapples, but since alternative development projects had promoted the crop widely, the fruit flooded the domestic market and prices dropped to $0.03 each. Juan made twenty-seven bolivianos (less than $4) on his crop. Farmers reported similar alternative development failures with crops such ginger root and palm hearts.

Coca grower frustration and distrust was only reinforced after visits to "model farms" in fancy agricultural stations, staffed by Bolivian professionals often earning in a month what farmers earn in a year. The presence of highly paid U.S. supervisors, racing back and forth in new jeeps from the Chapare to offices in one of Cochabamba's most luxurious office buildings, contributed to suspicions among farmers that the primary goal of the projects was to eradicate coca, not to create viable alternatives.

U.S. alternative development programs have been carried out against a backdrop of systematic and persistent harassment and repression of coca-growing families rather than being paired with regional initiatives that could help make alternative development successful. Police and military repression—not economic development—has consistently characterized U.S. policy. Coca growers on the ground have demanded just the opposite, wanting to trade in the international notoriety that coca has brought them for the kinds of resources that have never been available to Bolivia's rural indigenous poor. Teófilo Blanco expressed what coca growers have repeated for twenty years: "We have no potable water, health [services], or education systems. For us to give up coca, we have to have some of those things. We are demanding fair rights according to Bolivia's political constitution."[51]

Despite repeated promises for high levels of investment in basic infrastructure, few concrete results could be seen on the ground. Teófilo Blanco went on to explain: "They promised to build a bridge, but they haven't done it. I planted coffee but haven't been able to sell a single kilo. If you think I'm lying, I invite a high level commission to come to my farm to verify if there are any roads or development."[52] This frustration, combined with constant U.S.-financed militarized repression, created almost constant unrest throughout the 1990s in the Chapare, often disrupting the entire region.

Repeated failure was ensured by the United States' determination to condition assistance on coca eradication. This type of conditionality has long been perceived by U.S. officials as key to successful eradication programs.[53] Until the late 1990s, coca farmers were induced, usually through mounting repression, to give up coca in exchange for financial and technical assistance in switching to new crops. But often assistance arrived late or not at all or was insufficient when it did. With no work elsewhere in the country, and faced literally with concerns about survival, many growers went back to coca shortly after the eradicators left. Teófilo Blanco explained: "Many farmers have taken their kids out of school because they no longer have the economic means, and they're planting coca again."[54]

Alternative development programs have also historically been plagued by political considerations.[55] Until recently, USAID continually refused to see coca as anything other than a potential ingredient for cocaine and would not work with local peasant unions. From 1995 on, USAID also refused to work with the newly formed municipal governments, since they were dominated by the coca growers' political party, MAS. U.S. officials claimed that the poor peasant farmers—who make an estimated average one thousand dollars a year—were drug dealers. To override the existing local organizations, USAID created alternative structures, called "associations," which fomented suspicion and distrust. Some associations have existed on paper only, and many members kept a foot in both camps by retaining their union affiliation.

Coca grower Jorge Bautista explained: "I was one of the first producers in my zone to participate in alternative development programs.

I formed the first association of my region and four other associations. But now I am poorer and almost lost my house. I know I have deceived many of my fellow coca growers with these associations and that only through the union can we effectively push our demands."[56]

A Different Path

In the mid-1990s, two initiatives not associated with the United States brought new direction to alternative development and ultimately planted the seeds for a new vision forward. In 1994, a decentralization measure known as the Law of Popular Participation mandated that 20 percent of national tax revenues go to newly formed municipalities, accompanied by community oversight of the funds. Coca growers quickly appropriated this new political opening and won control of Chapare municipalities, forming a base that later became the MAS party.[57] The second initiative began with the European Union's (EU) Chapare Alternative Development Program in 1998. The EU's approach reflects the recommendations made by hundreds of experts on alternative development: focus on economic development without conditions requiring eradication.[58] According to Felipe Cáceres, the vice minister who was previously a coca grower and Chapare mayor, the EU program "in eight years, with one fourth of the money, achieved ten times what USAID accomplished in twenty years."[59]

In early 2003, U.S. policy began a gradual shift. Although it maintained its emphasis on eradication and its discourse that coca growers are drug dealers, USAID began to work directly with Chapare municipalities for the first time. By 2005, it had put a new face on its program by renaming it "integrated alternative development." The United States boasts that the value of alternative development crops and products leaving the Chapare in 2005 increased by a third in just one year, to a total of $34.9 million, demonstrating a modest success after twenty years.[60] It was not to be long-lived however. In 2004–2005 U.S. funding for economic aid dropped while funds for law enforcement increased.[61]

In the Yungas, the region associated with coca grown for traditional use, the United States has pursued a different strategy. In 2002, USAID started working through local municipalities, providing training for municipal employees and support for projects including construction of potable water systems, college scholarships, tourism infrastructure, and improved specialty coffee production for export.

The MAS Vision and Its Challenges

The Morales government, in its policy of *"coca si, cocaína no"* (coca yes, cocaine no) has aimed to redefine eradication and alternative development. The key strategic premise of its policy is centered on three points: cooperative eradication rather than forced eradication; a focus on alternative uses of coca in addition to alternative crops; and the industrialization of coca into new products and finding dependable legal markets for these products. This new approach has valued not only the leaf but also the producers as active decision makers in their own economic development.

In October 2006, President Morales announced a half-million-dollar project financed by the Venezuelan government to set up a coca industrialization plant in the Chapare. The plant would produce coca wine and tea, medicines and sweets, all of which will be purchased by Venezuela.[62] Two coca industrialization plants in the Yungas, built and then abandoned by the United Nations' AgroYungas project in the 1980s, have been reactivated to manufacture coca flour and bagged coca tea. By providing more legal market alternatives for coca, the Morales administration has hoped to build a new national economy supportive of indigenous communities and divert the sale of coca from the drug trade.[63]

To be sure, the new administration's policy faces a number of difficult challenges. Internationally, in order to open up markets, Bolivia will need to win approval to remove the coca leaf from the UN list of controlled substances, where it has been since 1961. The 1995 World Health Organization study, which indicates that coca has no deleterious effects, will be critical for the Bolivian government's argument to win a decision that would allow it to market coca teas, foods, and medicines. The United States' suppression of the report indicates just how political that fight will be.[64]

After attending a Vienna meeting of the International Narcotics Control Board in March 2006, Vice Minister Felipe Cáceres returned to Bolivia less optimistic about a quick overturn of coca prohibition. In March 2007, the UN officials reiterated their opposition to an increase in the promotion of coca. The Morales government, however, pledged to continue its push to develop a plan for international decriminalization of the leaf. In February 2008, the UN went an extra step, asking Peru and Bolivia to ban all uses of coca, including chewing the leaf and drinking coca tea. UN representatives claimed that their job was to ensure compliance with the UN convention of 1961.

Another challenge will be to unify coca growers, whose interests differ from region to region. This will include winning acceptance among all coca growers, particularly those outside the Chapare, of the one-*cato*-per-family limit on coca cultivation. In November 2006, Chapare coca grower Vitalia Merida explained the new scenario to a visiting delegation, revealing that disagreements between Chapare growers and the Morales administration could lie ahead: "Having Evo as president has changed things a lot. We don't need the police or military anymore. Union leaders meet to figure out who has extra coca and then they take it out themselves. But the permitted amount is not enough to cover our needs, even though for now we respect the agreement on it."[65] In other areas, such as the formerly protected legal zone of the Yungas, coca growers have openly disagreed with the *cato* limit. Developing a common platform among coca growers is crucial to opening opportunities for industrialization and the decriminalization of the leaf abroad.

While the MAS victory led the United States to moderate its long-standing hard-line position, a new path for the "war on drugs" and alternative development will depend on just how patient the United States is with Bolivia. After Morales's election in December 2005, U.S. officials began distinguishing between coca and cocaine for the first time ever. They initially expressed a willingness to work with the new administration, although they largely suspended aid to the Chapare after the election and failed to release other promised funding.

Despite this uncertainty, hope exists that a more effective and humane policy can emerge. To date, however, the Morales government has failed to concretely develop and implement rural development plans or an economic assessment of the *cato* and industrialization initiatives.[66] How long the United States—and coca growers—will wait patiently for the MAS government to act remains to be seen. After twenty years of suffering and failed promises, coca growers expect substantial changes, and the Morales government understands this. As Felipe Cáceres explained: "If there are real alternatives, the Coca Grower Federations will welcome them. My whole life has been involved in this, and this awful situation has to change. I really want something else for my children."[67]

CONCLUSION: A TALE OF TWO PERSPECTIVES

Coca leaf has been part of Bolivia's indigenous culture for nearly four thousand years. It is a leaf that represents the gifts of Pachamama to her people and that provides income for families that barely have enough to feed their children. To U.S. antidrug officials and others, the coca represents an addictive drug that spreads crime and destroys communities. It is the raw ingredient for a white powder against which successive U.S. governments have declared open war. It has also become a leverage point by which foreign governments have maintained their influence in Bolivia over several decades. The gap between these views could not be any wider, and each side is clearly willing to fight to support what they believe in.

It is because of this conflict of views that, in Bolivia, coca has become a symbol of resistance. In the face of foreign policies demanding its eradication by force, under the heavy hands of special military units, coca became an emblem for how foreign powers impose their will on Bolivians from abroad. Fierce resentment against these policies pushed coca growers to organize. A culture of social resistance that was born five hundred years ago, and again in Bolivia's mines and haciendas from the 1930s on, was reborn in the coca fields of the Chapare in the 1980s and 1990s, often among the children and grandchildren of miners. Coca grower *sindicatos,* or unions, became the defense mechanisms for those who wanted to protect their right to their economic livelihood and those who seek to preserve their cultural sovereignty. Those unions, in turn, became both catalysts and teachers for other resistance movements that followed, including the battles against the privatization of water and the bargain-priced exportation of Bolivian gas.

If the architects of the "war on drugs" want to understand why their strategies continue to meet unyielding resistance in Bolivia, it is because that war has chosen as its target a way of life that is rooted in centuries of history and is also key to many families' economic survival. In reality, the conflict in perspectives between U.S. officials and Bolivian coca growers is based more on blindness that an actual conflict of interests. There is no reason *cocaleros* cannot simultaneously defend their cultural and economic right to grow coca while also recognizing the real damage that this plant can cause elsewhere if turned over to the drug market and transformed into cocaine. On the other hand, the United States can certainly pursue its interests in fighting drug addiction without destroying the cultural richness and the economic necessity of Bolivian coca cultivation.

If both sides can see this, then Bolivia has a real chance now to adopt practical solutions that can serve the interests of both. Coca growers have already shown a willingness to limit coca cultivation in excess of legal uses. Creative solutions that involve the participation of coca-growing communities, rather than the use of force, could bring economic alternatives to farmers while bolstering community vigilance against those who do supply coca to the drug trade. For new constructive solutions to work, however, U.S. and other drug officials must recognize coca's long-standing cultural and economic significance and, most important, Bolivia's sovereignty to make its own decisions.

The United States has had two decades to apply its approach, and its effects can be measured in numbers. The number of dead can be counted in the dozens. The number of innocent people jailed can be counted in the thousands. The number of U.S. tax dollars spent can be counted in the millions. Yet cocaine availability in the United States and abroad continues unabated. The moment has come for a different approach, and it is Bolivia's turn to take the lead.

Doña Maria, outside her home in the village of Chuñu Chuñuni, weaves in the tradition passed to her from her mother and grandmother on a pre-Columbian loom. Photo: Melissa Draper (2006).

CHAPTER 7

Workers, Leaders, and Mothers

Bolivian Women in a Globalizing World

Melissa Crane Draper

Many of the chapters in this book deal with specific moments in Bolivia's history when its reality has intersected with global forces. This chapter takes a different tack, drawing us into the lives of six women, through a series of shorter case studies. Through them, we see globalization's dual nature: its opportunities and simultaneous threats, across class and ethnic lines. Just as opportunities are amplified through more global interconnectedness—from jobs to international labor organizing—so too are the threats globalization poses to Bolivia's most vulnerable groups. Who has access to those opportunities, and who is most threatened by their exclusion?

Perhaps most important, these women's stories remind us that globalization goes far beyond economics. Its influences have come not only in the form of neoliberal economic policies but also with the influx of foreign cultures and ideas that challenge women to decide how they want to be leaders, mothers, wives, professionals, and members of their communities.

Bolivian women have been an inextricable part of the process of global integration. Economic forces from abroad have increasingly dominated the country's experience in the past three decades. Macroeconomic policies brought neoliberal principles to the country through the privatization of mines and public services like water. Women's burden as wives and mothers in the face of mine closures and the unemployment of their husbands forced them to find new types of income, as vendors in a local market in Sucre or orange juice squeezers on the streets of Cochabamba.

More women across Latin America are entering the workforce. In Bolivia, they represent 40 percent of working adults. This is a workforce that has been forced to become more flexible in order to respond to the demand of efficiency and lower costs amid growing competition across continents. This increasing demand for flexible, independent workers has made women an easy target for lax and insufficient labor protections, because they are working more and more in the isolation of their homes, combining their responsibilities as mothers, wives, and workers.

The strands of economic globalization, however, do not paint the complete picture. Woven into the economic dimension are the changing perceptions of women's identity as a response to the influx of ideas and exchange with Western values that accompany that economic influence. What it meant to be a mother, a caretaker of the family, a worker, or a local leader just thirty years ago has morphed rapidly, challenging women to play more complex roles. In some cases, this means preserving local values of family or female identity that don't match principles introduced from abroad.

In the instance of water privatization policies, the economic impact on everyday lives included not just higher water bills but communities' reconsideration of their relationship to water. As caretakers of local water systems, women were among those community leaders who staunchly defended their culture of water in the face of its commercialization. Similarly, the changing demand for labor does not only mean that women must adapt to be more flexible, independent workers; it also means women taking on a new identity as a worker and struggling against the marginalization that comes with the lack of basic rights.

The ways in which women are frequently marginalized in a globalizing economy are reflections and amplifications of their standing in Bolivian society. In a country that is South America's poorest and most indigenous, women experience an extreme form of social and political exclusion. Two-thirds of Bolivian women are indigenous. Close to 40 percent of women living in rural areas cannot read. Education rates are consistently below those of men as is the level of pay for the same job. Average fertility rates are as high as six children in rural communities. More Bolivian women die in childbirth than in any other country in Latin America.

Machismo, or the belief that men are inherently superior to women, is a powerful current in Bolivian society that is the basis for women's exclusion in private and public life. Seven in every ten women experience domestic violence. Local community unions, particularly in rural areas, continue to exclude women from participating in processes of community decision making. In the case of labor unions that have begun to recognize the importance of women's participation, such as the coca growers unions of the Chapare region, most women's leadership has taken root only in the last fifteen years and lies strictly in the shadow of their male counterparts. Legal recognition of women as owners of land was promoted in the 1996 land reform law but has never been enforced. When discrimination against women, as a result of *machismo,* is combined with women's identity as indigenous people and rural farmers, that marginalization from Bolivian society intensifies. When global forces, largely defined along capitalist ideals, enter the mix—where the mobile, profit-seeking individual prevails—the exclusion of women is further compounded.

Bolivian women experience the opportunities and threats from global integration in very different ways. A woman in the wealthy La Paz neighborhood of Calacoto might identify more easily with a working mother in Bethesda, Maryland, than with an Aymara woman farmer who lives within an hour's drive of La Paz. Deep class and cultural divisions, reinforced by increasing economic inequality in the wake of neoliberal economic policies, means Bolivian women's access to globalization's opportunities are just as diverse as the identities they represent.

Consistent with neoliberal principles, an individual woman equipped with a good education, language ability, physical assets, and a network of contacts can get access to capital, build partnerships, and navigate foreign markets. These are the tools that unlock the financial, legal, and technological systems that provide access to the economic benefits of a neoliberal economy. They also allow a young mother to take out a loan from a bank to start a business or an entrepreneur to use the Internet to match locally produced weavings with art galleries on two different continents.

For the women who don't have those tools—the majority of Bolivian women—improving their lives through economic globalization can happen only indirectly, through intermediaries. As a result, the benefits risk parallel threats to labor protection, basic consumer rights, and female and community identities. On the macro level, those intermediaries are the political and economic elite who join forces with foreign institutions to determine macroeconomic policies for the country. At the local level, those intermediaries are foreigners or local elites who leverage their tools of education, resources, and contacts to open economic or social opportunities.

Ultimately, it is the identity of women as women—a unique feminine identity—that weaves all these strands of class and ethnic differences, trade-offs between opportunities and threats, access and exclusion, into one. Women are set apart by a shared adaptability and entrepreneurship, whether in business or in public leadership. They also share a susceptibility to exclusion as mothers, caretakers, and workers in the context of a male-dominated society.

This chapter looks into the lives of six women from across Bolivia's spectrum of class, ethnicity, and culture to see just how different the impact of globalization can be on women. The first two sections look at women and labor issues in the context of global changes to the workforce and the opportunities and threats those changes bring. First, a rural weavers' association leverages access to foreign markets for traditional Bolivian textiles, boosted by a foreign-funded development project that also promotes women's empowerment. And home-based workers in an urban knitting cooperative are satisfying the increasing demand of foreign markets for more flexible workforces.

In contrast, the second section introduces professional women who, backed by an education and other resources, take advantage of global integration as individuals. These women have no need for the intermediaries that negotiate global access for urban knitters and rural weavers. These two women's stories show how two very different professional women have negotiated globalization in their lives, one in the private sector and the other as part of the nonprofit sector.

Finally, we turn to the ways in which individual women, although from traditionally marginalized classes, have leveraged the globalization of solidarity and philanthropy to the advantage of the groups they represent at a local level. One takes the leadership of an all-female union of household workers to an international stage, while the other works in a male-dominated organization, supported by international counterparts, but is determined to keep the focus of change at the local level.

WOMEN WORKERS: RURAL, URBAN, AND GLOBAL

The lives of two women—one in the rural highlands of central Bolivia and the other in the urban setting of Cochabamba—show how economic globalization's windows of opportunity for women workers also provide some strong lessons about its limitations and threats. In both instances, intermediaries have supported the creation of jobs for women to increase their income and enable them to access foreign markets. In the case of the rural weavers' association, a development project provided structure and financial support so that the weavers could apply their skills in traditional Andean weaving techniques. The urban knitters' cooperative accesses foreign markets through a private business owner, who contracts them to make handmade goods that are not specifically Bolivian. Both cases also indicate that the primary goal of creating jobs and increasing income leads to other risks these women must confront in the face of globalization, including their identity as women and the threats to their basic rights as workers.

Severina Vargas: Life in the Rural Highlands

Chuñu Chuñuni (pronounced Choon-yoo Choon-yoo-nee) is a small community perched on the top of a barren hillside among Bolivia's high central valleys at fourteen thousand feet. It got its name from *chuño*, the naturally freeze-dried potato that it once used to pay its taxes. The village is accessible by car along a rough dirt road or by a two-hour walk along a narrow path from the highway connecting Cochabamba and La Paz. Small adobe houses, home to about sixty families, dot the hillside. From the footpath, the only other structures in sight are the llama and sheep corrals made of stone, a small white church, a one-room community building, and an elementary school. On the wall in the community building, where the locals hold weekly literacy classes, phrases in the indigenous Quechua language are scrawled across a big cream-colored piece of paper.

Alone in a Village Not Her Own

Severina is not a native of Chuñu Chuñuni. She first arrived there as the new bride of her husband, whose entire extended family lives in the village. A petite woman, she wears her hair in long braids. Her cheeks, burnt by the highland sun and wind, guard a surprising smile. She first left her own village of Caripuyo, in the neighboring department of Potosí, four years earlier. She decided to accompany some relatives in search of land and opportunity in the lowland coca-growing region of the Chapare. That's where she met her husband, Emilio, who insisted they return to Chuñu Chuñuni to be closer to his family and begin their own. In the three years that followed, they built their own house, returned to highland

BOX 7.1 | Women and Bolivia's Informal Economy

At least three-quarters of all Bolivian women who work do so outside of the formal economy, where there is no regulation or protection for workers.[1] In the rural areas, this includes the parts of the economy that do not operate with cash. Rural families work for their own consumption—growing food, raising animals, and sewing clothes—or they barter with one another. The rural informal economy also includes the cash a family might make selling crops or textiles, or running a small store.

In the urban informal economy, women work primarily as vendors, domestic workers, and caretakers, where there is no government regulation of their working conditions, salary, or hours. Although there are fewer women than men in the overall workforce, more women depend on the informal economy for their income. In Latin America, it is estimated that more than half of all employment, without counting rural farmers, falls within the informal sector. In Bolivia, that figure is even higher: six of every ten urban workers are part of the informal economy. Of every ten working women, seven are part of the informal economy.[2]

Why do women enter into the informal economy? In Bolivia, the general lack of jobs means there is little space in the formal economy for women, especially those with little education. Some entrepreneurial women choose to take advantage of the flexibility of running their own stand in the local market. Others, like young domestic workers, see working in a private home as their ticket to getting from rural areas to the city and building a self-sufficient life.

The mining sector reveals the stark link between globalizing forces and women in the informal economy. A sweeping privatization of Bolivia's mines, pushed by international institutions in the 1980s, shows us how women miners

---

farming, and had two children. In addition to growing potatoes, the family has kept llamas and sheep, and even chose to open a small store out of their house, where they sold cans of food, drinks, batteries, and light bulbs.

On a Wednesday in December 2003, soon after Severina found out she was pregnant with her third child, her husband was killed in a truck accident. He had been returning from market day in the city of Cochabamba with goods for their store when the truck he was in flew over the side of a cliff. Severina, now a widow and single mother of three at thirty-two, chose to stay in Chuñu Chuñuni. To provide for her family, she had to work much harder, compensating for what her husband would have done. She was lucky to get support from her mother-in-law and other community members. In just this way, the Andean concept of family is based on inclusion and shared labor.[1]

Severina is one of many single mothers struggling to make ends meet in Bolivia. In the department of Cochabamba, nearly one in three

and miners' wives were forced into unprotected work conditions. The *palliris*, or women miners, make up 40 percent of the informal mining sector that now dominates Bolivia. Dismal work conditions keep these women working in ill-equipped mines with no supervision or protection.[3] For the families who left the mines after privatization, their best option was to head for the cities in search of new jobs. Women carry a major part of the burden compensating for their husband's unemployment when economic crisis hits. One survey revealed that half of women street vendors in downtown Cochabamba are wives of former miners.[4] When there is a shortage of regulated, salaried jobs, Bolivian women have little option but to make what they can of the informal economy.

1. This is a conservative estimate including rural women farmers (rural farmers make up 40 percent of overall population) and the 74 percent figure (from Comisión para América Latina y el Caribe, CEPAL) of urban women working in the informal economy. See International Labor Organization (ILO), "Women and Men in the Informal Economy: A Statistical Picture," 2002, www.ilo.org/public/english/employment/gems/download/women.pdf.

2. Statistics are taken from the following sources in order: Comisión para América Latina y El Caribe (CEPAL), *Panorama social de América Latina, 1999–2000* (Social panorama of Latin America, 19992–000); Instituto Nacional de Estadísticas (National Institute for Statistics), 2002: http://www.ine.gov.bo/; Jaques Charmes, *Women and Men in the Informal Economy: A Statistical Picture* (Lima, Peru: OIT, 1994–2000), as cited by the Global Labour Institute, www.global-labour.org/la_economia_informal.htm.

3. Cristina Echavarria, "The Formalization of Artisan and Small-Scale Mining," speech transcript, www.idrc.ca/en/ev-61463–201–1-DO_TOPIC.html.

4. Caitlin Esch, the Democracy Center, Cochabamba, October 2006. Survey information available at www.democracyctr.org.

women identify as single mothers.[2] Single parents with multiple children are the most vulnerable to extreme poverty. In a rural community where income is closely related to the work capacity of the family and where men and women fulfill specific roles, the loss of a spouse is more than a traumatic emotional loss; it is a dire economic threat.

A Woman of Many Trades

My husband and I used to work together on almost everything. Since he died, things have been much harder. His parents help me prepare the potato fields and care for the llamas, but it's still a lot of work.[3]

Like many other rural campesino families, Severina has her hand in many economic activities at once. She grows potatoes; she sells nonperishable food and other goods from her small store; she shepherds llamas and sheep; and she weaves intricate *aguayos,* rectangular textiles used as carry-alls, from sheep's wool. It is common for rural families like Severina's to earn a living in five or six different ways. This limits their dependence on one source of income and lowers their risk in case of a bad harvest year or other unforeseen events.[4]

Rural life and the rural economy are central to Bolivia's identity and its national economy. While migration to urban areas is on the rise throughout Latin America, four of every ten Bolivians still live and work in the countryside.[5] The majority of small farmers identify themselves with Quechua, Aymara, or lowland indigenous groups and grow food for their own consumption. As in Severina's case, the indigenous campesino economy in Bolivia's rural areas is based on both cash and noncash income, which includes the cultivation of crops and the tradition of *trueque,* or barter, which is still common in many communities today.

Growing potatoes is central in Severina's life, since potatoes are her family's primary food staple. She spends October seeding her fields and April harvesting them, with help from her family. Severina also keeps two dozen sheep and a half-dozen llamas. They are not for sale, however. She kills one of these animals every other month to provide important protein for her children's diet. On rainy days and during the nights as the children sleep, Severina pulls out her loom— a simple lean-to loom whose design dates back before the arrival of Columbus—on which she weaves *aguayos* and personalized hatbands with creative designs of animals and geometric forms that are uniquely hers.

Weaving in rural Bolivia is primarily a woman's trade. Like most women in the region, Severina learned to weave when she was a girl watching her mother thread her polished llama bone swiftly through the vertical warps of her loom. As a young girl, she and her mother would spin the wool while walking and caring for their sheep and llamas. Weaving just one textile might take two weeks, maybe more, worked on in the spare spaces of time not spent in the fields or caring for the animals or the children. Weaving traditions in the Bolivian highlands go back to the Incas, the ancestors of the Quechua Indians of this region. One scholar described the importance of Andean tex-tiles, explaining that most Quechuas "still consider the skills of hand spinning, dyeing and weaving to be the essential criteria of human dignity."[6]

Severina's cash income comes mainly from her shop and the sales she makes on weavings in the city. In one month, she might make 40 or 50 bolivianos ($US5–6) from her store, while a hand-woven *aguayo* or a table cover woven for a shop in Cochabamba might bring her between 150 and 200 bolivianos ($US19–26) in profit. In studies of rural areas, an indigenous campesino family of six earns about 8,900 bolivianos annually (around $1,140), with some regions registering annual incomes as low as half that amount.[7]

Globalization touches Severina's life in Chuñu Chuñuni in two distinct ways. The first traces her role in the local union and women's group and how the relationship between men and women in Chuñu Chuñuni comes up against the imported concepts of gender equality through a rural development project. The other shows how the local association of weavers has leveraged an international market so their local weavings can provide cash income and support the life of those traditions for new generations.

Community Roles: Men versus Women

Women and men in Chuñu Chuñuni share responsibility but work in clearly divided ways. Women take care of the home and children, while men are mainly in charge of preparing the land for planting. Both men and women, however, work the harvest, and men often care for the house and children when the women cannot.[8]

The divide between men and women is more obvious when it comes to education. Severina attended primary school in her home village through the fourth year but then had to leave school to help her family. "My mother died when I was young, and my father drank. I needed to leave school so I could help take the sheep out to pasture and help with the potato harvest." Severina's story is common: on average, girls in rural villages receive less schooling than boys do.[9] Community member Patricio Mamani pointed out that education reform by the state in the mid-1990s had an impact in Chuñu Chuñuni: "My mother would tell me when I was little that things had gotten so much better in our village: there were now more girls going to school. When she was little there weren't more than two or three girls in school."

While leadership at the community level is traditionally dominated by men, three relatively new women's organizations within the community have opened up new spaces for women to interact and take leadership. Women first began to participate in 2004, when the central community organization, the union, opened up leadership to women.[10]

Each position in the organization has a male and female counterpart. But for many women, taking on a leadership role is not easy.

Virginia Mamani has to deal with the daily pressures of completing her own work in the house and caring for her bulls.[11] Her husband, Patricio, explained that during his wife's tenure as *dirigenta* he would take over some of her responsibilities at home. The women's organization, however, was very weak, since the men consistently resisted their wives' participation. "Most men don't like their wives serving as *dirigentas*. It complicates the other work they have," explained Patricio. Even for some of the women who aren't pressured by their husbands, leadership is a daunting idea. Severina admitted she is not interested in getting involved in local decision making.[12]

The two other local women's groups were actually born from forces originating outside of Bolivia. In 2001, in response to increasingly poor health standards in the rural areas, the U.S. Agency for International Development (USAID) partnered with a local contractor to help start a mothers' group. The idea was to help combat the region's high levels of child malnutrition by providing educational workshops and basic foodstuffs to mothers of children under two years old. Each mother received fortified flour, cooking oil, lentils, and vitamins, a collection of goods that Severina prizes. In response to the creation of the mothers' group, another group sprang up: women who did not have children also began meeting regularly. Imposing the identities of "mother" and "nonmother" in a rural community, Chuñu Chuñuni began to create subtle but false lines of separation among women that otherwise could have organized together. However unintentional, a simple health project carried out in the name of development by outsiders began to strain the internal dynamics of the community. Another project—this time focused on weaving—would prove to have a similar mixed impact. With the intention of raising incomes, a weaving project forced women to reevaluate their role within the community and their potential for leadership.

Women and Weaving in the Name of Development

In 2002, the community of Chuñu Chuñuni inaugurated a new building, one that was not like any of the adobe homes community members had constructed with their own hands. It was a brick structure with a blue tin roof and a yellow door. The plaque to the side of the door reads: "PRODEVAT" (Development Program for the Valleys of Arque and Tapacarí). The European Union (EU) had approved a five-year project to support development efforts in two highland valley provinces, Tapacarí and Arque, in the department of Cochabamba. One component of the program was to help revitalize cultural traditions through the support of local weaving skills. Chuñu Chuñuni was chosen as one of the five weaving centers, each of which grouped a series of smaller weaving communities together. It coordinated the work of local weavers in order to create a distribution network for the wool and the completed textiles to sell to tourists in a central shop built with an accompanying museum and lodge.

The textile project launched by the EU aimed to boost women's incomes and support cultural revival by recuperating traditional weaving skills and providing an outlet to sell those weavings. Over the long term, the project also intended to build greater respect for the weaving tradition and to empower women by increasing their income and their leadership opportunities. By the time the EU project finished in 2005, it had laid such a successful groundwork that community representatives chose to keep it going and found other funding to move toward full sustainability. All told, the association now provides income for nearly three hundred weaving families. This has allowed the project to help slow the trend of migration from these weaving communities to the city.

A major objective of the project was to promote women's involvement in the leadership of the weavers' association so they could be the producers and managers of the entire process. The project stumbled, however, when the women in the communities refused to lead the association. They were too busy already, they explained, so how could they possibly add the leadership position to their workload as mothers, wives, farmers, and shepherds? Let the men do it, they responded. According to research commissioned by the EU, the women's resistance to leadership was the result of two things. The first was a lack of education, especially reading skills, which made them less confident about managing documents and public speaking. General illiteracy rates in Bolivia hover around 7 percent for men and 20 percent for women; in the rural areas, more than one-third of women cannot read and write.[13] The second was the absence of other local examples of women as leaders.[14]

"Women's empowerment" became a catch phrase among development agencies in the 1990s, when major development institutions—led by the United Nations and including the World Bank—boldly recognized the centrality of women in the "fight against poverty." In 2000, gender equality and women's empowerment were included in one of eight development priorities—referred to as the Millennium Development Goals—ratified by 191 countries. The theory behind this goal is that if countries promote education for young girls, higher educational levels will have a profound impact on, among other things, the exclusion and poverty that women are vulnerable to later in life.

But how should "empowerment" be applied to isolated Quechua and Aymara communities without imposing foreign gender concepts that don't fit? Should outsiders determine what gender relationships look like, or should that be the decision of the men and women of each community? Those questions are part of a bigger struggle that Bolivia has with another aspect of its interaction with a globalizing world: the role of development programs directed by groups outside of Bolivia. In the case of the EU weaving project, intentions appeared to be nothing but positive, to inject funding to provide better incomes and recognition for weaving traditions. Bolivia, however, is a country saturated with development projects that are often associated with special interests or corruption. As a result, development initiatives in Bolivia generate a lot of skepticism.

That skepticism focuses particularly on nongovernmental organizations (NGOs). Instances of poorly spent foreign funds and low accountability to their target communities have given these civil society groups a bad reputation. In 2006, formal charges were brought by local women's unions in La Paz against two NGOs because, the unions claimed, the organizations were soliciting and receiving major funding from abroad in the name of the unions but without their involvement. Bolivian academics have suggested that NGO bureaucracies obstruct rather than support the process of indigenous and rural communities developing their own forms of citizenship.[15] This lapse has major implications for Bolivian women, who are a primary target group of local and international NGOs.

The weaving project is just one example of how fragile the relationship between foreign development programs and rural communities can be. Whatever the project—whether big or small and apparently free of political motivation—it inevitably brings unforeseen consequences to a community whose social structures are not fully understood by foreigners. In the instance of the USAID-led health project, the intentions and reported results, according to participants, were very positive. Women reported that the information and food given to them has helped them care better for their babies.[16]

On the other hand, the creation of a new women's organization, based on the singular identity of mother among the women, works against the more integrated and multiple identities of the women in the community and isolates the young mothers from other women who do not fall into the same category. This approach of development projects, to create new organizations that overlap or displace existing local groups, has been repeated across Bolivia, producing major disruption in communities from the Chapare lowlands in Cochabamba to the remote villages of the altiplano.[17] Ultimately, transparency and close coordination with local communities will ensure that future projects consider these subtle—but influential—dynamics.

What does this all mean for Severina? The weaving project is a boost for her monthly income and an additional strategy that keeps her from being dependent on just one or two sources of income. Without the infrastructure of the weaving association and the interest of foreigners, she may not have begun to teach her daughter the skills of weaving, which could have pushed the tradition further toward extinction. Now her community is recognized as a center of high-quality weaving, raising the appreciation—nationally and internationally—of the Quechua and Aymara highland weaving cultures. On the horizon are opportunities to export the weavings—in the form of pillows, table runners, and wall-hangings—to foreign markets in the United States and Europe. As for her leadership prospects, being a leader is not out of the realm of possibility, she said. Maybe when her children are older.

María Choque: Knitting for Saks Fifth Avenue

In the summer of 1994, María Choque left the small mining village of Colquechaca in the northern mountains of Potosí and came to the city. She was just twenty-two when she arrived in Cochabamba with her mother, father, and five brothers and sisters.[18] She had spent her entire childhood and adolescence in the community where her father mined tin, silver, and zinc. The mining camp sits at fourteen thousand feet above sea level, and her father worked in mines that were as high as fifteen thousand feet. Once famous for having produced more silver than any other mine in Bolivia in the 1800s, Colquechaca was shut down in 1994 by government decree, putting its miners out of work.[19] Colquechaca is one of many examples of mine closures required by economic restructuring, reforms promoted by institutions abroad and implemented by a Bolivian political elite.

María's education—and that of her siblings—is a topic of great pride for the family. Thanks largely to the strictness of her mother, all of the children graduated from high school. A university education was still out of reach, however. Their mother died after the family moved to Cochabamba, and her father's economic situation demanded that the children work, leaving no time for studying. When she was twenty-three, María married a young Cochabambino who worked whatever jobs he could get, from construction to driving a taxi.

When her first child was just a few years old, María found work as a knitter for a small private business based in Cochabamba that exports handmade clothes and bags. For more than nine years now, she has contributed to her family's income as a head knitter for the business that supplies high-end handbags to niche markets in the United States and Europe. She directs between twenty and forty local women knitters, all based in her neighborhood, who complete products designed in Los Angeles and New York. Overall, the business owner has a pool of four hundred workers.

The workers are organized into cooperatives like María's, and each works from home, coordinating with the head of their cooperative. "For us, it's more comfortable [to be at home] because we can be near our children and watch over them. Especially for those of us who have young children, you always have to keep an eye on them," explained María. María's job is like that of a manager running a small subcontracted company. She is the contact person who manages the knitters, with no oversight from the business owner. The owner receives an order for fifty baby sweaters from Italy; María offers an estimated time and cost of materials; she oversees the division of work among her group and delivers the products to the owner for payment once the sweaters are done.

Why have companies—like the one that employs María—begun to sprout up in developing countries from Guatemala to Thailand? With the single click of a button, products created by a local labor cooperative like María's are matched with foreign consumers thousands of miles away. In Cochabamba alone, estimates suggest that between five thousand and six thousand women work in informal cooperatives like María's, creating hand-knit sweaters and other products for export.[20] Technological advances and the ease with which products can be transported allow designers to outsource production halfway around the world to get the products they need for wages far lower than in the United States or Europe. As competition rises in the market, overhead and labor costs have to be minimized. Mass production moves to countries like China, where the supply of labor is nearly infinite. Niche market producers, like the one María works for, do not intend to compete with the Chinas of the world; they are specifically targeting small high-end markets where their comparative advantage is not the lowest wages and an endless number of workers but rather low(er) wages combined with skill and fine materials for smaller, more distinct product lines.

These characteristics of the global market demand a flexible workforce. The business model under which María works is a telltale example of how a small business creates a flexible, modular workforce to meet its need to stay competitive. Styles are updated and tastes change. For products to meet those demands, a workforce has to have a range of skills and the ability to turn out unique products in a short period of time. To keep costs low for the business, workers need to be hired only when orders are made and their specific skills required. As María explained: "We don't really have hours. When we have work, we have to work hard."

The growing demand for a flexible workforce, in the name of efficiency and competition in a global market, also translates to economic uncertainty and a total absence of labor protection for workers. Hours and salaries are not fixed. Benefits are not guaranteed. Organizing around labor issues becomes more difficult when work is done in individual homes and with minimal contact with fellow workers. In addition, young mothers are the most common profile for the growing number of home-based workers, which means their responsibilities are also split as the caretaker of the home and the family. Previously, María might have worked as a producer in a large factory with a unionized workforce, benefiting from collectively negotiated wages and government protections. In Bolivia and elsewhere, those models of employment are being supplanted with more flexible and fragmented ones, such as the cooperative that María runs.

This flexible labor regime starkly contrasts with the labor-organizing history for which Bolivia is so famous. Work conditions under the Tin Barons of Potosí and Oruro catalyzed the miners' labor movement in the early 1940s, which led the country to the 1952 Revolution and the creation of the Central Obrero Boliviano, the grandfather of Bolivian labor unions. By the 1960s, the women of Siglo XX, one of the mining communities under the control of Tin Baron Simón Patiño, successfully organized to support their miner husbands' fight for better pay and the freedom to organize. It is this legacy of organizing that has brought Bolivian women workers, from household workers to shoe factory workers, into a unionized world where they have leveraged their power to obtain better treatment and fair pay.

As access to global markets grows by the day, Bolivians and Bolivian women in particular need to respond to this changing demand for labor and create a way to safeguard their rights. Tens of thousands of women across the globe are home-based workers, invisible to government regulations and any recognition of labor rights regarding working conditions, pay, or benefits. The International Labor Organization began researching this growing workforce in the early 1980s, and several countries now legally recognize these workers. The Bolivian government lags, however, in recognizing home-based workers and in providing basic legal protections for working conditions.[21] This leaves the door open for business managers and owners to put profit and efficiency above the well-being of workers, disregarding basic labor guarantees.

In María's situation, the goodwill of the owner has helped compensate for the lack of formal labor protection. The owner operates an informal system of financial support for workers' health costs and has begun a dental care program to give her employees and their families regular checkups. Employer goodwill, however, is not a substitute for legal recognition and protection. For every employer like María's, there are numerous examples of others eager and willing to exploit flexible labor. Nightmare stories of labor sweatshops, in Bolivia and elsewhere, are well known.

Ultimately, workers need to advocate for a new framework of safeguards that responds to the demands for flexible labor. In the long term, that includes the passage of new labor laws and better vigilance by government agencies and workers' groups. Workers organizing will need to focus more on individual training regarding labor rights, channels for lodging complaints, and support for work inspectors. This new labor force of contractual workers also needs new ways to obtain basic benefits like insurance for health and retirement. As a result, labor organizing must use innovative strategies to lobby government to make such changes.

A new model of labor unions is emerging in response to this increasingly mobile and independent workforce. In the United States, consultants, freelance workers, and entrepreneurs have found ways to link together across professions to advocate for recognition as workers and to procure legal protections. The Freelancers Union, founded in 2003, is taking root in New York City and moving across the United States with more than forty thousand independent workers already signed up as members.[22] Currently the Freelancers Union is not taking on the full gamut of traditional union functions; it focuses more on getting members low-cost insurance rather than negotiating with employers. But it does pave the way for a large-scale advocacy group that can unite individual workers to ensure a basic safety net of benefits through negotiations with insurance carriers and pressure for legislation that favors independent workers. In Bolivia, a similar umbrella advocacy organization could benefit home-based workers, independent gardeners, and construction workers alike. According to a local labor activist based in Cochabamba, initial attempts have been made to create such a union for Bolivian workers, especially for women, but they have met with limited success. In the eyes of the government, these workers still do not exist.[23]

The "gatekeeper" phenomenon is another major threat for Bolivian women workers. The business owner's central role in bridging local production and foreign clients illustrates just how dependent a local workforce can be on a single access point in order to take advantage of jobs created through the growing interconnection of global markets. As with the weavers' association, the way grassroots groups or lower-class urban workers access foreign markets is most often through a highly educated and connected individual. In the two cases examined here—the rural weaving group and the urban knitting cooperative—one or two foreigners are the pivot points of the business, at least at its inception. In this way, the workers' relationship to the market, prices, and consumers is entirely moderated by these individuals who are specialized in their ability to bridge cultures, satisfy foreign client expectations, and manage international business relations. Similarly, the head knitters are a type of gatekeeper between the knitters' groups and the central administration. This works to further isolate the women workers and frees the head knitter and the business owner from any accountability in questions of fair treatment and pay. On the one hand, the flexibilities required offer special benefits for women, in particular the ability to work near their children and with flexible hours that can also combine well with home responsibilities. On the other hand, absent legal protections, globalization's demand for flexible labor markets also opens new doors for abuse.

In addition to a new economic framework that challenges workers to adjust to a new type of workforce and its lack of safeguards, these knitters, like many other sectors in Bolivia, also face another challenge from an increasingly interconnected economy: they must struggle with the volatility of jobs influenced by foreign trade rules written a continent away.

BOX 7.2 | The Feminization of
Bolivian Global Migration

In the course of just two months in late 2006, local newspapers reported that thirty thousand Bolivians left the country for Spain.[1] With seven of every ten of those Bolivians being women, that translates to twenty-one thousand women leaving Bolivia within just sixty days.

This "feminization" of migration is a phenomenon that will continue to grow if Bolivia cannot develop more opportunities for Bolivians at home. The consequences of inadequate or misguided economic policies and development programs that have fallen short of their goals in the past two decades—and particularly without a necessary focus on women's stability in the economy—are playing out in the mass exodus of Bolivians to places like Europe and neighboring countries.

The emigration factor takes a heavy toll on Bolivian women. The growing trend of out-migration is a clear consequence of the lack of jobs in Bolivia combined with the demands for labor in countries like Argentina, the United States, and Spain. As Bolivians looking for work, women are drawn by a high foreign demand for caretakers, particularly of children and the elderly. This mirrors the increase of women in Europe and elsewhere who are working more outside the home. As caretakers of their own family, Bolivian women are forced to abandon their own children, creating painful family divisions. The family as an economic unit is disrupted, and women are forced to adjust to new roles. (For more on Bolivian emigration, see chapter 8.)

1. "Más de 30 mil bolivianos viajaron a España en los últimos dos meses" (More than 30,000 Bolivians traveled to Spain in the last two months), *Opinión*, January 8, 2007.

U.S. Trade Policies and Cochabamba Knitters

María lives a long way from the offices in Washington where global trade decisions are made, but the choices made there affect her life a good deal. Political negotiations surrounding trade preferences between the United States and Bolivia have potential consequences for María and her fellow knitters in Cochabamba. (For more on trade issues and Bolivia, see chapter 5.)

Since 1991, Bolivia has had special access to U.S. markets under trade preferences for textile exports, preferences that directly benefit María and the other producers in Cochabamba. First, those preferences came under the Andean Trade Preferences Act and then from 2002 through 2006 under the Andean Trade Promotion and Drug Eradication Act. The agreements allowed Colombia, Ecuador, Peru, and Bolivia to export various products, including textiles and leather goods, to the United States without having to pay any type of tariff. These trade preferences are a part of U.S. antidrug policies, because, the United States reasons, more jobs in textile and leather industries means fewer people will grow coca to make cocaine. The preferences have also served as a "carrot" to governments to keep up their antidrug measures in order to boost exports of textiles to the United States. In 2006, Republican leaders in the U.S. Congress tried to use the preferences as a "stick" as well on the issue of free trade, threatening to end the agreement as punishment for Bolivia's opposition to the Free Trade Area of the Americas agreement.[24] In February 2008, the Andean Trade Promotion and Drug Eradication Act was renewed for an additional ten months following a diplomatic initiative by the Morales administration.

Trade preferences like these are important to businesses like the one María works for, and by extension, for the jobs it creates for women like her. However, access to U.S. markets ultimately lies in the hands of Bolivian trade negotiators and U.S. politicians. If the United States were dedicated to economic development in countries like Bolivia, its politicians would promote these preferences alongside development assistance to ensure that growth is sustainable. However, too often those decisions are based on political reasoning rather than Bolivia's needs for economic development.

WOMEN PROFESSIONALS

Women associated with Bolivia's social movements and the country's three primary indigenous groups—the Quechua, the Aymara, and the Guaraní—dominate the literature on women in Bolivia. While an analysis of Bolivia cannot exclude those groups, it would also be incomplete without considering middle- and upper-class women who play an important role in the development of Bolivia—politically, economically, and socially.

Among those benefiting from economic globalization in Bolivia are many of its professional women. Equipped with a huge set of advantages, such as access to education, salaried jobs, and a network of contacts, these women have negotiated opportunities to their advantage. Rosa Hernández is an unequivocal supporter of the principles of neoliberal economic policies, which have opened new markets in which she can expand her private business and have lowered the costs of products she wants to consume. Teresa Hosse has grasped opportunities through global philanthropy that have allowed her to apply her knowledge to the challenges facing women and communities in Bolivia's rural areas. Both have leveraged their education, familial support, and their own inner drive to create successful lives as mothers, wives, and also as professionals.

Rosa Hernández: A Winner within the Global Economy

On March 8, 2007, with her husband at her side, Rosa Hernández gave birth to her first child, Andrés. Unlike the majority of women in Bolivia who give birth under conditions of grave poverty and with no access to medical care, Rosa had a room to herself in one of Cochabamba's private hospitals. In a country that has one of the worlds' highest maternal mortality rates, Rosa's situation is a rare one. As many as one in one hundred babies born in rural, indigenous areas lose their mother.[25]

Rosa is like many other Bolivian women in that she is a strong-willed survivor. Her mother was told by doctors when Rosa was born that she would die within a few days. Against all odds, she fought back—a precursor to the spirit of persistence that has helped her build a successful career, a marriage, and now, a family. She is one of globalization's success stories, and she is the first to identify herself as one of its major proponents.[26]

Education was highly prized in her family of five, and she followed her older sisters' lead in completing her college degree—in business administration—and going on to get an extra certification in insurance. After graduating from the private Catholic university in Cochabamba, Rosa entered the private sector working as a marketing and sales manager for a local dairy company. After switching to a position in the insurance department of the bank where her mother worked, she and her mother joined forces in 2006 and created their own company as insurance brokers. Building on her mother's original portfolio of clients, they have now quadrupled their business to nearly 2,500 clients, and the business continues to grow.

Generational Changes

Abuelita, as Rosa refers affectionately to her grandmother, never knew anything more than being a housewife: taking care of the family, cooking, and caring for the house. Rosa ascribes her own success to the example her mother offered. A housewife for the first ten years of Rosa's life, her mother began working in insurance when she was forty years old. Entirely new to the industry, her mother was determined to master it. And yet, she was able to do so without losing close contact with her children, thanks in large part to the support her family got from the abuelita living with them, helping to run the house and care for the children. But even Rosa is challenging her mother's model of a professional mother. She worked until the day of Andrés's birth, thanks to the fact that she and her mother are their own bosses. She was able to return to work full-time within two weeks of giving birth since she could keep her son with her at all times.

Without Abuelita, however, neither Rosa nor her mother could work without having to hire household help. Rosa's grandmother is in charge of almost all the household responsibilities—from cooking the daily lunch for six people to caring for the house. However, Rosa and her mother are the ones who clean the house and do the laundry, tasks they do after a full day's work. The familial network frees the younger women of the house to hold demanding, well-paying jobs, even as they continue to contribute to chores at home. As more and more women become professional, and mothers and grandmothers are not available for child care, young women will depend even more heavily on assistance from domestic workers for the care of their children and their homes. It is the crucial role of the household worker that allows professional women and mothers to leave the house and duties of the family, to be teachers, bankers, and lawyers. While this could translate to double opportunity—in terms of women entering the workforce—respect and recognition for the household worker's role in that relationship, as a formal worker, remains largely overlooked by society.

Perceptions of Opportunity

Rosa's job was created by the needs of a globalizing world. Her clients are active in international commerce, and her ability to do her job is made possible by her immediate access to information and the ability to communicate constantly with counterparts abroad via the Internet. For her, globalization represents opportunity. She points to her mother, who has applied her entrepreneurial spirit and is now a businesswoman who has generated employment for six other people just within their office.

Rosa's work is based on a national and international network of insurers. She maintains contact with companies in Argentina and Chile so her clients' transport companies can have seamless coverage as they cross Bolivian borders. She insures truck companies, wood floor exporters, and businessmen who travel abroad regularly. When a local company in Bolivia exports wood products to Germany, Rosa is the one who arranges inspections and reimburses clients if shipments arrive damaged.

The opportunity of a globalizing world is also what Rosa's sister, Anamaría, seized upon when the job market turned sour for her in Cochabamba in 2001. Trained as an industrial engineer, Anamaría worked as a private consultant for various projects for the municipal and regional governments. "She was always a workaholic," Rosa said about her sister. "But it was impossible for her to keep working [in Bolivia]. She did not feel like she was respected for her skills." Repeated changes in government meant her clients rarely paid her on time, if at all. She took a risk and moved to the United States, where political instability would no longer inhibit her chance to work. In the course of five years, she has become a top manager in a private firm outside of Washington, D.C., where she lives amid a burgeoning Bolivian migrant community. She has just bought her own house and now supervises more than thirty people at her job.

Rosa finds it hard to understand how the majority of Bolivians selectively criticize the forces of globalization when they benefit every day from products imported from abroad and income received from foreign aid. "Think about cell phones," she said. "They used to cost $1,500 when they first started arriving. Now, thanks to the international market and competition, prices have dropped to $40—an amount that almost any Bolivian can scrape together. It lets us communicate, do work, be more efficient." A more interconnected world, she argues, allows women in Bolivia to have contact with others and to see opportunities beyond their traditional role in the home. For Rosa, globalization is a vehicle that challenges an entrenched *machismo* and redefines the limitations society places on women.

Teresa Hosse: Leading a Nonprofit in Rural Development

It was 1982 and student protests were more the norm than the exception on the downtown streets of Cochabamba. The students of the city's public university were the major protagonists in the struggle against the dictatorial regime of García Mesa, and Teresa Hosse was among them.[27] It took her seven years to finish college because of political interruption in the university schedule. Soldiers supervised each classroom, and students and their parents were required to sign agreements promising to keep their children from getting involved in politics.

Teresa comes from a comfortable middle-class home, where her biggest challenges were the strictness of her father and surviving as the only girl among three brothers. Her mother took a subordinate role to her father, who was a doctor and the only breadwinner. Her mother, however, would push Teresa to think beyond the world of the housewife to become a professional. One of the best students in her college class, Teresa began working simultaneously at one of Cochabamba's earliest NGOs. That work planted the seed that transformed the way Teresa saw the world: "In the city you have everything you could ever need. You go two hours outside of Cochabamba and what do you find? An entirely different logic about the world and how to live," she explained. The work Teresa became involved in was a marketing project for a small community producing wool sweaters. She was fascinated by what she found: a total and utter contrast to the city world she knew so well. Teresa's interest was piqued. So, when someone offered to connect her with a group creating bilingual newspapers for the rural areas as a contact for developing her college thesis, she jumped at the opportunity.

From 1984 until 1987, the village of Raqaypampa became Teresa's second home. A remote community in the southeastern extreme of the department of Cochabamba, Raqaypampa is not only famous for its intricate weavings and traditional production of potatoes, but also as an area impacted by foreign aid directed at agriculture. The Green Revolution had been introduced to Bolivia following a severe drought in 1982–83. The "revolution," led by U.S.-based foundations and USAID, promoted new farming technologies—pesticides, fertilizers, and irrigation systems—to increase agricultural production in developing countries. A surge of NGOs had focused on the Cochabamba region to import their green revolution. What Teresa found in the rural area of Raqaypampa, however, was not the success they expected. Communities employing the green revolution technologies were actually worse off in terms of nutrition.

Teresa's work merged with that of her mentor, Pablo Regalsky, who founded the Center for Communication and Andean Development (CENDA) in 1985. Teresa worked as part of the research team looking at the diverse strategies that peasant farmers use in the production and sale of their crops. She credits Pablo, an Argentinean who has been working in Bolivia with rural communities for more than twenty-five years, with recognizing these impositions from abroad and bringing awareness to the rural communities about the value of their traditional systems of production. "CENDA was like a school for us," she explained. "All of us evolved together under Pablo's guidance."

General suspicion of NGOs, most of them funded by foreign governments and foundations, was something Teresa and her colleagues had to deal with from the first moment they visited Raqaypampa. It soon became obvious to the people of the community that Teresa and her colleagues had a long-term commitment and willingness to exchange, not just dictate, ideas and knowledge. Teresa always arrived with gifts of the Spanish-Quechua bilingual newspaper CENDA produces. From these experiences, Teresa said she witnessed the slow process by which the Raqaypampa community began to reflect on and really appreciate their relationship to the land and traditions of their Quechua culture.

Despite her love for field research, Teresa's new role as a mother in 1987 led her to stay closer to home, and she became more involved in collection and analysis of data from the research team. Just three years later, in 1990, she was asked to join the executive administrative team for CENDA. Teresa's preference for being in the field remained, but her new administrative role in the planning and financial supervision of the organization paralleled her need to be closer to her husband and their daughters.

Teresa was able to carry a full workload and still spend time with her family because she could rely on her mother and a household worker to care for her daughters and keep the house in order. Her husband coordinated with her so the two would never travel at the same time, and they even struck an agreement that allowed each of them to pursue a master's degree during different years, while the other looked after the family and home. The sharing of responsibilities was key to making both Teresa's and her husband's careers successful and setting an example for their daughters to follow a similar path. In 2000, CENDA broke with tradition and named a woman to its top post when Teresa was invited to become its director.

The Global Threads of Development: Threats and Opportunities

Factors from abroad have left their imprints on CENDA and on Teresa's professional experience. While Rosa's private-sector perspective draws on the positive impact of global forces, Teresa has witnessed a mixed bag of globalization's consequences through her work. As a thesis student, she learned about the ill-prescribed solutions of foreigners to deal with Bolivia's struggle against drought in the early 1980s. Foreign governments and foreign-funded NGOs initiated technology-driven development projects that were applied with little respect for long-standing knowledge from the communities themselves.

CENDA's fundamental principle for its work lies in respect for a community's existing knowledge and experience. CENDA does not impose foreign concepts. Instead, it encourages community members to reflect on their situation, give them tools, and present them with examples while respecting the systems they already have in place. If an idea takes hold, then it can grow amid the community's own values. "It's not easy," Teresa admitted.

Particularly in the instance of gender equality, Teresa has to distance the values she upholds in her own household with her two teenage daughters and those of the rural communities with whom CENDA works. "We as an institution begin from the point that you have to understand the logic of a community in relation to a woman's role," she explained. Just as with improving women's participation—which most outsiders would agree is an obvious goal—"you must follow [the community's] rhythms, and ultimately it has to be a process that comes from them." The process involves a long commitment, a willingness to learn, and patience on the part of people working in development projects—a rare combination of characteristics for a web of institutions that require tangible results to justify costs.

Despite its constructive critique of foreign pressures and shortsightedness, CENDA's existence still depends on the global force of foreign philanthropy. The organization makes its decisions cautiously, selecting funders who will not place conditions on CENDA's work, so that it can maintain its full independence. Teresa shares the other major benefit she sees that globalization has brought to CENDA's work: in recent years CENDA has been able to open new channels of exchange with other groups doing similar work with indigenous communities in other parts of the continent, such as Ecuador. Unlike the early 1980s, when it worked in relative isolation, CENDA can now share its lessons learned from Raqaypampa and make useful comparisons to similar work carried out thousands of miles away.

WOMEN LEADERS: FROM LOCAL TO GLOBAL

Bolivian women have an unusual propensity for leadership. The challenge of unprecedented class inequalities and the exceptional will of Bolivia's people to demand their rights are the ingredients for a powerful mix that has produced an ample number of committed grassroots civic leaders. The image of Bartolina Sisa can be found in offices, assembly rooms, and schools across the country. An Aymara Indian, Bartolina fought the Spanish alongside indigenous leader Tupac Katari and died at the age of twenty-six in 1782, brutally killed by Spanish forces.[28] She has become a symbol for indigenous pride, women's leadership, and utter commitment—to the death—to fight discrimination and subordination by foreigners.

Domitila Chungara lived through the conflicts in the mines during the age of the dictators, the fearless leader of the housewives' association in the Siglo XX mining community. The exploitation of miners and the strong hand of dictators through the 1960s and 1970s pushed her to speak out about mistreatment, imprisonments, and even massacres of miners and their families. Though she was imprisoned and beaten and her family blacklisted, she refused to stay quiet: "I have a deep rancor in my heart, for all the outrages we have suffered. . . . Repression is very strong and the family suffers a great deal. It is precisely for this [reason] that I believe that I ought not to be quiet since we have suffered so much."[29]

The legacy of the violence and suffering in the mines has not been forgotten, nor has the means of organizing against anything perceived as heavy-handed foreign imposition. The children and grandchildren of the miners, many of whom relocated to the lowland coca-growing regions after many mines were closed in the mid-1980s, brought the concept of labor unions with them. The daughters and granddaughters of those miners felt the same rancor that Domitila did when U.S.-promoted forced coca eradication began in the late 1980s and local communities were once again exposed to violence and mistreatment.

Symbols of female heroism permeate all regions of Bolivia. Nicolasa de Cuvene is to the lowland Moxos Indians what Bartolina Sisa is to the Aymara and Quechua women. Born around the time Bolivia was founded in 1825, Nicolasa refused to betray her husband when the Spaniards tortured her for information.[30] Local women use her name to evoke steadfastness, loyalty, and resistance. Leadership programs bear her name to this day. Many generations later, the Moxos women again played a role in history in the thirty-four-day March for Territory and Dignity in 1990, which started in the eastern lowlands and ended in La Paz, gaining new visibility for the demand for greater participation of indigenous groups in the Beni department. From this legacy comes the stories of two Bolivian women whose contemporary heroism shows how present-day leadership is shaped by global forces.

BOX 7.3 | *Cocalera* Leadership,
Courtesy of the "War on Drugs"

Nuqanchik warmis jina sumaq organizasqa kanchik imaptinchus kay injusticia kaptin.
(Thanks to injustice, we as women are organized.)

In the Chapare coca-growing region, this Quechua saying points out just how deeply the U.S.-promoted "war on drugs" has affected the development of women's leadership.[1] Women began organizing in the 1980s in response to the beginning of forced eradication of coca plants, primarily in support of the all-male coca-growing unions. By the mid-1990s, male coca-growing leaders realized these women were an untapped resource in their resistance efforts to protest the increasing militarization and violence associated with the antidrug policies from abroad. In 1997, women participated for the first time in the Chapare's union elections, where they formed a parallel leadership structure to that of the men.

The Chapare's example of women's leadership has stretched far beyond the lowland jungle regions and inspires social movement leaders across Bolivia. "The Chapare is our school," explains one female leader of a highland community. By raising the visibility of women as community leaders, other communities once resistant to women's participation have begun to open new, formal positions for their leadership. As they assume these new roles, however, many women continue to struggle to find the balance of shared power alongside their male counterparts, to which there is still underlying resistance.

Since 2005, under the MAS government, *cocalera* leaders are making even more of a mark at the national and international levels. Three of these women now occupy top posts in the Morales administration: president of the National Constituent Assembly, the MAS party leader, and the minister of justice. (For more on coca and the "war on drugs," see chapter 6.)

1. Draper, Melissa. "Women's Voices Rise from the Chapare," *Cultural Survival Quarterly* (Winter 2003): 67–69.

Casimira Rodríguez: From Trafficked Adolescent to Justice Minister

One sunny Sunday afternoon in late 1979, when she was just thirteen years old, Casimira Rodríguez said good-bye to her family, got into a truck in her small village of San Vicente, and headed for the city.[31] A couple that had visited her village repeatedly had spoken kindly to her parents that afternoon in the family's humble adobe home in their native language, Quechua. Now they were taking her to Cochabamba where an education, new clothes, and a job awaited her. She would even be able to send money back to her parents, they had promised, so they could have vegetables one day during the week to vary the repetition of corn and potatoes that were the basis of their diet. Her nervousness was mixed with the excitement of the idea that she would be able to help her family have a stable income.

The butterflies in her stomach quickly subsided when she realized her new life was not going to be what she had imagined. She was taken to the house of these "friends," a lower-middle-class home on the south side of the city. She was locked in the house and told she could not leave. For two years Casimira worked seventeen hours a day without pay, while cooking, cleaning, and caring for a family of fifteen. The only time she was allowed out of the house was to carry a foul-smelling chemical solution to nearby Lake Alalay, where she was told to dump it discretely. She didn't know that the noxious liquids were precursor chemicals used to make cocaine. She found that out when the police burst into the house one night. She was fourteen years old.

Casimira's luck turned the day there was a quiet knock on the door and she heard her mother's voice whisper in Quechua that she was there to steal her back. A mutual friend had gotten word back to San Vicente about Casimira's situation. Never had Casimira thought she would be so glad to return to her village, some ten hours by bus on bumpy dirt roads from the city. For another year, she stayed with her family and continued her studies in San Vicente before deciding to return to Cochabamba in search of her own work, again as a household worker. It was 1981. Soon after, she began to organize some of her fellow domestic workers, exchanging experiences and survival strategies. Four years later, in December 1985, she helped to found the union of domestic workers of Cochabamba. Little did she know then that it would ultimately project her onto the global stage.

Building a Movement of Women Workers, Locally and Globally

Household workers are more difficult to organize than workers in any other sector. Latin American labor organizers tried for decades to help these women organize, but their invisibility made it too hard to reach them.[32] Unlike other labor groups, domestic workers do not have a central, physical place—like a factory, a university, or an office—where they regularly collect for work and where they could begin to organize. These women work in isolation, behind closed doors.

Before 1985, there was no support for Bolivia's household workers. They are virtually all women and come from Quechua, Aymara, or other indigenous communities. The majority migrate from the rural areas before the age of fifteen with very little education and barely enough Spanish to help them navigate the city and their work. Some come to work for several years and then return to their village to start a family. Others never leave the city.[33] Estimates suggest that 90 percent live in the homes where they work. Without any protection under labor laws until 2003, they were some of the most marginalized workers in Latin America.[34] Their invisibility makes it impossible to confirm estimates of how many homes employ household workers. Although a new law requires a monthly minimum wage of 500 bolivianos ($US60), some still receive nothing. Casimira estimates that 40 percent of employers comply with the minimum wage, while half of all employers pay less than the minimum wage.

Unlike most other labor groups, household workers have connections to every niche of society. If a person is not directly related to a domestic worker, then they likely benefit from their labor in their own home. The majority of impoverished rural and urban families are related to someone—a sister, mother, daughter, cousin—who works in a home to cook, clean, and care for children or the elderly. Not only do top business executives and national politicians depend on the work of these women, so do lower-middle-class schoolteachers and local government workers.

The domestic workers' union is distinct from the other grassroots unions and organizations in Bolivia because its constituency and leadership are entirely made up of women. Other social movements have developed parallel structures of women's leadership in the upper parts of those organizations, but the nature of the mixed-gender membership and tradition still keeps key decision making in men's hands.

The household workers have successfully built strategic alliances with other social movements. Building solidarity with other women's groups, however, has not been so easy. Even though household worker organizing aims at breaking down society-wide discrimination toward women and indigenous people and domestic work, these women still face discrimination. According to some domestic workers, this even includes other women among Bolivia's social movements and especially middle- and upper-class women. The teachers, government workers, and businesswomen who are freed up to work outside of the home by having a household worker consistently fail to support them. This shows just how deep discrimination runs, even among women and particularly between classes.[35]

By the early 1990s, key leadership that included Casimira began organizing unions of domestic workers in each of Bolivia's five major cities, and a movement began pushing for the creation of a national-level union. In the process of forming a central union, the women began to exchange experiences, organize workshops, create trainings, and develop the idea of a national law establishing labor rights for house-hold workers. In 1993, the National Federation of Household Workers of Bolivia was founded in Cochabamba, and the proposal for the law gained new allies among other social movement leaders and politicians. Casimira was elected head of the national union from 1996 through 2001. In February 2003, with Casimira as its most prominent proponent, the Law on Salaried Household Work was passed by the National Congress. For the first time ever, domestic workers had the right to demand paid vacation time, fair treatment in the workplace, and a minimum wage.

Global Support Transforms Household Workers and Leadership

Standing in front of eight thousand Methodist women in a packed indoor stadium in Anaheim, California, just a mile from Disneyland, Casimira Rodríguez described her life as an adolescent girl: a slave in a home where verbal abuse was the norm and where hope had no place.

Throughout her terms as a local and national leader in Bolivia, Casimira drew interest from abroad and worked to match the domestic worker organizations with global partners. Foundations and nonprofit organizations from Europe and the United States began to support small projects, national assemblies, and exchanges to foreign countries where household workers could share their experiences. By the 1990s, several multilateral organizations such as the International Labor Organization and UNICEF were becoming active supporters of household workers by conducting regional studies on workers' conditions, hosting conferences, and creating new forums for exchanges with the household workers on relevant topics such as emigration and human trafficking.

Casimira's personal leadership entered the international sphere when she was elected in 2001 to serve as secretary general of the International Confederation of Latin American and Caribbean Domestic Workers. Founded in 1988 in Bogotá, Colombia, the confederation became the platform for household workers across Latin America to take their movement global. As the main representative of the international union through 2006, Casimira expanded the movement's contacts and support to countries far beyond Latin America, including India, the Netherlands,

Italy, and the United States. With speaking tours that included Harvard University, workshops at the World Social Forum in India, and exchanges in Germany, the woman who was once an enslaved household worker in Cochabamba was able to help share the experiences of household workers around the world. She explained: "I have been lucky to learn from other women. I listen to the stories of a woman in the Middle East and a domestic worker in Mexico. We sleep on the floor together, we share our strategies, we learn from one another. We are stronger for it."

Casimira's experience is but one example of how international support for women's leadership has grown exponentially in the past two decades. Grassroots leaders such as Casimira have carved out spaces to share their stories and build their leadership skills so they can become bridges by which foreigners and Bolivians create further partnerships. International movements and networks have proliferated now that travel and the Internet have become accessible to people around the globe. In 1992, the Via Campesina was founded as a network of peasant groups that transcends national borders to coordinate peasant organizations—including peasant women. Via Campesina has worked with the Bartolina Sisa National Federation of Bolivian Peasant Women and even demanded the release of women leaders when a previous Bolivian government arrested women associated with the coca growers' movement. In 2001, activists from forty-one countries descended on Cochabamba as the People's Global Action (PGA) network gathered to address topics of land, women's rights, and global economic policies that were common to countries on five continents. The PGA Web site organizes international protests and shares information in eight different languages.[36]

The benefits of global exchange are clear. Sharing ideas and experiences builds strategies and encourages collaboration. It also opens up space for rising leaders at home, as it did in Casimira's case. The local union in Cochabamba and the Bolivian national union now have a new generation of leaders in their young twenties who are taking on responsibility and leading a growing movement. "We have opened up a lot since 1999," Casimira explained. "As new doors opened for me beyond the household workers, my *compañeras* began to represent [the local and national unions] across Bolivia and in other parts of Latin America."

When local leadership goes global, however, the opportunities for leaders are tempered by threats to their accountability if they do not stay closely rooted to their constituency. The international jet-setting of grassroots leaders can threaten the very foundation of their legitimacy.

When conferences and projects abroad take leaders from their community, they can easily lose a connection to their constituents and fellow leaders. One man in Cochabamba spoke about a social movement leader who has become known internationally. "He has no *base* anymore. He keeps going on these fancy trips out of the country, but he has forgotten about where he comes from," the man said.[37] In a country where social movements are based on community action to fight historical inequalities, the rise of a leader to international stardom quickly draws questions and criticism.

A New Face in Bolivian Politics

The call came late the night of January 19, 2006, just two days shy of Evo Morales's inauguration as Bolivia's first indigenous president. Bolivia's leader-to-be called Casimira Rodríguez that night to ask her to come to La Paz immediately. The next day, in person, he repeated a question he had half jokingly asked her several times over the previous few years: when I become president, will you be one of my ministers? Her response that day would chart a very different course for her life than she had imagined just days before.

At her first 5 A.M. staff meeting in the Government Palace, she looked around to see twelve men and three other women, none of whom had the long black braids or the traditional *pollera* skirt that she wears every day. Though a symbol of pride for many Aymara and Quechua women, the skirt, lace shirt, and shawl that were adopted from the Spaniards often brings discriminatory looks from other Bolivians, even today. As the minister of justice for Bolivia's first indigenous-led administration, Casimira quickly became a face of the radical change from previous governments. In the past, she had rejected repeated offers from the MAS party to run as a party candidate because she was not interested in getting into politics. However, as a representative of the majority indigenous population in the country—and with a constituency that reaches almost every home in the country—she chose to accept the appointment as minister.

Casimira was not without her detractors: the national association of lawyers called for her resignation because she was not trained as a lawyer. One adviser to a prominent U.S. female politician, citing Casimira's lack of formal education, complained that she was "set up for failure" and was a dangerous example of incompetence that could be damaging to women's role in politics. Casimira was not the conventional female politician, but her appointment as minister sparked an important dialogue across the country and the continent about the representation of historically excluded indigenous people and especially women. Only with examples of leadership will there begin to be changes to such deep-seated discrimination.

The role of women in politics in Bolivia has had a dismal history. For decades, women's representation in Congress was in the single digits, a condition that changed only when, in 1997, a system of quotas was created requiring that one-third of the party candidates be women. But a greater number of women candidates has not translated into a similar number of women elected to office. And an increase in women's representation does not necessarily mean that those officials take action on issues affecting women.

The issue of competence compounds the challenges women have in taking office. When education is considered a luxury for the majority of Bolivian women, few have the experience or background that prepares them to be savvy politicians. When that combines with long-standing *machismo*, women become a target for criticism by opposition parties and the press. Critics of President Morales's appointment of a female president of the Constituent Assembly, for example, pointed to her as yet another example of a male politicians' strategy to appoint women whose loyalty is valued more than their competence.

The rise of these women leaders is inextricably linked to globalization. The election of the first indigenous-led administration in Bolivia's history—largely based on broad discontent with economic prescriptions from abroad over the last two decades—has brought more women into the high ranks of politics. The Morales administration boasts the highest number of women in high-ranking posts in Bolivia's history. "Women have to be a part of this profound change in our country," remarked Casimira. The support those women leaders get, in politics and among social movements and civil society groups, has grown over the last twenty years with a strong sense of globalized solidarity from counterparts in other countries and foreign funders. And now that women are becoming more visible leaders, especially among indigenous groups, they will continue to be challenged to define their own style of leadership, one that does not conform to a cookie-cutter Western model but is particular to them and their communities. It starts with examples of women leaders like Casimira who begin to break down long-standing stereotypes, challenging preset concepts of what it means to be a woman, indigenous, and a leader.

Casimira formally stepped down as minister of justice in January 2007 in a ceremony at the Presidential Palace in the same salon where she had been sworn in just a year earlier. She gets stopped in the street by random passers-by to thank her for her time in the government. "You give us hope," they repeat. "We have great trust in you," they say. Young adolescent girls in El Alto, near the city of La Paz, say the same. "You hear her story and the young women just light up. It gives them so much hope to know there is a woman who has overcome so much to succeed as she has," reported a local teacher.[38] Casimira does not fit the example of a highly educated high-society female politician that is held up as the ideal in the Western model. She is poised, diplomatic, confident, and perhaps most important, she is honest and committed in her representation of a sector of society that has been excluded from Bolivia's political system since its inception.

Carmen Peredo: A Leader behind the Scenes

Nine-year-old Carmen Peredo was holding her uncle's hand as she crossed the Prado, the long street that cuts through the center of La Paz. When the gunshots rang out, she gripped her uncle's hand tighter and looked in horror to see a student wounded, lying on the ground. Others fell at the student's side. Later, she asked her uncle what had happened, but his explanation was futile. She could not grasp how a government could kill its own people.[39]

It was early 1971, a tumultuous period in Bolivian history. General Juan José Torres was president—a position he would keep for less than one year before General Hugo Banzer Suárez would overthrow him in a military coup and usher in a new wave of repression and violence. Now forty-five years old, Carmen still remembers that moment. She claims it has guided her life's work, which has put her at the forefront of one of her country's key globalization struggles: keeping control of Bolivia's water.

Born to a family of twelve in the small town of Tiquipaya, outside of Cochabamba, Carmen was sent to La Paz to live with relatives to lessen the burden on her parents. The incident on the Prado made her question everything about her country. She returned to her family in Tiquipaya for junior high, where she began reading and inquiring insatiably about the current political situation. By the time she entered high school, she was already a local leader in one of the community organizations that worked with peasants and women in particular. By the age of fifteen, Carmen had become an active member of the national socialist party.

Water Users Unite: The Federation of Irrigators

The spark Carmen felt that day on the Prado has fed a deep-rooted commitment that is most evident in her work as a founder of and now primary adviser to Bolivia's Federation of Irrigators. Community-led water management is common in parts of Bolivia, especially in regions that government services have never reached and where traditional community structures have remained intact. As new systems of management— some through water privatization schemes—have been introduced in some areas, local communities have fought hard to obtain recognition for their traditional management systems.

Carmen's role in that struggle began in 1992, when she started working with the local water users in Tiquipaya. Two years later, an idea took root: communities in the region needed a central federation that could unite hundreds of local water committees and lay the groundwork for joint action. In October 1997, the Federation of Irrigators was founded. Two years later, the forces of globalization would thrust Carmen to the forefront of a national battle.

In November 1999, the executive committee of the federation decided to call an emergency meeting of key social movement leaders in Bolivia: behind closed doors the national government had signed a water privatization deal giving a consortium of foreign companies control over the Cochabamba public water system. The deal also threatened to give foreign companies control over the rural water systems as well. Seven days later, irrigation leaders met with the leader of Cochabamba factory workers, Oscar Olivera, and together they formed the Coalition for Water and Life that led the now-famous 2000 water revolt. (For more on the Cochabamba Water Revolt, see chapter 1.)

After the water revolt was won by the coalition of community groups, the federation began conducting workshops around the country that initiated an important nationwide discussion about water, its importance to indigenous and peasant communities, and how management should be handled. From this dialogue came the proposal to establish a national umbrella organization that could push for water policies favorable to the traditional structures of water supervision. Currently the organization coordinates with communities in seven of the nine departments in Bolivia.

"Some people think I am the property of the federation," Carmen joked. The hours she spends each day at the federation would make you think she is nothing less. She is not an elected leader; she is the one who makes general plans a reality, and as a result she has gained the respect and trust of the local leaders and local water users. She calls herself an "adviser." She takes regular calls from President Evo Morales, with whom she has worked closely—from organizing street protests around the Cochabamba Water Revolt in 2000 to distributing tractors donated by the Venezuelan government for local farmers in 2006.

Digging a little deeper, one finds that the federation functions smoothly—from every workshop to conferences to intraorganizational coordinating—thanks to five competent women, all under the direction of Carmen. While all of the community-elected leaders that make up the executive committee are men, it's the women who really get things done. With only a few days' notice, these women mobilized eighteen thousand community members to march on the Cochabamba soccer stadium to call attention to water issues as South American heads of state met at the Presidents' Summit in December 2006. "And that's just a fraction of the [irrigation committees'] constituency," noted Carmen.

Now that the president of the federation, Omar Fernández, has become a Senator in the National Congress, Carmen reflects on the fact that she too could have had the chance to be in the Morales government. In the end, she says she's glad to have stayed with the federation in Cochabamba, because Fernández's work at the national level is complemented by her work within the federation, resulting in a far more effective network than the federation has ever had. "We've gotten more things done this year [2006] with [Fernández] in La Paz and me here. It's incredible," she said.

Women and Water

My grandmother was an irrigator too. I remember
when I was little how I would watch the waters pass
near her house, but I didn't understand quite how it all
worked. Later, I realized that I had always been surrounded by a culture of water.[40]

                                    Carmen Peredo

Across Latin America and in developing countries around the world, women have always had a strong connection to water. Studies show that they are the ones primarily responsible for the collection and care of the household's water supply, particularly in rural areas.[41] And when water resources are threatened—whether through contamination, drought, or privatization—women are often the first to deal with the consequences. They are forced to reprioritize household needs if water becomes more expensive. Even young girls are affected because they are the ones pulled from school to help their families find water in times of scarcity or when water prices go up.

When global forces promote privatization of basic services in developing countries, women are among those most affected. When water resources were privatized in Cochabamba in 1999, water prices leapt by an average of 50 percent and often more. Household budgets—which are mainly managed by women—had to be turned inside out to compensate for the new high cost of water. Those higher prices meant money could not be spent on health, education, and food expenses. For the most impoverished women, the high price was not a question of reprioritizing the budget; it became a question of basic survival. At the community level, the water systems coordinated by women like Carmen and her grandmother before her were threatened with disruption to enable a for-profit entity to create a new distribution system that incorporated none of the native knowledge passed down over generations.[42] It is clear that in the development of water resources, women's role in management and access must be taken into account if that development is going to be sustainable.

What is true for water is true for other natural resources and public services that are privatized. When privatization of any basic service is accompanied by a rise in prices, the most disadvantaged groups—including women, indigenous people, and geographically isolated communities—are the first to lose out. Couple that with political systems that already exclude those voices from decision making and the result is compounded.

Roots of Leadership: The Local and the Global

Leaders rise in response to the needs of a society. In its organic, grass-roots form, the creation of leaders has nothing to do with leadership seminars, elite universities, or corporate networking. When people's basic rights to survival and dignity are threatened, leaders step forward to voice opposition and to propose solutions. Most of Bolivia's social movement leaders have risen in response to the crises, conflicts, and deep-seated discrimination that have defined Bolivia's history. Many of those struggles have been related to Bolivia's global integration. Just as the coca growers' movement produced leadership in response to the "war on drugs," so too did the crises over water and unjust discrimination against domestic workers.

Forces beyond Bolivia's borders have influenced these leaders in many ways. These forces have repeatedly helped to create the crises and conflicts that call forth new leaders, from Bartolina Sisa, who stood up against the Spaniards, to Carmen Peredo, who fought water privatization by foreign companies. The discontent with foreign-prescribed economic models and "development" over the past twenty years made way for the election of Bolivia's first indigenous-led government, which has also opened doors for women, who have been historically sidelined, such as Casimira Rodríguez. At the same time, one should not underestimate the positive impact that some global forces have brought these same leaders—whether in the form of exchange, resources, information, or solidarity. As Carmen explained, "There is that other side to globalization . . . globalizing solidarity. It is an important thing for us, and yet I realize how important it is that we continue to build *locally*."

CONCLUSION

Bolivian women have intrigued visitors, intellectuals, and activists for decades, not only because of the vitality and wisdom with which they represent the country's thirty-four different cultural groups, but because they continue to challenge the categories outsiders attempt to place on them. The Moxos women in the Beni region are not the same as the urban social movement leaders of Cochabamba, the urban professional women of La Paz, or the highland Quechua weavers of Chuñu Chuñuni. Their culture and traditions are not the same, and the impacts of a globalizing world on each of them vary. The diversity that defines Bolivian women is the same diversity that challenges a country like Bolivia to negotiate its own unique form of globalization.

However, the identity that binds women together across cultural groups and deep class lines is the common ground they have as women and mothers. In the face of globalizing forces, all women are faced with a rapidly increasing influx of ideas about what it means to relate to men, the family, their work, and their community. That feminine identity is a strong bond, and yet Bolivia shows us how class, ethnic, and regional loyalties can be an even more pervasive force. Culturally, the majority indigenous population—diverse unto itself—shares few values with a small but powerful elite. The strength of those loyalties along cultural and class lines reinforces the huge gap between those Bolivian women who have access to resources and opportunities and those who do not. When global factors are added to the mix, two things happen:

the disadvantages women have become amplified, and divisions among women are intensified.

Bolivia is characterized by extreme marginalization. Through the lens of women's lives, we see how the disadvantages of Bolivian women are rooted in *machismo,* coupled with long-standing discrimination against class and ethnic groups. Global forces exaggerate those disadvantages. Since access to the benefits of economic globalization depends on, among other things, level of education, type of employment, and level of participation, it is marginalized women who lose out. As these disadvantages intensify, class divisions among women deepen.

The marginalization of women becomes amplified when economic globalization brings privatization, as in the instance of water. Women are hit the hardest because they are the ones most connected to the basic needs of the family, with responsibility for providing water for the household. Lower-class women are hit even harder because they have fewer resources with which to cope with the higher cost of privatized services. And rural indigenous women are most affected because they are disadvantaged not only as caretakers of the home, but as women with few resources, and conflicting conceptions—on a cultural level—of what it means to put community water under the control of foreign private business. A woman in a *machista* society in the poorest country on the continent carries the brunt of exclusion when global forces are brought into the mix.

The second way global forces impact Bolivian women is by intensifying divisions among them. In Bolivia, women identify more strongly with their communities, class, and regions than as women. Everyday politics and local conflicts highlight ethnic, class, and regional divisions. As active members of the social movements—from irrigators to coca farmers—women have put the struggle for their community or class cause above any demands that challenge the existing balance of power between men and women. In politics, women representatives in Congress clearly place a priority on issues benefiting their communities and show little interest in pressing for change to political structures that are unfriendly to women's participation.

Global forces deepen those divisions in two ways. First, women have a range of resources and access to globalization, which means they benefit in highly unequal ways, if at all. Middle- and upper-class women, who strive to claim their benefits from new markets and mobile employment, can limit access for women with fewer resources. When those women are resistant to giving up their own privilege, they may become "gatekeepers" by moderating the benefits of globalization to women who work for them. This can lead to exploitation on one hand and resentment on the other as women with fewer resources watch their "gatekeepers" access resources they cannot. The gatekeeper phenomenon is not relegated to the economic sphere: even social, grassroots leaders are also known to exploit their role as leaders for privileged access, to the detriment of their constituencies.

The resistance to global integration creates another source of division. Policies imposed from abroad have reinforced women's loyalty to their sector rather than to issues facing women. The succession of "wars" over drugs, water, and gas—all reactions to foreign imposition—have strengthened social movements and civil sectors around single issues, while simultaneously drowning out any focus on women's issues. That resistance also elicits a strong reaction from those who generally support globalization. There are strikingly opposing views of how Bolivians envision their country's role in a global economy. In a country like Bolivia, where repeated resistance to globalization comes in the form of weekly road blockades, protests, or marches that can paralyze an entire city, those who support the course of globalization resent that resistance, often accusing protesters of holding back the country's "progress."

Examples from outside of the economic sphere are a reminder that other types of global forces—like the influx of ideas and cultural mores—can exacerbate class and ethnic divisions. Foreign intellectuals and activists—often with Bolivian counterparts—have repeatedly alienated women with the imposition of foreign concepts of gender. For many Bolivian women, *feminism* is marked as a bad word, appropriated by intellectuals and local elites to further their own causes. This, too, has worked to separate, rather than unify, women across class lines.

Creating more common ground despite these influences from abroad will require three major initiatives from within. First, key leaders—including women leaders and male allies—need to reach across cultural, class, and regional divides to offer examples of unity. Second, that leadership needs to lay out an initial and inclusive platform of priorities based on actions and not rhetoric, with which they can build a dialogue across groups and regions. This may include both nationwide priorities, such as how to improve education and participation for women around the country, and locally focused actions that are tailored to the needs of each region. Third, in coordination with local representatives, these leaders need to create an action plan of public campaigns, lobbying, and local projects that directly supports implementation of the platform.

Building solidarity in the midst of deep divisions is not an easy proposition. Bolivia is a country that will always challenge unity. Global forces—from economic pressures to political and diplomatic influence—will continue to incite conflicts that deepen class, regional, and ethnic differences. However, women have a unique opportunity to foster a common cause to build unity rather than deepen existing divisions. In Bolivia, it is not uncommon for the will of the people, coupled with remarkable leadership, to make far-flung dreams become reality.

In late 2006, nearly five hundred Bolivians left the country every day to seek employment and opportunity abroad, most of them with sad farewells like this one in the airport in Cochabamba. Photo: Aaron Luoma (2007).

CHAPTER 8

And Those Who Left

Portraits of a Bolivian Exodus

Lily Whitesell

For decades, Bolivia has seen an exodus of its people emigrating abroad. In late 2006, nearly five hundred Bolivians were leaving every day, boarding buses and planes to seek opportunity and employment abroad. Nearly one out of every four people who were born on Bolivian soil now live elsewhere. Mothers leave their children, fathers leave behind their families, and recent graduates leave their homes, all to seek some slice of opportunity that, for many, they can't find at home.

Based on interviews with Bolivian immigrants in Buenos Aires, Washington, D.C., and Barcelona, as well as with families in Bolivia, Lily Whitesell traces the stories of the Bolivian diaspora. Why do they leave? What are their dreams? What becomes of their lives in their new homes? Will they ever return to Bolivia? In Bolivia's emigration story we hear the voices of those who have left and those who have been left behind.

PORTRAITS

Leonardo Fernández, Argentina, 1992

When Leonardo Fernández was three years old, his father left him, his older sister, and his mother to find a better life in Argentina.[1] A year later, in 1992, Leonardo's father sent for his family. Leonardo's earliest memories from Bolivia include his seven-year-old sister's tears after the disappearance of their father. In Argentina, he remembers playing with other workers' kids outside the factory where his parents worked late into the night and being heartbroken by petty insults about his Bolivian background by Argentinean kids at school.

Simona Velásquez, Argentina, 2005

Simona Velásquez lived in El Alto, La Paz's sister city, managing her own health problems while trying to support six children and an alcoholic husband by making traditional skirts and Andean *ponchos*. When relatives invited her to Buenos Aires to work in their clothes factory, she was nervous. She had heard about the rough working conditions for Bolivians at many of those factories, but she never imagined she would be working from eight in the morning past midnight every day. When her boss threatened to fire her if she spoke out against the working conditions, she set out on her own to find something better.

Julia García, United States, 1973, 1988, 1994

Growing up in rural Cochabamba, Julia García was a girl with two long black braids and a strong sense of family, culture, community, and justice. She suffered teasing and discrimination at school for her Quechua accent but made a career of it. After college, she began teaching Spanish and Quechua to foreigners and got a short internship in the United States in 1973. After years of serving as a translator for development projects and leading bilingual education programs in rural Bolivia, she opened a small store in downtown Cochabamba. When the store failed in 1988 and she risked losing her house to the bank, she left her children behind and headed north once again to the large Bolivian enclave in Arlington, Virginia.

Carlos Arrien, Spain, 1971; United States, 1972

In 1971, when Carlos Arrien was in his first year studying architecture at the Universidad Mayor de San Andrés in La Paz, Bolivian dictator Hugo Banzer closed the public universities and targeted university students as "enemies of the state." When a graduate student Carlos knew was shot trying to negotiate with the police, Carlos's parents decided it was time to take advantage of a special travel deal and they sent him to study in Spain. As Carlos explained thirty years later in a food court outside his workplace in downtown Washington, D.C., the irony was that Spanish dictator Francisco Franco was doing the same thing in universities in Spain.

Medardo Villarroel, Spain, 1996

Growing up in a rural coca-growing region of Bolivia, Medardo Villarroel dreamed of leaving for the city. As a young man, he moved to Cochabamba, opened up a bike shop, and got married. When his young wife told him she was pregnant, Medardo knew that his meager profits at the shop would not be enough to support a family of three. He weighed his options and decided to leave again, this time for Spain. When Medardo arrived in Barcelona in 1996, the Bolivian community was still small and sparse. He suffered police harassment, discrimination at work, and gawking stares from people in the street. At first, Medardo planned to stay in Spain for two years, dreaming of saving enough to buy a car and return to Bolivia as a taxi driver. Ten years later and still in Barcelona, he has new dreams, a new family to take care of, and a new life to lead.

Arminda Solíz, Argentina, 1990s; Spain, 2002

Arminda Solíz went to Buenos Aires during the boom years of the 1990s, but when Argentina fell into economic crisis in 1999, she went back to Santa Cruz, Bolivia's rapidly growing eastern city, and opened up a small hardware store. Never one to pass up a new opportunity, Arminda was intrigued when a Spanish friend came and visited her at the store. She asked him what kind of business one could set up in Spain, and the next day she bought her ticket to leave Bolivia for the second time—with her brother, her little girl, and the intention of opening up a Bolivian restaurant in Barcelona.

WHY THEY LEFT:
A BRIEF HISTORY OF BOLIVIAN EMIGRATION

If there is a starting point to Bolivian migration abroad, it is with the groups of indigenous Guaraní that crossed over Bolivia's remote southern border to work in Argentina's sugarcane harvest in the late nineteenth century. Tales of the vast Argentinean plantations spread quickly through Bolivia's rural areas. That emigration grew in the first half of the twentieth century to satiate northern Argentina's need for rural laborers.[2] Thousands of Bolivian farmers became Argentinean sugar-cane harvesters, and most stayed close to the Bolivian border. As late as 1947, nearly nine out of ten Bolivians in Argentina were still concentrated in the two northern provinces closest to Bolivia, Salta and Jujuy.[3]

In the late 1930s, Argentina's tobacco plantations and vineyards were booming, and landowners began to hire Bolivian workers for more than just the sugarcane season. With work that was now year-round, Bolivian migrants settled down and even began buying their own land.[4] To this day, many of the great farms and plantations in northern Argentina are owned by descendents of those first Bolivian migrant workers.[5]

Around the same time, Chile also began drawing Bolivians. Julia García's great-uncles were among those who were attracted by opportunities there, escaping the forced-labor system of the haciendas.[6] They carried crates of vegetables on mules and trains to sell in border towns. Julia, who would later leave for the United States, recalled that as a girl, "Everything Chilean was in style. [Everyone was] curious about what the *pampas* were like; we all wanted to go. Even up until the 1960s, we would play the latest Chilean *cuecas* at our get-togethers and parties." However, what eventually transformed Bolivian emigration from modest border crossings to Argentina and Chile into a full-blown national exodus was not only opportunity abroad but economic and political turmoil at home.

The Great Upheavals: Revolution and Repression

On April 15, 1952, after a broad-based popular movement in Bolivia won a stunning victory in national elections and the existing government refused to recognize the results, Bolivia's miners, farmers, and laborers led a national revolution. That revolution put Víctor Paz Estenssoro in power as Bolivia's newest president and triggered a wave of political change.[7]

As his first major act as president, Paz Estenssoro nationalized the lucrative mines of the western highlands of the country, the majority of which were held by three so-called Tin Barons.[8] After the revolution, working for the new national mining company meant having a stable, well-paying job. Bolivians of working age left their homes and flocked to the mines.[9]

In August 1953, the government passed a sweeping agrarian reform law, distributing hundreds of thousands of acres of hacienda landholdings to the indigenous peasants who had worked the land for generations.

Before the reform, less than 5 percent of the population controlled 70 percent of Bolivia's land.[10] The land redistribution sent a small wave of wealthy rural hacienda owners, now nearly landless, to the cities. It also gave the former slaves and sharecroppers, now landowners, the freedom to buy and sell land—and move away from it.[11] This new freedom would plant the seeds for what would later become the mass movement of Bolivians abroad.

In the mid-1960s, Bolivia entered a period of historic political instability: nineteen presidents in twenty-one years.[12] In 1971, a coup led by General Hugo Banzer Suárez set off a decade of repressive dictatorships. The universities were closed, and political enemies and their families were killed, disappeared, or exiled. Students who could afford to leave the country did, like Carlos Arrien. He had just finished his first year studying architecture at the Universidad Mayor de San Andrés in La Paz when Banzer came into power. Carlos explained: "After Banzer's coup, they closed the universities for two years, and there really wasn't anything to do. I left partially because of that. In truth, though, my parents really sent me out of the country because they were afraid of what could happen to me. They said, 'If we don't send him out of here, he's going to get involved in some political movement and end up dead in the streets.'" Carlos left for Spain that very year, ironically trading one repressive dictatorship for another. After more than a year of waiting for Spanish universities to open, he decided to try his luck in the United States.

Repression and the search for political and economic stability also sent a wave of emigrants to rapidly industrializing Argentina. Buenos Aires drew immigrants from the heart of Bolivia to build manufacturing and textile factories—and to work in them. Many were also drawn to rural areas just outside the city to cultivate fruit and vegetables to feed the growing population. These new emigrants left their families, homes, and communities, not only for the harvesting seasons, but for years at a time.[13]

The New Wave: Neoliberalism's Bitter Fruit

What sparked Bolivia's current exodus abroad was neither revolution from the left nor repression from the right. The root of that exodus lies in Bolivia's profound economic poverty and the harsh impact of a package of market-driven reforms brought to Bolivia from abroad in 1985. The heart of those reforms involved privatizing national industries, gutting labor protections, and cutting back on government expenditures.[14] (For more on these policies, see chapter 4.)

The miners were the hardest hit by the privatizations, with more than twenty thousand laid off in two years.[15] The newly unemployed and their families began to flock to Bolivia's three largest cities: La Paz, Cochabamba, and Santa Cruz. They also left for the tropical lowlands of the Chapare to grow coca.[16] One emigrant described what happened this way: "When the state-owned mines closed, it provoked an exodus. The [former miners] left the mines like bullets shot from a gun and scattered across the country. Those who arrived in the Chapare established the coca growers' communities. At first, they grew coca for domestic consumption [chewing], but then the era of cocaine began—'82, '84, '86, '88. They all had [U.S.] dollars, and every woman had her revolver. . . . That's how it was when the DEA [U.S. Drug Enforcement Agency] arrived." (For more on coca and the "war on drugs," see chapter 6.)

At the same time, farmers living in Bolivia's rural highlands suffered chronic droughts and cuts to farm assistance and began leaving the land their families had cultivated for generations. Parents sent their children to the cities or saved up to send them abroad. Bolivia was transformed from having a mostly rural population to having 65 percent of its people living in urban areas in just three decades.[17] La Paz's sister city of El Alto starkly illustrates the extent of Bolivia's rural exodus. El Alto was founded in March 1985 by migrants from the agricultural and mining areas of the altiplano (Bolivia's highland plains). In less than twenty-five years, its population has come to equal that of La Paz, making it one of the largest cities in Bolivia.[18]

Today, residents of El Alto like Simona Velásquez help fuel Bolivia's exodus. Simona left for Argentina in economic desperation. She earned so little making and selling traditional Bolivian attire that her oldest children, just starting high school, had to work eight-hour days after their classes. Even with her children working, they could barely make ends meet. "Everything we earned only paid for our food; there was no way to save anything," Simona explained. When she left for Buenos Aires, she never once looked back.

THE DESTINATIONS

As Bolivians will eagerly tell you, local eating and drinking favorites such as *pique a lo macho* and Taquiña beer can be found in nearly every corner of the earth. By far, the biggest Bolivian communities are in Argentina, Spain, and the United States.[19] Each represents a very different history of migration, and each is home to a very different population of Bolivian emigrants.

Argentina:
Estimated Bolivian Population: 1,500,000

To Bolivians looking abroad for better opportunities in the 1980s and 1990s, Argentina seemed like the place to go.[20] Its economy was booming, there was no language barrier, and to get there, all you had to do was get on a bus. Emigrants from all over Bolivia flocked to its capital, Buenos Aires. When Leonardo Fernández's father left for Argentina in 1991, most immigrants worked in construction, the service sector, or in textile factories.[21] His father landed in a large textile factory filled with Bolivian immigrant workers. With Argentina's peso pegged to the dollar, Bolivians were able to save up, send money home, and even have enough to buy their own machines and start up factories of their own. Leonardo's father was one of them—he set up a small workshop out of his home.

Argentina, however, was not as economically stable as many immigrants hoped. In the 1990s, it was going through the same program of radical deregulation, privatization, and trade liberalization recommended by the International Monetary Fund (IMF) that Bolivia had experienced in the 1980s.[22] In 1999, crisis hit Argentina. The government refused to pay back its debt to the IMF, banks refused to let their customers take out money, and the peso was unpegged from the American dollar.[23] The result was an economic meltdown. In the years leading up to the crisis, many Bolivians sensed that trouble was brewing and returned to Bolivia or left directly for other destinations like the United States and Spain.[24]

Before the crisis, the Bolivian emigrants who left for Argentina often had access to resources far exceeding the price of a bus ticket to Buenos Aires. Since the crisis, however, the Bolivians who have left for Argentina have come from Bolivia's most destitute areas.[25] For many young people living in Bolivia's rural highlands, the choice is not whether or not they will stay in the lands their parents farmed and mined, but whether to go to El Alto or Buenos Aires.[26] Today, the Bolivian community in Argentina, with roughly 1.5 million immigrants, is splitting at the seams. Established immigrants contrast sharply with the new arrivals, dividing the community along economic and often political lines.[27]

United States:
Estimated Bolivian Population: 300,000

Over the last fifty years, hundreds of thousands of Latin American emigrants have looked to their northern neighbor to provide opportunities not available in their own countries.[28] Thousands of Bolivians have been among them.

In 1987, informal street vendors began to set up shop on the sidewalk outside Julia García's electronics store in downtown Cochabamba. They paid no taxes and sold the same wares for up to fifty dollars less. Julia's sales faltered and she defaulted on her bank payments. She was close to losing her home, which she'd put up as collateral for her loan. She described leaving for the United States as her "only option." A friend who lived in Virginia found work for her, and Julia left, determined to make enough to pay off her loan within two years.

In Bolivia, if someone tells you they have family in the United States and you ask where, more times than not it will be Arlington, Virginia, affectionately known among Bolivians as "Ahrrlingtohn." Arlington has long been the heart of the Bolivian community in the United States. Through the 1960s and 1970s, it consisted of a few thousand professionals and students whose wealthy families could afford the visa and plane fare.[29] In the 1980s, a broader swath of Bolivians began to arrive, crossing the U.S.-Mexican border or getting visas through the U.S. government to reunite them with parents or children already there.[30] By 2006, the Bolivian enclave in Arlington had grown from a few thousand transplants to a well-established community estimated to be 150,000, half the total number of Bolivians in the United States and enough to count as the eighth-largest city in Bolivia.[31]

Spain:
Estimated Bolivian Population: 250,000

Ten years ago in 1996 when [I decided to leave for Spain], immigration here was like a leaky faucet, there were only two or three other Bolivians coming in drips and droplets, but now, here in Spain, Bolivian immigration is pouring.

Medardo Villarroel

Medardo Villarroel's arrival in Spain predated the boom of Bolivian emigration to that country by several years. However, in the first years after 2000, as Argentina was dealing with its crisis and the United States was tightening its immigration policies, Bolivia's economic situation was not improving. Working as a nanny or construction worker in Spain was becoming more and more attractive.[32] Within a year of her arrival in Spain, Arminda Solíz was doing well caring for an affluent elderly woman in Barcelona. She sent money home to bring over the rest of her family and began making plans to open her restaurant.

The stream of Bolivian emigration abroad jumped across the Atlantic and grew to a torrent. This new emigration was significantly different from past waves—it was no longer dominated by men. Nearly seven out of every ten emigrants from Bolivia were women. While the feminization of Bolivia's emigrant population was fairly new, it had been a growing trend in world migration for the previous three decades. Bolivian women have left for Spain to fill the demand for domestic workers and home care for children and the elderly.[33] As Bolivian women have taken over tasks in their homes, Spanish women have had the chance to enter the workforce more than ever before.[34]

Authorities estimated that by the end of 2006, more than 250,000 Bolivians were living in Spain, mostly in Barcelona and Madrid. Over the course of a few short years, that country has nearly surpassed the United States as the home of the second-largest Bolivian expatriate community, after Argentina, in the world.[35]

THE BOLIVIAN EXODUS, ONE BY ONE

The number of Bolivians who have made the decision to leave is staggering—even though the actual size of that exodus is hard to measure. Because large numbers of the Bolivians living abroad are undocumented, official estimates tend to undercount them. The most comprehensive research shows that roughly 2.5 million Bolivians live abroad, which means that nearly one out of every four people born in Bolivia now lives in another country.[36]

In 2005, 61 percent of Bolivians reported that they were considering leaving the country.[37] But when emigrants are faced with the decision of where to go, their options are not limited to Argentina, the United States, and Spain. The Bolivian community in Brazil has seen patterns of growth similar to those of neighboring Argentina, though not in the same vast numbers. Bolivians have also formed smaller communities all over the world, in places as far off as Italy, Switzerland, Japan, and Israel.

The pattern of Bolivian emigration is determined only in part by the ebb and flow of global economics and immigration rules. It is also the product of hundreds of thousands of individual decisions, most of them hard ones. Bolivian emigrants are influenced by their perception of opportunities in other countries, their own economic situation, and their responsibilities to their parents, siblings, spouses, and children. They also make their decisions based on the invitations they receive from relatives, friends, and former neighbors living abroad.

Those who make the decision to leave are not only young single men and women without families of their own. The Bolivian population abroad is also made up of mothers and fathers who have left young children behind, often with relatives or neighbors. One twenty-two-year-old mother fought back tears as she explained making the choice to go to Spain: "I have been married five years. I work so hard. My husband works so hard. But what do we have to show for it? Nothing. We work to pay for food and rent; that's all." In 2006, she left behind her five-year-old son and her husband and went to Barcelona to be a nanny for other people's children so she could send her savings home.

Those decisions are heartbreaking and can even make some potential emigrants change their mind. Cynthia, who washes clothes for a living, to this day has never traveled out of Cochabamba. She explained: "Three years ago, I was supposed to leave. My plans were all set. My aunt is in Spain. She had been there nearly five years, but I just couldn't bring myself to leave my one-year-old baby."[38]

The force that drives many Bolivians to leave their families has its roots in traditional Andean ties of solidarity. That solidarity manifests itself in a commitment to provide for their family—a commitment so powerful that it drives emigrants to leave them. According to Bolivian sociologist Leonardo de la Torre Ávila, traditional family ties "continually remind our emigrants that their family, their community, and their land are anticipating their support at home." Those ties of solidarity also operate at the community level to create strong networks of emigrants in the new country, often from the same Bolivian town or village, that finance, support, and sustain newcomers.[39] For those who do leave, making that difficult decision and choosing where to go are only the first steps. They soon face the challenge of getting in.

GETTING IN

Ever since nations first drew their borders, migrants have been crossing them. No country in the world has been untouched by immigration—but each nation's immigrant history and policies are very different. The rules they impose shape their immigrants' experience even before they leave home.

Guards at the Door

Argentina: A Tradition of Open Borders

Argentina is known for being a country of immigrants. Its open-border tradition is even inscribed in its constitution.[40] Argentina's first immigrants came from Europe with last names like Schmidt and Bocchini. Since then, Argentineans have spoken with pride about their connection with Europe. But when darker-skinned immigrants with last names like González and Mamani started to arrive from Bolivia, many were treated with suspicion, discrimination, and contempt.[41]

As early as 1936, the Argentinean legislature began to pass laws to discourage and control immigration into its border provinces, but few were successful. While it was much harder to obtain legal residency than before, it was still easy to get in as a tourist. For decades, most of the immigrant population there lacked official status.[42] Faced with a large undocumented population, the government considered its alternatives and decided that the best course of action was to grant an immigrant amnesty. The Argentinean Department of Migration recognized that immigrants' "hard work did not generate income for our society, only for the informal economy. Their lack of documents resulted in marginality and inequality, exposing human beings to all manner of degradation."[43] For those reasons, the government saw that it was to its advantage to grant immigrants legal status. Argentina gave broad amnesties to its booming immigrant population on five different occasions from 1958 to 1992. In that period, more than a million newcomers became legal residents.[44]

When Argentina faced economic crisis in the late 1990s, however, the Argentinean public took the tack that would be repeated in the United States and elsewhere—they blamed the immigrants. In 1995, the governor of Buenos Aires promised to fight unemployment by conducting raids and deporting immigrants. Argentinean unions attributed deteriorating workplace safety standards and lower salaries to those coming from Bolivia and Paraguay. When the economic crisis hit bottom four years later, anti-immigrant sentiment exploded. Responding to political pressure, police teams detained undocumented foreigners in the street. New laws toughened entry requirements and increased deportations.[45]

However, with the country's economic turnaround and the installation of a new progressive government led by President Nestor Kirchner in 2003, Argentina's immigrant policies were relaxed. Instead of trying to keep immigrants from neighboring countries from gaining full rights, new legislation made it easier for them to obtain legal residency. With just a birth certificate and proof of no criminal record, Bolivians were able to get their National Identification Document. To make the process easier for those who were afraid of Argentinean authorities, community and immigrants' rights groups became certified to serve as official intermediaries between the Argentinean government and the immigrants.[46]

The United States: From Ellis Island to the U.S.-Mexican Border

In 2006, the Hispanic and Latino community became the largest minority group in the United States. In the same year, the number of undocumented immigrants in the United States, most of them Latin Americans, was estimated at more than 12 million.[47] One Bolivian related the following interpretation of Latin American immigration, told from a Mexican perspective: "Years ago, we lost our lands by force. We had no military might, and the United States took them from us [in the U.S.-Mexican War of 1847]. But now we are advancing forward—without violence. We've gotten behind enemy lines bit by bit, but it's a peaceful invasion. Latinos have already occupied a quarter of the United States and [Americans] don't have a clue."[48]

The story of immigration to the United States began long before the current wave of Latin Americans, however. In the first two decades of the twentieth century, 25 million immigrants landed at Ellis Island with little restriction, despite complaints that newcomers "stole jobs, were ignorant, criminal and showed no desire to become citizens."[49] With anti-immigrant fears running high, the United States tightened the rules on entry in the early 1920s. Congress established immigration quotas based on nationality for the first time; the U.S. Border Patrol was created; and restrictions on deportations disappeared. The quotas shifted in the mid-1960s, placing new limits on immigration from Latin America.[50] From the 1960s to the 1980s, hundreds of thousands of undocumented immigrants from Mexico, Central America, and South America found their way into the country, many of them fleeing repressive governments or wars backed by the United States. Some crossed the U.S.-Mexican border, and others arrived as tourists but never left.

Like Argentina, the United States eventually responded to its huge undocumented immigrant population with an amnesty program. From 1986 to 1987, almost 3 million newcomers became "legal." That amnesty, implemented by President Ronald Reagan, was supposedly only open to migrant farmworkers, but many saw the program as an opportunity to finally legalize their status after years of living in the United States.[51] Carpenters and restaurant workers got false migrant laborer certifications to present a believable story in the visa interview.[52] After the 1986 legalization, however, immigrants continued flowing into the United States—with and without documents.

After terrorists took over four airplanes on the morning of September 11, 2001, anti-immigrant sentiment in the United States flared once again. Lawmakers increased border security and toughened entry requirements. Their efforts were met with mixed success. In border-crossings, the overall numbers of undocumented immigrants entering the country through Mexico did not decrease, but the difficulty and cost of crossing grew significantly for those immigrants. While immigrants got across for an average of $6,000 in 2002, crossings cost an estimated $12,000 in 2005. The latest immigrants to cross the border have told of costs as high as $15,000 to $30,000.[53] One young Bolivian woman who traveled to Mexico and hired a coyote, the agents who guide those entering illegally, made it across only after a series of tense days.

> At four in the morning the car dropped her off on the side of an interstate. When the bus arrived, she got on and the driver motioned to a man sitting alone in the back. The man carefully and quietly told her, "I am your coyote. When I tell you to, get off the bus and go into the McDonald's across the street. Don't act scared, keep your head up, and don't say anything." After several hours, she got off and followed the directions. A man sat down at the table next to her. "The car is outside. When you finish your food, walk calmly out the door on the left and get in." That's how she got here, moving carefully from one place to the next.[54]

A month later, she was finishing her high school degree and living with relatives in Arlington, Virginia.

U.S. anti-immigrant policies didn't stop with tightening border security. In February 2006, two members of Congress proposed legislation to turn undocumented immigrants into felons and to criminalize any private institution providing any support or social services to undocumented residents. Uproar erupted in Latin American immigrant communities. Massive rallies in March and April 2006 across the United States revealed immigrant pride and strength to the American public, provoking newspaper headlines such as "We decided not to be invisible anymore."[55]

Spain: Colonialism Reversed

When addressing the United Nations in September 2006, Bolivian president Evo Morales expressed the great irony of current Latin American emigration to Europe: "Before it used to be the Europeans that invaded

Latin America, especially Bolivia, but now it seems that the situation has changed. It is now the Latin Americans, or the Bolivians, that are invading Europe."[56]

Compared with Argentina and the United States, Spain has a short record of immigration. In its modern history, Spain saw more migration out until the late 1980s, when it began to attract immigrants from Eastern Europe and Africa. Makeshift boats crossed the Strait of Gibraltar from Morocco and landed in the Canary Islands from Africa's western coast. In the early 1990s, Latin Americans also began to arrive, mostly from Ecuador and Colombia.[57]

At first, Spain discouraged immigration from Africa as well as Latin America. As recently as 2002, Spanish officials "promoted a tough line" on fellow European Union (EU) countries who were "doing nothing" about undocumented immigration.[58] Spain, however, was tailor-made for new immigrants. It had the lowest birth rate in Europe, facing an aging labor force and declining population. With immigrants' arrival and addition to the workforce in the late 1990s, Spain's economy boomed, encouraging even more immigrants to come—2.8 million of them over six years. Spain's immigrant population has increased fourfold since 2000, and the economy has continued to grow. Spain alone created half of all new jobs in the EU from 2001 to 2006.[59]

When a new socialist president, Jose Luis Rodriguez Zapatero, came into power in 2004, Spain's immigration politics also changed. The new head of state reframed the debate in the country. In November 2006, the Spanish ambassador to Bolivia defended (legal) Bolivian immigration: "Spain is in need of foreign workers, and Bolivians are contributing in great measure to our country's wealth."[60]

Even when Spain shut its doors to other Latin American countries like Colombia and Ecuador in 2001 and 2003, Bolivia's emigrants to Spain could still enter without a visa. Then Bolivia became Spain's top source of undocumented immigrants.[61] Spain faced mounting pressure from other members of the European Union to stop the growing numbers of Bolivian "tourists" who never left. In August 2006, Spain gave notice that it was considering imposing a new visa requirement on Bolivians.[62] Spanish officials touted the new visa requirement as the way to end exploitation and workplace abuse of those who lived there illegally, but Bolivian emigrants were not convinced.

After that announcement, Bolivians flooded travel agencies and passport offices, rushing to make it in before the door closed. In October 2006, newspapers reported that more than thirty thousand Bolivians had left for Spain in just two months.[63] Bolivian airlines purchased new jumbo jets just to meet the demand for tickets to the Old World.[64] On April 2, 2007, however, the day after the visa deadline was imposed, the airplanes to Spain were nearly empty and travel agents lazily watched the clock. The mad rush was over, reduced to a trickle.

Getting In, Legally and Illegally

One of the girls I know tried three times before she got in. The first time, they got her when she was getting off the plane in New York. Someone ratted out her coyote, and they took her in and deported her. Fifteen thousand dollars down the drain. The second time, she came in through Mexico, and [the coyotes] drove her to California. She got there, and they got her again. The third time, she crossed the border and she didn't want to risk taking a plane, so she took buses all the way to Washington, D.C. She got here, but she had to pay.

Julia García

After choosing where to go, Bolivian emigrants have to find a way to get there. Some will face greater challenges than others, but for each one, that decision is carefully calculated. Will a Bolivian already in the United States apply for a residency visa for a family member? Will the emigrant be economically secure enough to pass as a tourist with Spanish immigration officials in the Madrid airport or in an interview with the United States consulate in La Paz? Or will the emigrant try to get in clandestinely, risking personal safety and an investment of thousands of dollars to cross the U.S.-Mexican border?

Visa in Hand

When I first came to the United States, I was fourteen. I had never met my dad—he left for the U.S. while my mom was still pregnant with me. When I was eleven, he got papers for my mom and she left to start getting papers for the rest of us. Two years later, everyone's papers arrived except mine. They had gotten lost in the mail, and I had to wait another year in Bolivia so they could send the new ones.

Arturo Sezano

The most desirable but also the most difficult and least common way of emigrating is with a work permit or residency papers. Since the visa requirements were put in place, emigrants hoping to get a Spanish visa need to arrange a work contract through family, friends, or acquaintances already there. However, getting a work visa for Spain is now nearly as difficult as getting one for the United States. A few hundred thousand U.S. immigrant visas are given out worldwide each year— usually when family members who already have citizenship sponsor their children, parents, or siblings for residency. The demand for the immigrant visas is so strong that some new applicants are given wait times of up to twelve years until they can get a visa. Over the last ten years, an average of 664 Bolivians have gotten immigrant visas to the United States each year.[65]

The Tourists Who Never Leave

I went to a travel agency, bought my ticket, and left
with my daughter and my brother. I came in as a
tourist without any problems. The tour took me from
Madrid to Barcelona, and from there, I went to the
hotel. The first job I had was cleaning that very hotel.
I stayed there for two months.

                                                    Arminda Solíz

Entering a country as a tourist and staying illegally—whether in Argentina, the United States, or Spain—is one of the oldest tricks in the immigrant's book. After a couple of hours on a plane or bus, Argentinean immigration officials will give a Bolivian immigrant a tourist stamp for ninety days without a second glance. The ease of entering as a tourist and getting papers once there has meant that most Bolivian immigrants to Argentina have used this method, often not bothering to try for a residency visa.[66]

Applying for a tourist visa to the United States is much different. The application fee for the visa is over one hundred dollars, nearly two months' salary on Bolivia's minimum wage. Once the paperwork is in, the applicant has to go through the U.S. visa interview process notorious among Bolivians—a process daunting even to accomplished Bolivian academics and previously admitted international consultants.[67]

One Bolivian recalled that the worst part was the wait. "The day began and everyone was patient and optimistic. But one by one, we watched others go in for the interview, and over and over again, they were rejected."[68] More than 2 million tourist visa applicants to the United States are rejected each year worldwide. In a country with scarce economic resources, the hundreds of thousands of dollars that are collected each year by the U.S. Embassy on Bolivia's rejected visa applications are a source of bitter resentment for the Bolivian people.[69]

The vast majority of Bolivians who have left for Spain have entered that country as tourists. Starting in 2001, the number of Bolivian travel agencies grew from 11 to 166 in just five years, though many were not legally registered.[70] They advertised packages to Spain on giant brightly colored signs in the largest plazas of the cities, promising airplane tickets and hotel stays to guarantee entry. Bolivians were told to wear Hawaiian shirts and take travel gear; women cut off their long braids and left their traditional attire at home.[71] But even with all their precautions, once they got to immigration, their fate was out of their hands. In the rush to get in before the visa requirements were put in place, fifty Bolivians were sent back every day. In 2006 alone, there were at least two instances of entire planeloads being detained for intense interviews and up to half of the travelers being deported.[72]

One If by Land: Clandestine Border Crossing

One of the young men in the traditional Bolivian dance
group took three months to get here. He came with
fourteen others—six women and the rest men. They
put together a *Tinku* dance group and flew to Panama,
bringing their costumes with them. In Panama they
found the Bolivian Embassy and put together a show.
They earned some money and left for Costa Rica. They
did the same thing in Costa Rica. Dancing, dancing,
dancing, one country after another, they arrived in
Mexico. In Mexico they also performed, but they had
already found their coyote to cross the border. That
very night, they left for the border. They left their costumes, everything, in Mexico, but they paid their passage with the money they had made performing. They
spent three months doing it, but they made it in.

Julia García

No one really knows how many immigrants cross borders every day by sneaking past or around border guards. Many of the Bolivians living in the United States and some of those in Argentina probably did so without registering at the border.[73]

Those who are rejected by the U.S. Embassy for a tourist visa have one last option. They leave for Mexico, find a coyote, and invest thousands of dollars to cross the U.S.-Mexico border, often borrowing from everyone they know. The only Central American country Bolivians can get into without a visa is Panama, and so the trip across the U.S.-Mexico border begins with a flight to Panama, like the one taken by the fourteen-member Bolivian dance group. Entrusting your fate to an unknown coyote has its dangers. Julia García tells another woman's story: "I know an older woman who came with her daughters. Her story is very different, much more painful. The coyotes raped her daughters and left them on the side of the path. Another group that was crossing found them there, crying and in shock, and helped them across."

Staying In

"They want to stop us, keep us from coming in?" explained one immigrant. "We're already here. There's no way they can kick us all out."[74] Even so, the threat of deportation is constantly on the minds of immigrants who have arrived without legal status. In Argentina, the United States, and Spain there have been different strategies for finding undocumented immigrants. In Spain and Argentina, the most common method is by stopping people on the street. In Spain, Medardo Villarroel recalls being stopped by the police and asked to show his documents frequently. Once, when he forgot to bring his residency card with him, he was taken into custody and forced to stay in jail for a day and a half while he waited for a friend to bring his documentation. Leonardo Fernández remembers fear spreading throughout the Bolivian community in Argentina when Immigration Control conducted its street raids. In the United States, immigrant raids usually target the workplace. In December 2006, the United States conducted raids on meatpacking plants, restaurant chains, and other large immigrant employers across the country. Immigrants reported being struck with fear that they or their loved ones could be hit.

When anti-immigrant sentiment runs high, mass deportations are used by politicians to respond to public pressure. However, the cost of finding all the undocumented immigrants in Argentina, the United States, or Spain would be prohibitive. A recent study estimated that the cost of deporting undocumented immigrants from the United States would be in the tens of billions of dollars every year—due mostly to the projected $140 billion overall cost of apprehension.[75] There is also no guarantee that those deported won't come back, and many do just that.

The one way immigrants without legal papers can escape the constant fear of deportation is by finding a way to legalize their status. The terms of amnesty programs vary widely from one country to another. Most involve paying a fine to recuperate the costs of processing the applications. Many also require proof of residency—leases, utility bills, or even bus fare stubs or receipts.

At the end of 2005, President Kirchner of Argentina heralded a new immigration amnesty law with these words: We have "the intention to integrate, to expand opportunities, we want to value immigrants' work, we want to value that work but also not devalue the work of those already here. May [this law] serve to end undocumented work and promote legitimate employment and may its central focus be the human being. [With this new law, we will have] equal responsibilities, equal rights, equal opportunities, and a great country."[76] Argentina's latest amnesty was one more manifestation of the government's openness to immigration. While that country, like the United States and Spain, implemented more restrictive policies in the past, the most recent plan combines the open-border rhetoric of the Kirchner presidency with a concerted effort to provide opportunities for immigrants from nearby countries. In its 2005 amnesty, Spain was slightly more restrictive than Argentina, targeting only working immigrants. Spain has periodically opened the doors to citizenship over the last decade, letting undocumented immigrants obtain a residency for three years with proof of work. After a two-year process, they can gain citizen status.[77]

The United States has had only a few broader legalizations of undocumented immigrants, most notably the two-year farmworker amnesty of 1986. However, the majority of recent U.S. legalizations have occurred through individual sponsorships. Bolivian undocumented immigrants in the United States search for employers who will sign sponsorship papers or ask newly legalized family members to sponsor them for a green card. After five years of having permanent resident status, immigrants can apply for citizenship to give them the right to vote, greater preference in sponsoring a family member for residency, and greater access to higher education, health care, and the legal system.[78]

Through their recent amnesty programs, Argentina and Spain have shown how serious they are about not wanting a large undocumented population like the one the United States has. Those programs and the U.S. project to build a wall on its southern border are very different approaches to the same problem—that undocumented workers can drive down local wages. Argentina and Spain see the solution to that problem in bringing the workers up into the formal economy, while the United States has tried to push those workers out of the economy altogether.

There are hundreds of minute policy decisions that countries have to make about immigration, from which travelers need visas to enter their countries to what documents they require for immigrants to legalize their status. But if you boil all those decisions down, they are really about how those countries receive their immigrants. Throughout their histories, Argentina, the United States, and Spain have received immigrants in very different ways. At some points, they have welcomed immigrants with open arms. At others, they have shut their doors. In the end, if there continue to be large disparities between the opportunities that immigrants can find abroad and those they can find at home, immigrants will keep coming. Their experience will be determined by the balance countries choose between the rules for immigration and the lives of human beings.

LIFE IN THE NEW COUNTRY

I heard them say, Benito's son is coming through
Mexico. They rejected his visa application; we're going
to help him. One said, I'm going to put down a
thousand, another, two thousand, another, five hundred, to pay the coyote. Good, they said, now where
will he stay? One said, he can stay with me. Another
said, I'll get him clothes. And who will find work for
him? Everyone looked for work.

When Benito's son was there in Mexico next to the
coyote, they wired him the money. They all went to
give him a hearty welcome. They helped him until he
was up on his own two feet, until he had paid back
each member of the group and begun to save and send
money home. Then he was automatically indebted to
the group. When another immigrant came—a nephew,
relative, neighbor—it was a moral obligation. He had
to help. That is the moral commitment of our lives—it's
in our blood, in our souls, in our culture, in our tradition. We help each other, we have to. That's reciprocity,
our *ayni*.

Julia García

Even being met with a dozen welcoming faces of those who came before does not free a newly arrived immigrant from the challenges he or she will face. While the newcomers often do find the opportunities they have come in search of, the new world they have arrived in can also hold exploitation, discrimination, loneliness, culture shock, and heartache. It all begins with the arrival.

When four-year-old Leonardo Fernández, his older sister, and his mother got off the bus in Buenos Aires in 1992, they met his father's anxious embrace. A year earlier, his father had been welcomed by the timid smiles of distant relatives. Medardo Villarroel got off the plane in Barcelona clutching a slip of paper with the addresses of his aunt and sister tightly in his hand. Julia García and Arminda Solíz each had a friend waiting to pick them up at the airport.

Knowing how hard it is to be alone in a new society, Bolivians take care of their newest arrivals. They offer their houses and resources to friends and family out of compassion and respect for their shared experience, their tightly knit hometown communities, and as Julia García pointed out, as a matter of personal integrity and culture.

Finding Work

[I came to Spain] like every other immigrant, thinking
that money [was] going to fall from the trees.

Medardo Villarroel

The first job of all immigrants is getting one. Many have borrowed everything their families could scrape together to pay for a plane ticket or a coyote's fee. They get off the plane with enormous debt, immediately start the scramble to find work, and don't rest until they have a steady paycheck.

Medardo Villarroel arrived in Barcelona anxious to find work. For four months he lived on his sister's tightly stretched finances and quickly ebbing goodwill. He spent every day looking for a job, but as soon as he found a lead, it seemed to disappear just as quickly. Desperation and depression set in. Finally, he found another Bolivian who helped him find a construction job. From that moment on, he began to believe that the risk he had taken might be worth it.

Immigrants often find themselves in a vulnerable position when they apply for a job. Language can be the first problem, particularly in the United States. Even if that is not an obstacle, however, many have no

reference point for negotiating a fair wage. Those who lack documentation also carry a visceral fear of the legal system. Those who find work—
as day laborers, carpenters, mechanics, textile factory workers, domestic
workers, nannies, or caring for the elderly—rarely have a contract or
other protections.[79]

In the Washington, D.C., area, half of all domestic workers make
salaries, below the federal minimum wage, and nearly six out of ten day
laborers report having been denied wages at least once.[80] Workers tell of
employers who string them along for months and then never pay them,
of bosses who accuse them of damaging tools and then deduct the cost
from their pay. Live-in domestic workers reported working sixteen-hour
days and having to be on call throughout the night. Those who have
tried to file suits against employers have won only years of legal compli-
cations and delay.

Immigrant workers are not just confronted with exploitation. They
also face blatant discrimination. Medardo Villarroel bitterly remembered leaving a job in Barcelona when he realized after years that only
Spaniards would be promoted. He never had a chance, he said, just
because he was an immigrant.

Immigrants are also forced into jobs where they are sure to receive
the poorest treatment. Even many Bolivian doctors and lawyers end up
working on the bottom rung of the economic ladder. Carlos Arrien,
who spent his first year abroad trying to study in Spain, found nothing
but subhuman working conditions when he moved to New York City in
1972. He recalled how he and other immigrants waiting in the job lines
outside a toy factory were, in his words, treated like animals. "The inter-
viewer literally opened your mouth and looked at your teeth!" He had
never been treated that way before, and it only got worse when he got
the job: "I swear the factory was straight out of Dickens; it looked like
an old train station: black walls, ten minute breaks, harsh discipline on
the assembly lines, with a tower in the middle from which they shouted
at you to move faster. It was like a prison."

The worst cases of mistreatment are told by Bolivian workers in the
textile factories of Buenos Aires. When Simona Velásquez arrived in the
Argentinean capital, her work hours started at 8 A.M. and didn't end
until 1 a.m., seven days a week. At the end of the workday, she and her
six children slept in a back room of the factory they shared with other
workers. Simona's fingers swelled up with rheumatism, and her children
began coughing incessantly from breathing the harsh factory air. When
she complained about it, the owner told her, "We brought you here to

work, not to get sick," and threatened to send her back to Bolivia. Shortly after she left the factory, her oldest son's chronic coughing turned into a severe case of tuberculosis. He never recovered. Despite treatment, he died weeks later. Left with few options and six mouths to feed, Simona scoured the city and found a workers' textile factory cooperative where tasks were shared and she was able to earn a decent wage on an eight-hour shift.

A year later, in March 2006, a fire in a textile factory drew international attention to the conditions of Argentinean factories. The deaths of six Bolivian immigrants who had been locked inside their workplace sparked public charges of exploitation. The testimony of Simona and other workers filled the pages of local and foreign newspapers. Unfortunately, inspections only pushed many of the owners to move their factories further out from the city and deeper underground. Simona and her co-workers even received threats from Argentinean and Bolivian factory owners angry over their lost profits.[81]

Not all Bolivians' work experiences are filled with exploitation and mistreatment. Many are able to find the opportunity they left their country for. In exchange for taking care of her employer's elderly mother for three years, Arminda Solíz was not only paid a good salary, her employer also sponsored her for residency and helped her get a permit for the restaurant she had long dreamed of opening.

Another immigrant, Emma Violand Sánchez, told of the opportunities she found in the United States. She first worked as a nanny as a young woman in the 1960s. After going to college and getting her master's degree in education and counseling, she returned to her country to begin her profession. After eight years in Bolivia, however, she reached a point of stagnation as a professional woman. She could not advance any further or continue her studies, so she decided to return to the United States to get her doctorate. Now, Violand Sánchez directs the Arlington Public Schools' extensive English for Speakers of Other Languages program. For her, leaving Bolivia meant finding possibilities she never would have had in her home country.[82]

For those who have not found the same opportunities as Violand Sánchez, why is emigrating worth the risk? They take that risk for two main reasons—their commitment to save money and their promise to send it home. As one immigrant in the United States frankly put it, "We don't come here to live comfortably. We come here to work."[83] Julia García explained that when she left for the United States in 1988 in fear of losing her house to the bank, she was able to save enough in two years to pay back her thirty-thousand-dollar loan, recover her house, and go home with an additional twenty thousand dollars.

While some immigrants bring the money they save back with them, most stay and send remittance payments home. Three brothers who left for Barcelona in their mid-twenties freed their aging farmer parents from having to work into their elderly years.[84] A middle-aged father in Arlington expressed his pride in having sent each of his four children to private schools and colleges at home.[85] Others send money back to buy houses or land or to pay for others to join them.

Not all remittances go directly to families. In keeping with Bolivians' strong community tradition of mutual reciprocal help, emigrants also send assistance home for their communities. An Arlington soccer league made up of transplants from rural Cochabamba requires each member to pay an entrance fee in order to play. Those fees—totaling between seven thousand and fifteen thousand dollars per season—are sent back to the hometowns of the players to be invested in schools, churches, and new roads.[86]

Finding Community

Our people are very close. Wherever we go, we find
each other and help each other. Someday I would like
to discover and understand—what is that force that
binds us together everywhere we go?

Julia García

In Buenos Aires, Barcelona, and Arlington, emigrants have created Little Bolivias. The neighborhoods are dotted with grocery stores that stock traditional ingredients and restaurants that serve Bolivian dishes. Bolivian newspapers, radio stations, and television programs broadcast news from home. Professional associations of doctors, lawyers, businessmen, and businesswomen meet and help one another. Soccer leagues carry the names of Bolivian cities and towns. *Folklórica* music groups play Andean instruments brought from Bolivia, and cultural groups don elaborate costumes to perform Bolivia's countless traditional dances in parades and festivals.[87]

If immigrants don't find community at first, they create one. After Arminda Solíz arrived in Barcelona and found a job, she started to look for other Bolivians. There were people with Andean features everywhere, but they all seemed to be from Ecuador. When she finally opened up her restaurant, she called it El Cochabambino, determined to create a little corner of home in Barcelona.

In 1973, Julia García took a work-sponsored trip from Bolivia to New York to teach English and Quechua for four months. She ached for Bolivia and arranged to visit some friends in the growing Bolivian community in Arlington, Virginia. When she tasted home-cooked Bolivian food for the first time in months, she was surprised to find something so familiar in a country where she had felt so out of place. When Julia returned to the United States in 1988, the difference was astonishing. Immigrants from single towns in rural areas had filled entire apartment complexes. One even took the name of a small village back in Bolivia, which became known as "Tarata-town." After several years of teaching at a middle school in the heart of the community, she began directing the Escuela Bolivia, a Saturday cultural and educational program. She has found and created her community—fighting to expand Escuela Bolivia, leading traditional dance groups, teaching Quechua, and passing on her rich ancestral culture to classes filled with young Bolivians.

Facing Discrimination

There is discrimination. Why? Perhaps it is because we come with a different way of thinking, a different mind-set, that doesn't fit with theirs. Our beliefs, our views, the way we plan our lives are very different. We don't fit into their system.

Julia García

Discrimination does not just occur in the workplace—immigrants face prejudice from the moment they step outside their community. When he first arrived in Spain, Medardo Villarroel felt like he was always offending someone everywhere he went. He was uncomfortable making noise or drawing any sort of attention to himself. "People would insult you; they would call you 'Sudaca' [a derogatory term for a South American] and all kinds of names." In Argentina, Leonardo Fernández also suffered in his elementary school. It was tough to be the new kid and the only dark-skinned foreigner. He remembered the teasing and discrimination clearly: "At that age, even one little word hurts."

Facing discrimination as a young girl in Bolivia, Julia García's mother taught her "to learn to make people respect you." When she went to the United States, she took that lesson with her. On her daily train ride to work, she noticed that while most people were reasonably polite, some people's good behavior seemed forced. One day, she confirmed her suspicions when the train stopped suddenly, sending passengers tumbling over one another. Julia was thrown onto an elegantly dressed woman, who hissed at her, "Dirty Hispanic! Why don't you go somewhere else!?"

Struggling with Integration

I am Bolivian and I will always be Bolivian. Even if I
were to stay here in Spain a hundred years, I would
never belong here. I will always be Bolivian and my
country will always be my country.
                    Arminda Solíz

The other struggle Bolivian immigrants face is internal: a struggle to hold on to their language, their culture, and their identity while they integrate into a new world. In the United States, Bolivians trying to fit in are confronted with an entirely new language. Some immigrants become fluent quickly; others never learn enough English to order lunch at an American restaurant. For some immigrants from Bolivia, it is not their first time learning a new language—Spanish is a second language after Quechua or Aymara.

Bolivian emigrants work hard to preserve and pass on those indigenous Andean languages. Leonardo Fernández proudly told the story of the family gathering in Buenos Aires when his godfather started speaking in Aymara. Leonardo's parents responded in Spanish at first, but his godfather insisted until the whole family was speaking Aymara by the end of the evening. Because of his godfather's persistence, Leonardo's family began to speak Aymara at home.

The same forces that have preserved the Aymara and Quechua languages for centuries have also preserved their cultures, a source of great Bolivian pride. Immigrants worry that moving to a new country implies putting their culture, pride, and identity on the carving block. However, many have found ways of adapting to their new country without sacrificing their culture.

Others have even rediscovered their culture in the new country. Growing up in La Paz, Carlos Arrien daydreamed about being an American hippie. He was far more interested in learning to play Bob Dylan's latest hit on his guitar than anything else. Spanish friends challenged that mind-set for the first time by pressing him for music from his birthplace. Carlos realized he would have to look for his identity—beyond his teenage dreams of being an American hippie. When he moved to the D.C. area, he attended an Andean *folklórica* music performance and was inspired. He asked a few Bolivian

---

BOX 8.1 | Assimilation and Adaptation:
One Bolivian Woman's View

We live in two worlds. We are two strangers staring at each other. [Americans], how they wish we would assimilate! But for me to be able to assimilate, I would have to forget everything I am, erase myself, and try to be like them. They would have to take out the blood that runs through my veins, from my head all the way down to my toes, and put in someone else's. Even then, I would never be able to be like the others; it's ridiculous to try to be something you're not. That's how I understand assimilation.

But adaptation, I can understand. I can adapt to living side-by-side, so as not to bother you, watching and learning what frustrates you, what you find agreeable, respecting you and being careful not to offend you. That's what we were taught to do. I will respect you, but I will never be the same as you. I will never think the same way you do, feel the same way you do. All we can do is be respectful and do our best to live in harmony with each other.

[The gap between our cultures] will narrow, bit by bit. It's hard to stop the progression of time. Sometimes progress means something valuable gets destroyed. And we will begin to mix. That will mean assimilation. That's inevitable. You can't stop that. No one can stop humanity from changing.

Julia García

---

friends to join him in putting together a group: he played guitar, one friend picked up the *charango* (a traditional Bolivian stringed instrument), and another learned the Andean panpipes and reed flute. The group became a hub for Latino cultural activities in the area. They brought together writers, artists, actors, and musicians from across Latin America and coordinated Latino music festivals. Carlos explained it this way: "I have always maintained my ties with Latin American culture through music. I was always with friends, singing and playing. We created an environment which in some sense was one of the reasons I was able to stay here—perhaps if I hadn't had those ties, that environment, I would have gone back."

Immigrants' children, raised as Spaniards, Americans, or Argentineans, do not always hold on to their culture as tightly as their parents do. Leonardo Fernández lamented that there are schools in the heart of the Buenos Aires Bolivian community where students don't even recognize their Bolivian identity. But for some, like Leonardo, the desire to discover the mystery of their homeland and to pass on their culture is strong. Some cultural loss is always going to occur in any immigrant community. But what is most basic—pride in the Bolivian heritage, the family, and the community and the rich traditions of Bolivian cuisine, music, and dance—will survive.

El Volver: *The Return*

I had a really hard time [in Barcelona]. I wanted to go
back—a lot of people do at first. In one sense, it's great
to be able to make a little money, buy things you've
always wanted but never could in Bolivia—a television,
a car. Never in my life would I have dreamed I would
be able to own a car. Here, a few months of work and
you've got a car, you've got a house, you've got a TV.
[But] this is no paradise; paradise is my country. To be
completely honest, for me, paradise is Bolivia . . . fresh
air, open land, peace, and tranquility.

Medardo Villarroel

El volver refers to going back, returning. It is a nostalgic longing for a time when things seemed simpler. The desire to rediscover a place where life is familiar, where there is no constant renegotiating of the tiniest details of living, where old friends and family are always nearby, where the warmth and comfort of a familiar culture and community surround you.

When Leonardo and his family arrived in Argentina, one of the first things they did was become legal residents, which was a rare choice among Bolivian immigrants in Argentina. "Many people think they're going to work for three or five years and then go back," so they never get their residency. Even in the case of Leonardo's family, the decision to get their papers in order had more to do with getting into public schools than with an intention to stay. Leonardo explained: "In my family, we all have the dream of going back to Bolivia. The only thing keeping us here is finishing our studies and getting our degrees. Then we'll go back to Bolivia. For us it has to do with our identity, our family, and where we truly belong."

The forces that pull on emigrants are strong and contradictory. Once drawn away from their homeland, the force pulling them back starts to exert itself. At the same time, they make ties in the new country that keep them there: family, friends, a house, and a job, a world in which they have invested their time, energy, and money.

Medardo Villarroel planned to stay in Barcelona for two years to save up to "buy a little Toyota Corolla and then go back and make [his] living as a taxi driver in Bolivia" with his wife and child. However, Medardo did what many other immigrants do: he started a new life in Barcelona.

Ten years later, living with his new wife and three little girls, he is resigned to his fate, asking himself, "If I were to go back with a little money, I'd get there, spend it, and then what?" Simona Velásquez still feels strongly about why she left. She has found peace in Argentina; her children are getting a good education. She no longer has to stretch half a pound of meat to feed eight people or deal with a husband who's always drinking. She asks herself, with a life like this, "Why would I go back?" For another Bolivian emigrant, the idea of returning "is something that sticks with you. You're here [in the United States], but you're only here for a little while, and you have to go back. All of this here, it's like it's something borrowed, like none of it is really yours. No one says they want to stay. There are people who have been saying 'I'm going back, I want to go back' for years [and they never do]."[88]

In the Bolivian community in Arlington, Julia García has found a middle ground. "I want to go back. But maybe *el volver* is not a physical return. Perhaps it is about returning to something that is yours, wherever you are. The desire to go back is really about regaining something you have in your mind and in your heart."

BACK HOME IN BOLIVIA

The story of Bolivian emigration does not unfold only among those who leave for Barcelona, Arlington, and Buenos Aires. A big part of that story takes place back home in Bolivia. It is the story of the families left behind; it is the story about what happens to the money that is sent back. In some cases, it's a story about those who do choose to return. And it's also a story of a government struggling to provide jobs to keep its people at home.

Long-Distance Families

My sister is the one who suffered the most. When my father left [for Argentina], she missed him terribly. [Just imagine that] from one day to the next your father disappears and you don't understand why. . . . I was only four and didn't realize what was happening; I only have a few memories. When I went back to Bolivia after ten years and saw my aunts and uncles and cousins, I barely even recognized them. [What I regret the most is not having grown up with] my grandfather, who died years later. I only got to see him once in my life.

Leonardo Fernández

When a Bolivian emigrant boards an airplane or a bus to begin the journey abroad, it is usually after a tearful farewell with aunts, uncles, cousins, parents, siblings, and sometimes even sons or daughters. When mothers and fathers leave their children behind, those children face the anxiety and the emotional impact of losing their parents. They also suffer a higher likelihood of mistreatment and emotional or psychological problems later on.

A recent study in Cochabamba concluded that the increased feminization of Bolivian emigration is taking a particularly harsh toll on children. Of 180 cases of abused children, nearly half are children of recent women emigrants.[89] Another study showed that eight out of every ten adolescents in Cochabamba that are in trouble with the law are children whose parents have emigrated.[90] Living without a mother or father can also force children to grow up very quickly. When Vanesa, a university student in the city of Cochabamba, was left in charge of her sixteen-year-old brother, she felt as though the pressures of being both a mother and a father had been placed on her shoulders. When her mother called from Barcelona, she would try to put on her best stoic voice, but she couldn't hide the anxiety she really felt.[91] Children are not the only ones who suffer because of Bolivia's emigration. Parents left behind talk about their children's departure as the hardest experience of their lives.[92] Many are faced with the choice of leaving their homes to join their children abroad or seeing their children and grandchildren only once every few years if they return to Bolivia at all.

Bolivian Investments: Remittances and Development

If all of the emigrants that are here send a little money
home, then more money will begin to circulate in
Bolivia, the situation there will begin to improve, and
Bolivia will grow and develop.

                                                    Arminda Solíz

Salaries in the countries where Bolivians emigrate average six times the salaries at home.[93] Many Bolivians take advantage of how far those earnings can be stretched in their home country by saving their salaries and sending money home. Nearly 10 percent of Bolivia's gross domestic product comes from its emigrants' monthly remittances, the highest percentage in South America. In 2005, more than $800 million was sent to Bolivia from abroad.[94]

Bolivia also holds the regional record for using remittances to invest in the future. Fifty-five percent is used for investments—to buy property, invest in children's education, or start a business.[95] As opposed to foreign aid, which can get stuck in the pockets of intermediaries, that money is sent directly to the families when they most need it. In rural Cochabamba, for example, remittances have allowed farmers to plant more than just corn or potatoes, and they are now seeing growing returns from their new peach orchards.[96]

Within a family, "remittances constitute one of the largest and most effective poverty relief programs," as the Inter-American Development Bank observed in a recent study.[97] Vanesa, the university student left in charge of her sixteen-year-old brother, can attest to the impact of the money her parents have sent home. Using the money her parents earned first in Buenos Aires, then in Barcelona, Vanesa's family has been able to buy land, build a house, and stop worrying about finances. Vanesa has lived from her parents' remittances through high school, and they have paid her college tuition. Even after her father came back to Bolivia, Vanesa knew that "no matter what happens, my mom [who cares for an elderly woman in Spain] will send home to give us what we need."[98]

In the United States, Carlos Arrien, who has only his parents left in Bolivia, marveled at the commitment to family that Bolivian remittances demonstrate: "Their generosity, their values, not just the value of money, but the value of family, the value of providing for those left at home— my God, this is an example of what real family values are. Their sacrifice. No one expected this phenomenon to happen—that a population would leave and keep sending [so much] home. They haven't forgotten their people. They haven't separated themselves from their family. They are an example for all of us."

Those Who Choose Bolivia

Some emigrants do more than just talk about returning. Professors, doctors, housewives, and taxi drivers all over Bolivia can tell the long stories of why they chose to stay in Bolivia or how they made the decision to come back. Choosing to come home is sometimes as risky as leaving. Immigrants who don't have papers lose the option of reversing their decision—if they change their mind once they're back in Bolivia, they have to find a way to get in all over again. After immigrants have established themselves and adapted to their new life, returning to

Bolivia can be just as hard as leaving it was. Few make the choice lightly. Sometimes they return when they complete a specific goal, like Shirley Girón, who left for Barcelona for the sole purpose of saving enough to buy a house. During those two years, she counted down the days and months until she could return to her children.

Like Arminda Solíz during Argentina's crisis, some return because economic conditions are no longer attractive enough to keep them abroad. A 2007 slowdown in the housing and construction market in the United States left day laborers and construction workers there faced with the decision of staying in the country without work, hoping their luck would change, or going home empty-handed.[99] Others have even cited feelings of patriotism as their reason for staying in Bolivia: "Look, I'm here because we can't all leave. I want to stay here and work to improve my country."[100]

Some simply decide they don't want to live so far away from their friends and family. One Bolivian who has lived in the United States describes her cousin's situation there: "She's got one kid now and one on the way. She's just not happy. I always think, 'What are you doing there?' There is so much support for her here; her mother or cousins could help take care of the kids; she could finish college. And what is there to do? If you don't have a car, you basically have to sit at home all day."[101]

Bolivian Policy: Trying to Make the Dream Possible at Home

In a preinaugural speech, Evo Morales said:

> What have these [neoliberal] economic policies left us with? Unemployment. We have seen the results up close. Our nation invests in the education of our young people; our families invest in their children's education. A young person can get a college degree, but then there's no work. These days, they leave for Europe to wash dishes. How many relatives do we have in Argentina, the United States, or Europe? How many of our neighbors are there? We have so many natural resources, but still our people leave. We have the responsibility to settle this economic and historical social error. Together we will correct the mistakes [of the past].[102]

The Bolivian exodus has not gone unnoticed by its policy makers. When Evo Morales was inaugurated in January 2006, he promised a new kind of governing that would focus on doing what was best for Bolivia, not foreign interests, and that would work hard to relieve the nation's poverty.

In its first year, the new government drew in record gas and oil revenues, negotiated continued trade preferences from the United States, and made announcements of labor plans to provide work for those most susceptible to the call of emigration. In current government officials' minds, the key to combating Bolivia's poverty is to obtain access to foreign markets. Addressing the United Nations in September 2006, President Morales said: "All of you, here in North America as well as in Europe, know that there are many Bolivians who leave in search of work. Why? Because right now, there is no job creation [in Bolivia]. Instead of my sisters and brothers going to Europe—how much better would it be if products went and not human beings? I believe that if we want to resolve the issue of immigration, [we need] fair trade, trade for people, trade which resolves the unemployment problem."[103]

But trying to hold back Bolivian emigration is like trying to stop a tidal wave. The shift of underlying policies that sent hundreds of thousands of Bolivians moving across oceans began decades before. Even Morales's promises of tens of thousands of new jobs have done little to stop it.[104] While Bolivians who wish to stay in Bolivia ask for economic growth, those who wish to find opportunities elsewhere have other requests for their government. They ask for migration accords with wealthy countries to help them go in legally and for assistance from Bolivian embassies once they arrive.

CONCLUSION

The story of Bolivian emigration is made up of thousands of individual decisions, thousands of individual lives. A close look shows that three common threads run through almost all of them—the search for opportunity, the value of family, and the demand for fairness. Behind those threads is also the story of global economic change that goes well beyond individual choices.

In Bolivia, people do what people do all over the world. They look at their future, survey their options, and make the best choices they can. Each year, one by one, hundreds of thousands of Bolivians decide that the economic conditions they face at home mean that their best option is to leave. Even Bolivians who have spent years getting college or post-graduate degrees, establishing careers or shops, or raising a family decide that their best chance for success is to leave all that behind. Although that opportunity is elusive for some, others tell of starting at the bottom in a new land and working their way up. They tell of restaurants that have become successes, careers that have blossomed, futures that hold new promise. That search for opportunity is not just about individuals finding success. It is also about the vast gap in opportunity between nations like Bolivia—plagued by poverty, inequality, and unemployment—and the countries emigrants leave for. To be sure, emigrants face difficulties and hardships on the way. But migration, at its best, allows regular people all around the world to find new hope abroad.

The decisions Bolivians make to emigrate are not merely personal expressions of choice. They are a reaction to global forces that the individuals involved do not control. Many of those leaving Bolivia have been impacted directly or indirectly by the economic fallout of privatization, relaxation of labor protections, and other parts of the neoliberal economic formula that their governments so eagerly adopted in the 1980s and 1990s under foreign pressures. Emigration from Bolivia, and from many other countries in a similar position, is just as much a part of global economic change as the global movement of capital and corporations.

There is also a paradox of family in the Bolivian emigration story. To provide for their parents and children, many Bolivians conclude that they must leave them. Commitment to family, a commitment that runs deep in Bolivia, pushes fathers across a border to finance their children's schooling. Commitment to family sends mothers across an ocean in hopes of gaining a foothold in a better life for their families. That commitment fills Bolivian airports with tears and distraught faces as loved ones bid farewell for what they know will be years. It is easy for some to criticize the decisions mothers and fathers make to leave their children to work abroad. The separation of parents from their children is not without consequences for a family, community, or country. On the other side, it is just as easy to idealize them for the sacrifice they make for their families. None of it makes the tug-of-war decision any easier. None of it lessens an emigrant's commitment to their family or makes a child any less important to a mother or father.

Bolivians' decision to leave throws them into the fates of other countries' immigration policies. Those policies plunge Bolivians into new risks and unfamiliar territory—navigating Mexican deserts, bearing subhuman working conditions, and being forced to place their trust in unknown strangers. Thousands of undocumented Bolivians live their lives in fear—even as they chop vegetables in restaurant kitchens, scrub floors in luxurious homes, and lay the foundations for new bridges and skyscrapers. They know that their new lives can be taken away from them at any moment.

The decisions made now by the nations receiving immigrants will have a profound effect on their people's stories and histories. A century from now, the U.S.-Mexican border will feature just as prominently as Ellis Island in the stories of how young children's families came to the United States. But instead of poetry about the welcome that immigrants receive, those stories will be about the fear of getting in—and the relief they felt when they finally received documents.

The public choices that governments make will ultimately decide how much pain and suffering those immigrants will have to endure along the way. When Simona and her co-workers spoke out about the exploitation they faced—and when Bolivians joined together with other immigrants on the steps of the U.S. capitol in April 2006—it was not only to demand an end to that suffering. It was also to demand the respect they deserve: a place at the negotiating table, a say in the rules that govern their lives, and the dignity of being treated as fellow human beings.

The debate about migration will continue to change, but migration itself is certain. The pull of foreign ports is relentless, inevitable, and timeless. Since the beginning of human history—long before the era of modern global economics—the real force of globalization has always been the movement of people across borders. Long after the existing economics that govern people's lives shift and change, people with limited options and resources at home will choose to leave, hoping to change their family's fate by emigrating to foreign lands.

Conclusion

What Bolivia Teaches Us

Jim Shultz

This book began with a question: What is globalization? It ends with another: What do Bolivia and its stories teach us about how to make globalization a force for justice and equity, instead of a recipe for exploitation and abuse?

THEORY VERSUS REALITY

One lesson Bolivia teaches us is about the wide gap between theory and reality. On the one hand, much of the force behind economic globalization comes from the unwritten rules of free markets. Capital flows to where it can maximize profit. Workers head for lands where they can earn better wages. Nations trade goods because buyers and sellers benefit. But economic globalization is also shaped dramatically by other rules that are written down and that are a matter of choice, not destiny. Crafted and policed by a remarkably small number of people and institutions, those global rules are based on a set of theories about how the world works. For two decades, Bolivia has been a test lab for those theories, and the experiment hasn't gone well.

Time and time again global institutions such as the World Bank and the International Monetary Fund (IMF) advised and coerced Bolivia to make their theory Bolivia's practice. Successive governments, led by a small and affluent national elite, adopted the rules wholesale, out of both ideology and self-interest. They privatized public water systems and the nation's valuable gas and oil reserves into foreign corporate hands. They sold off state-owned businesses, also to foreign companies. They cut public spending and raised taxes in order to pay off foreign debt.

And time and time again the theories failed to deliver what they promised. Privatizing water sent rates skyrocketing and priced a resource essential to life beyond many people's reach. Giving foreign corporations control of Bolivia's gas and oil never produced the revenue and jobs the theorists promised, but it did produce an environmental disaster. IMF demands for budget discipline translated into new taxes on the working poor and a rebellion that left thirty-four people dead. Economic dislocation helped trigger an exodus of hundreds of thousands of emigrants abroad.

In Bolivia, the gap between globalization theory and globalization reality could hardly have been wider. As the theories floundered and the protests mounted, the foreign architects had a ready response. Bolivia just implemented the theories badly. Bad implementation became the new theory.

This lesson from Bolivia is not about complex economics but about human nature. Economists and policy makers a hemisphere away decided that they knew what was best for Bolivia more than the people who lived there. Large numbers of Bolivians, however, believed otherwise. They believed that giving control of their water and gas to foreign corporations was a bad idea. They understood that it was wrong to tax people with the lowest incomes to pay off foreign loans that had mainly benefited the privileged. They knew these things not from theory but from direct experience. Bolivians, and many of their South American neighbors, have rejected the policies imported from Washington, not because of ideology, but because at a very practical level the policies failed.

Officials at international financial institutions do not wake up each morning asking themselves, "What can I do today to make life harder for the poorest?" The problem is actually twofold. First, even if global rule makers mean well, they operate largely in a world of theory and assumptions that often bear little relation to how things actually work out on the ground. Second, they are completely unaccountable to the people whose lives they so dramatically affect. It is also a fact that these institutions serve, not coincidentally, the corporate and economic interests of the wealthy nations that control them. Democracy is fundamentally about the people affected by public decisions having the ability to choose the decision makers and influence their actions. By that measure, it is hard to imagine a system less democratic than the influence that the World Bank, the IMF, and others wield over nations like Bolivia.

In Bolivia, there is also an important homegrown flipside to this gap between theory and reality—the gap between what globalization's critics seek to create and how hard it is to actually accomplish that creation. While the people of Cochabamba won the water revolt victory that has become known around the world, they are still a very long way from fulfilling the revolt's promise; the public water company they retook remains inefficient and poorly managed. President Evo Morales embarked on a historic step with his decree to "nationalize" Bolivia's privatized gas and oil industry, but his government has been plagued by a lack of expertise and resources to make that promise real.

Bolivians have been courageous and inspiring in their declarations of what they *do not* want. But they are still struggling to create the policies and institutions that build the nation they *do* want. Governing and public administration require very different skills than protest, and even the most glorious of public visions must still be built from nuts and bolts. Bolivia's new political majority is still struggling with those nuts and bolts. This too is partly the fruit of the reforms hatched from abroad. Two decades of disassembling state enterprises and putting economic conservatives and foreigners at the reigns has left little opportunity for others to gain the experience they need to govern.

OPPORTUNITIES, BUT FOR WHOM?

One of the great arguments made in favor of economic globalization is about its potential to open up new opportunities for people worldwide. Workers find new markets for what they produce, consumers find access to cheaper goods, and investors find new openings for profit. Bolivia's experiences with globalization ask the question, however, opportunities for whom, and at what cost?

Looking at the results of Bolivia's two-decade dance with neoliberalism, it is clear that the biggest economic winners have been the foreign corporations that used the new rules to pick up lucrative bargains at the nation's expense. Foreign oil firms, for example, were given control of a state oil and gas industry worth billions of dollars, without having to pay the Bolivian treasury a cent for those assets. Also among the big winners are the Bolivian government officials who made the new rules and then, not coincidently, benefited from them personally. Leaders who helped bury the nation in foreign debt also profited handsomely from the loans. President Gonzalo Sánchez de Lozada, who directed the privatization of Bolivia's oil and gas pipelines to Enron and Shell, also reaped a big personal benefit from a side deal that constructed a line directly to his gold mine.

Bolivia's globalization winners also include the civil servants who became agents of foreign institutions, among them the "antidrug" prosecutors paid by the U.S. Embassy and the hundreds of officials who received special "plus" salaries from the World Bank, the IMF, and others. Their personal opportunities came at the expense of their country's sovereignty.

On the other side, who has lost economically in Bolivia under the new global rules? Those who rely on public services—education, health care, and other basics—have lost because privatization deals with foreign companies diminished resources for the national treasury. Tens of thousands became unemployed overnight from the sale of state enterprises. Bolivia's environment has also suffered, from the destruction caused by foreign companies left unregulated by Bolivia's government.

In short, Bolivia's experience underscores a deep problem with the new global economic order worldwide. For those with access to power, formal education, and capital, new opportunities do exist. Some of those opportunities are genuine and honest, such as the woman in Cochabamba who leveraged herself into the international insurance industry. Other new opportunities are not so benign. More important, Bolivia's experiences show us that the opportunities of globalization still flow most to those who hold the classic keys of privilege. If globalization is going to increase equity instead of disparity, the rules of the game are going to have to be very different than the ones on display in Bolivia for the last two decades.

BOLIVIA'S CHALLENGE: GLOBALIZATION OF A DIFFERENT KIND

Bolivia is not saying no to integration in the global economy. It seeks foreign markets for its gas and oil, forms "people's trade agreements" with its neighbors, and courts foreign investors. Bolivia is saying yes to globalization but challenging it to be something different.

One of the things Bolivia is challenging globalization to be is fair instead of exploitative. It is demanding a reasonable price for its rich gas reserves and the chance to both own that gas for itself and to industrialize those reserves to create jobs and local opportunity. It is seeking fair access to U.S. markets for its textiles and products. It seeks to relieve itself of foreign debt and dependency. Reconfiguring globalization into something more equitable means changes at every level—from changes in trade laws to the creation of microenterprises that can tap into niche markets for handmade goods, in the way that the weavers of Chuñu Chuñuni have done with their textile creations.

Bolivia is also challenging globalization's assault on national sovereignty. Citizens in the United States, for example, would never accept foreign interference in their national debate over private versus public health care. In Bolivia similar public-versus-private debates on issues like water and gas were taken out of Bolivian hands through the aid conditions set down by the World Bank and the IMF. By backing away from IMF loans, by ending the U.S. bonuses to drug prosecutors, and by setting its own economic and political course, Bolivia is also demanding a form of global integration that leaves its national sovereignty intact.

Finally, Bolivia offers a lesson about globalization's potential that is not about economics; it is about the power of popular democracy. The social history of developed countries for the last century is filled with efforts to create democratic movements and institutions that can address the limits and excesses of an uncontrolled marketplace—from labor protections to environmental safeguards. Today the markets are global and citizen democracy is playing catch-up.

In their struggles with foreign corporations and foreign governments, Bolivian activists have built networks of solidarity and support that are worldwide and powerful. Bolivia's domestic workers have organized internationally. Debt cancellation was the product of a global effort. Cochabamba's victory against Bechtel's $50 million water revolt claim was won by a coalition of more than three hundred organizations in forty-three countries. Bolivia has shown us, in a powerful way, how to make activism global, creating exchanges, networks, and understanding that have a global impact.

Through all of these challenges—economic, cultural, and political—Bolivia is resisting that aspect of globalization that troubles not only nations but individuals as well, the push toward global conformity. As the Encyclopedia Britannica tells us, globalization includes a relentless push to make the "experience of everyday life standardized around the world." In the face of that push toward conformity, Bolivia's challenge echoes a countermovement worldwide to maintain our national and our individual uniqueness.

There is also an echo of David versus Goliath in the stories of Bolivia's challenge to globalization. Here, over and over again, humble people have taken on the world's giants and they have won, even in some cases with just a slingshot in their hand. What is it that has driven people in Bolivia to take on such fights? I heard the answer to that question one day, standing on a windswept hill in Cochabamba. A fifteen-year-old boy told me about how he became political, a step that eventually made him one of the young "water warriors" in Cochabamba's water revolt: "I remember one day my mother sent me to the store to buy some bread that would cost us one boliviano. But she told me that we had no money and to ask the store owner if we could pay later. I thought to myself, 'my mother works so hard and still we have to borrow one boliviano to buy bread.' That was when I knew something wasn't right."

For two decades, Bolivia has been told by foreign governments and institutions what it needed to do in order to prosper in a globalizing world. The so-called experts had the answers. Bolivians, who have experienced the results of that advice firsthand, have come to the same conclusion as that boy on the hill—something isn't right. With great courage they have fought for a future very different from the one prescribed for them by others, a future of their own design.

Contributors

Nick Buxton (author) a U.K. native, served as communications manager for the Jubilee 2000 campaign against debt and has published chapters on the successes and limitations of this historic global movement. He has also worked with Fundación Solón, a Bolivian organization that conducts research, holds cultural events, and publishes on issues of free trade, water, and women.

Carol S. Conzelman (contributor) received her Ph.D. in cultural anthropology at the University of Colorado at Boulder. As a Fulbright Scholar, she conducted ethnographic fieldwork in the Bolivian Andes in 2003–2004, studying democracy and development in a legal coca-growing region. She examined municipal and community democratic practices, rural development, adventure tourism, and the impact of the U.S. "war on drugs." Carol also teaches university anthropology courses on globalization, development, and democracy.

Melissa Crane Draper (editor) earned her master's degree in International Relations at Johns Hopkins University (School of Advanced International Studies) with a focus in women's issues in development. A graduate of Dartmouth College, she worked for two years with women in grassroots organizations in Bolivia and also in rural Maharashtra, India. She returned to Bolivia in 2005 as an Earhart Fellow to work on issues of women and globalization in coordination with the Democracy Center. Melissa has lived in Bolivia for four years.

Caitlin Esch (contributor) is a graduate of George Washington University who has spent a year and a half living and writing from South America, including both Argentina and Bolivia. She served as editor of the Democracy Center's magazine from Bolivia, *Jallalla!*, during 2006.

Linda Farthing (contributor), a writer, educator, and activist, has worked on Bolivia for twenty-five years and has lived there for eight. She has extensive experience in grassroots community development in both Bolivia and Nepal. In addition, she has written and produced over fifty articles and radio reports on Bolivia, most recently publishing *Impasse in Bolivia: Neoliberal Hegemony and Popular Resistance* (Zed Books, 2006) with Ben Kohl.

Roberto Fernández Terán (contributor) is a professor at the Universidad Mayor de San Simón in Cochabamba. He has written extensively on issues of Bolivia's experiences with foreign economic policies, including his book *FMI, Banco Mundial y estado neocolonial: Poder supranacional en Bolivia* (The IMF, the World Bank, and the neocolonial state: Supranational power in Bolivia), Plural Press, 2003.

Gretchen Gordon (author) is pursuing a master's degree in Latin American studies at the University of California at Berkeley. The former director of the Citizens Trade Campaign in Washington, D.C., Gretchen researches and writes extensively on Latin America and globalization. Her work has been published by Pacifica News Service, *The New Internationalist,* and *Dollars and Sense* among others. She has worked in advocacy around trade and globalization issues for seven years.

Christina Haglund (author) has made Latin America her home for five years, starting out as a Peace Corps volunteer in Paraguay. In addition to her work with the Democracy Center researching the Enron/Shell oil spill, she is a photographer and participates in projects related to rural and urban education, health, and empowerment.

Aaron Luoma (author) received his master's degree from the School for International Training and has lived in Cochabamba on and off since 2002. While spending most of the last fifteen years abroad, Aaron has been both a teacher and coordinator of intercultural exchange programs. He also spent two years working with immigrants on the U.S.-Mexican border in El Paso, Texas.

Marcela Olivera (contributor), a graduate of the Catholic University in Cochabamba, Bolivia, served for four years as the key international liaison for the Coalition for the Defense of Water and Life in Cochabamba. In 2004, she worked with Public Citizen in Washington, D.C., to develop an international citizens' network on water rights, Red Vida.

Leny Olivera Rojas (contributor) is a graduate of the Universidad Mayor de San Simón in Cochabamba. For five years, she has been an activist with Bolivian youth organizations and social movements, in particular with the efforts of Bolivians to address issues related to water, oil, and gas. She has been active in international exchanges on popular education in Bolivia, Sweden, and Tanzania.

Aldo Orellana López (contributor) is a Bolivian activist who is part of the Coalition for the Defense of Water and Gas of Cochabamba and Indy Media Bolivia. He works as a researcher with the Democracy Center and studies economics at the Universidad Mayor de San Simón in Cochabamba.

Jim Shultz (editor) is the Democracy Center's executive director. A graduate of the University of California at Berkeley and Harvard University, he is the author of two books, most recently the award-winning *Democracy Owners' Manual*

(Rutgers University Press, 2002). His writings on global issues have been published in magazines and newspapers across the United States, Canada, and the United Kingdom. His on-the-ground reporting on the 2000 Cochabamba Water Revolt won top honors from Project Censored. Jim has lived in Bolivia for ten years.

Lily Whitesell (author) is a graduate of the University of Virginia. She first came to Bolivia in 2003 through the School for International Training, studying the sociopolitics of urbanization in Cochabamba. Prior to returning to Bolivia in 2007, Lily worked in social justice advocacy in the Washington, D.C., area and with Bolivian organizations in Arlington, Virginia. She has lived in Bolivia for three years.

Coletta A. Youngers (contributor) is an independent consultant and Senior Fellow at the Washington Office on Latin America and has monitored developments in Bolivia for twenty years. She is co-editor of *Drugs and Democracy in Latin America: The Impact of U.S. Policy* (Lynne Rienner Publishers, 2005), author of *Violencia política y sociedad civil en el Perú: Historia de la Coordinadora Nacional de Derechos Humanos* (Instituto de Estudios Peruanos, 2003), and numerous book chapters on U.S. international drug control policy.

Notes

1. THE COCHABAMBA WATER REVOLT

1. UNICEF, "At a Glance: Bolivia," www.unicef.org/infobycountry/bolivia.html.

2. Instituto Nacional de Estadística, "2001: Resultados Censo Nacional de Población y Vivienda Departamento de Cochabamba" (2001: Results of the National Census on Population and Housing, Cochabamba Department), www.ine.gov.bo.

3. Osvaldo Pareja, "Desarrollo regional y participación: Análisis crítico de la realidad regional, la importancia de planificación: El caso SEMAPA" (Regional development and participation: Critical analysis of the regional reality, the importance of planning: The SEMAPA Case), (Cochabamba, Bolivia: Ediciones Runa, 2002), pp. 61–64.

4. Off-the-record interview with the author.

5. Drawn from a presentation of the study by Universidad Mayor de San Simón economics professor Carmen Ledo, "Inequidad y exclusión social en el acceso al servicio de agua potable en Cochabamba" (Inequity and social exclusion in access to drinking water services in Cochabamba), presented in Cochabamba, February 2000, www.aguabolivia.org/PublicarX/GESTION/TEMA5B.htm.

6. On corruption charges, see, for example, Luis González Quintanilla, "Misicuni: El túnel de la intransigencia" (Misicuni: The tunnel of the intransigence), *La Razón*, October 27, 2000, www.aguabolivia.org/prensaX/Prensa/2000/Noviembre/28–3/MIb271000.htm.

7. From the introduction to "Privatizing Water and Sanitation Services," a set of World Bank policy papers available at http://rru.worldbank.org/Papers Links/Privatizing-Water-Sanitation-Services.

8. Quoted in "Leasing the Rain," an episode of the PBS series *Now* that aired on July 5, 2002; see www.pbs.org/now/transcript/transcript125_full.html.

9. "Promoting Privatization," in *The Water Barons* (Washington, D.C.: Center for Public Integrity), February 3, 2003; see www.publicintegrity.org/water/report.aspx?aid=45.

10. "Banco Mundial es claro: Sin privatización de SEMAPA no hay agua potable para Cochabamba" (The World Bank is clear: Without privatizing SEMAPA there will be no drinking water for Cochabamba), *Primera Plana* (La Paz), February 29, 1996, p. 10.

11. "Organismos multilaterales, presionan al gobierno: Condonaran $US 600 millones de deuda si privatizan SEMAPA de Cochabamba..." (Multilateral organizations pressure the government: They will forgive $US 600 million of debt if SEMAPA is privatized), *El Diario* (La Paz), July 1, 1997, p. 5.

12. "Bolivian Water Management: A Tale of Three Cities," Washington, D.C., World Bank, Spring 2002, p. 1.

13. "The Bechtel Report 2008," Bechtel, San Francisco, CA, p. 4; see www.bechtel.com/annual-report.html, and Bechtel's corporate history at www.bechtel.com/history.htm.

14. Laura Peterson, "Bechtel Group Inc.," in *Windfalls of War* (Washington, D.C.: Center for Public Integrity), March 31, 2004; see www.publicintegrity.org/wow/bio.aspx?act=pro&ddlC=6.

15. Interview with the author, November 11, 2001, Cochabamba.

16. Interview with the author, October 18, 2006, Cochabamba.

17. "Cochabamba and the Aguas del Tunari Consortium," Bechtel Corp., San Francisco, CA, March 2005, p. 3, www.bechtel.com/pdf/cochabambafactso 305.pdf.

18. "Bechtel vs. Bolivia: The Water Rate Hikes by Bechtel's Bolivian Company," www.democracyctr.org/bolivia/investigations/water/waterbills-global.htm.

19. Unless otherwise cited, all quotes from Olivera are from a September 29, 2006, interview with the author in Cochabamba.

20. Unless otherwise cited, all quotes from Fernández are from a November 11, 2001, interview with the author in Cochabamba.

21. Correspondence between the Democracy Center and Bechtel in January 2006 would later reveal that the company had invested less than $1 million in Bolivia.

22. This account of the events between the government, the archbishop, and the Coordinadora is drawn from a set of off-the-record interviews with direct participants.

23. "Leasing the Rain," transcript.

24. Interview with the Democracy Center via e-mail, November 13, 2006.

25. Oscar Olivera, *Cochabamba* (Cambridge, MA: South End Press, 2004), p. xi.

26. A transcript of Mr. Wolfensohn's comments was provided to the Democracy Center by a Finnish journalist present at the news conference on April 12, 2000.

27. "Leasing the Rain."

28. Óscar Olivera, *Cochabamba*, pp. 81–82.

29. Tim Padgett, "A Voice on the Left," *Time*, May 28, 2006, www.time.com/time/magazine/article/0,9171,1198906,00.html.

30. The $50 million figure comes from a January 10, 2007, interview by the author with Eduardo Valdivia, the Bolivian government's chief negotiator on the case.

31. "ICSID Cases," World Bank, www.worldbank.org/icsid/cases/cases.htm.

32. "Leasing the Rain."

33. Bechtel's admission that it knew its rate hikes would be "difficult socially" are included in correspondence from the company to the Democracy Center, available at http://democracyctr.org/bechtel/bechtel_letters.htm.

34. Interview with the author, Cochabamba, January 2006.

35. Team member Raquel Gutiérrez writing in Olivera, *Cochabamba*, p. 63.

36. Interview with the author, Cochabamba, October 1, 2006.

37. SEMAPA report, "Informe de gestión—gerencia comercial" (Management report—commercial management), Cochabamba, 2004, p. 4.

38. Ibid., p. 43.

39. Interview with the author, Cochabamba September 19, 2006.

40. Off-the-record interview with the author, June 2006.

41. Interview with the author, September 10, 2006, La Paz.

42. "Bolivia Public Expenditure Review, Executive Summary," World Bank, Washington, D.C., June 14, 1999, p. 1.

43. Interview with the Democracy Center, October 12, 2006, Cochabamba.

2. A RIVER TURNS BLACK

1. Carlos Villegas Quiroga, *Privatización de la industria petrolera en Bolivia: Trayectoria y efectos tributarios* (Privatization of the petroleum industry in Bolivia: Trajectory and impacts), 2nd ed. (La Paz, Bolivia: Plural Editores, 2004), 174.

2. Centro de Estudios Superiores Universitarios de la Universidad Mayor de San Simón (CESU), *Gas, petróleo e imperialismo multinacional en Bolivia, una visión Crítica del poder y su relación con las contribuciones petroleras, 1985–2003* (Gas, petroleum and multinational imperialism in Bolivia, a critical vision of power and its relation to contributions by petroleum companies, 1985–2003), (Cochabamba, Bolivia: CESU, September 2005), 9.

3. Institute for Policy Studies, "Enron's Pawns: How Public Institutions Bankrolled Enron's Globalization Game," March 22, 2002, www.seen.org/PDFs/pawns.pdf (accessed on August 19, 2006).

4. CESU, *Gas, petróleo e imperialismo*, 16.

5. Ibid., 24.

6. Roberto Fernández Terán, interview with the author, Cochabamba, Bolivia, September 8, 2006.

7. ENSR International, *Auditoria ambiental del derrame de hidrocarburos en el Río Desaguadero* (Environmental audit of the oil spill on the Desaguadero River), vol. 2 (Bolivia, April 2001), 11.

8. Porfiria Marca de Castillo, interview with the author, May 21, 2006.

9. ENSR, *Auditoria ambiental*, vol. 2, 13.

10. Maria McFarland Sánchez-Moreno and Tracy Higgins, "No Recourse: Transnational Corporations and the Protection of Economic, Social, and Cultural Rights in Bolivia," *Fordham International Law Journal* 27 (2004): 7.

11. ENSR, *Auditoria ambiental,* vol. 2, 10–11.

12. Sánchez-Moreno and Higgins, "No Recourse," 20.

13. Roger E. Carvajal, "Análisis de los riesgos toxicológicos en la salud humana" (Analysis of the toxicological risks on human health), Annex of Environmental Audit (Bolivia, March 2001), 39.

14. ENSR, *Auditoria ambiental,* vol. 2, 11.

15. Transredes S. A., *Derrame OSSA-2 al Río Desaguadero; Informe socioeconómico y acciones del equipo CLO's* (Oil spill OSSA-2 on the Desaguadero River), (Oruro: Transredes, July 2000), vii.

16. Vidal Aguilar, interview with the author, El Choro, Bolivia, March 5, 2006.

17. Bird's-eye-view photo of Lake Poopó taken from Google Map Service, http://209.15.138.224/bolivia_mapas/s_theAltiplanoLakePoopoBolivia.htm (accessed on August 20, 2006).

18. ENSR, *Auditoria ambiental,* vol. 6, 20.

19. Dictionary.com, http://dictionary.reference.com/browse/negligence (accessed August 21, 2006).

20. Sánchez-Moreno and Higgins, "No Recourse," 20.

21. Ibid., pp. 20, 7.

22. ENSR, *Auditoria ambiental,* vol. 7, 4.

23. Sánchez-Moreno and Higgins, "No Recourse," 8.

24. ENSR, *Auditoria ambiental,* vol. 7, 4.

25. Transredes memo to the Democracy Center, March 21, 2007.

26. Ibid.

27. Environmental Resource Management, www.erm.com/ERM/Showcase.nst (accessed August 21, 2006).

28. *Telepaís,* channel 13, February 7, 2000; *Noticias Central,* channel 5, February 21, 2000; "Súper: Transredes no actuó rápido" (Super: Transredes does not act rapidly), *La Prensa,* February 10, 2000.

29. Jorge Lazzo Valera, "Transredes se comprometió a remediar efectos de derrame de petróleo en Oruro" (Transredes promised to fix Oruro oil spill effects), *Presencia,* February 6, 2000.

30. *Noticias Central,* Channel 5. February 5, 2000.

31. Transredes press release, *La Prensa,* March 8, 2000.

32. *Noticias PAT,* channel 42, February 15, 2000.

33. Ibid.

34. Community members of Ulloma, in a meeting with the author, May 11, 2006; Hans Möeller, interview with the author, June 14, 2006; community members in Acopata, interview with the author, May 18, 2006.

35. Guisoni, Oscar, "Aguas negras: Derrame en el desaguadero. Una historia que se vuelve a repetir" (Black waters: Oil spill on the Desaguadero, a history that will be repeated), *La Prensa,* February 6, 2000.

36. "Área contaminada debe ser declarada zona de desastre" (Contaminated area should be declared a Disaster Zone), *La Patria,* February 3, 2000.

37. Don Juan del Díos Castillo Villegas, interview with the author, May 16, 2006.

38. Tom Pellens, economist, Centro de Investigación y Promoción del Campesinado (CIPCA), interview with the editor, Cochabamba, Bolivia, March 14, 2008.

39. ENSR, *Auditoria ambiental,* vol. 7, 39.

40. Transredes memo to the Democracy Center.

41. Details of the meeting come from a meeting with the author on May 11, 2006; ENSR, *Auditoria ambiental,* vol. 2, 107.

42. Jorge Lazzo Valera, "Comunidades afectadas por derrame de petróleo viven en la incertidumbre" (Communities affected by the oil spill live in uncertainty), *Presencia,* February 18, 2000.

43. ENSR, *Auditoria Ambiental,* vol. 7, 8.

44. Ibid., 3.

45. "Derrame: Comunarios de Chuquiña claman justicia" (Oil spill: Community members from Chuquiña call for justice), *La Prensa,* December 12, 2001.

46. ENSR, *Auditoria Ambiental,* vol. 7, 10.

47. "Limpiaron el 80% del crudo derramado" (Eighty percent of oil spill has been cleaned up), *La Razón,* March 26, 2000.

48. "Gobierno detecta malos trabajos de limpieza en el río Desaguadero" (Government discovers poor quality of cleaning job on the Desaguadero), *La Razón,* March 31, 2000.

49. "Transredes y CARE comienzan con los proyectos de desarrollo" (Transredes and CARE begin with development projects), *Ultima Hora,* August 4, 2000.

50. ENSR, *Auditoria ambiental,* vol. 2, 107.

51. ENSR, *Auditoria ambiental,* vol. 7, 39.

52. Juan Carlos Montoya Ch., *Efectos ambientales y socioeconómicos por el derrame de petróleo en el Río Desaguadero* (Environmental and socioeconomic impacts due to the oil spill on the Desaguadero River), (La Paz, Bolivia: Fundación PIEB, 2002), 16.

53. ENSR, *Auditoria ambiental,* vol. 2, 186.

54. ENSR, *Auditoria ambiental,* vol. 7, 11.

55. "El proceso de compensación de Transredes registra importantes avances" (The process of Transredes's compensation shows important advances), Transredes press release as printed in *La Razón,* June 7, 2000.

56. ENSR, *Auditoria ambiental,* vol. 2, 186; ENSR, *Auditoria ambiental,* vol. 7, 12.

57. Don Teodisio Liquepe, interview with the author, May 17, 2006.

58. "El proceso de compensación," *La Razón,* June 7, 2000.

59. ENSR, *Auditoria Ambiental,* vol. 7, 13.

60. Hans Möeller, interview with the author, June 13, 2006.

61. Montoya, *Efectos,* 165.

62. "Derrame en el Desaguadero crea polémica" (Oil spill on the Desaguadero creates controversy), *El Mundo,* March 16, 2000.

63. ENSR, *Auditoria ambiental,* vol. 2, 157.

64. Transredes S. A., "Derrame OSSA-2 al Río Desaguadero: Tercer informe intermedio, conclusión de las operaciones de limpieza y actualización de compensación" (Oil spill OSSA-2 on the Desaguadero River: Third intermediate report, conclusion of the clearing operations and compensation update), Annex G: Contrato Transaccional, Clausula Cuarta.

65. Community members of Ulloma, in a meeting with the author on May 11, 2006.

66. Transredes S. A., "Derrame OSSA-2 al Río Desaguadero: Tercer informe intermedio," Annex G.

67. Vidal Aguilar, interview with the author, Cruz Choro Viri-Viri, Bolivia, March 5, 2006.

68. Community members of Ulloma, in a meeting with the author on May 11, 2006.

69. Foro Boliviano de Medio Ambiente y Desarrollo Oruro (FOBOMADE), "Análisis y evaluación del proceso y los conflictos socioambientales derivados de la contaminación por el derrame de petróleo en el Río Desaguadero: Un año después del desastre ambiental" (Analysis and evaluation of the process of the socioenvironmental conflicts as a result of the contamination from the oil spill on the Desaguadero River: One year after the environmental disaster), (Oruro, Bolivia: January 2001).

70. Transredes S. A., "Derrame OSSA-2 al Río Desaguadero: Informe socio-económico y acciones del equipo CLO's" (Oil spill OSSA-2 on the Desaguadero River: Socioeconomic report and actions of the CLO team), (Transredes: Oruro, July 2000), 4–5.

71. Anonymous former CLO employed by Transredes, interview with the author, November 17, 2005.

72. Transredes S. A., "Derrame OSSA-2 al Río Desaguadero," 40.

73. "29 mil barriles de crudo reconstituido se derramaron en el río Desaguadero" (29,000 barrels of reconstituted crude oil spill into the Desaguadero River), Presencia, March 25, 2000.

74. "Sigue la contaminación en Desaguadero" (Contamination in the Desaguadero continues), La Razón, July 23, 2000.

75. Patch Safety Services Ltd., "Conclusions of Analysis," June 2000.

76. See www.odi.org.uk/speeches/corporations2002/report7.html.

77. Sánchez-Moreno and Higgins, "No Recourse," 16.

78. Victor Rico, informal interview with the author, La Paz, Bolivia, May 8, 2006.

79. ENSR, Auditoria ambiental, vol. 7, 15.

80. Vidal Aguilar, interview with the author, El Cruz Choro Viri-Viri, Bolivia, March 5, 2006; Ulloma community members, interview with the author, May 11, 2006; Sánchez-Moreno and Higgins, "No Recourse," 16.

81. Transredes memo to the Democracy Center.

82. Sánchez-Moreno and Higgins, "No Recourse," 16.

83. This figure is based on the calculation that of the 3,938 families that were compensated, with each family unit having an average of five members.

84. ENSR, Auditoria ambiental, vol. 2, 184.

85. Ibid.

86. Ibid.

87. Ibid.

88. "Violenta protesta de comunarios de Chuquiña contra Transredes" (Violent protest by the Chuquiña community members against Transredes), El Diario, June 16, 2000.

89. "Marcha de campesinos contra Transredes y la contaminación" (Farmers' march against Transredes and the contamination), *La Patria,* February 8, 2000.

90. Rufino Choque, interview with the author, Poopó, Bolivia, March 13, 2006.

91. "Mujeres y niños uru muratos enferman por falta de alimento" (Uru murato women and children fall sick due to lack of food), *Presencia,* June 2, 2000.

92. Sánchez-Moreno and Higgins, "No Recourse," 11.

93. "Transredes trató de interferir la marcha de Uru-Muratos" (Transredes tried to interfere in the Uru-Murato march), *Ultima Hora,* April 6, 2000.

94. "Funcionarios de Transredes rehenes en Toma Toma" (Transredes officials taken hostage in Toma Toma), *Presencia,* April 7, 2000.

95. Saul Apaza, interview with the author, Oruro, Bolivia, March 3, 2006.

96. Saul Apaza, interview with the author, Cochabamba, Bolivia, November 23, 2006.

97. Sánchez-Moreno and Higgins, "No Recourse," 21.

98. Victor Orduna, "Qué tú crees, que esto es Suiza?" (What do you think, that this is Switzerland?), *Pulso,* February 25, 2000.

99. Sánchez-Moreno and Higgins, "No Recourse," 3.

100. Ibid.

101. *Estudio Abierto,* channel 4, February 9, 2000; "Comité cívico enjuiciará a Transredes: Parlamentarios dicen que la empresa desinforma" (Civic committee will bring a case against Transredes: Parliamentary members say the company misled), *La Razón,* February 9, 2000.

102. See www.transredes.com/pdf/memoria/MA2005ENG/parte1ing.pdf.

103. Sánchez-Moreno and Higgins, "No Recourse," 21.

104. "Brazil Battles Oil Spill Threat," BBC News, July 18, 2000, http://news.bbc.co.uk/1/hi/world/americas/838826.stm.

105. Felipe Coronado, interview with the author, Oruro, Bolivia, November 17, 2005; Hans Möeller, interview with the author, La Paz, Bolivia, June 13, 2006.

106. Felipe Coronado, interview with the author, November 17, 2005.

107. FOBOMADE, "Análisis y evaluación."

108. Hans Möeller, interview with the author, June 13, 2006.

109. Transredes, *Derrame OSSA-2 al Río Desaguadero: Informe socio-económico,* vii.

110. Hans Möeller, interview with the author, June 13, 2006.

111. Ibid.

112. "How an Oil Spill Helped a Bolivian Energy Company to Become a Model of Corporate Citizenship," *IDB America,* October 5, 2005.

113. Environmental Services (ENSR), www.ensr.aecom.com/MarketsAndServices/46/65/index.jsp (accessed June 29, 2006).

114. Carvajal, "Análisis de los riesgos toxicológicos," 4–5.

115. Ibid., 5.

116. Ibid., 38.

117. Ibid., 39.

118. ENSR, *Auditoria ambiental,* vol. 7, 12.

119. Ibid., 15–16.

120. "Comunarios y Transredes definirán plan de remediación"(Community members and Transredes Hill define a remediation plan), *La Prensa,* October 18, 2001.

121. "Enron Deals Under Scrutiny in Bolivia," *Hawaii Reporter,* April 5, 2002.

122. Tomás Villegas Castillo, interview with the author, May 20, 2006.

123. Transredes press release in *La Prensa,* March 8, 2000.

124. Transredes press release in *La Razón,* June 7, 2000.

125. ENSR, *Auditoria ambiental,* vol. 7, 13.

126. Transredes memo to the Democracy Center.

127. Ibid.

128. Santiago Castillo Ramos, interview with the author, May 23, 2006.

129. Inter-American Development Bank, www.iadb.org/csramericas/2003/doc/henshaw2.pdf (accessed May 11, 2006).

3. OIL AND GAS

1. Most of the research for this chapter was completed in early 2007, with critical updates added through March 2008.

2. Mensaje a la nación del presidente de la república (Message from the nation's president), Evo Morales Ayma, from Carapari, La Paz (May 1, 2006). Translation by authors.

3. Andrés Soliz Rada, Bolivia's hydrocarbons minister, from resignation letter, (September 15, 2006), text translation found at http://mrzine.monthly review.org/solizrada190906.html.

4. James Dunkerley, *Rebellion in the Veins: Political Struggle in Bolivia, 1952–82* (Thetford, UK: Thetford Press, 1984), 6.

5. Ibid., 7.

6. Ibid., 14.

7. Centro de Documentación e Información Bolivia (CEDIB), *La gestión de los recursos naturales no renovables de Bolivia* (Management of nonrenewable natural resources of Bolivia), *No.* 2 (Cochabamba, Bolivia: Live Graphics SRL, 2005), 97; John Crabtree, *The Great Tin Crash* (London: Latin America Bureau, 1987).

8. Mirko Orgaz García, *La guerra del gas: Nación versus estado transnacional* (Gas war: The nation versus the transnational state) (La Paz: CEDLA, 2005), 139. Translation by authors.

9. Paul Roberts, *The End of Oil: On the Edge of a Perilous New World* (New York: Houghton Mifflin, 2004), 168.

10. Ibid., 167.

11. Energy Information Administration, "December 2006 Monthly Energy Review: Table 9.11 Natural Gas Prices," http://tonto.eia.doe.gov/merquery/mer_data.asp?table=T09.11; Roberts, *End of Oil,* 177.

12. "Más de 57 mil vehículos dejaron la gasolina por el gas natural" (More than 57 million vehicles give up gasoline for natural gas), *Opinión,* September 1, 2006.

13. Ibid.

14. Carlos Rojas, interview with the authors, La Paz, March 28, 2006.

15. Carlos Royuela Camboni, *Cien años de hidrocarburos en Bolivia: 1896–1996* (One hundred years of hydrocarbons in Bolivia: 1896–1996) (Cochabamba: Los Amigos del Libro, 1996), 35–36; Centro de Estudios para el Desarrollo Laboral y Agrario (CEDLA), *Los hidrocarburos en la historia de Bolivia* (Hydrocarbons in the history of Bolivia) (La Paz: CEDLA, 2005), 8.

16. Enrique Mariaca Bilbao, "Petróleo en Bolivia" (Petroleum in Bolivia), in *Temas sociales 22 foro YPFB vs. capitalización* (Social topics 22, forum of YPFB vs. capitalization) (La Paz: Universidad Mayor de San Andrés, Facultad de Ciencias Sociales, 2001), 19; Dunkerley, *Rebellion,* 27.

17. "Standard Oil: La primera nacionalización en 1937" (Standard Oil: The first nationalization in 1937), *Opinión,* May 23, 2006.

18. Mariaca Bilbao, "Petróleo en Bolivia," 19. Translation by authors.

19. Mirko Orgaz García, *La nacionalización del gas: Economía, política, y geopolítica de la 3ra. nacionalización de los hidrocarburos en Bolivia* (Gas nationalization: Economy, politics, and geopolitics of the third nationalization of hydrocarbons in Bolivia) (La Paz: CEDLA, 2005), 100. Translation by authors.

20. CEDLA, *Los hidrocarburos,* 8.

21. Orgaz García, *La nacionalización,* 108.

22. Ibid., 107.

23. Herbert S. Klein, *Bolivia: The Evolution of a Multi-Ethnic Society,* 2nd ed. (New York: Oxford University Press, 1992), 240.

24. Aid statistics are from 1954–64. Mariaca Bilbao, "Petróleo en Bolivia," 22.

25. CEDLA, *Los hidrocarburos,* 16; Dunkerley, *Rebellion,* 112.

26. CEDLA, *Los hidrocarburos,* 15.

27. Orgaz, *La nacionalización,* 111.

28. CEDLA, *Los hidrocarburos,* 15.

29. Camboni, *Cien años,* 123.

30. Augusto Céspedes, *Antientreguismo: Una política del pueblo, foro nacional: Gas y petróleo, liberación o dependencia* (Anti-deliverism: Politics of the people, national forum: Gas and petroleum, liberation or dependency) (Cochabamba: UMSS Editorial Universitaria, November 29, 1967), 132. Translation by authors.

31. Camboni, *Cien años,* 141. Translation by authors.

32. Marcelo Quiroga Santa Cruz, *Oleocracia o Patria: Obras Completas* ("Oil-cracy" or homeland: Complete works), vol. 5 (La Paz: Plural Editores, 1977), 62. Translation by authors.

33. Dunkerley, *Rebellion,* 165.

34. "1969: Marcelo Quiroga y el decreto de nacionalización de la Gulf Oil" (1969: Marcelo Quiroga and the decree of Gulf Oil nationalization), *Opinión,* May 14, 2006.

35. CEDLA, *Los hidrocarburos,* 17–18.

36. Benjamin Kohl and Linda Farthing, *Impasse in Bolivia: Neoliberal Hegemony and Popular Resistance* (New York: Zed Books, 2006), 112.

37. Camboni, *Cien años,* 151.

38. J. Osvaldo Calle Quiñónez, *El que manda aquí soy yo: Guía rápida para entender la capitalización* (I am the one who commands here: A rapid guide to

understanding capitalization) (La Paz: Fundación Chuquiagu, 2000), 141; Pablo Ramos Sánchez, "Los recursos hidrocarburíferos en la economía Boliviana" (Hydrocarbon resources in the Bolivian economy), in *Temas sociales 22 foro YPFB vs. Capitalización* (Social topics 22, forum of YPFB vs. capitalization) (La Paz: Universidad Mayor de San Andrés, Facultad de Ciencias Sociales, 2001), 87.

39. Mariaca Bilbao, "*Petróleo en Bolivia*," 27.

40. Álvaro García Linera, "Los impactos de la capitalización: Evaluación a medio termino" (Impacts of capitalization: An evaluation on average terms), in *Luces y sombras: 10 años de la capitalización* (Lights and shadows: Ten years of capitalization), Delegación presidencial para la revisión y mejora de la capitalización (La Paz: December 2004), 227.

41. Carlos Villegas Quiroga, interview with Gretchen Gordon, La Paz, June 2005.

42. Roberto Fernández Terán, *FMI, Banco Mundial y estado neocolonial: Poder supranacional en Bolivia* (IMF, World Bank, and neocolonial state: Supra state power in Bolivia) (La Paz: Universidad Mayor de San Simón, July 2004), 86.

43. Calle Quiñónez, *El que manda aquí,* 29.

44. Osvaldo Calle Quiñónez, "'Bolivia la nueva': El despertar de un acto de ilusión" (The new Bolivia: Upon awakening from an act of illusion), in *Temas sociales 22 foro YPFB vs. capitalización* (Social topics 22, forum of YPFB vs. capitalization) (La Paz: Universidad Mayor de San Andrés, Facultad de Ciencias Sociales, 2001), 48.

45. Orgaz García, *La nacionalización,* 136.

46. Ibid.

47. Mirko Orgaz García, interview with the authors, March 27, 2006.

48. Claire McGuigan, "The Benefits of Foreign Investment: Is Foreign Investment in Bolivia's Oil and Gas Delivering?" *Christian Aid/CEDLA* (November 2006): 37, 41.

49. Carlos Arce, interview with the authors, La Paz, March 27, 2006.

50. García Linera, "Los impactos de la capitalización," 227.

51. Orgaz García, *La nacionalización,* 137.

52. Orgaz García, *La guerra del gas,* 223.

53. García Linera, "Los impactos de la capitalización," 235; CIA World Factbook, 2005; International Monetary Fund, "Bolivia: Ex Post Assessment of Longer-Term Program Engagement—Staff Report and Public Information Notice on the Executive Board Discussion" (2005), 6.

54. García Linera, "Los impactos de la capitalización," 232.

55. Ministerio de Hidrocarburos, "Estadísticas—upstream—producción" (Statistics-upstream-production) (July 28, 2005); "Comportamiento de los impuestos sobre hidrocarburos" (Behavior of the hydrocarbon taxes)," unpublished data from CEDLA (La Paz, March 19, 2007). Author-calculated average.

56. Óscar Zegada Claure, "Los impactos de la capitalización: Evaluación a medio término" (Impacts of capitalization: Midterm evaluation), in *Luces y sombras: 10 años de la capitalización* (Lights and shadows: Ten years of capitalization), Delegación presidencial para la revisión y mejora de la capitalización (La Paz: December 2004): 222; García Linera, "Los impactos de la capitalización," 230.

57. "La fiscalía de La Paz cierra el caso de la quebrada empresa Enron" (Prosecutor's office of La Paz closes the case of Enron bankruptcy), *La Razón,* December 21, 2006; Calle Quiñónez, *El que manda aquí,* 135.

58. "Denuncian un gasoducto de uso privado" (Charges of a gas pipeline for private use), *Opinión,* November 15, 2002.

59. Enrique Menacho Roca, interview with the authors, April 25, 2006.

60. Orgaz, *La guerra del gas,* 193–94.

61. Luis A. Gómez, *El Alto de pie: Una insurrección Aymara en Bolivia* (El Alto stands up: An Aymara insurrection in Bolivia) (La Paz: Textos Rebeldes, 2004), 41.

62. Orgaz, *La guerra del gas,* 194.

63. *Gas: Debate nacional* (Gas: National debate) (La Paz: El Pulso del País: 2004), 96.

64. "Marchas pacíficas por gas paralizan varias ciudades" (Peaceful marches on gas issue paralyze various cities), *Los Tiempos,* September 20, 2003.

65. Gómez, *El Alto de pie,* 22.

66. *Memoria testimonial de la "guerra del gas"* (Testimonial statement from the "gas war") (La Paz: Cepas-Caritas, 2004), 30.

67. Supreme Decree 27209, October 11, 2003. Translation by authors.

68. Néstor Salinas Malléa, interview with Gretchen Gordon, Mar del Plata, Argentina, November 2005.

69. Néstor Salinas Malléa, e-mail interview with authors, May 2007.

70. "Mesa ratifica su alejamiento de Goni y asegura que nada justifica la muerte" (Mesa confirms his distance from Goni and assures that nothing justifies death), *Opinión,* October 17, 2003. Translation by authors.

71. Gómez, *El Alto de pie,* 99.

72. Ibid., 104. Translation by authors.

73. "Cronología de la caída del ex presidente" (A chronology of the fall of the ex-president), *Correo del Sur,* October 18, 2003. Translation by authors.

74. "EEUU apoya a Goni y dice que no reconocerá otro gobierno" (U.S. supports Goni and says that it will not recognize another government), *La Razón* (October 14, 2003). Translation by authors.

75. Forrest Hylton and Sinclair Thomson, "The Chequered Rainbow," *New Left Review* 35 (September/October 2005), 56.

76. Ibid., 57.

77. Sixty of the sixty-seven deaths were certified to have causes related to military actions. Source: Legal archive of the Comité Impulsor del Juicio de Responsabilidades.

78. Swearing-in address of Constitutional President Carlos Mesa Gisbert, La Paz, October 17, 2003. See www.bolivia-usa.org/discurso_presidente_mesa. htm. Translation by authors.

79. "Mesa mantiene alto nivel de apoyo mientras Evo Morales cae a sólo 8%" (Mesa maintains a high level of support while Evo Morales falls to a mere 8%), *La Capital,* March 21, 2005.

80. Carlos Villegas Quiroga, interview with Gretchen Gordon, La Paz, June 2005.

81. "Documentos de coyuntura" (Documents of current events), vol. 9 (La Paz: CEDLA, December 2004), 21. Translation by authors.

82. Hylton and Thomson, "The Chequered Rainbow," 58.

83. "FMI: Bolivia solo es viable si exporta gas" (IMF: Bolivia is only viable if it exports gas), *Econoticias Bolivia,* March 11, 2004. Translation by authors.

84. www.bolivia/especiales/2004/referendum/resultados, citing the National Electoral Court.

85. Comisión Andina de Juristas y Red Andina Democrática, Alerta Informativa Democrática (Andean Commission of Jurists and the Democratic Andean Network, Democratic Information Alert), "Últimos acontecimientos en Bolivia" (Latest events in Bolivia), April/May 2005, www.cajpe.org.pe/Nuevoddhh/alerta_informativa_democr%C3%A1tica-Bolivia.pdf.

86. Ibid.

87. Carlos Arce and Pablo Poveda, *La nueva ley de hidrocarburos* (The new hydrocarbon law) (La Paz: CEDLA, May 2005), 5.

88. "Senador adelanta que Mesa promulgará la ley mañana" (Senator says Mesa will promulgate law tomorrow), *Los Tiempos,* May 7, 2005.

89. Carlos Rojas, interview with the authors, La Paz, March 28, 2006.

90. "Congreso e iglesia definen futuro del país" (Congress and church define the future of the country), *Los Tiempos*, June 7, 2005. Translation by authors.

91. Hylton and Thomson, "The Chequered Rainbow," 60.

92. Ibid.

93. Ibid.

94. "Propuesta para una nueva Bolivia con progreso y paz: Programa de gobierno 2006–2010" (Proposal for a new Bolivia with progress and peace: Government program 2006–2010), Podemos 2005 election pamphlet. Translation by authors.

95. "Nacionalización con compra progresiva" (Nationalization with gradual purchase), *La Razón*, October 24, 2005. Translation by authors.

96. Movimiento al Socialismo (MAS), "Ayuda memoria: Diez medidas para cambiar Bolivia" (Helpful statement: Ten measures to change Bolivia), 2005 MAS election document. Translation by authors.

97. Address by Evo Morales Aima to Bolivian Congress, La Paz, January 22, 2006. Translation by authors.

98. "Bush Warns of 'Erosion of Democracy' in Venezuela, Bolivia," *Bloomberg,* May 22, 2006.

99. "El Presidente asumió el cargo con el 74% de aprobación" (The president assumed the role with 74% approval), *La Razón,* January 22, 2007.

100. "Bolivia: Petroleras firman acuerdo" (Bolivia: Oil companies sign agreement), *BBC Mundo.com,* October 29, 2006; "Presidente Evo Morales: 'De aquí a 10 años, Bolivia ya no será ese país mendigo'" (In 10 years, Bolivia will not be this beggar country), United Press International, October 31, 2006.

101. Roberto Fernández Terán, interview with the authors, Cochabamba, March 21, 2006.

102. "El gobierno inició la industrialización del gas" (The government began the industrialization of gas), *El Deber,* December 11, 2006. Translation by authors.

103. Juan Patricio Quispe, interview by telephone with the authors, October 23, 2006.

104. "Evo: La nacionalización es un proceso que está a medio camino" (Evo: The nationalization is a process that is on its way), *Bolpress*, February 14, 2007, www.bolpress.com/art.php?Cod=2006103115&PHPSESSID=da1dodf57b.

105. Supreme Decree #28701, "Heroes of the Chaco." Translation by authors.

106. Centro de Documentación e Información Bolivia (CEDIB), "Análisis del decreto supremo #28701, 'Héroes del Chaco,' emitido por el gobierno de Evo Morales 1ro de mayo de 2006" (Analysis of supreme decree #28701, "Heroes of the Chaco," announced by the Evo Morales government, May 1, 2006) (CEDIB: Cochabamba, Bolivia, 2006), 25.

107. "Bolivia Reclaims Oil Refineries," *BBC News*, June 27, 2007, http://news.bbc.co.uk/2/hi/americas/6243802.stm.

108. Robert Conrad, interview by phone with the authors, May 3, 2006.

109. Centro de Estudios para el Desarrollo Laboral y Agrario (CEDLA), *Legitimando el orden neoliberal: 100 días de gobierno de Evo Morales* (Legitimizing the neoliberal order: 100 days into the government of Evo Morales) (La Paz: CEDLA, May 2006), 6.

110. "Ahora, las petroleras operan para YPFB" (Now, the oil companies operate for YPFB), *La Razón,* October 30, 2006; "La nacionalización bajo la lupa" (Nationalization under the magnifying glass), *Boletín económico, análisis de coyuntura no. 4* (La Paz: Fundación Milenio, August 2006), citing data from the Hydrocarbons Ministry and YPFB.

111. Centro de Estudios para el Desarrollo Laboral y Agrario (CEDLA), "Contratos petroleros que consolidan la vieja política neoliberal" (Petroleum contracts that consolidate the old neoliberal policy), *Hora 25*, no. 45 (December–January 2007).

112. "Bolivia exportó de enero a octubre más que durante todo 2005" (Bolivia exported from January to October more than the total in 2005), *Los Tiempos,* November 16, 2006, author's calculation; "Trago amargo de Bolivia hace a Brasil buscar su propio gas" (Bitter swallow from Bolivia makes Brazil look for its own gas), *Terra,* September 28, 2006, http://actualidad.terra.es/nacional/articulo/trago_bolivia_brasil_1112463.htm.

113. Dan Keane, "Bolivia's Natural Gas in Demand," *Associated Press*, March 11, 2008.

114. "Bolivia recibirá $US 110 millones adicionales por la venta de gas" (Bolivia will receive an additional $110 million USD for its gas sale), July 17, 2006, www.hoybolivia.com/news.php?seccion=78&d3=36396.

115. Conal Walsh, "Gazprom's Huge Venezuela Gas Deal Alarms U.S.," *Observer,* August 6, 2006.

116. "Petroandina instalará 15 nuevas estaciones de servicio en el país" (Petroandina will install 15 new service stations in the country), *Los Tiempos,* December 8, 2006.

117. "La nacionalización tropieza en su principal actor, YPFB" (Nationalization stumbles over its main actor, YPFB), *La Razón,* August 12, 2006. Translation by authors.

118. "Spain's Repsol Threatens Bolivia with Legal Action," Reuters, August 27, 2006.

119. "Tarija busca asociarse a las petroleras" (Tarija looks to associate itself with oil companies), *Los Tiempos,* February 3, 2006.

120. "Errores técnicos afectan nacionalización hidrocarburos Bolivia" (Technical errors affect Bolivian hydrocarbon nationalization), Reuters, March 13, 2007. Translation by authors.

121. Carlos Villegas, interview with Gretchen Gordon, La Paz, June 2005.

122. Robert Conrad, interview by telephone with the authors, May 3, 2006.

123. Joseph Stiglitz, "Who Owns Bolivia?" *Daily Times,* June 23, 2006.

124. *Territorios indígenas y empresas petroleras* (Indigenous territories and petroleum companies) (Cochabamba: Ceidis, 2005), 71.

125. Guadalupe Montenegro, interview with the authors, Santa Cruz, April 24, 2006.

126. "La nacionalización bajo la lupa," *Boletín económico, análisis de coyuntura no. 4* (La Paz: Fundación Milenio, August 2006), 85; "Bolivia exportó de enero a octubre más que durante todo 2005," *Los Tiempos,* November 16, 2006.

127. Néstor Ikeda, "Bolivia busca 5.800 millones en inversión privada" (Bolivia looks for 5,800 millions in private investment), Associated Press, July 19, 2006, translation by authors; Daniel Schweimler, "Bolivia Unveils Anti-poverty Plan," *BBC News,* June 17, 2006, http://news.bbc.co.uk/2/hi/americas/5090850.stm.

128. Jane Monahan, "Bolivia's Nationalisation Plans in Trouble," *BBC News,* August 17, 2006, http://news.bbc.co.uk/1/hi/business/4801233.stm.

129. Economic Commission for Latin America and the Caribbean, United Nations, "Foreign Investment in Latin America and the Caribbean," chap. 4 in *Hydrocarbons: Investments and Corporate Strategies in Latin America and the Caribbean,* 2001.

130. Néstor Salinas Malléa, e-mail interview with authors, May 2007.

4. LESSONS IN BLOOD AND FIRE

1. Bolivia shares its seat of government between two cities. La Paz is home to the executive and legislative branches, while the judicial branch is based in Sucre, the historical capital. In 2007, serious political conflicts erupted in Bolivia over this issue.

2. Joseph E. Stiglitz, *Globalization and Its Discontents* (New York: W. W. Norton, 2003), 11.

3. International Monetary Fund, "The Origins of the IMF," 2004, www.imf.org/external/pubs/ft/exrp/what.htm#origins; Carol Welch, "The IMF and Good Governance," in *Foreign Policy in Focus,* vol. 5, no. 13 (Washington, D.C.: Institute for Policy Studies and International Relations Center, October 2001), www.fpif.org/briefs/vol5/v5n13imfgov_body.html; and Stiglitz, *Globalization,* 12.

4. Stiglitz, *Globalization,* 12.

5. John Braithwaite and Peter Drahos, "Bretton Woods: Birth and Breakdown," in *Global Business Regulation* (Cambridge: Cambridge University Press, 2000), 97–101.

6. International Monetary Fund, "The IMF's Role at a Glance," 2004, www.imf.org/external/pubs/ft/exrp/what.htm#glance.

7. Ibid.

8. Ibid.

9. Welch, "IMF and Good Governance."

10. Stiglitz, *Globalization*, 13.

11. Roberto Fernández Terán, *FMI, Banco Mundial y estado neocolonial: Poder supranacional en Bolivia* (The IMF, the World Bank, and the neocolonial state: Supranational power in Bolivia), 2nd ed. (Cochabamba, Bolivia: Plural Editores, 2004), 28–29.

12. International Monetary Fund, "IMF Members' Quotas and Voting Power, and IMF Board of Governors," 2005, www.imf.org/external/np/sec/memdir/members.htm.

13. International Monetary Fund, "Articles of Agreement of the International Monetary Fund," 2005, www.imf.org/external/pubs/ft/aa/aa.pdf.

14. William Finnegan, "The Economics of Empire: Notes on the Washington Consensus," *Harpers*, May 2003, 45.

15. Fernández Terán, *FMI*, 27.

16. International Monetary Fund, "Who Makes Decisions at the IMF," 2004, www.imf.org/external/pubs/ft/exrp/what.htm#origins.

17. Fernández Terán, *FMI*, 25.

18. International Monetary Fund, "Highlights in the Evolution of IMF Lending," 2004, www.imf.org/external/pubs/ft/exrp/what.htm#highlights.

19. Fernández Terán, *FMI*, 25.

20. U.S. Congressional Budget Office, "Historical Budget Data," 2005, www.cbo.gov/showdoc.cfm?index=1821&sequence=0.

21. Gross domestic product (GDP) refers to the total of all goods and services produced by a nation within the borders of that nation. The standard measure of public deficits is as a percentage of a nation's GDP. U.S. budget numbers are from U.S. Congressional Budget Office, "The Budget and Economic Outlook: Fiscal Years 2008 to 2017," January 2007, http://www.cbo.gov/ftpdoc.cfm?index=7731.

22. Benedict Clements, Sanjeev Gupta, and Gabriela Inchauste, "Fiscal Policy for Economic Development: An Overview," in *Helping Countries Develop: The Role of Fiscal Policy* (Washington, D.C.: International Monetary Fund, 2004), www.imf.org/external/pubs/nft/2004/hcd/index.htm.

23. Despite the seriousness of the events of Febrero Negro and despite the IMF's clear relationship to those events, fund officials in Washington refused to be interviewed on the record for this report, despite repeated requests that they do so. Officials at the IMF did, however, agree to speak off the record about general IMF policy.

24. Arthur MacEwan, "Economic Debacle in Argentina: The IMF Strikes Again," in *Foreign Policy in Focus* (Washington, D.C.: Institute for Policy Studies and International Relations Center, January 2002), www.fpif.org/pdf/gac/0201argentina.pdf.

25. Stiglitz, *Globalization*, 12–13.

26. Bethan Emmett and Max Lawson, "The IMF and the Millennium Goals, Failing to Deliver for Low-Income Countries," (Washington, D.C.: Oxfam International, 2003), 1–2.

27. Ibid., 2.

28. International Monetary Fund, "Bolivia: Transactions with the Fund, Disbursements and Repayments Detail from January 01, 2004 to December 31, 2004," 2005, www.imf.org/external/np/tre/tad/extrans2.cfm?memberKey1=70& valueDate=2004&yearType=C&acctType1=GRASDA&extrans_flag=Y.

29. Mariano Baptista Gumucio, *Historia universal y de Bolivia* (Universal and Bolivian history), 10th ed. (La Paz, Bolivia: n.p., 1994), 192–94.

30. Marc Lindberg, "Bolivia: Stabilization and Adjustment 1985–88: Did It Work?" Kennedy School of Government Case Study # C16–90–951.1 (Cambridge, MA: Harvard University, 1990), 1.

31. Fernando Canelas Tardio and Carlos Mesa Gisbert, *Bolivia milenio* (Millenial Bolivia) (Cochabamba, Bolivia: Editorial Canelas/Los Tiempos, 1999), 107.

32. IMF and World Bank blacklisting from comments by former Bolivian president Gonzalo Sánchez de Lozada in Noel Ramírez and Marc Lindberg, "Bolivia: Controlling Hyperinflation 1985–86," Kennedy School of Government Case Study # C16–90–951.0 (Cambridge, MA: Harvard University, 1990), 4.

33. Lindberg, "Bolivia: Stabilization and Adjustment," 1.

34. Ramírez and Lindberg, "Bolivia: Controlling Hyperinflation," 4–5.

35. Ibid., 5.

36. Government of Bolivia, International Monetary Fund, and the World Bank, "Bolivia Enhanced Structural Adjustment Facility Policy Framework Paper, 1998–2001," (Washington, D.C.: International Monetary Fund, August 25, 1998), www.imf.org/external/np/pfp/bolivia/index.htm#I; and Letter of Intent between the Bolivian government and the IMF, "Bolivia: Memorandum of Economic and Financial Policies," (Washington, D.C.: International Monetary Fund, May 25, 2001), www.imf.org/external/NP/LOI/2001/bol/01/ index.htm.

37. Bolivia, IMF, and the World Bank, "Bolivia Enhanced Structural Adjustment."

38. Memorandum of understanding between the Bolivian government and the International Monetary Fund, "Memorandum of Economic Policies of the Government of Bolivia," (Washington, D.C.: International Monetary Fund, March 21, 2003), www.imf.org/External/NP/LOI/2003/bol/01/index. htm.

39. Instituto Nacional de Estadística de Bolivia, "Bolivia: Indicadores de pobreza moderada por año según área geográfica, 1999–2002" (Bolivia: Poverty indicators moderated by year according to geographic area, 1999–2002), www.ine.gov.bo/cgi-bin/piwdie1xx.exe/TIPO.

40. Centro de Estudios para el Desarrollo Laboral y Agrario (CEDLA), "Economía boliviana: Evaluación y tendencias" (Bolivian economy: Evaluation and tendencies) (La Paz, Bolivia: CEDLA, January 31, 2005) www.cedla.org/ pub/pubfree.php?cod_pubfree=32.

41. Ibid.

42. Centro de Estudios para el Desarrollo Laboral y Agrario (CEDLA), "El crecimiento económico sólo favorecerá a pocos exportadores" (Economic growth favors only a few exporters) (La Paz, Bolivia: CEDLA, July 9, 2004), www.cedla.org/noticias/noticia.php?cod_noti=2.

43. "Bolivian Water Management: A Tale of Three Cities," World Bank, Spring 2002, 1.

44. Vincent Gouarne and John Briscoe, "Don't Shut the Tap on Private-Sector Water," *Globe and Mail*, May 18, 2000.

45. For a complete analysis of the water rate hikes, see "Bechtel vs. Bolivia— The Water Hike by Bechtel's Bolivian Company (Aguas del Tunari): The Real Numbers," the Democracy Center, www.democracyctr.org/bechtel/waterbills/waterbills-global.htm.

46. Bolivia and IMF, "Memorandum of Economic Policies."

47. Carlos Villegas Quiroga, *Privatización de la industria petrolera en Bolivia: Trayectoria y efectos tributarios* (Privatization of the petroleum industry in Bolivia: Trajectory and impacts), 2nd ed. (La Paz, Bolivia: Plural Editores, 2004), 93; and Roberto Fernández Terán, interview with the author, La Paz, March 23, 2005.

48. Ministerio de Hidrocarburos, "Estadísticas—upstream—producción" (Statistics-upstream-production), July 28, 2005; "Comportamiento de los impuestos sobre hidrocarburos" (Hydrocarbon tax behavior), unpublished data from CEDLA (La Paz, March 19, 2007), author-calculated average.

49. Unidad de Análisis de Políticas Sociales y Económicos (UDAPE), "Evaluación de la Economía" (Evaluation of the economy) (La Paz, Bolivia: UDAPE, 2004, www.udape.gov.bo.

50. Centro de Estudios para el Desarrollo Laboral y Agrario (CEDLA), "Análisis comparativo del PGN 2005" (Comparative Analysis of GDP 2005) (La Paz, Bolivia: CEDLA, 2005), www.cedla.org.

51. International Monetary Fund, "Memorandum of Economic Policies, April 8, 1999," 2004, www.imf.org/external/NP/LOI/1999/040899.HTM.

52. U.S. Congressional Budget Office, "Historical Budget Data."

53. "President Discusses Homeland Security Department," White House press release, June 7, 2002, www.whitehouse.gov/news/releases/2002/06/20020607-4.html.

54. "Debt and Deficit Quotes," http://zfacts.com/p/467.html.

55. Bolivia and IMF, "Memorandum of Economic Policies."

56. "En muchos aspectos el modelo falló" (In many aspects the model failed), *El Deber*, October 28, 2001.

57. The figures are extrapolated from the World Bank's estimate of Bolivia's 2003 GDP at $7.8 billion and figures from CEDLA reporting a 2002 Bolivian budget of $3.055 billion.

58. Francisco Baker, IMF spokesman, from a written statement to the author, Washington, D.C., February 22, 2003.

59. The interview with President Carlos Mesa for this report took place in May 2003, when he was still vice president of Bolivia. Mesa became president five months later. President Carlos Mesa, interview with the author, La Paz, May 26, 2003.

60. Edwin Aldunate, interview with the author, La Paz, May 25, 2003.

61. George Gray Molina, interview with the author, La Paz, February 12, 2005.

62. Ibid.

63. Molina reported that the population that would pay the tax was 360,000, and Bolivia's population in 2002 was estimated at 8.1 million.

64. President Carlos Mesa, interview with the author, La Paz, May 26, 2003.

65. Asamblea Permanente de Derechos Humanos and others, "Para que no se olvide: 12–13 de febrero 2003" (So it is not forgotten: February 12–13, 2003) (La Paz, Bolivia: Asamblea Permanente de Derechos Humanos and others, 2004), 21.

66. Ibid.

67. Juan Forero, "Economic Crisis and Vocal Opposition Test Bolivia's President," *New York Times*, February 16, 2003.

68. This and all quotes from David Vargas are from an interview with the author, La Paz, February 10, 2005.

69. Asamblea Permanente de Derechos Humanos and others, "Para que no se olvide," 22.

70. Ibid.

71. President Carlos Mesa, interview with the author, La Paz, May 26, 2003.

72. Unless otherwise noted, the chronology of events in Plaza Murillo on February 12 is based on the excellent moment-by-moment account from Asamblea Permanente de Derechos Humanos and others, "Para que no se olvide," 21–29.

73. Asamblea Permanente de Derechos Humanos and others, "Para que no se olvide," 200.

74. Asamblea Permanente de Derechos Humanos and Coordinadora de la Mujer, "El caso de Ana Colque" (Ana Colque's case) (La Paz, Bolivia: Asamblea Permanente de Derechos Humanos and Coordinadora de la Mujer, 2004), 18.

75. Sacha Llorenti, interview with the author, La Paz, February 10, 2005.

76. Vicenta Quispe de Colque, interview with the author, La Paz, February 10, 2005.

77. Asamblea Permanente de Derechos Humanos and Coordinadora de la Mujer, "El caso de Ana Colque," 20–21.

78. The presence of the IMF mission in Bolivia during February 12–13 was described by President Carlos Mesa, George Gray Molina, and Edwin Aldunate, from interviews with the author in La Paz.

79. Asamblea Permanente de Derechos Humanos and others, "Para que no se olvide," 28.

80. Advertisement in *Los Tiempos*, February 14, 2003, A12.

81. Reuters, "Bolivia's Crisis-Ridden Leader to Reshuffle Cabinet," *Yahoo! News*, February 13, 2003.

82. "Goni anuncia recortes, diálogo y un presupuesto que no sea del FMI" (Goni announces [budget] cuts, dialogue, and a budget that is not the IMF's), *Opinión*, February 17, 2003, 2.

83. Data from the Bolivian government's Ministerio de Hacienda, www.hacienda.gov.bo/.

84. Francisco Baker, IMF spokesman, from a written statement to the author, Washington, D.C., February 22, 2003.

85. International Monetary Fund, "IMF Staff and Bolivia Agree on Economic Framework for 2003," press release, February 22, 2003.

86. International Monetary Fund, "IMF Managing Director Rodrigo de Rato's Statement at the Conclusion of His Visit to Bolivia," press release, February 18, 2005.

87. "IMF to Extend 100 Percent Debt Relief for 19 Countries Under the Multilateral Debt Relief Initiative," news release, International Monetary Fund, Washington, D.C., December 21, 2005, www.imf.org/external/np/sec/pr/2005/pr05286.htm.

88. Centro de Estudios para el Desarrollo Laboral y Agrónomo (CEDLA), October 13, 2006, unpublished statistical analysis requested by author.

89. Asamblea Permanente de Derechos Humanos and others, "Para que no se olvide," 197–203.

90. Organization of American States, "Informe de la Organización de los Estados Americanos (OEA) sobre los hechos de febrero del 2003 en Bolivia" (OEA report on the events of February 2003 in Bolivia), May 2003, www.bolpress.com/documentos.php?Cod=2002066843.

91. Amnesty International, "Bolivia: Crisis and Justice, Days of Violence in February and October 2003," (London: Amnesty International, November 2004), http://web.amnesty.org/library/index/engamr180062004.

92. Ibid.

93. Vicenta Quispe de Colque, interview with the author, La Paz, February 10, 2005.

94. President Carlos Mesa, interview with the author, La Paz, May 26, 2003.

95. Quoted in "Quotations by John Maynard Keynes," www-groups.dcs.st-and.ac.uk/~history/Quotations/Keynes.html.

5. ECONOMIC STRINGS

1. María Luisa Ramos, personal interview with the author, La Paz, December 2, 2006.

2. See "IMF Members' Quotas and Voting Power, and IMF Board of Governors," International Monetary Fund, www.imf.org/external/np/sec/memdir/members.htm. In the World Bank the top ten nations control 50 percent of the votes. Bolivia has only 0.11 percent of the votes; it shares a director with Argentina, Chile, Peru, Paraguay, and Uruguay. See also http://go.worldbank.org/O9SoUoIOA0.

3. E. Lora, "Structural Reforms in Latin America: What Has Been Reformed and How to Measure It," Inter-American Development Bank working paper no. 348, 2001.

4. Hans Huber Abendroth, Napoleón Pacheco Torrico, Carlos Villegas Quiroga, Álvaro Aguirre Badani, and Hugo Delgadillo Barca, *La deuda externa*

de Bolivia: 125 años de renegociaciones y cuántos más? Desde la operación secreta del gobierno y los Meiggs hasta la iniciativa HIPC (Bolivia's external debt: 125 years of renegotiation and how many more? From the secret government operation and the Meiggs to the HIPC initiative) (La Paz: CEDLA, 2001), 41–45.

5. Ibid., 64–66.

6. Ibid., 156.

7. "Brown, Köhler Stress Need for Global Cooperation," *IMF Survey* 30, no. 22 (November 26, 2001): 367, www.imf.org/external/pubs/ft/survey/2001/112601.pdf.

8. All the Bolivia national debt statistics in this chapter up to 1998 are taken from Abendroth et al., *La deuda externa,* which draws on figures provided by the Bolivian Central Bank. The statistics for years after 1998 are drawn directly from the Bolivian Central Bank figures, www.bcb.gov.bo/deudaexterna.

9. Abendroth et al., *La deuda externa,* 107.

10. José Pimentel Castillo, personal interview with the author, La Paz, November 23, 2006.

11. The rise in international interest rates was prompted by a sharp rise in U.S. interest rates, orchestrated by Paul Volcker, chairman of the Federal Reserve under President Reagan.

12. Abendroth et al., *La deuda externa,* 283.

13. Ibid., 286.

14. Inocencia Apaza, personal interview with the author, Guaqui, November 21, 2006. Also see analysis in Jerry R. Ladman, and Ronald L. Tinnermeier, "A Model of the Political Economy of Agricultural Credit: The Case of Bolivia," *American Journal of Agricultural Economics* 63, no. 1 (February 1981), 66–72.

15. Abendroth et al., *La deuda externa,* 286.

16. Jeffrey Sachs, *The End of Poverty: Economic Possibilities for Our Time* (London: Penguin Books, 2006), 91.

17. Noel Ramírez and Marc Lindberg, "Bolivia: Controlling Hyperinflation 1985–86," Kennedy School of Government Case Study # C16–90–951.0 (Cambridge, MA: Harvard University, 1990), 4–5.

18. Juan Carlos Águilar, personal interview with the author, La Paz, December 1, 2006.

19. Mamerto Pérez Luna, "Apertura comercial y sector agrícola campesino: La otra cara de la pobreza del campesino andino" (Commercial liberalization and the peasant agricultural sector: The other face to poverty of the Andean farmer) (La Paz: CEDLA, November 2003), 62.

20. Inocencio Apaza, personal interview with the author, Guaqui, November 21, 2006.

21. CEPAS/CARITAS, "Ricos y pobres, la brecha se ensancha" (The wealthy and the poor, the gap widens) (La Paz, April 2004), 28.

22. Fernando Landa Casazola and Wilson Jimenez Pozo, "Bolivia: Crecimiento pro pobre entre los años 1989 y 2002" (Bolivia: Pro poor growth between the years 1989 and 2002) (La Paz: UDAPE, 2003).

23. CEDLA, "Área urbana estructura del empleo 2003–4" (Urban structure of employment, 2003–4), based on INE, "Encuesta continua de hogares

2003–4" (Surveys continue in homes 2003–4). Bolivian sociologist Silvio Escobar reported in 1991 that there was a street seller for every three families in Bolivia's cities (Duncan Green, *Silent Revolution: The Rise of Market Economics in Latin America* [London: LAB/Cassell, 1995], 7), while NACLA reported that between 1990 and 1995, eighty-four out of every one hundred new employees in Bolivia worked in the informal sector (NACLA report no. 3, November–December 1997).

24. Christian Aid, "Personal Stories: The Human Face of the Debt Crisis" (London: July 1998), 9.

25. Calculated from Bolivian Central Bank figures.

26. Republic of Bolivia, "Poverty Reduction Strategy Paper" (La Paz, March 2001), 33–38. National poverty statistics don't exist for the years before 1997, but a study of urban poverty suggests that income levels deteriorated significantly in the 1980s, improved slightly in the 1990s, and deteriorated further from 1999 to 2004. The overall picture has not changed significantly since the 1970s.

27. George Gray Molina, "Una economía más allá del gas" (An economy beyond gas) (La Paz, UNDP, August 2006), 6.

28. Green, *Silent Revolution,* 7.

29. C. McGuigan, "The Benefits of FDI? Is Foreign Investment in Bolivia Delivering?" (London, Christian Aid, January 2007), 60.

30. Andrés Soliz Rada, "La telaraña del poder en la venta del gas" (The spiderweb of power in gas sales) *Voltaire Network,* September 15, 2002, www.voltairenet.org/article120342.html.

31. Inequality increased by almost 20 percent according to the Gini coefficient, a commonly used measurement of distribution of income and wealth. Fundación Jubileo, "Cuestión de justicia: Desigualdad y pobreza en Bolivia" (A matter of justice: Inequality and poverty in Bolivia) (La Paz, March 2006), 5–6.

32. Juan Carlos Carranza, personal interview with the author, La Paz, November 25, 2006.

33. Letter of intent from the Bolivian government to the IMF, August 14, 1998, www.imf.org/external/np/loi/081498.htm.

34. Mark Weisbrot and Luis Sandoval, "Bolivia's Challenges," Center for Economic and Policy Research, March 2006, 3, www.cepr.net/documents/bolivia_challenges_2006_03.pdf. Based on real per capita GDP based on purchasing power parity (PPP).

35. Benjamin Kohl and Linda Farthing, *Impasse in Bolivia: Neoliberal Hegemony and Popular Resistance* (London: Zed Books, 2006), 73.

36. Statistics calculated from Bolivian Central Bank figures.

37. Asesoría de Política Económica, Sector Externo, "Bolivia y la iniciativa HIPC, documento de trabajo" (Bolivia and the HIPC Initiative, Work Document) (La Paz: BCB), 6–9. Also calculated from Gerencia de Operaciones Internacionales, Departamento Deuda Externa, "Evolución de los desembolsos de la deuda externa pública" (Evolution of the public external debt payment) and "Servicio de la deuda externa publica" (Payments of the public external debt) (La Paz: BCB, 2005).

38. Much of the analysis in this section owes a considerable debt to the investigatory work of Roberto Fernández Terán: *FMI, Banco Mundial y estado neocolonial: Poder supranacional en Bolivia* (The IMF, the World Bank, and the neocolonial state: Supranational power in Bolivia) (La Paz: Plural Press 2003).

39. Interview by Havard Haarstad, Ph.D. student, La Paz, November 24, 2006.

40. Joseph Stiglitz, "Mi aprendizaje de la crisis económica global" (What I learned from the global economic crisis), *Nueva Sociedad*, no. 168 (July-August 2000): 106–115, as cited in Fernández Terán, *FMI*, 48.

41. Abhijit Banerjee, Angus Deaton, Nora Lustig, and Ken Rogoff, "An Evaluation of World Bank Research, 1998–2005," The World Bank (September 2006), 7, 20, http://siteresources.worldbank.org/DEC/Resources/84797–11093 62238001/726454–1164121166494/RESEARCH-EVALUATION-2006-Main-Report.pdf.

42. Kati Murillo, personal interview with the author, La Paz, November 8, 2006.

43. Fernández Terán, *FMI*, 69.

44. *Hoy*, "Asalariados de instituciones internacionales" (Wage-earners from international institutions) (La Paz, July 28, 1988), as cited in Fernández Terán, *FMI*, 113.

45. Javier Gómez, personal interview with the author, December 1, 2006.

46. World Bank, "Bolivia Poverty Report, Latin America and the Caribbean Region," report no. 8643-BO, Country Operations Division I, Country Department III, October 3, 1990, chapter 4, page 50, as cited in Fernández Terán, *FMI*, 114.

47. María Luisa Ramos, personal interview with the author, La Paz, December 2, 2006.

48. UNRISD/CESU-UMSS, "Temas globales en Bolivia: Deuda externa y comercio justo en tiempos de cambio" (Global topics in Bolivia: External debt and fair trade in times of change) (La Paz, May 2006), 11.

49. Anthony Gaeta, spokesman for the World Bank, quoted in *PR Week*, April 16, 1999.

50. Fabien Lefrancois, "Leading a Horse to Water: Is There a Role for the IMF in Poverty Reduction?" Bretton Woods Project, November 25, 2003, www.brettonwoodsproject.org/art-27842.

51. World Bank, "El Banco Mundial y el FMI respaldan la elegibilidad de Bolivia para recibir US$1300 millones en alivio de la deuda dentro de la iniciativa HIPC ampliada" (The World Bank and the IMF back the eligibility of Bolivia to receive $1.3 billion USD in relief debt under the HIPC initiative), press release 2000/198/S, http://web.worldbank.org/WBSITE/EXTERNAL/TOPICS/EXTDEBTDEPT/0,,contentMDK:20046632~isCURL:Y~pagePK:641 66689~piPK:64166646~theSitePK:469043,00.html.

52. IMF, "Bolivia: Ex Post Assessment of Longer-Term Program Engagement—Staff Report and Public Information Notice on the Executive Board Discussion," IMF Country Report, No. 05/139 (April 2005), 24.

53. Kati Murillo, personal interview with the author, La Paz, November 8, 2006.

54. Institute of Social Studies, "The Bolivian Poverty Reduction Strategy: Yet Another Brilliant Idea?" (Hague, December 2003), 9.

55. "This inverted Bolivian pyramid explains why amongst other things, an economic strategy based solely on growth has little impact." George Gray Molina, "La economía más allá del gas" (The economy beyond gas) (La Paz: UNDP, August 2006), 34.

56. There were still some criticisms of the Foro Jubileo for not including some popular movements and for being church-dominated. See Christian Aid, "Participating in Dialogue? Estrategia Boliviano por la reducción de la pobreza" (London, January 2002).

57. Unidad de Programación Fiscal (Fiscal Programming Unit), "Comportamiento de los recursos HIPC II" (Behavior of the HIPC II Resources) (Boletín Informativo 5, June 2006), 2.

58. Javier Comboni, personal interview with the author, La Paz, November 27, 2006.

59. Republic of Bolivia, "Poverty Reduction Strategy Paper" (La Paz, March 2001), 170.

60. Juan Carlos Parra, head of education for La Paz municipality, in personal interview with the author, La Paz, November 22, 2006.

61. Adhemar Esquivel Velásquez, "Reflexiones sobre el recurso humano del sector salud en Bolivia" (Reflections on human resources in the health sector of Bolivia) (La Paz: UDAPE, July 2006), 6; and Fundación Jubileo, "Fin de la deuda o deuda sin fin" (End of debt or debt without end) (La Paz, February 2005), 90.

62. "Cuarto informe de progreso de los objetivos de desarrollo del milenio" (Fourth progress report on the objectives of millennium development) (La Paz: UDAPE, November 2006), 39, 44.

63. World Bank, "For the Well-Being of All Bolivians" (La Paz, 2006), 8.

64. For the IMF, determining a sustainable level of debt meant evaluating whether a country "can meet its current and future external debt service obligations in full, without recourse to debt rescheduling or the accumulation of arrears and without compromising growth," from IDA and IMF, "The Challenge of Maintaining Long-Term External Debt Sustainability" (Washington, April 2001), 6; www.imf.org/external/np/hipc/2001/lt/042001.htm.

65. Bolivia's budget was equivalent to $47 billion bolivianos, which calculates at $5.8 billion dollars at an exchange rate in March 2007 of $US1 to 7.99 bolivianos, http://vmpc.hacienda.gov.bo/ppto/ppto2006/index.htm.

66. Many experts believe that because of a lack of human resources only 200 municipalities out of 327 are viable. Fundación Jubileo, "Fin de la deuda," 51.

67. For example, a study by Action International Health in 2003 showed that the hiring of new medical staff had predominantly taken place in urban and developed areas rather than rural areas, where 97 percent of the population live in economic poverty. AIS Bolivia, "Seguimiento a la EBRP, la iniciativa HIPC y su impacto en el sector salud" (Follow-up on EBRP, the HIPC initiative, and its impact on the health sector) (La Paz, 2003), 48–56.

68. José Pimentel Castillo, a mining leader from Potosí, was appointed vice president of the National Mechanism for Social Control in his region. He recounts that he had to wait a year for regulations, was given no space in

government apparatus, and had no resources to work. The mechanism was eventually dissolved, as "there was no political will to make it work."

69. Teresa, personal interview with the author, La Paz, November 13, 2006.

70. Weisbrot and Sandoval, "Bolivia's Challenges," 3.

71. Fundación Jubileo, "Cuestión de Justicia," 5.

72. Letter of intent from the Bolivian government to the IMF, October 7, 2005, www.imf.org/external/np/loi/2005/bol/100705.pdf.

73. Fundación Jubileo, "Después de la condonación del BID, el desafío es el endeudamiento responsable" (After IDB's debt forgiveness, the challenge is responsible indebtedness in the future) (La Paz, January 23, 2007).

74. Total debt in February 2007 according to Bolivian Central Bank was $2.5 billion, which has been divided by the population estimates of the National Institute of Statistics of 9.6 million people. INE estimated that 64 percent of the Bolivian population earn an average of $1.25 a day (10 bolivianos).

75. Fundación Jubileo, *Revista Jubileo,* no. 6 (La Paz, January–February 2007), 2–3.

76. Ibid., 2.

77. Raúl Mendoza, personal interview with the author, La Paz, November 23, 2006.

78. David Adams, "Mistrust Stole Bolivia's Shot at Reform," *St. Petersburg Times,* November 26, 2004, http://pqasb.pqarchiver.com/sptimes/access/745934831.html?dids=745934831:745934831&FMT=FT&FMTS=ABS:FT&date=Nov+26%2C+2004&author=DAVID+ADAMS&pub=St.+Petersburg+Times&edition=&startpage=23.A&desc=Mistrust+stole+Bolivia%27s+shot+at+reform.

79. "Empleo y percepciones socio-económicas en las empresas exportadoras bolivianas" (Employment and socioeconomic perceptions of Bolivian export companies) (La Paz, UDAPE, April 2006), 52.

80. Aid is also clearly another key tool of influence. In 2007, for example, Bolivia presented its National Development Plan to the Consultative Group (association of donors to Bolivia). It called for roughly $4 billion for a $6.8 billion plan, which gives considerable leverage to donor governments.

81. Pablo Solón, personal interview with the author, La Paz, December 2, 2006.

82. USA's GDP (based on purchasing power parity) was estimated to be $12.98 trillion in 2006, compared to $27.21 billion for Bolivia. Central Intelligence Agency, *The World Factbook,* www.cia.gov/cia/publications/factbook; Oxfam, "Song of the Sirens. Why the U.S.-Andean FTAs Undermine Sustainable Development and Regional Integration," Oxfam Briefing Paper 90 (June 2006), 7.

83. "NAFTA Anxiety: Trade Agreement Has Not Produced Expected Gains in Mexico's Economy," *Washington Post,* January 10, 2007.

84. "El ALBA y el TCP comienzan a andar con ocho convenios" (ALBA and TCP begin with eight agreements), Bolpress, May 23, 2006, www.bolpress.com/politica.php?Cod=2006052312.

85. The price was increased from $3.18 dollars per million British Thermal Units (BTUs) to $5.5 dollars per million BTUs from the beginning of 2007. See "Argentina, Bolivia Agree on Price Increase for Bolivian Gas Exports," *People's*

Daily Online, June 28, 2006, http://english.people.com.cn/200606/28/eng200 60628_278102.html.

86. "Evo Morales no pagará la deuda externa de Bolivia" (Evo Morales will not pay Bolivia's external debt), *Los Tiempos,* January 1, 2006, www.lostiempos. com/noticias/03–01–06/03_01_06_nac3.php. Translation by author.

6. COCA

1. Timothy Plowman, "Botanical Perspectives on Coca," *Journal of Psychedelic Drugs* 11, no. 1–2 (1979): 103–17; James A. Duke, David Aulik, and Timothy Plowman, "Nutritional Value of Coca," *Harvard University Botanical Museum Leaflets* 24, no. 6 (1975): 113–19; also in William Carter, ed., *Ensayos científicos sobre la coca* (Scientific essays about coca) (La Paz: Librería Editorial Juventud, 1996). This research shows that the normal amount of coca chewed by an indigenous worker in one day—about one hundred grams—more than satisfies the U.S. recommended dietary allowance for these vitamins and minerals.

2. Roderick E. Burchard, "Una nueva perspectiva sobre la masticación de la coca" (A new perspective on chewing coca), *América Indígena* 38, no. 4 (1978): 809–35.

3. Wade Davis, *One River: Explorations and Discoveries in the Amazon Rainforest* (New York: Simon and Schuster, 1996), p. 419. For more on calcium of coca leaf, see Paul T. Baker and Richard B. Mazess, "Calcium: Unusual Sources in the Highland Peruvian Diet," *Science* 124 (1936): 1466–67; and Carter, *Ensayos científicos,* 67–70.

4. Fernando A. Montesinos, "Metabolism of Cocaine," *Bulletin on Narcotics* 17, no. 2 (1965): 11–17; see also Carter, *Ensayos científicos,* 99–111; Andrew Weil, "Letter from the Andes: The New Politics of Coca," *New Yorker,* May 15, 1995, pp. 70–80.

5. Enrique Mayer, "El uso social de la coca en el mundo andino: Contribución a un debate y toma de posición" (The social use of coca in the Andean world: A contribution and position taken in a debate), *América Indígena* 38, no. 4 (1978): 849–65.

6. Anthony Henman, *Mama coca: Un estudio completo de la coca* (Mother coca: A complete study of coca) (La Paz: Hisbol S.R.L., 1992 [1978]), p. 85.

7. Silvia Rivera Cusicanqui, "Liberal Democracy and *Ayllu* Democracy in Bolivia: The Case of Northern Potosí," *Journal of Development Studies* 26, no. 4 (1990): 97–121.

8. John V. Murra, "Introducción al estudio histórico del cultivo de la hoja de coca (*Erythroxylum coca*) en los Andes" (Introduction to the historic study of coca leaf cultivation), in *El mundo andino: Población, medio ambiente y economía* (The Andean world: Population, environment, and economy) (Lima: IEP Ediciones, 2002 [1992]), p. 360.

9. John Hemming, *The Conquest of the Incas* (London: Macmillan, 1970), p. 354.

10. James M. Malloy, *Bolivia: The Uncompleted Revolution* (Pittsburgh, PA: University of Pittsburgh Press, 1970), p. 17.

11. William E. Carter and Mauricio Mamani, *Coca en Bolivia* (Coca in Bolivia) (La Paz: Librería Editorial Juventud, 1986).

12. June Nash, *We Eat the Mines and the Mines Eat Us: Dependency and Exploitation in Bolivian Tin Mines* (New York: Columbia University Press, 1993 [1979]).

13. Gabriel Carranza Polo, *Inal Maman Sarta Wipa: El levantamiento de la madre coca* (Inal Maman Sarta Wipa: The rise of mother coca) (La Paz: 2001), p. 23. Translation by author.

14. Pablo Stefanoni and Hervé Do Alto, *Evo Morales, de la coca al palacio: Una oportunidad para la izquierda indígena* (Evo Morales, from coca to the palace: An opportunity for the indigenous left) (La Paz: Malatesta, 2006).

15. Davis, *One River*, p. 414.

16. Lynn Sikkink, "A History of Coca, Part 1: Andean Folk Medicine and Victorian Tonic," *South American Explorer* 72 (2003): 6–11; and "Coca, Part II: Casualty of the Drug Wars," *South American Explorer* 73 (2003): 6–11; Richard Davenport-Hines, *The Pursuit of Oblivion: A Global History of Narcotics* (New York: Norton, 2002); Dominic Streatfeild, *Cocaine: An Unauthorized Biography* (New York: St. Martin's Press, 2001); P. Gootenberg, ed., *Cocaine: Global Histories* (London: Routledge, 1999); Madeline B. Léons and Harry Sanabria, eds., *Coca, Cocaine, and the Bolivian Reality* (Albany: State University of New York Press, 1997); Roberto Laserna, *Veinte juicios y prejuicios sobre coca-cocaína* (Twenty judgements and prejudices about coca-cocaine) (La Paz: Edición Clave, 1996); Davis, *One River*; and Henman, *Mama Coca*. See also the Washington Office on Latin America, www.wola.org; and the Andean Information Network, www.ain-bolivia.org.

17. José Agustin Morales, *Monografía de las provincias de Nor y Sud Yungas (Departamento de La Paz)* (Monograph of the North and South Yungas Provinces—Department of La Paz), 157. (Ayacucho, Peru: Imp. Artística, 1929).

18. Ibid., p. 159; Paul Gootenberg, "Reluctance or Resistance? Constructing Cocaine (Prohibitions) in Peru, 1910–1950," in Gootenberg, *Cocaine: Global Histories*, p. 56.

19. Davis, *One River*, p. 417. Accepted estimates of traditional use of coca is closer to four thousand years.

20. For a comprehensive history of the legal control of coca leaf and cocaine, see "Coca Yes, Cocaine No?" Transnational Institute Drugs and Democracy Programme Debate Paper #13, June 2006, www.tni.org/drugs/index.htm.

21. Davis, *One River*, p. 418; Harold Osborne, *Bolivia: A Land Divided* (London: Oxford University Press, 1964), p. 116.

22. While Bolivia was never fully decertified, in 1994 and 1995 it was granted a national security waiver, which eliminated the sanctions to protect U.S. national security. The certification process was modified in 2002. See Coletta A. Youngers and Eileen Rosin, eds., *Drugs and Democracy in Latin America: The Impact of U.S. Policy* (Boulder, Colo.: Lynne Reinner Publishers, 2005), p. 372.

23. Kathryn Ledebur, "Bolivia: Clear Consequences," in Youngers and Rosin, *Drugs and Democracy*, p. 151; and Theo Roncken, "El enigma boliviana:

Bilateralizar la agenda bilateral" (The Bolivian enigma: Bilateralize the bilateral agenda), in *Democracias bajo fuego: Drogas y poder en América Latina* (Democracies under fire: Drugs and power in Latin America), ed. Martin Jelsma and Theo Roncken (Montevideo, Uruguay: Ediciones de Brecha, no date), p. 305.

24. Washington Office on Latin America (WOLA) interview with former Bolivian government official, October 1, 2006.

25. U.S. Department of State, International Narcotics Control Strategy Report 2002, Bolivia section.

26. WOLA interview with Godofredo Reinicke, former Human Rights Ombudsman in the Chapare, August 11, 2005.

27. Kathryn Ledebur, *Coca and Conflict in the Chapare,* Washington Office on Latin America's Drug War Monitor series, July 2002, p. 13.

28. Ibid., pp. 164, 170.

29. Andean Information Network (AIN)/WOLA meeting at the U.S. Embassy in La Paz, November 2002.

30. Ledebur, *Coca and Conflict,* p. 164; and written communication from Kathryn Ledebur, August 11, 2005.

31. AIN/WOLA interview with Phil Chicola, U.S. State Department, July 15, 2002.

32. This section is based on Kathryn Ledebur and Coletta A. Youngers, *Crisis or Opportunity? Bolivian Drug Control Policy and the U.S. Response,* WOLA/AIN, June 2006.

33. "Morales reitera a EE.UU. necesidad de alianza" (Morales reiterates need for alliance to the U.S.), *El Diario,* January 23, 2006.

34. Carol Conzelman, "Yungas Coca Growers Seek Industrialization of Coca but Split on Its Legalization," AIN Report, February 8, 2007.

35. AIN/WOLA interview with Juan Alanoca, director of Radio Fides Chapare, September 28, 2006.

36. AIN/WOLA interview with Col. Miguel Vásquez Viscarra, October 4, 2006.

37. The names in this section have been changed to protect people's privacy and safety.

38. Personal interviews with the author, Cochabamba, June–July 1999.

39. Figures based on data from the Régimen Penitenciario del Departamento de Cochabamba (Prison Authority for the Department of Cochabamba), received upon written request February 2007.

40. Personal interview with the author, July 1999, Cochabamba.

41. U.S. State Department, International Narcotics Control Strategy Report, Volume 1: Drug and Chemical Control, March 2006, www.state.gov/p/inl/rls/nrcrpt/2006/vol1/html/62106.htm (accessed April 2, 2007).

42. This is based on the personal observation of the author, who was present at the trial.

43. Personal interview with the authors, November 4, 2006, Eterazama, Bolivia.

44. To date, there have been many fluctuations in the exchange rate between the boliviano and the U.S. dollar. Throughout this chapter, the exchange rate is based on the numbers from late 2006, approximately eight bolivianos to one U.S. dollar.

45. Personal interview with the authors, November 29, 2006, Cochabamba, Bolivia.

46. Personal interview with the authors, January 4, 2007, Parajti, Bolivia.

47. "Los precursores, el blanco del nuevo plan antidrogas" (The precursors, the target of the new antidrug plan), *La Razón,* August 31, 2006. Translation by author.

48. Estimate based on data from C. Araníbar and A. Alarcón, *Desarrollo alternativo y erradicación de cultivos de coca* (Alternative development and coca crop eradication) (La Paz: Viceministerio de Desarrollo Alternativo, Ministerio de Agricultura, Ganadería y Desarrollo Rural, 2002); General Accounting Office, *Drug Control Efforts to Develop Alternatives to Cultivating Illicit Crops in Columbia Have Made Little Progress and Face Serious Obstacles* (Washington, D.C.: GAO, 2002; M. Lifsher, "In U.S. Drug War, Ally Bolivia Loses Ground to Coca Farmers," *Wall Street Journal,* May 13, 2003; and the U.S. Agency for International Development, "The USAID Assistance Program in Bolivia," http://bolivia.usaid.gov. Considerable variation exists in these numbers, with some estimates ranging as high as $700 million up to 2002 if PL 480 funds (U.S. food aid program) are taken into account. G. A. Potter, *Rhetoric vs. Reality: Alternative Development in the Andes: Final Report* (New York: Drug Policy Alliance, 2002).

49. Personal interview with the authors, November 4, 2006, Eterazama, Bolivia.

50. Personal interviews with the authors, January 4, 2007 (Juan), and November 29, 2006 (Cintia).

51. Andean Information Network, "Coca Grower Views on Alternative Development" (Cochabamba: AIN, 2002), 6.

52. Ibid.

53. United States Agency for International Development (USAID), "USAID Vision Statement on Conflict" (Washington, D.C.: USAID, 2004).

54. Ibid.

55. Linda Farthing and Benjamin Kohl, "'Conflicting Agendas': The Politics of Development Aid in Drug Producing Areas," *Development Policy Review* 23 (2005): 183–98.

56. AIN, "Coca Grower Views on Alternative Development."

57. Benjamin Kohl and Linda Farthing, *Impasse in Bolivia: Neoliberal Hegemony and Popular Resistance* (London: Zed Books. 2006).

58. German Enterprise for Technical Cooperation and the United Nations Drug Control Program, "The Role of Alternative Development in Drug and Development Co-operation" (2002).

59. Interview with Felipe Cáceres, July 31, 2003, Villa Tunari.

60. USAID/Bolivia, "Integrated Alternative Development Strategic Objective 2006," www.bolivia.usaid.gov/U.S./5ID.htm, (accessed February 28, 2007); USAID/Bolivia, "Licit Economy in Coca Growing and Associated Areas Increasingly Sustainable."

61. Ibid.

62. "En diciembre comienza industrialización de la coca y Venezuela comprará toda la producción" (Coca industrialization begins in December and

Venezuela will buy the products), Agencia Boliviana de Información, October 8, 2006, www.cocasoberania.org/131020061.html.

63. Conzelman, "Yungas Coca Growers."

64. Susan Taylor Martin, "U.S. Policy Not Limited to Borders," *St. Petersburg Times,* July 29, 2001.

65. E-mail communication from Andean Information Network, November 16, 2006.

66. E-mail communication from Andean Information Network, October 20, 2006.

67. Interview with the author, July 2003.

7. WORKERS, LEADERS, AND MOTHERS

1. Silvia Rivera, "Familias que no 'conyugan' e identidades que no conjugan: La vida en Mizque" (Families that don't "fit" and identities that don't combine: Life in Mizque)," in *Ser mujer indígena, chola, o birlocha en la Bolivia post-colonial de los años 90* (Being an indigenous woman, Chola, or Birlocha in a postcolonial Bolivia in the 90s), ed. Rivera et al. (La Paz: Ministerio de Desarrollo Humano, 1996), 101.

2. Rivera, "Familias que no 'conyugan,'" 102.

3. Severina Vargas (pseud.), interview with the author, Cochabamba, December 4, 2006.

4. José Luis Eyzaguirre, Composición de los ingresos familiares de campesinos indígenas: Un estudio en seis regiones de Bolivia (Composition of familial incomes of indigenous peasants: A study of six regions of Bolivia) (La Paz: Plural Editores, 2005), 205.

5. Ibid., 16.

6. Grace Goodell, "The Cloth of the Quechuas," *Natural History* (December 1969): 48.

7. Eyzaguirre, *Composición de los ingresos familiares,* 80.

8. ProActiva Consultores, "Informe preliminar: Fortalecimiento de la Asociación de Artesanos Andinos de los municipios de Arque, Tacopaya y Tapacarí" (Preliminary report: Strengthening of the Andean Artesan Association of the municipalities of Arque, Tacopaya and Tapacarí) (unpublished manuscript, Cochabamba, October 2004), 15.

9. Based on a six-region study. Eyzaguirre, *Composición de los ingresos familiares,* 49.

10. Patricio Mamani, interview with the author, Cochabamba, February 22, 2007.

11. Virginia Mamani, interview with the author, Chuñu Chuñuni, August 5, 2006.

12. Severina Vargas (pseud.), interview with the author, Cochabamba, December 4, 2006.

13. "The Situation of Women in Bolivia," UNICEF report, www.unicef.org/bolivia/children_1538.htm (accessed March 17, 2007).

14. Olivia Román Arnez, interview with the author, Cochabamba, August 4, 2006.

15. Rivera, "Familias que no 'conyugan,'" 23.

16. Group interview with author, Chuñu Chuñuni, August 6, 2006.

17. This includes alternative development in the Chapare, projects for domestic workers in Cochabamba, and a "mother's club" in the Qaqachaka. Rivera, "Familias que no 'conyugan,'" 25.

18. María Choque (pseud.), interview with the author, Cochabamba, August 15, 2006.

19. Ibid.; statistics from Michelle Hall-Wallace, "Minerals from the Andes: Emeralds, Golds and Silver from the Sky," *Rocks and Minerals,* January 2003, www.encyclopedia.com/doc/1G1–96194330.html.

20. Ibid.

21. "Quitarles la máscara de invisibilidad: Los trabajadores a domicilio y la economía mundial" (Taking off the mask of invisibility: Household workers and the global economy), Género, Formación y Trabajo, Organización Internacional de Trabajo, CINTERFOR, The Inter-American Centre for Knowledge Development in Vocational Training, www.cinterfor.org.uy/public/spanish/region/ampro/cinterfor/temas/gender/doc/cinter/pacto/cue_gen/tra_dom.htm.

22. Steven Greenhouse, "Labor Union, Redefined, for Freelance Workers," *New York Times,* January 27, 2007, www.nytimes.com/2007/01/27/us/27freelance.html?ex=1183608000&en=7fa478324387b94e&ei=5070.

23. Claudia López, interview with the author, Cochabamba, June 30, 2007.

24. "Andean Trade Benefits Expiring," *Newsletter of the U.S. Labor Education in the Americas Project,* October 2006, www.usleap.org/Recent%20Headlines/October%202006/Andean%20Trade%20Benefits%20Expiring.htm.

25. "The Situation of Women in Bolivia," UNICEF, 2001, www.unicef.org/bolivia/children_1538.htm.

26. Rosa Hernández (pseud.), interview with the author, Cochabamba, August 14, 2006.

27. María Teresa Hosse, interview with the author, Cochabamba, October 18, 2006.

28. "Nietas herederas de Bartolina Sisa rinden homenaje" (Bartolina Sisa's granddaughters and heirs pay homage), *Boletín Red-Ada* 53 (January–August 2006): 16.

29. Quoted in June Nash, *We Eat the Mines and the Mines Eat Us: Dependency and Exploitation in Bolivian Tin Mines* (New York: Columbia University Press, 1993), 115.

30. Sonia Brito Sandoval, *Mujeres indígenas protagonistas de la historia* (Indigenous women protagonists of history) (La Paz: Tijaraipa, 1998), 46–47.

31. Personal accounts from this section are drawn from a series of formal and informal interviews. Casimira Rodríguez, interviews with the author, Cochabamba, November 15, 2006, and March 4, 2007.

32. William Douglas, personal interview with the author, February 22, 2005.

33. Denise Arnold and Juan de Dios Yapita, "Los caminos de género en Qaqachaka" (Paths of gender in Qaqachaka)," in *Ser mujer indígena,* 309.

34. CONLACTRAHO, *Las condiciones de vida de las trabajadoras del hogar en la ciudad de La Paz, Bolivia* (Life conditions of household workers in

the city of La Paz, Bolivia) (La Paz: OIT, 2003), 27; Elsa Chaney and Mary Garcia Castro, eds., *Muchacha, cachifa, criada, empleada, empregadhina, sirvienta y . . . nada más: Trabajadoras del hogar en América Latina y el Caribe* (Girl, maid, servant, and . . . nothing more: Female household workers in Latin American and the Caribbean) (Mexico City: Editorial Nueva Sociedad, 1993), 14.

35. Casimira Rodríguez, interview with the author, Cochabamba, March 4, 2006.

36. The PGA Web site can be found at www.nadir.org/nadir/initiativ/agp/index.html.

37. Ramiro Sánchez (pseud.), interview with the author, Cochabamba, December 10, 2006.

38. Personal interview with Margaret Foggarty, Cochabamba, March 26, 2007.

39. Personal details throughout the sections are taken from a personal interview with Carmen Peredo, Cochabamba, December 13, 2006.

40. Carmen Peredo, interview with the author, Cochabamba, December 13, 2006.

41. Renu Mandhane, "What Is the Effect of Water Privatization on the Right to Water?" Association for Women's Rights in Development, 2005, www.awid.org/go.php?stid=822.

42. Elizabeth Peredo, "The Women of Cochabamba Valley: Water, Privatization and Conflict" (La Paz: Fundación Solon, 2003), 7.

8. AND THOSE WHO LEFT

1. Unless otherwise noted, all references to Medardo Villarroel, Arminda Solíz, Julia García, Carlos Arrien, Leonardo Fernández, and Simona Velásquez throughout the chapter come from the following sources: Medardo Villarroel, interview with Aldo Cardoso, Barcelona, Spain, November 2006; Arminda Solíz, interview with Aldo Cardoso, Barcelona, Spain, November 2006; Julia García, interview with the author, Arlington, Virginia, December 29, 2006; Carlos Arrien, interview with the author, Washington, D.C., November 9, 2006; Leonardo Fernández, interview with Aldo Orellana López, Buenos Aires, Argentina, December 1, 2006; Simona Velásquez, interview with Aldo Orellana López, Buenos Aires, Argentina, December 3, 2006.

2. Geneviève Cortes, *Partir para quedarse* (Leaving to stay) (La Paz: IRD, IFEA, 2004), 153, 155.

3. Alejandro Grimson, "La migración boliviana en la Argentina" (Bolivian migration in Argentina), in *Migrantes bolivianos en la Argentina y los Estados Unidos* (Bolivian migrants in Argentina and the United States) (La Paz: Programa de las Naciones Unidas para el Desarrollo, 2000), 14–15.

4. Ibid., 15.

5. Alfonso Hinojosa, "Bolivia for Export," in *Temas de debate* (Debate topics) (La Paz: Programa de Investigación Estratégica en Bolivia, November 2006), 2.

6. Leonardo de la Torre Ávila, *No llores, prenda, pronto volveré: Migración, movilidad social, herida familiar, y desarrollo* (Don't cry, my dear, I will be

home soon: Migration, social mobility, family wounds, and development) (La Paz: Fundación PIEB, 2006), 70–71.

7. Presidencia de la República de Bolivia, "Galería de Presidentes de la República de Bolivia" (Gallery of Presidents of the Republic of Bolivia) www.presidencia.gov.bo/Presidentes_Bolivia/pr_Bolivia.htm.

8. Herbert S. Klein, A Concise History of Bolivia (New York: Cambridge University Press, 2003), 213.

9. de la Torre Ávila, No llores, 77.

10. Ángel Jemio-Ergueta, "La reforma agraria de Bolivia" (Bolivia's agrarian reform), Nueva Sociedad (July-August 1973): 19–37.

11. de la Torre Ávila, No llores, 77.

12. Presidencia de la República de Bolivia, "Galería de Presidentes."

13. Cortes, Partir, 154–55; Roberto Tenencia, "Familias bolivianas en la producción hortícola de la provincia de Buenos Aires" (Bolivian families in horticulture production in Buenos Aires province), in Migraciones transnacionales: Visiones de Norte y Sudamérica (Transnational migrations: Visions from North and South America) (La Paz: Centro de Estudios Fronterizos, 2004), 203–6.

14. Klein, Concise History of Bolivia, 245.

15. Ibid.

16. Cortes, Partir, 126.

17. Ibid., 56; Monte Reel, "Bolivia's Rural Women Are Remaking Cities, Lives," Washington Post, March 6, 2007, A01.

18. Ciudad de El Alto, "Reseña histórica" (Historical review), www.ciudadelalto.org.bo/elalto.htm.

19. Hinojosa, "Bolivia for Export," 2.

20. Estimates of the size of Bolivia's expatriate communities vary widely from one source to another. I have used the following source: Alfonso Hinojosa, "Bolivia for Export," in Temas de debate (La Paz, Bolivia: Programa de Investigación Estratégica en Bolivia, November 2006), 2.

21. Ibid.

22. Fernando L. Solanas, Memoria del saqueo (Memory of the pillage) (Argentina: Cinesur S.A., 2004).

23. Ibid.

24. de la Torre Ávila, No llores, 132.

25. Ibid., 72; "Dos de cada tres bolivianos tienen parientes que viven fuera del país" (Two of every three Bolivians have relatives who live outside the country), La Razón, April 9, 2006.

26. Anonymous high school senior, interview with the author, Copacabana, Bolivia, April 1, 2007.

27. Hinojosa, "Bolivia for Export," 2; Marie Trigona, "Bolivian Migrant Workers Fight Neoliberal Fashion," Dollars and Sense (January 2007): 28.

28. Mae Ngai, "How Grandma Got Legal," Los Angeles Times, May 16, 2006.

29. Julia García, interview with the author, Arlington, Virginia, December 29, 2006.

30. de la Torre Ávila, No llores, 80; Cortes, Partir, 158.

31. de la Torre Ávila, *No llores,* 33; Instituto Nacional de Estadística de Bolivia, "Bolivia: Población total proyectada, según ciudades de 10.000 habitantes y mas, 2005–2010" (Bolivia: Total projected population, by cities of 10,000 inhabitants and more, 2005–2010), www.ine.gov.bo/cgi-bin/piwdie1xx.exe/TIPO.

32. Arminda Solíz, interview with Aldo Cardoso, Barcelona, Spain, November 2006.

33. Hinojosa, "Bolivia for Export," 3.

34. Pilar Marrero, "Immigration Shift: Many Latin Americans Choosing Spain Over U.S.," Pacific News Service, December 9, 2004.

35. Hinojosa, "Bolivia for Export," 2.

36. Ibid.

37. Bendicen and Associates, "Encuesta de opinión publica de receptores de remesas en Bolivia" (Public opinion survey of receivers of remittances in Bolivia) (Santa Cruz: MIF FOMIN, October 5, 2005): 40.

38. Cynthia, interview with the author, Cochabamba, Bolivia, March 21, 2007.

39. de la Torre Ávila, *No llores,* 45.

40. From the preamble of the Argentinean constitution. For the entire text, see Honorable Senado de la Nación, "Constitución Nacional, Preámbulo" (Preamble of the National Constitution) www.senado.gov.ar/web/interes/constitucion/preambulo.php.

41. Grimson, "La migración," 31.

42. Ibid., 14, 17; Cortes, *Partir,* 155–56.

43. Plan Nacional de Normalización Documentaria Migratoria (National Plan for Migratory Documentation), "Importancia" (Importance), www.patriagrande.gov.ar/html/importancia.htm.

44. Grimson, "La migración," 17, 13; Cortes, *Partir,* 156.

45. Grimson, "La migración," 26–28.

46. Plan Nacional de Normalización Documentaria Migratoria, "Guía para migrantes del MERCOSUR y estados asociados" (Guide for migrants from MERCOSUR and associated states) www.patriagrande.gov.ar/html/doc_mercosur.htm; "Gobierno quiere legalizar gratis a los emigrantes" (Government wants to legalize emigrants for free), *La Prensa,* April 11, 2006.

47. Nedra Pickler, "Bush Says Deportation 'Ain't Gonna Work,'" Associated Press, June 8, 2006.

48. As told by Julia García, interview with the author, Arlington, Virginia, December 29, 2006.

49. Ngai, "How Grandma Got Legal."

50. Ibid.

51. Ibid.

52. de la Torre Ávila, *No llores,* 80–81.

53. Ibid., 84–85; story told by Julia Garcia, interview with the author, Arlington, Virginia, December 29, 2006.

54. Story told by Julia García, interview with the author, Arlington, Virginia, December 29, 2006.

55. Dan Balz and Darryl Fears, "'We Decided Not to Be Invisible Anymore'; Pro-Immigration Rallies Are Held Across Country," *Washington Post,* April 11, 2006.

56. Evo Morales, "We Need Partners, Not Bosses," address to the United Nations, September 22, 2006, www.counterpunch.org/morales09222006.html.

57. Giles Tremlett, "Spain Attracts Record Levels of Immigrants Seeking Jobs and Sun," *Guardian,* July 26, 2006; Marrero, "Immigration Shift."

58. Paul Anderson, "Stopping the New Spanish Armadas," *BBC News,* June 22, 2002.

59. Tremlett, "Spain Attracts Record Levels."

60. Eduardo García, "European Immigration Plans Spark Bolivian Exodus," Reuters, November 7, 2006.

61. Rickard Sandell, "Spain's Immigration Experience: Lessons to Be Learned from Looking at the Statistics," Real Instituto de Estudios Internacionales y Estratégicos, January 12, 2006, www.realinstitutoelcano.org/documentos/277.asp.

62. Katiuska Vásquez "Dos países piden frenar la migración" (Two countries request putting the brakes on migration), *Los Tiempos,* August 4, 2006; "España tendrá que pedir visa a los bolivianos" (Spain will require visa for Bolivians), *La Razón,* August 8, 2006.

63. "Mas de 30 mil bolivianos viajaron a España en los últimos dos meses" (More than thirty thousand left for Spain in the last two months), *La Opinión,* January 8, 2007.

64. García, "European Immigration Plans."

65. U.S. Department of State Bureau of Consular Affairs, "Visa Statistics," http://travel.state.gov/visa/frvi/statistics/statistics_1476.html; New American Opportunity Campaign, "Immigration Basics: Family-Sponsored Immigration," January 2005, www.cirnow.org/content/en/basics_family.htm.

66. Aldo Orellana López, interview with the author, Cochabamba, Bolivia, February 22, 2007.

67. The U.S. visa interview process is so notorious in Bolivia that Juan Carlos Valdivia, a popular Bolivian filmmaker, used it as the basis for his 2004 movie, *American Visa.*

68. Anonymous Bolivian, conversation with the author, Cochabamba, Bolivia, April 14, 2007.

69. U.S. Department of State Bureau of Consular Affairs, "Visa Statistics."

70. Katiuska Vásquez, "Llega la visa: Las agencies multiplican sus anzuelos" (The visa is coming: Agencies multiply their bait), *Los Tiempos,* January 28, 2007; José Andrés Sánchez, "La gran estafa: Cómo el sueño migratorio muere antes del viaje" (The great swindle: How the migration dream dies before the trip), *El Deber,* January 7, 2007.

71. García, "European Immigration Plans"; Eduardo García, "Spain Dream Ends for Hundreds of Bolivians," Reuters, March 31, 2007.

72. "Retienen en aeropuerto de Madrid a 200 bolivianos" (200 Bolivians detained in Madrid airport), *Los Tiempos,* February 7, 2007; "Cada mes ingresan cerca de 15 mil bolivianos a España" (Each month nearly fifteen thousand Bolivians enter Spain), *La Razón,* October 31, 2006.

73. de la Torre Ávila, *No llores,* 84.

74. Julia García, interview with the author, Arlington, Virginia, December 29, 2006.

75. Center for American Progress, "Deporting the Undocumented: A Cost Assessment," Center for American Progress, 2005, www.americanprogress.org/issues/2005/07/b913099.html.

76. Nestor Kirchner, speech on the Plan Nacional de Normalización Migratoria, Buenos Aires, Argentina, December 14, 2005.

77. Aldo Cardoso, telephone interview with the author, Barcelona, Spain, March 12, 2007.

78. New American Opportunity Campaign, "Immigration Basics: Naturalization," January 2005, www.cirnow.org/content/en/basics_naturalization.htm.

79. Hinojosa, "Bolivia for Export," 3.

80. "Wage Theft: How Maryland Fails to Protect the Rights of Low-Wage Workers" (Silver Spring, MD: CASA of Maryland, 2007), 7.

81. Trigona, "Bolivian Migrant Workers," 28–29.

82. Emma Violand Sánchez, interview with the author, Arlington, Virginia, December 20, 2006.

83. Otilia Huayta, interview with the author, Upper Marlboro, Maryland, December 22, 2006.

84. Fredy Campos, interview with Aldo Cardoso, Barcelona, Spain, November 2006.

85. Wilder Aranibar, interview with the author, Arlington, Virginia, October 28, 2006.

86. de la Torre Ávila, No llores, 101–2.

87. Grimson, "La migración," 33; Emma Violand Sánchez, interview with the author, Arlington, Virginia, December 20, 2006.

88. Julia García, interview with the author, Arlington, Virginia, December 29, 2006.

89. "La migración de la madre causa más casos de abuso" (Mothers' migration causes more abuse cases), La Razón, March 7, 2007.

90. Red Ada bulletin (Cochabamba, Bolivia: June 6, 2006).

91. Vanesa Gonzáles Martinez, informal conversations with the author, May 2005.

92. Mother of a Bolivian emigrant, interview with the author at the Bolivian consulate, Washington, D.C., January 5, 2007.

93. "Las remesas de los migrantes latinos alcanzaran este año a $US 60 millones" (Latino migrant remittances reached $US 60 million this year), Opinión, October 19, 2006.

94. "Mas de 30 mil bolivianos," Opinión, January 8, 2007.

95. Bendicen and Associates, "Encuesta de opinión publica," 27.

96. de la Torre Ávila, No llores, 159.

97. "Las remesas de los migrantes latinos alcanzaran este año a $US 60 millones," Opinión, October 19, 2006.

98. Vanesa Gonzáles Martinez, informal conversations with the author, March 2007.

99. Nick Miroff, "Immigrants' Jobs Vanish with Housing Slowdown," Washington Post, December 27, 2006, A13.

100. Ximena Moscoso, interview with the author, Cochabamba, Bolivia, January 13, 2007.

101. Daniela Rivero, interview with the author, Cochabamba, Bolivia, January 13, 2007.

102. Evo Morales, preinaugural speech at Tiwanaku, Tiwanaku, Bolivia, January 21, 2006, www.barrioflores.net/weblog/archives/2006/01/index.html.

103. Evo Morales, "We Need Partners."

104. Gustavo Ondarza, "El plan laboral no frena el éxodo" (The labor plan does not stop the exodus), *El Deber*, October 8, 2006.

Index

Text: 10/13 Sabon
Display: Sabon
Compositor: International Typesetting and Composition
Printer and binder: Sheridan Books, Inc.